RENEWALS: 691-4574
DATE DUE

**WITHDRAWN
UTSA LIBRARIES**

Urbanization
in History

Urbanization in History

A Process of Dynamic Interactions

Edited by

AD van der WOUDE
AKIRA HAYAMI
JAN de VRIES

CLARENDON PRESS · OXFORD
1990

Oxford University Press, Walton Street, Oxford OX2 6DP
Oxford New York Toronto
Delhi Bombay Calcutta Madras Karachi
Petaling Jaya Singapore Hong Kong Tokyo
Nairobi Dar es Salaam Cape Town
Melbourne Auckland
and associated companies in
Berlin Ibadan

Oxford is a trade mark of Oxford University Press

Published in the United States
by Oxford University Press, New York

© IUSSP 1990

All rights reserved. No part of this publication may be reproduced,
stored in a retrieval system, or transmitted, in any form or by any means,
electronic, mechanical, photocopying, recording, or otherwise, without
the prior permission of Oxford University Press.

This book is sold subject to the condition that it shall not, by way
of trade or otherwise, be lent, re-sold, hired out or otherwise circulated
without the publisher's prior consent in any form of binding or cover
other than that in which it is published and without a similar condition
including this condition being imposed on the subsequent purchaser

British Library Cataloguing in Publication Data
Urbanization in history: a process of dynamic interaction. —
(International studies in demography)
1. Urbanization, history
I. Woude, Ad van der II. Hayami, Akira III. De Vries,
Jan IIII. Series
082 307.7609
ISBN 0-19-828679-1

Library of Congress Cataloging in Publication Data
Urbanization in history : a process of dynamic interactions/edited
by Ad van der Woude, Akira Hayami, and Jan de Vries.
Selected papers from a seminar held in Tokyo, Japan, Jan. 1986,
sponsored by IUSSP Committee on Historical Demography.
1. Urbanization—History—Congresses. 2. Sociology, Urban—
Methodology—Congresses. 3. Rural–urban migration—History—
Congresses. 4. Population—History—Congresses. I. Woude, A. M.
van der. II. Hayami, Akira, 1929–. III. De Vries, Jan, 1943–
IV. International Union for the Scientific Study of Population.
Committee on Historical Demography.
HT361.U726 1990 307.76'09—dc20 89-70901
ISBN 0-19-828679-1

Typeset by Pentacor Ltd., High Wycombe, Bucks
Printed in Great Britain by
Bookcraft Ltd., Midsomer Norton, Avon

Acknowledgements

IN 1983, when the International Union for the Scientific Study of Population set up its new Committee on Historical Demography, it was decided to make the Committee's chief object the encouragement of research on past demographic processes outside Europe and North America. It is well known that there have been vigorous developments in the study of historical demography since the 1950s, first in Europe, and later in the United States and in Canada. During the course of this process historical demography has evolved to become one of the most fruitful areas of scholarly research both by demographers and by historians. Its claim to existence is now securely recognized by scholars in both disciplines on both continents.

The situation is very different in other parts of the world. There are several reasons for this. The attention of demographers concerned with the study of developing countries was fixed, for obvious reasons, on the practical problems connected with the population explosion of the period following the Second World War. Time and energy could not always be spared for retrospective long-term studies based on sound scholarship. In addition, historical research in these countries reacted slowly to the new trends in American and European historical studies that were directed towards the social sciences. This presented obstacles to the development of historical demography as a branch of history.

A very important contributory reason for this relative neglect was the fact that—with the important exception of Latin America and the Philippines—the nature of the documentary sources in the developing countries differs fundamentally from those in Europe or North America. In the latter, research has benefited from the records kept by the Christian Churches. It is not a coincidence that the study of (historical) demography began in the West. Its birth was occasioned in large degree by the existence of registers of vital events that arose from the needs of the Churches. The introduction of historical demography to the non-Christian world requires that attention be paid to other sources that could furnish demographically useful information.

The long-term policy of the IUSSP Committee on Historical Demography is to stimulate the search for sources in the non-Christian world that would be of value to demographic research. Only when historians and demographers know more about the existence and character of such sources can historical demography develop into a fully-fledged field of scholarly research in the non-Western world. As a short-term measure, the Committee decided to stimulate interest in the historical demography of the non-Western countries by organizing seminars in those parts of the world so that the most promising scholars from those countries could be brought together with European and

North American colleagues. The first of these seminars met in December 1984 in San José, Costa Rica, and discussed 'Orphanhood and the Measurement of Adult Mortality in the Past'. A selection of the papers presented to that seminar has been published in *Notas de Población. Revista Latinoamericana de Demografía*, 13: 37, 38 (1985).

A second seminar met in January 1986 in Tokyo, its subject being 'Urbanization and Population Dynamics in History'. Some fifty scholars from Europe, the Americas, and Asia participated in the seminar, at which thirty-eight papers, organized in six sessions, were presented and discussed. The session titles and chairmen were: 'Urban demography' (Jacques Dupâquier); 'Migration' (Étienne Hélin); 'Rank-size distributions and urban networks' (Roger Schofield); 'East Asian urbanization patterns' (Akira Hayami); 'Agricultural productivity, transport capacity, and urban growth' (Sølvi Sogner); and 'The concept of the city' (Massimo Livi Bacci). In addition to these participants, approximately twenty-five local scholars and students also attended the seminar. An editorial committee consisting of Akira Hayami, Jan de Vries, and Ad van der Woude was set up and has selected nineteen of the papers submitted for publication.

To organize the scholarly aspects of the seminar, the Committee on Historical Demography appointed a subcommittee consisting of Alain Bideau, Akira Hayami, Roger Schofield, and Ad van der Woude. In addition, logistical and social arrangements were handled by a local organizing committee under the direction of Akira Hayami, whose other members were Hiroshi Kito, Shunsaku Nishikawa, Osamu Saito, and Minoru Yasumoto. All of them deserve our heartfelt thanks.

Two persons deserve special mention. Without the extraordinary efforts of Akira Hayami this seminar would never have been held. He, more than anyone else, made its realization possible, and all participants are in his debt. The work of Marc Lebrun, co-ordinator for the IUSSP, was also crucial. The preparatory discussions, correspondence, and much of the organizational work which preceded the seminar were in his capable hands.

The seminar became a reality with the financial and material support of many institutions and individuals. It is my great pleasure to acknowledge the assistance of Jan de Vries, of the University of California at Berkeley, for his help in developing the draft of a proposal of possible issues to be discussed at the seminar, which we formulated as a guideline to participants during our common stay at the Netherlands Institute for Advanced Study in the Humanities (NIAS) at Wassenaar in the spring of 1983; and again for his editorial work on the papers that were presented.

An essential precondition for the realization of the seminar was the financial assistance received from many supporters and donors. They were: Keio University, the Tokyo Metropolitan Administration, the Japan Society for the Promotion of Science, the Commemorative Association for the Japan World Exposition, the Kajima Foundation, Japan IBM Co., Ohsekai

(Graduates from Professor Hayami's seminar), Canon Inc., Esso Sekiyu K.K., Shimizu Construction Co. Ltd., Taisho Marine and Fire Insurance Company Ltd., Hattori Seiko Co. Ltd., the Chiyoda Mutual Life Insurance Company, the Daiichi Mutual Life Insurance Company, Maruzen Co., as well as several private persons. As chairman of the Committee I am grateful for the kind and generous way in which these donors supplemented the resources of the IUSSP to enable this seminar to take place. The editorial committee would also like to express its special thanks to Mr E. Grebenik for his help in putting the manuscript into its final form. As a result of his work, a number of faults and inconsistencies in the original papers have been corrected. The individual authors and the editorial committee, of course, accept responsibility for any remaining errors or omissions.

A.v.d.W.

List of Contributors

PAUL BAIROCH, Département d'Histoire Économique, Université de Genève, Genève, Switzerland

JAN de VRIES, Department of History, University of California, Berkeley, California, USA

JEAN-PIERRE BARDET, EHESS, Laboratoire de Démographie Historique, Paris, France

TOMMY BENGTSSON, Department of Economic History, Lund University, Lund, Sweden

ÉTIENNE FRANÇOIS, Unité de Formation et de Recherche des Sciences Historiques et Géographiques, Université de Nancy I, Nancy, France

GUNNAR FRIDLIZIUS, Department of Economic History, Lund University, Lund, Sweden

AKIRA HAYAMI, Department of Economics, Keio University, Tokyo, Japan

HANS CHRISTIAN JOHANSEN, Department of Economic History, University of Odense, Odense, Denmark

PAUL M. HOHENBERG, Department of Economics, Rensselaer Polytechnic Institute, Troy, New York 12181, USA

BERNARD LEPETIT, EHESS, Laboratoire de Démographie Historique, Paris, France

TS'UI-JUNG LIU, The Institute of Economics, Academia Sinica, Nankang, Taipei, Taiwan, Republic of China

MARGARETA MATOVIĆ, Stockholms Universitet, Historiska Institutionen, Stockholm, Sweden

ALFRED PERRENOUD, Département d'Histoire Économique, Université de Genève, Genève, Switzerland

CAROL A. SMITH, Department of Anthropology, Duke University, Durham, North Carolina, USA

DAVID S. REHER, Faculdad de Ciencias Politica y Sociologia, Universidad Complutense de Madrid, Madrid, Spain

GILBERT ROZMAN, Department of Sociology, Princeton University, Princeton, New Jersey, USA

OSAMU SAITO, The Institute of Economic Research, Hitotsubashi University, Kunitachi, Tokyo, Japan

AD van der WOUDE, Department of Rural History, Agricultural University, Wageningen, The Netherlands

E. A. WRIGLEY, Cambridge Group for the History of Population and Social Structure, Cambridge, UK

MINORU YASUMOTO, Department of Economics, Komozawa University, Setagaya-Ku, Tokyo, Japan

Contents

List of Figures	xiii
List of Maps	xv
1. Introduction: The Hierarchies, Provisioning, and Demographic Patterns of Cities Ad van der Woude, Jan de Vries, Akira Hayami	1
2. Types of City-Size Distributions: A Comparative Analysis Carol A. Smith	20
3. Problems in the Measurement, Description, and Analysis of Historical Urbanization Jan de Vries	43
4. East Asian Urbanization in the Nineteenth Century: Comparisons with Europe Gilbert Rozman	61
5. Patterns of Settlement and Political Changes: The French Revolution and the National Urban Hierarchy Bernard Lepetit	74
6. The German Urban Network between the Sixteenth and Eighteenth Centuries: Cultural and Demographic Indicators Étienne François	84
7. Brake or Accelerator? Urban Growth and Population Growth before the Industrial Revolution E. A. Wrigley	101
8. Agricultural Productivity, Trade, and Urban Growth during the Phase of Commercialization of the Swedish Economy, 1810–1870 Gunnar Fridlizius	113
9. The Impact of Crop Yields, Agricultural Productivity, and Transport Costs on Urban Growth between 1800 and 1910 Paul Bairoch	134
10. Migration into and out of the Danish City of Odense Hans Christian Johansen	152
11. Mobility and Migration in Pre-industrial Urban Areas: The Case of Nineteenth-Century Cuenca David S. Reher	165

12. Migration, Wages, and Urbanization in Sweden in the
    Nineteenth Century   186
    Tommy Bengtsson

13. The Changing Structure of Urban Employment and its Effects
    on Migration Patterns in Eighteenth- and Nineteenth-Century
    Japan   205
    Osamu Saito

14. Migration, Family Formation, and Choice of Marriage Partners
    in Stockholm, 1860–1890   220
    Margareta Matović

15. Aspects of Fertility Decline in an Urban Setting: Rouen and
    Geneva   243
    Alfred Perrenoud

16. Innovators and Imitators in the Practice of Contraception in
    Town and Country   264
    Jean-Pierre Bardet

17. Urbanization and Demographic Behaviour in Spain, 1860–1930   282
    David S. Reher

18. Economic and Demographic Implications of Working-Class
    Housing in Early Victorian Leeds   300
    Minoru Yasumoto

19. Demographic Aspects of Urbanization in the Lower Yangzi
    Region of China, c.1500–1900   328
    Ts'ui-jung Liu

20. The City: Agent or Product of Urbanization   352
    Paul M. Hohenberg

    Index   365

List of Figures

2.1.	Metropolitan districts: 100 largest in the United States in 1940, ranked in order of decreasing population size	21
2.2.	Argentina, 1859–1960: city-size distribution at each census date (best-fitting line of slope −1 drawn, excluding largest city in all, except first census date)	23
3.1.	Three phases of early modern urbanization	52
3.2.	The stylized urban transition	54
3.3.	The stylized urban demographic transition	58
4.1.	Rank-size distribution: China (1840s) and Japan (1875)	68
5.1.	Urban hierarchies: model distributions	77
5.2.	Urban hierarchies, 1700–1836	79
5.3.	Urban hierarchies, theoretical distributions, 1750 and 1840	82
8.1.	Population increase in rural and urban Sweden, 1810–1900	114
8.2.	Population increase in the towns according to their geographical location	115
8.3.	Population increase in Malmö and the county of Malmöhus	115
8.4.	Terms of trade for Malmö and the whole country, 1831–70	118
8.5.	Freight factors on corn shipped from Göteborg to London, 1840–69	122
8.6.	Total population increase, net migration, and natural increase in Malmö (a), urban Sweden excluding Stockholm (b), and Stockholm (c), 1821/30–1891/1900	126
8.7.	Crude birth- and death-rates in Malmö (a), urban Sweden (b), and Stockholm (c), 1821/30–1891/1900	127
8.8.	Age-specific mortality rates 1821/30–1891/1900 in the age-group 25–50	128
8.9.	Real wages for agricultural workers, 1751–1880 (5-year moving average)	132
10.1.	Births and deaths in Odense, 1723–90	154
10.2.	Age pyramid for the population of Odense, 1787	161
12.1.	Population change in Malmö, Göteborg, Stockholm, all towns, and the whole country, 1800–1900	186
12.2.	Population increase in Malmö, 1821–59: (A) actual increase, (M) increase with actual migration and zero natural increase, and (N) increase with actual natural increase and zero migration	187

xiv   *List of Figures*

12.3.	In- and out-migration from Malmö, 1821–59	189
12.4.	Age pyramids for the towns and some regions of Sweden, 1850	190
12.5.	Diffusion of real wages in Sweden 1805/9–1910/14: coefficients of variation for nominal wages, cost of living, and average real wages for all counties based on 5-year averages; coefficient of variation for nominal wages for all counties, excluding the four northernmost	196
12.6.	Dispersion of nominal wages and prices of rye in Sweden 1735/9–1910/14: coefficients of variation for all counties based on 5-year averages	197
12.7.	Nominal wages in the towns and in the countryside of Scania, 1821–59	198
15.1.	Sum of age-specific fertility rates, current (Rouen) and marriage cohorts (Geneva)	248
15.2.	Adjusted legitimate fertility rates by age of women at marriage and date of marriage (Geneva)	250
15.3.	Adjusted legitimate fertility rates, by age of women at marriage and social origin, for different marriage cohorts	260
16.1.	Adjusted completed family size by 20-year period of births	268
16.2.	Mean of birth intervals	271
16.3.	Adjusted theoretical completed family size by 20-year birth periods	275
18.1.	Working-class housing (back-to-back houses)	301
18.2.	Middle-class housing (terrace houses)	302
18.3.	Age structure in Leeds	305
18.4.	Sex ratio in Leeds	306
18.5.	Overall labour-force participation rate	310
18.6.	Labour-force participation rate excluding resident servants and visitors	311
18.7.	Contribution made by co-resident offspring to the household economy	318
18.8.	Distribution of age at death (cumulative)	323
20.1.	Intersectoral flows in a transitional economy	360

List of Maps

6.1.	Geographical location of the 33 largest German towns about 1600 (frontiers of 1789)	85
6.2.	Geographical location of the 36 largest German towns about 1800	87
6.3.	Geographical location of the 33 main publishing towns in Germany (by number of titles listed in book fairs 1610–19)	91
6.4.	Geographical location of the 35 German towns with the largest numbers of publishers during the sixteenth and seventeenth centuries	92
6.5.	Geographical location of the 33 largest German publishing towns by 10-year average of titles appearing in catalogues, 1765–1805	95
6.6.	Geographical location of the 34 German towns with the largest numbers of authors, 1806	96
16.1.	Geographical location of sample	266

1 Introduction
The Hierarchies, Provisioning, and Demographic Patterns of Cities

AD van der WOUDE, JAN de VRIES, AKIRA HAYAMI

Department of Rural History, Agricultural University, Wageningen, The Netherlands.
Department of History, University of California, Berkeley, California, USA.
Department of Economics, Keio University, Tokyo, Japan.

In preparing the conference on 'Urbanization and Population Dynamics in History' the organizers formulated a series of questions for the guidance of contributors. The questions were intended to lend coherence to the academic discussion, and we shall repeat them here to introduce the nineteen papers in this volume which have been selected from the thirty-eight presented at the conference. The main points touched upon in the questionnaire referred to three aspects of the process of urbanization: urban hierarchies and networks, distinctive characteristics of the urban demographic system, and urban–rural relationships.

Study of the first of these topics is motivated by a desire to move beyond conventional concepts of urbanization. Indeed, urbanization remains an elusive object of study to the historian and social scientist alike, largely because of the multi-dimensional character of urbanization. The aggregative dimension, so familiar to us in summations of city populations used to calculate the percentage urban, indicates the 'weight' of the urban sector. But when we seek to interpret the possible meaning of this information, our attention necessarily turns to how the urban sector 'throws its weight around'. One approach, familiar to the historian and demographer alike, is to inquire in detail into the inner workings of the city: its economy, social structure, vital rates, migration flows, etc. The assumption underlying this approach is that the individual city is a microcosm of the larger urban sector as a whole.

A second approach, relatively new to historical studies, is to inquire into the relations among cities as expressed in administrative hierarchies, trade and communication flows, migration patterns, and other patterned phenomena. The assumption underlying this approach is, to quote the paper contributed by Carol Smith, that 'the true significance of the local case-study is revealed by situating it within an overarching, functionally differentiated hierarchical structure'. Jan de Vries expresses the compatible position that the *arrangement* of cities is as revealing as the *aggregation* of cities in interpreting urbanization.

In this volume we present five chapters (by Carol Smith, Jan de Vries, Gilbert Rozman, Bernard Lepetit, and Étienne François) that all explore the possibilities inherent in studying the relations between cities. Among the questions considered are: how do urban hierarchies (or systems, or networks) develop over time? By which methods and with which sources and dimensions (i.e. population, function, infrastructure) should the hierarchies be defined and measured? How should the patterns of urban arrangements revealed by these methods be categorized? And finally, what meaning can be attributed to the varying patterns that emerge from these studies? The historical study of urban systems is still such a new field of inquiry that questions of method, questions of ultimate meaning, and almost everything in between are still subject to debate.

Although central-place theory and related methods of identifying hierarchical arrangements are important in the study of urban systems, the principal techniques are based on the analysis of rank-size distributions. The chapter by Carol Smith provides a state-of-the-art discussion of the scholarly literature on rank-size distributions and a thoughtful analysis of the problems of method, description, and interpretation revealed by that literature. On the basis of her own investigations of Central American urban systems Carol Smith offers her considered opinion on most of the outstanding issues. She establishes categories for the varying 'arrangements' of cities into systems, she urges that 'infrastructure' rather than population be used as the basic measurement of the urban system, and she argues that the phenomenon of primacy (where the largest city(ies) is(are) overly large) should be seen as being due to other causes (such as colonialism, the exercise of state power, and administrative tradition) than those bringing about changes in the rank-size distribution as a whole. These suggestions often have provocative implications, not least for comparative historical research.

Gilbert Rozman examines changes in the urban structures of Japan and China, and compares them with Europe. At a level of generalization rather higher than Carol Smith's, he explores gross differences in the design of urban networks in order to establish a research agenda for students of Asian urbanization. Yet his ultimate concern is compatible with Carol Smith's—to acquire the insights that might make it possible to assess what sort of urban system makes a society 'well positioned for modernization'.

This question has imbedded within it an important implication: that an urban system is not a *product* of industrialization and modernization, but is itself a *precondition* for those phenomena. This suggestion has interesting theoretical consequences, but it also imposes new demands on the method of measuring urbanization itself. To the extent that current conventions have found favour precisely because they call attention to those features of urbanization that we regard as flowing from modern industrialization, they are bound to be inadequate to reveal the process that led to the construction of Rozman's 'pre-modern urban networks'. In his contribution, Jan de Vries presents a critical survey of measurement techniques and analytical concepts, with the objective of finding more inclusive models, and measurements that uncover the several dimensions of urban development.

Opinions differ about the proper use of rank–size distributions. Carol Smith emphasizes their theoretical meaning and values their prescriptive possibilities; de Vries is sceptical of attributing theoretical meaning to rank-size distributions and urges that they must be treated as empirical data. In conjunction with other data, they can provide diagnostic possibilities. Of greater importance than this difference of approach is the striking agreement in these contributions that the proper use of rank–size distributions is historical, and historical-comparative, and not, as in the older geographical and regional planning literature, chiefly cross-sectional and static. In other words, it is now recognized that urban network formation reflects deeply rooted historical structures. Modern networks are neither the product of recent influences, nor are they quickly altered by transitory policies.

Correspondingly, most contributors discuss the evolution of urban hierarchies over very long periods, some extending over several centuries. An exception is Bernard Lepetit's study, in which he tests the usefulness of rank-size distributions for shorter-term analysis by examining the impact of a strong, sudden, exogenous shock: the French Revolution. The revamping of France's administrative system from one of thirty-odd historic regional capitals to eighty-six new departmental seats provides Lepetit with something approaching a laboratory experiment with which to measure the impact of a spatial redistribution of administrative functions on the rank–size distribution of cities. His use of the rank-size distribution is noteworthy in that attention is paid to the *entire* distribution and to the measurement of the manner in which the different points in the hierarchy are related to each other. Authors of earlier studies too often confined attention to the very largest cities, and were satisfied with *ad hoc* descriptions of patterns in the rank-size distributions.

However much the use of rank–size distribution appeals to us as a conceptual tool, we must not lose sight of the limitations that are inherent in the use of city populations as the universal measure of rank in the urban hierarchy. It can, in fact, be quite misleading. Peter Xenos—in a paper presented at the Tokyo seminar but not included in this volume for reasons of space—provided an analysis of the Philippine urban system that alerted us to the fact that urban settlements established by Spanish colonial policy differed significantly from Western norms. The difficulty of separating the rural from the urban populations of *pueblos* and the long-continued policy of carving new settlements out of the territory of existing *pueblos* make interpretations of population data treacherous. Xenos also called attention to the minor role played by population redistribution (i.e. migration) in nineteenth-century Philippine urban growth. This growth occurred chiefly by natural increase, which means that cities grew large without necessarily raising the percentage urban of the whole nation.

This brings us back to the remarks of Carol Smith, who, like Peter Xenos, bases her observations on an urban system of Spanish heritage. She argues that it would be preferable to employ functional indicators to avoid the pitfalls of reliance on purely demographic measurements. In his chapter, Étienne François provides us with an attempt to analyse an urban system with the help of a functional approach. However, the theoretical appeal of a functional specification of urban hierarchies quickly yields practical problems. Which functional measurements are unambiguously superior to population size? No single indicator seems ideal, yet the deployment of multiple indicators may be very useful in revealing the complexity of the urban hierarchy.

François's study compares the development of Central Europe's urban system between 1600 and 1800 as it is revealed by the conventional demographic indicators, and also by the functional 'cultural' indicators of book production, presence of publishers, and presence of writers. The differences revealed by these two kinds of indicators raise intriguing questions about our understanding of the concept 'urban hierarchy'. In Germany, it appears that a well-defined cultural hierarchy emerged in advance of widespread economic integration (as revealed by the demographic indicator), which, in turn, preceded the political unification of the nineteenth century. By this imaginative use of the rank–size distribution technique, François considers the methodologically important question of the causal relationship among the economic, political, and cultural sectors of society. The patterns he reveals seem neither to fit Marxist views, nor the scheme advocated by Braudel.

At the seminar, a promising approach for the future may have been presented in an unpublished paper by William Skinner. Instead of the rank–size distribution he took central-place theory as his starting-point. Within natural (geographically delimited) regions, Skinner tried to uncover mutually reinforcing patterns of differentiations between centre and periphery that involve systematic differences in population size, occupational distribution, wage rates, price levels, and demographic behaviour. The 'centrality' index he devised is specific to a given region; it does not illuminate directly higher levels of urban-system integration. But it goes beyond existing work in its attempt to provide a comprehensive indicator of urban position. We hope that Skinner's contribution to the seminar will soon be ready for publication.

As is so often the case, at least as many new questions are raised as are answered. We now know more about the methodological issues concerning the measurement of urbanization and the description of urban systems. But at the same time we are alerted to the need to study more deeply the ways in which population-size distributions of cities are related to social, political, and economic forces. The historical perspective of these contributions has helped to clarify the methodological issues; a dynamic historical approach should also be of value in studying the evolving relationship between urban populations and societal structures.

Rank–size distributions and concepts of urban networks and hierarchies have been shown to be useful for achieving a deeper understanding of urbanization processes, yet even their most fervent advocates must acknowledge that they are incomplete by themselves. Urbanization has its inter-urban dimension, to be sure, but it is also strongly conditioned by urban–rural relations. 'No pre-industrial country', to quote Wrigley's contribution to this volume, 'could become urbanized to the degree which is now commonplace throughout the industrial world. The ultimate reason for the comparatively low levels of urbanization in pre-industrial societies is not far to seek. To live, one must eat.' The conference organizers wished to see this topic explored in as broad a context as possible, by an investigation of what one might call the logistics of urban growth. Alongside the question of urban food supplies, it seemed necessary to consider energy supplies, investment in urban infrastructure, and the production of transport services.

A second, related, topic of investigation of particular importance to pre-industrial urbanization concerns the relationship between urban and *rural non-agricultural* populations. Was the growth of rural non-agricultural populations competing with, or complementary to, the urban sector? For example, would growing rural non-agricultural populations compensate for declining urban demand, or did the two more often decline together, causing markets for agricultural products to contract? A third topic that requires attention is, of course, the character of urban–rural relations during the period of transition to the industrial era. We have selected three papers in which these urban–rural dimensions of urbanization are explored. E. A. Wrigley's contribution deals with the apparently unique character of English urbanization during the pre-industrial period; Gunnar Fridlizius presents the case of southern Swedish urbanization during the early stages of industrialization; Paul Bairoch marshals macro-economic data and reflects on the overall urban development of Continental Europe during the nineteenth century.

The triad—urbanization, economic growth, and population increase—is at the core of Wrigley's contribution. His aim is to gain more insight into why English urbanization during the two centuries before 1800 differed so markedly from Continental experience. The Ricardian doctrine of declining marginal returns in agriculture leads inexorably to the proposition that the level of urbanization has tangible upper bounds—and that the boundary is not far distant. In principle, this should result in a stationary urban state, for which eighteenth-century France may serve as an example. But the Ricardian paradigm also seems capable of explaining the less benign phenomenon of reversals in urbanization as experienced—at some point between 1600 and 1800—in Spain, Italy, Central Europe, and the Netherlands. The example of England stands as a happy exception to Ricardo's dismal proposition. There, the urban population consistently grew more rapidly than that of the nation as a whole, despite the substantial overall population growth rate of the seventeenth and eighteenth centuries. Moreover, English cities grew in the face of a rapid growth of the rural non-agricultural population. English urbanization seems to have been complementary to 'proto-industrialization', while Continental urbanization seems to have been competitive with it.

Wrigley argues that for all this to happen agricultural productivity must have increased substantially. In his vision, the causal linkage is not agricultural development-urbanization. Rather, he argues that towns—first London, and later the port cities and the new manufacturing towns—played the driving role in the virtuous cycle of population growth, urbanization, and economic development. The growing supply of urban goods available to the rural consumers increased incentives to expand agricultural production.

It is interesting to note that in the Swedish case, as analysed by Fridlizius, trade between town and country also acted as a catalyst to both urbanization and general economic growth. Fridlizius focuses his attention on Malmö, which was the chief port for the export of Scanian cereals. At first Scanian grain found its principal markets in other parts of Sweden, but after the abolition of the British Corn Laws the trade became international in character and its volume increased remarkably. And, as the grain trade grew, so did Malmö. The rise of Malmö as an exporter of a primary product did not lead to the creation of an enclave-economy oriented exclusively to foreign markets. Fridlizius describes a city that functioned as the accelerator in a process of regional market integration and commercialization. This process had begun earlier, so that an urban merchant class was already established and well placed to orchestrate economic growth, when the international grain trade began. Merchant houses stimulated farmers and landlords to introduce new farming methods, and supplied credit in many forms. Taking advantage of economies of scale, the merchants became more specialized and introduced new commercial techniques.

In rural Scania these multiple initiatives resulted in a remarkable growth of agricultural productivity whose proximate causes were an extensive enclosure movement, an increase in the number of hours worked per labourer, and organizational changes that increased labour productivity. Of particular importance was a growth of productivity in the transport sector. The railways did much to lower transport costs, of course, but Fridlizius argues that many cost-reducing measures had preceded railways, and that, here too, merchants had played a major role. In this whole process of market integration both parties, town and countryside, profited; it well illustrates the truth of Adam Smith's maxim that the mutal trade between town and country was 'the great commerce of every civilized society'. In this relationship the town was certainly not parasitic, draining human and material resources from the countryside. The town benefited from the relationship, but so did the countryside.

What Fridlizius elucidates through a micro-historical focus on a region of Sweden, Paul Bairoch analyses with macro-economic calculations drawn from all of nineteenth-century Continental Europe (excluding Russia). Bairoch traces the effects of crop yields, agricultural productivity, and transport costs on urban growth. Of these three factors, the fall in transport costs emerges as the most striking. In Bairoch's view, transport costs fell in the course of the nineteenth century by a factor of ten. The gains in agricultural productivity (about 150 per cent) and of combined vegetable and animal yields per unit of land (75–80 per cent), impressive as they were, pale in comparison.

Bairoch is interested in measuring the specific contribution of each of these factors to urbanization. Strong assumptions were needed to carry out this exercise, but the results are quite surprising. Bairoch assumes that the population is evenly spread over a geographical plane whose only feature is cities, each of the same size, all located at regular intervals. He can then show that higher crop yields have an effect equivalent to a reduction of the area required to feed the city population. This reduces the average distance that food needs to be transported (and that urban goods need to be transported to reach rural consumers). The improvement in crop yields in nineteenth-century Europe was such, reckons Bairoch, that they could account for no more than an increase of 2.3 per cent in the size of the urban population. This small impact of an increase in crop yields is less astonishing than one might think. During the nineteenth century United States crop yields hardly increased at all, yet the percentage urban rose from 5.3 to 41,6.

More important than the increase of output per unit of land was the increase in output per unit of labour. The increase of 150 per cent in the productivity of agricultural labour during the nineteenth century was capable, under Bairoch's assumptions, of accommodating an increase of 440 per cent in the urban population. That is, this factor alone could account for all the urbanization that took place during the nineteenth century, and much more besides.

The dramatic fall in transport costs during the nineteenth century had little impact on the lifting of the ceiling on urbanization. Here, Bairoch's simplifying assumptions are particularly constraining. In fact, cities are not evenly spaced, nor are they all of equal size. On the contrary, urban-systems concepts teach us to expect a strongly hierarchical and spatially unequal urban world. Bairoch recognizes this point, and notes that lower transport costs had an important effect on the growth of very large cities, cities that simply could not exist when transport costs were high.

The simplifying assumptions employed by Bairoch bear a certain resemblance to the theoretical model first presented by von Thünen in *Der isolierte Staat in Beziehung auf Landwirtschaft und Nationalökonomie* (Hamburg, 1826). Such a simplified rendering of complex phenomena makes possible theoretical insights into locational processes, but its ability to explain real historical developments is necessarily limited.

In view of the importance of urban provisioning to the potential urbanization of pre-industrial societies, it may not be amiss to delve further into this issue here. Historians are inclined to simplify the situation by concentrating on the provisioning of foodstuffs—and to simplify further by focusing attention on the supply of breadgrains. Yet every society has at least four basic material needs—food, clothing, shelter, and heating—and the countryside is the source for all the required raw materials: wool, flax, and hemp for cloth; timber, bricks, and tiles for construction; firewood, peat, and coal for heating energy; and, of course, all foodstuffs. In contemplating the consequences of this elementary fact it must be kept in mind that the land, labour, and transport requirements for the production and urban supply of each of these raw materials are to some extent competitive.

We can illustrate the importance of this fact by pausing to consider the implications of the claim made by Bairoch that each city-dweller in pre-industrial Europe consumed between 1.0 and 1.6 tons of firewood annually. A town of only 10,000 inhabitants would need to witness the annual arrival of between 10,000 and 16,000 horse-drawn carts, each carrying one ton of firewood. This amounts to thirty to fifty carts per day. By way of comparison, we can estimate such a city's breadgrain requirements at approximately 3,500 tons (assuming a consumption for all purposes of one kilogram per head per day). This would require a daily average of ten carts loaded with a ton of grain each to enter our city of 10,000 inhabitants. It is evident that supplying a growing city with firewood by means of horse-drawn carts quickly ran up against an unyielding constraint: simply providing fodder for the horses and food for the teamsters would withdraw arable acreage needed for the food supply of the urban population itself, while lengthening distances from forest to city would drive firewood prices rapidly upward. Clearly, the provisioning of a substantial city with fuel required the availability of water transport. Wherever this was not available, and wood remained the dominant source of heating energy, the maximum attainable level of urbanization faced definite limits. It will now be clear why von Thünen in his *Der isolierte Staat* located the sources of urban firewood as close to the city as possible. Only land devoted to the production of the most perishable foodstuffs deserved to be located closer to the city markets than the woodlands.

The above estimates are rough, but suffice to demonstrate the pressure the energy demands of a growing urban sector placed on pre-industrial transport facilities. The same overwhelming pressure can be shown to have been placed on rural labour supplies. Oral inquiries made in Austria among small farmers old enough to have experienced wood-cutting before the advent of mechanized saws and tractors revealed that a farmer needed to labour between six and eight weeks in order to provide his farmstead with firewood for the year. By extension, a pre-industrial society in which half the population was urban would require each rural household to labour for three months in order to provide firewood for itself and an urban household. Specialized foresters can be assumed to have attained a rather higher productivity than the Austrian peasants on whose experience this calculation is based, but they would also have been more distant from urban markets. In any event, it is clear that the provision of firewood diverted labour from agriculture, just as its transport diverted livestock and crop land from human consumption.

A third constraint that stood in the way of providing a large urban sector with firewood was the sheer surface area required to grow the necessary timber. Calculations for the heavily urban Dutch Republic of the seventeenth and eighteenth centuries show that a permanent forest preserve of 800,000 hectares—one-quarter of the country's total surface area—would have been necessary to harvest annually the nation's heat energy needs. If well-managed forests could yield an annual average of two tons of firewood per hectare, and if town dwellers required, following Bairoch, between 1.0 and 1.6 tons per year, a forested area of 0.5 to 0.8 hectares needed to be reserved for every urban inhabitant. Thus a town of 10,000 inhabitants needed a forest reserve of between 50 and 80 square km; one of 100,000 inhabitants needed between 500 and 800 square km. As cities grew in size and number, the conflict between the need for agricultural land and the need for forests became unavoidable.

A particularly telling illustration of the constraint imposed by fuel supplies is provided by the experience of Tokugawa Japan, which neither imported nor exported staple products of any sort from 1635 until 1854.[1] After the suppression of the constant internal warfare that had marked sixteenth-century Japan, a long era of internal and external peace ensued. In this benign environment the population grew from about 12 million around 1590 to 30 million by the 1720s. From then on, the population oscillated around that level until the 1820s. Agricultural production appears to have more than kept pace with population growth, particularly after 1720; as output grew while the population remained stationary, the standard of living rose. Presumably the substantial urbanization experienced by Tokugawa Japan was related to this economic growth, but here, too, a ceiling was reached (when the urban population stood at about 15 per cent of the total) which proved unyielding, despite the continued growth of agricultural output.

However accommodating agriculture might have been, the same could not be said for Japan's forest reserves. The large-scale temple, castle, and urban construction of the seventeenth century resulted in severe deforestation. Simultaneously, the growing peasantry exploited forests more intensely than before for lumber, fuel, and fertilizer. In response, the villages restricted their members' access to the communally owned woodlands. The growing value of forest land caused the government to see it as a potentially important source of revenue; this set in motion a prolonged effort on the part of the *daimyo* to appropriate village-owned forests.

Wood became an important source of public revenue as, by the early

---

[1] For the history of forest depletion and management in Japan see M. M. Osaka, 'Forest preservation in Tokugawa Japan', in R. P. Tucker and J. F. Richards (eds.), *Global Deforestation and the Nineteenth-century World Economy* (Durham, NC, 1983), 129–145; C. Totman, *The Origins of Japan's Modern Forests, The Case of Akita*, Asian Studies at Hawaii, no. 31 (Hawaii, 1985); C. Totman, 'Logging the Unloggable. Timber Transport in Early Modern Japan', *Journal of Forest History* (1983), 180–91.

eighteenth century, virtually all Japan's remaining high-quality forests had fallen into the hands of the *shogun* and *daimyo*. Such forests were all too scarce, however, and policies of conservation and afforestation were gradually enacted. As a result late nineteenth-century Japan was once again well endowed with majestic woodlands. The striking feature of this thumbnail sketch is the coincidence of a crisis in the supply of forest products, and the cessation of overall urbanization. No comparable link can be found between food production and urbanization.

The closed character of the Japanese economy during the Tokugawa period seems to invite bold generalization. The working of these constraints could be shown for pre-industrial Europe as well, although the more open economies add a complicating factor. Just as in Japan, in Europe as a whole the percentage urban did not exceed 15 per cent. But there were some notable regional exceptions to this rule; by examining their solutions to the energy constraint we may better understand the nature of the problem.

In Flanders a dense network of large cities was already in existence during the high Middle Ages, and neighbouring Brabant soon followed its example.[2] By the early sixteenth century over 30 per cent of this region's population lived in cities with more than 10,000 inhabitants. How did these cities secure their fuel supplies? During the early stages of this process of urban growth (during the tenth to twelfth centuries) the region was still heavily wooded, and the numerous waterways permitted the transport of wood from considerable distances. As the woodlands disappeared, the cities turned to peat, which was abundant in the large bogs between Bruges and Antwerp. By the fifteenth century these nearby bogs were exhausted, and the cities— Antwerp was by now the largest and most dynamic—reached further and further afield for new peat supplies. First, the extensive reserves available north of Antwerp (between Breda and Bergen op Zoom) were taken in hand. By the mid-sixteenth century, bogs straddling the border between Utrecht and Gelderland were being developed by an Antwerp entrepreneur.

We know little about the fuel sources available to the southern Netherlands' cities after the Dutch Revolt, but when they began to grow again at the end of the eighteenth century they shifted to coal, available from Liège and Hainault, and pushed ahead with an extensive programme of road and canal improvements.

[2] The data on Belgium can be found in A. Verhulst, *Histoire du paysage rural en Flandre. De l'époque romaine au XVIIIe siècle* (Brussels 1966); B. Augustyn, 'De Turfwinnersdorpen Kieldrecht en Verrebroek in 1394', *Annalen van de Koninklijke Oudheidkundige kring van het Land van Waas*, 88 (1985), 241–56; B. Augustyn and E. Thoen, 'Van veen tot bos. Krachtlijnen van de landschapsevolutie van het Noordvlaamse Meetjesland van de 12^e tot de 19^e eeuw', *Historisch-Geografisch Tijdschrift*, 5 (1987), 97–112; K. A. H. W. Leenders, *Verdwenen Venen. Een Onderzoek naar de ligging en exploitatie van thans verdwenen venen in het gebied tussen Antwerpen, Turnhout, Geertruidenberg, en Willemstrad (1250–1750)*. (Wageningen, 1989). H. Soly, *Urbanisme en Kapitalisme te Antwerpen in de 16^e eeuw* (Brussels, 1977); C. Vandenbroeke, 'Zuinig stoken. Brandstofverbruik en brandstofprijzen in België en Frankrijk Sinds de 15^e eeuw', *Economisch en Sociaal-Historisch Jaarboek*, 51 (Amsterdam, 1988), 93–125.

Urbanization came later in the northern Netherlands than in Flanders and Brabant, but attained even higher levels: during the early sixteenth century 31 per cent of the population lived in cities, and by 1675 45 per cent of the Republic's population were urban. In the province of Holland these figures were higher still; over half the population were urban throughout the seventeenth and eighteenth centuries.[3] One derivation of the name 'Holland' is that it was originally 'Holt-land', i.e. woodland. By 1600, there was precious little evidence to support the plausibility of that explanation. The Republic was substantially deforested.

A thorough study of the Republic's energy supplies makes clear how much this highly urbanized area depended on the exploitation of peat bogs.[4] Today very little remains of the layer of peat that once covered much of the northern and western portions of the Netherlands. By calculating the size of the original peat bogs, and subtracting what now remains, it becomes clear that over the years some 6.2 billion cubic metres of peat have been removed, mostly in the seventeenth, eighteenth, and nineteenth centuries. Before 1800, some 700 hectares were stripped of peat each year, yielding some 15.5 million cubic metres of peat. This required 7,000 man-years of labour. Since peat-digging was a seasonal activity, the actual number of labourers was easily three times this figure. The density of peat is such that ten cubic metres weigh about one ton, and the heating value of a ton of peat is equal to that of a ton of wood. Remembering the amount of land and labour needed to produce firewood illustrated above, we find that, if the Dutch Republic had relied on forests, some 22,000 man-years of labour would each year have had to work a permanent forest reserve of 800,000 hectares—one-quarter of the country's land area.

The Dutch could exploit their peat bogs efficiently, because nearly all were located at or just below the water table. Water transport was essential to the economical digging and transporting of this bulky commodity. Had road transport been used to bring the peat to its urban markets, 110,000 horses would have been required, and to feed these horses 230,000 hectares—one-third of the nation's arable land—would have been withdrawn from the production of crops destined for human consumption.

One reason why the alternatives to peat are so patently impossible in the Dutch Republic is that the cheap availability of peat turned this urban region into an intensive user of heat energy. Peat supplies sufficed to supply four million kilocalories per head per year during the seventeenth and eighteenth centuries, a multiple of the normal pre-industrial level. With such abundant supplies, the Dutch supported a wide array of energy-intensive industries,

---

[3] A. M. van der Woude, 'La Ville néerlandaise', in A. Lottin, G. P. Poussou, H. Soly, B. Vogler, and A. van der Woude (eds.), *Études sur les villes en Europe occidentale. Milieu de xviie siècle à la veille de la révolution française* (Paris, 1983), 307–85 (esp. tables 4, 6).

[4] J. W. de Zeeuw, 'Peat and the Dutch Golden Age. The Historical Meaning of Energy-Attainability', *A. A. G. Bijdragen,* 21 (Wageningen, 1978), 3–31.

such as brewing, distilling, brick, tile, pipe, and faïence factories, salt and sugar refineries, madder and chicory works, bleaching and dye works, etc.

If the numerous cities of the Low Countries could grow in the favourable environment created by peat deposits and water transport, what was the key to the rapid urbanization of England, where 20 per cent of the population lived in cities with more than 10,000 inhabitants by 1800, and, even more remarkably, Europe's first city of one million inhabitants emerged in the form of London? Both features of England's urbanization—its rapid growth and its concentration in one great city—appear to be related to the character of its energy supply. Until the end of the eighteenth century neither peat nor extensive waterways existed to supply numerous points with cheap energy. What did exist were coal deposits. In the north-east, mines were very near the coast, so that the coal could be carried cheaply to distant markets—as long as they were accessible by coastal vessels. This became the source of cheap fuel for London; as the city grew throughout the eighteenth century so did its consumption of coal: from 775 kg. per head in 1701–25 to 1,250 kg. per head in 1776–1800.[5]

While the mines of Northumberland lifted the energy constraints on London's growth, the existence of coal deposits did not automatically solve this problem for most other urban locations. Only towards the end of the eighteenth century, with the construction of a canal system linking the major navigable rivers of England into a comprehensive system of internal waterways, did it become possible to supply coal cheaply to the commercial and industrial towns of the interior. Their impressive early growth could now continue, ultimately reaching levels of urbanization far higher than had been achieved in the Low Countries.

One final zone of very high urbanization remains to be considered: Italy. It was, indeed, the first heavily urbanized part of Europe, but we have left it to the last because its example raises more questions than it provides answers. Almost every part of Italy was highly urbanized by the standards of medieval and early modern Europe, but the extreme case was northern Italy, with about 15 per cent of its population in cities with more than 10,000 inhabitants from at least 1500. But urban provisioning could hardly have been less of a challenge further south, where cities such as Palermo, Rome, and, the largest of all, Naples, each concentrated well over 100,000 inhabitants within their walls as early as 1600.

How did these numerous, large cities acquire their heating energy? At present there is no convincing answer to this question. We know that Venice imported wood from the Dalmatian coast and even from the Black Sea. But this must have been timber for building rather than for firewood. Could the many cities of the Po valley have supplied themselves with wood from the

---

[5] Quantities calculated from data in P. H. Deane and W. A. Cole, *British Economic Growth, 1688–1959* (Cambridge, 1962), and in E. A. Wrigley and R. S. Schofield, *The Population History of England, 1541–1871* (London, 1981).

slopes of the Alps, making use of the numerous rivers and streams that feed the Po? Where, then, should we begin to look for the energy supplies of cities such as Florence, Rome, and Naples?

It is possible that the key to this historical problem is to focus on demand rather than supply. The milder climate of the Mediterranean basin must have reduced the need for home heating fuel from the levels obtaining in northern Europe. In fact, the discomfort reported by northern visitors to Italy during the winter months hints at the possibility that Mediterranean homes made little, if any, provision for space heating, requiring the inhabitants simply to endure the (relatively brief) periods of extreme cold.[6]

A related matter concerns the fuel needed for the preparation of food. Is this requirement roughly the same in all cultures, or is it possible to identify 'fuel-intensive' and 'fuel-sparing' cuisines? It would be interesting to compare the average daily fuel use of the Italian (and Japanese?) kitchens with that of, say, the German, Scandinavian, or English kitchen. One thing is certain, the common drinks of northern Europe, beer and distilled spirits, required far more heat energy in their preparation than did the wine of the Mediterranean lands.

This brings us to a third component of demand for fuel, the fuel-using industries. Did the industrial structure before the Industrial Revolution differ regionally according to relative energy availability? If so, there would have been substantial interregional differences in fuel consumption, and these would have been most strikingly different in the cities, where industrial production was disproportionately concentrated.

Although we do not have firm answers to the many questions raised above, it now seems possible to speculate that the range of fuel needs per head of town-dwellers offered by Bairoch (1.0 to 1.6 tons of firewood annually) may require modification: there may have been fuel-saving economies (Italy, other Mediterranean countries, Japan?) which consumed fuel at or below the low end of Bairoch's range, while fuel-intensive economies (north-western Europe) consumed near the high end of the range.[7] The difference is by no means insignificant to the potential for pre-industrial urbanization.

We began these remarks with the observation that the city depended on the countryside for its basic needs of food, clothing, housing, and heating. We have stressed a fact not sufficiently recognized, that transport acted as a

---

[6] For perceptions of Mediterranean winter climate see F. Braudel, *The Mediterranean and the Mediterranean World in the Age of Philip II* (Eng. trans., New York, 1972), 255–6.

[7] Factual information seems difficult to find. H. Chr. Johansen put at our disposal concrete data on the imports of firewood, peat, and coal during the years 1784–94 in the Danish cities of Copenhagen (about 100,000 inhabitants) and Odense (about 5,000 inhabitants). In Copenhagen the calorific value of these three sources of energy put together was approximately equal to 1.5 tons of wood per city-dweller. This is clearly at the upper end of the range given by Bairoch. The city of Odense received from the countryside on average about 15,000 cart-loads of firewood and 12,000 cart-loads of peat each year. This certainly surpasses the calorific value of Bairoch's upper level of 1.6 tons of firewood given as an average per city-dweller. But Odense contained such energy-intensive industries as sugar refineries and soap works within its walls.

severe bottleneck in the urban provision of energy supplies, and that energy supplies, save in exceptional circumstances, actively constrained urban growth until the age of coal and railways. Urban populations need food, of course, but in most of Europe in early modern times this constraint remained theoretical. The percentage urban did not actually press against the limits imposed by agricultural productivity. In the case of fuel supplies the situation may have been very different; here the constraint to urbanization seems to have been not simply theoretical but real.

While the pre-industrial city could not exist without raw materials from the countryside, neither could it exist without the immigration of country people. This statement is widely accepted as a veritable rule of pre-industrial urban demography, but in fact migration is the least known dimension of population history. Analyses of migration patterns are not numerous, and this is understandable when one reflects on the extremely limited and imperfect documentation of this phenomenon available before the late nineteenth century.

Migration, and the related subject of the marriage market, are particularly good vantage points from which to approach the larger topic of the urban demographic system. The questionnaire drafted to guide contributions to the Tokyo seminar sought to direct attention to the demographic behaviour of migrants. The age, sex, and marital status of migrants to the towns could, in the aggregate, profoundly influence the overall urban demographic system. A particularly neglected topic is out-migration from the cities, the selective character of which could likewise influence the urban demographic system. Finally, attention was directed towards the ways in which migrants were integrated into the urban communities. Here, the marriage market is the single most important institution. All these issues contribute to a more complete understanding of the ways migration influenced urban fertility levels. In describing and analysing the 'demographic transition', attention is focused on fertility and mortality. In its urban setting, this transition concept needs to be placed in a broader social context—one that incorporates migration patterns.

The five papers included in this section of the volume (Johansen, Bengtsson, Reher, Matović, and Saito) underscore the central role of migration in the pre-industrial urban demographic system. At the same time they warn that the single most common measure of migration, the net migration to the city, can be a treacherously misleading indicator of the larger phenomenon. Johansen, in his study of the Danish city of Odense, observes that the difference between net and gross migration rates did not change greatly between 1750 and 1900. Out-migration was regularly between 6 and 8 per cent higher than in-migration. The combination of the two ensured that the city experienced each year a substantial turnover of population. At any given time, a majority of adults had been born outside the city; belonging to the second or third generation of an Odense family was altogether exceptional.

In mid-nineteenth-century Scania (southern Sweden), Bengtsson measured gross migration rates of between 5 and 12 per cent in the rural districts and between 12 and 15 per cent in the towns. In one year an incredible 22 per cent of the population had just arrived in Scania's towns. Bengtsson's migration findings are broadly consistent with those of Johansen: net out-migration in rural districts was only 0.2 per cent per year, but this sufficed to maintain an average level of urban in-migration of 1.2 per cent. Despite this, nineteenth-century urban Swedish population growth owed nearly as much to natural increase as to migration. Only in Sweden's largest city, Stockholm, did the demographic situation differ markedly from that in the smaller towns examined by Johansen and Bengtsson. Stockholm experienced severe economic stagnation between 1750 and 1850, and not until the 1860s did the capital's population record a natural increase—and only after 1880 did this natural increase play any significant role in the city's growth. During the entire second half of the nineteenth century net in-migration accounted for fully 80 per cent of the city's growth. During this period net in-migration oscillated between 2.0 and 3.5 per cent of the population.

Lest we ascribe these migration patterns to Scandinavian peculiarities the example of a small Spanish provincial city can be introduced. Reher's study of mid-nineteenth-century Cuenca reveals the same key role played by migration, and emphasizes the large differences that could emerge between trends in the net and the gross migration rates. Between 1844 and 1847 this somnolent town of some 5,500 inhabitants experienced an annual net out-migration of 2.5 per cent. But this net figure was the result of gross in-migration rates of 13.7 per cent and out-migration rates of 16.2 per cent. Each year, well over 10 per cent of the town's population was new to Cuenca.

These four examples can be added to others available in the literature to strengthen our belief that high rates of in- and out-migration have long characterized European cities of all sizes. This can account, perhaps, for the occasional very rapid growth or decline of town populations observed in the historical records. Given the high rates of gross migration, an imbalance could quickly generate a substantial change in total population. A corollary to this is the observation that the long-term stability of a town's population is unlikely to reflect the absence of migration; rather, it most probably is the product of a balance between substantial in- and out-migration streams.

The demographic impact of these migration streams depends sensitively upon their age distributions. Reher shows that migration in Cuenca affected all age groups. Comprehensive age-at-migration data are not available from the other studies, but they are all in agreement that both in- and out-migration is most intense among people between 15 and 35 years of age. What did differ from town to town was the relative importance of migration of males and females. Stockholm and Cuenca received far more female migrants than males; in Odense and the Scanian towns the two migration flows were generally in balance; in Japan males dominated migration to the towns, although this dominance gradually diminished during the course of the eighteenth and early nineteenth centuries.

These studies also show that the vast majority of migrants (both in and out) were single. This directs our attention to the marriage market as an institution regulating the integration of migrants into the urban community. Matović's contribution is highly instructive with regard to the difficulties that migrants could face in securing a marriage partner. She found that the large surplus of female migrants to mid-nineteenth-century Stockholm put them in a weak competitive position in finding a spouse. But male migrants did not enjoy a strong position in the marriage market either, since their frequent inability to secure permanent employment and earn a steady income made them unattractive marriage partners. In this context, Matović observes, many migrants remained celibate, and many more entered into informal unions. These extra-marital 'families', in which the women were commonly much older than the men, reflected a 'poverty culture' where economic insecurity placed 'respectable' marriage out of reach.

The inequalities that placed marriage out of reach for many migrants also affected partner choice within marriage. The strongest position in the Stockholm marriage market was that of the native-born, particularly that of men. The native-born enjoyed better access to secure employment, but the women among them suffered from the overall surplus of women in the city. This general situation may prove to have been common to many of Europe's cities, where high sex ratios were typical. It has been shown to have been true of Amsterdam at the beginning of the nineteenth century.[8] Reher's finding that Cuenca's native-born married earlier on average than migrants provides additional confirmation of the disadvantages faced by migrants. Perrenoud's contribution shows the same phenomenon to have prevailed in Geneva throughout the seventeenth and eighteenth centuries: on average, native women married at least four to five years earlier than migrant women.

With these differences between migrants and natives we have only begun to explore the many differences in demographic behaviour that characterized urban communities. Cities were invariably more like 'melting-pots' than were rural communities. The socio-economic, ethnic, and religious groups could vary enormously one from another. For this reason, it is futile to think of urban demography as a unity to be set beside rural characteristics. We must not lose sight of the fact that the composite urban pattern is invariably composed of distinct, socially differentiated patterns.

Approaches to historical urban demography stressing social differentiation bore very useful fruit in the contributions on migration and marriage just discussed. This line of attack proved to be essential to the two papers in which the urban demographic system as a whole was considered, and specifically, the practice of family limitation within marriage. Perrenoud's comparative

---

[8] H. A. Diederiks, *Een stad in verval. Amsterdam omstreeks 1800* (Meppel, 1982), 70–85.

study of Geneva and Rouen differentiated between migrants and natives, and among social groups in Geneva. Bardet compared Rouen to its hinterland and sought to isolate the demographic behaviour of rural migrants to Rouen to see how urban life changed that behaviour.

If Rouen and Geneva can be taken as representative of French cities as a whole the following picture of demographic change emerges: the practice of family limitation became widespread during the second half of the seventeenth century. Between 1670 and 1800, the average completed family size fell from about eight to four. The higher strata of society took the lead in this development, but the middle classes followed their superiors within a generation. It seems to have taken another thirty to forty years before family limitation spread to the lower classes. By the beginning of the nineteenth century social differences in fertility restriction had largely disappeared; the practice of family limitation had become diffused throughout urban society.

Within each social class, these studies show that the lead in adopting family limitation within marriage was taken by couples who married early in life. Among Genevan women who married before their twentieth birthday, average completed family size fell from 9.6 to 5.3 within a century; during the same period women who married between the ages of 30 and 34 reduced their average completed family size from 4.3 to 3.6 Fertility control was clearly parity specific; there was little evidence for it during the first decade of marriage. However, as the eighteenth century progressed this characteristic became less marked and fertility declines can also be seen in the second quinquennium of marriage.

What of those women who were newcomers to urban life? How strongly did their fertility behaviour differ from that of women long accustomed to urban life? The total fertility of migrant women was somewhat lower than that of the urban born as a consequence of their higher average age at marriage. After the age of 30 these differences all but disappear, however, and at the higher parities migrant women adopted family limitation practices just as their native-born sisters did. This similarity in reproductive behaviour runs counter to our preconceived notions. The common assumption that family limitation practices would take time to diffuse to migrant populations rests on the assumption that migrants were disproportionately poor, ill-educated, even dispossessed. In the case of Rouen, Bardet is able to show that the literacy level of migrants to the city was well above the average of that of the rural population from which they were drawn, and even surpassed the level of those born in Rouen. If migrants tended to be disproportionately drawn from the more enterprising rural folk, it should not surprise us that they quickly grasped the advantages in the urban setting of restrictive procreative behaviour.

Combining the findings on migration with those on the adoption of family limitation practices seems to suggest that among the large number of women who migrated out of the cities, or returned to their villages after a stint in the city, there must have been many who had had experience of fertility-restricting behaviour. In Rouen, for example, as many as 25 per cent of all women who bore at least one child in the city left before the end of their child-bearing years. Did such migrants spread family limitation practices to the small towns and villages?

Bardet examines this question by comparing the development of marital fertility in Rouen, in surrounding villages, in more distant villages of the Vexin, and in the small provincial town of Meulan. Until the mid-eighteenth century Rouen's behaviour was hardly emulated in any of these other places. After about 1730, the inhabitants of Meulan began to limit their fertility, but rather hesitantly until 1790, when fertility fell rapidly. In the villages, the process can first be observed after 1760, with proto-industrial villages apparently taking the lead over purely agricultural ones. At the current stage of this study, Bardet notices an interesting difference between fertility-restricting behaviour in city and country: in Rouen birth intervals remained short and restriction was achieved on a parity-specific basis; in the countryside fertility was reduced through the lengthening of the average birth interval.

The socially and geographically differentiated analyses by Perrenoud and Bardet move the study of the origins of modern contraceptive behaviour a large step forward. A generation of family reconstitution studies can begin to release answers to our questions about French uniqueness, and the dynamic of the fertility transition once the urban cornerstones are in place. Consider the question of the time and place when deliberate fertility restriction within marriage began. If further research confirms our suspicion that it began in urban France during the second half of the seventeenth century, the question remains, why? Perrenoud and Bardet adhere to the hypothesis first developed by Maurice Garden, that the habit of wet-nursing that was widespread among urban French families during the seventeenth century and confronted these families with so large a rise in fertility as to force the search for a solution to the too-frequent incidence of pregnancy. Perrenoud's chapter offers concrete data on the rise of fertility on the eve of the adoption of family limitation practices. His suggestion that rural fertility behaviour should be seen as imitating urban experience makes even more urgent the continued study of urban demography.

Despite our best efforts to organize current research on historical urban demography around a few themes, there are inevitably important and interesting research agenda that fall beyond the boundaries of our categories. Human ingenuity is not easily channelled into predetermined paths. And we must be grateful for the three final research contributions, which add a challenging variety to this volume. Ts'ui-jung Liu's chapter serves as a demonstration of the potential richness of Chinese genealogical records and local literary evidence as a source of demographic information. The contribution by Reher on Spanish urbanization after 1860 fits well into the general themes of this volume, but differs radically in method. Here, in Reher's second chapter, highly aggregative historical data are deployed to evaluate the influence of several variables on urbanization. The influence of the Princeton Fertility Project,[9] whose methods hold promise for specifically urban analysis in the future is obvious in this chapter.[10] Yasumoto's chapter offers an exercise in social demography. Precisely because the city is—so much more than the countryside—a composite of different social groups we should expect to find many applications of social demography here.

In editing the contributions to a conference it is nearly impossible to retain the intellectual atmosphere created by the participants. We have the chance to convey something of that atmosphere because the conference was fortunate to have ended with the concluding remarks of a scholar capable of presenting a clear summary and penetrating critical reflections. Paul Hohenberg's contribution echoes much of the spirit of the discussion; at the same time it poses new questions. His remarks served well in closing the conference, and they serve well to round out this volume with guidance for future research.

[9] For a survey of these publications and their results, see A. J. Coale and S. C. Watkins, *The Decline of Fertility in Europe* (Princeton, 1986).

[10] The method is spreading beyond the Princeton group proper. See e.g. O. W. A. Boonstra and A. M. van der Woude, 'Demographic Transition in the Netherlands. A Statistical Analysis of Regional Differences in the Level and Development of the Birth Rate and of Fertility, 1850–1890', *A A. G. Bijdragen*, 24 (Wageningen, 1984), 1–57 (also publ. Utrecht, 1984); and in a regional case-study, T. L. M. Engelen, *Fertiliteit, Arbeid, Mentaliteit. De vruchtbaarheidsdaling in Nederlands-Limburg, 1850–1960* (Assen, 1987).

2 Types of City-Size Distributions
A Comparative Analysis

CAROL A. SMITH
Department of Anthropology, Duke University, Durham, North Carolina, USA

Most scholars concerned with variation in urbanization have concentrated their attention on differences in levels and rates of urbanization. But urbanization is more than the growth in urban population, it is also the reorganization of the urban system, which can be seen and measured by the different forms the urban system takes. That is, in addition to growing, the cities resulting from urbanization take on hierarchical relations with other cities manifest in particular city-size distributions (e.g. rank size, primate, and 'flat-topped' or immature).[1] In this chapter I focus on explaining the different distributions that emerge in systems of cities during the urbanization process.

There is at present no theory that adequately accounts for the full range of empirical variation in urban forms over time and space—though general theories of urban forms abound, most of them developmental. One reason why most general theories fail the test of history is that they are based on inadequate distinctions among urban forms. In addition, most theories fail to distinguish between different aspects or features of urban size—i.e. size in terms of urban infrastructure against size of urban population. I hope to show here how explanations of the developmental patterns of urban distributions can be improved by making finer distinctions among them and by distinguishing urban forms based on infrastructure from urban forms based on population.

1. Forms of the city-size distribution

Empirical studies, mostly based on the relative sizes of the largest cities in a national urban system, show three basic urban forms: (*a*) the first-ranking city may be much larger than twice the size of the second-ranking city (primate); (*b*) it may be only twice the size of the second-ranking city (rank size); or (*c*) it

---

[1] I use the term 'immature' to describe the city-size distribution first described and named by C. Vapñarski, 'The Argentine System of Cities: Primacy and Rank-Size Rule', in J. Hardoy (ed.), *Urbanization in Latin America* (Garden City, 1975). The distribution has a shallower slope than the 'mature' or rank-size distribution described below, and often has a 'flat top' as well.

may be close to the same size as the second-ranking city (no standard term has been given to this pattern).[2] Geographers concerned to understand these patterns have found that the top-ranking cities in a national system must be contextualized within the national system of cities. Zipf, for example, observed that if the city populations in the United States were plotted against city rank on a double logarithmic scale, the result was approximately a straight line with a slope of -1 (see Fig. 2.1).[3] In other words, each city was half the size of the city next higher in rank to it. This is known as the 'normal' rank-size distribution.

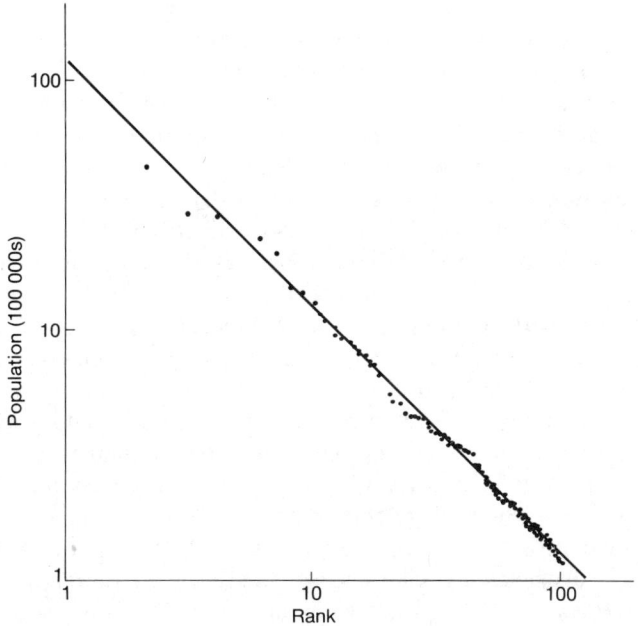

Figure 2.1. Metropolitan districts: 100 largest in the United States in 1940, ranked in order of decreasing population size

Brian Berry must be credited with carrying out the most sustained treatment of city-size distributions extant; much of the present orthodoxy about urban primacy and about the rank-size distribution rests on his work, which I briefly summarize here.[4]

---

[2] M. Jefferson, 'The Law of the Primate City', *Geographical Review*, 29 (1939), 226–32; G. K. Zipf, *Human Behavior and the Principle of Least Effort: An Introduction to Human Ecology* (Reading, Penn., 1949); N. Ginsberg, *Atlas of Economic Development* (Chicago, 1961).
[3] Zipf, *Human Behavior*, did not discover the rank-size rule, but was the first to try to explain it. The phenomenon had been noted much earlier (cf. F. Auerbach 'Das Gesetz der Bevölkerungskonzentration', *Petermann's Geographische Mitteilungen*, 59 (1913), 74–6).
[4] B. J. L. Berry, 'City Size Distribution and Economic Development', *Economic Development*

Berry's comparative work showed that normal rank-size distributions were typical of the following countries: those with developed economies (the United States being the prime example); those with many cities and large populations (China provides one such case); and those in the process of developing (El Salvador is one example). Primate systems had the opposite characteristics. The comparative work also suggested that urban primacy could result from the improper specification of an urban system: a small country whose urban hinterland extended well beyond its national boundaries (Portugal, for example, with its several overseas colonies) might have an over-large first-ranking city because that city headed a larger than national urban system. Berry also linked the development of rank-size regularity to central-place theory, proposing that a rank-size distribution resulted from the regular increments of population in cities at different levels of a central-place hierarchy.[5] On the basis of his theoretical work, as well as his comparative and longitudinal studies, he proposed an evolutionary theory of urban primacy which suggested that it preceded economic development (and represented an immature phase of urban growth). Economic development brought about the later emergence of a rank-size distribution.

On the basis of studies such as these, it became customary to define urban primacy as deviation from the rank-size rule. Normal or developed urban systems were assumed to conform to the rank-size distribution, while first-ranking cities in abnormal or undeveloped systems were assumed to be 'over-large'. Measures of urban primacy (such as Ginsberg's index) are in fact predicated on the rank-size distribution.[6] If the first-ranking city is more than twice the size of the second-ranking city, or is larger than the sum of the populations of the second, third, and fourth cities, it is larger than the rank-size rule predicts. On the basis of this comparison, moreover, it is *too* large. (This last statement is true, of course, only if evidence supports the notion that rank-size distributions characterize mature, well-integrated urban systems.) Theories of urban primacy, in fact, revolve around the contrast between primacy and rank-size distributions. Given that the very definition of urban primacy rests upon this contrast, it is reasonable for any study of urban

---

and *Cultural Change*, 9 (1961), 571–87; B. J. L. Berry and W. L. Garrison, 'Recent Developmnts of Central-Place Theory', *Regional Science Association: Papers and Proceedings*, 9 (1958), 107–20; B. J. L. Berry, 'City Size and Economic Development', in L. Jakobson and V. Prakesh (eds.), *Urbanization and National Development* (Beverly Hills, 1971).

[5] Central-place theory is concerned with the spacing of cities relative to their sizes. Size is, however, defined in terms of urban functions, especially those for rural consumers, rather than in terms of population. Central-place theory was developed by W. Christaller, *Central Places in Southern Germany*, trans. C. W. Baskin (Englewood Cliffs, 1966). and by A. Lösch, *The Economics of Location*, trans. W. F. Stolper (New Haven, 1954). A review of its basic predictions and assumptions can be found in C. A. Smith, 'Regional Economic Systems: Linking Geographical Models and Economic Problems', in C. A. Smith (ed.), *Regional Analysis*, i. *Economic Systems* (New York, 1976), 3–63.

[6] Ginsberg's index measures primacy by considering the relative sizes of only the top four cities in a national system. Cf. Ginsberg, *Atlas of Geonomic Development*.

primacy to be concerned with rank-size distributions. But is it reasonable to assume that urban primacy is the only deviation from the rank-size rule?

In fact, it is not reasonable to make such an assumption, as Cesar Vapñarski demonstrated in 1966.[7] Not only may top-ranking cities be larger than would be expected from the rank-size rule, they may also be smaller (see Fig. 2.2). That is, Vapñarski found that while Buenos Aires was a primate city

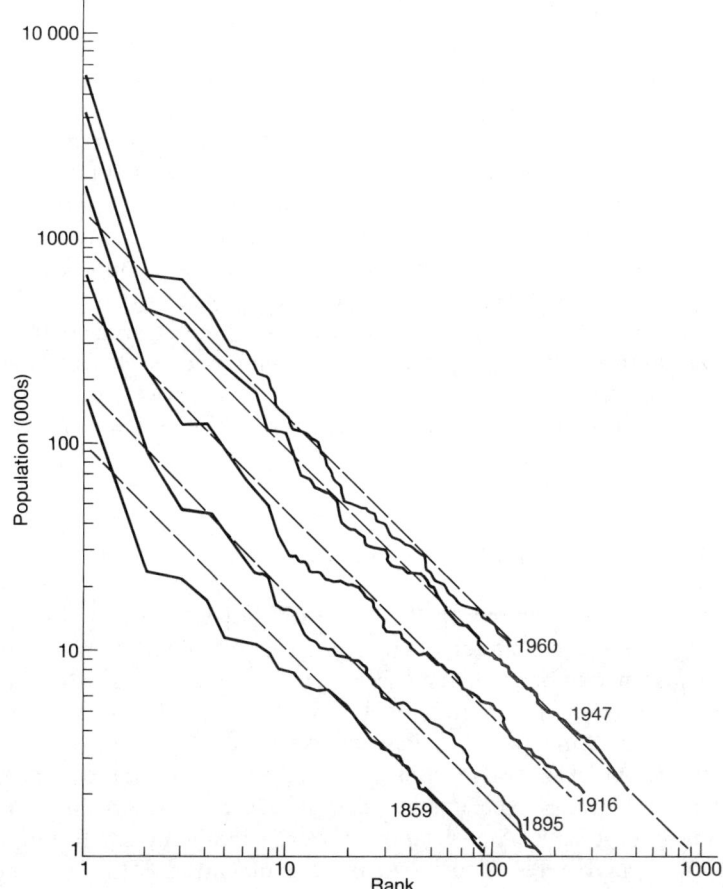

Figure 2.2. Argentina, 1859–1960: city-size distribution at each census date (best-fitting line of slope −1 drawn excluding largest city in all, except first census date)

and thus larger than predicted by the rank-size rule, the next group of cities were all much smaller than predicted. He also found that during the twentieth century Buenos Aires continued to grow even larger than would be expected

[7] Cf. Vapñarski, 'Argentine System of Cities'.

on the basis of the rank-size distribution, at the same time as the secondary cities grew to a point approximating the rank-size distribution (see Fig. 2.2). In other words, Argentina's urban system became more primate at a time when it also came to conform more closely to the rank-size rule. Vapñarski concluded that primacy was not fully inconsistent with a rank-size distribution. What was inconsistent with the rank-size distribution was the distribution that Vapñarski found for Argentina in 1869, when most Argentine cities were 'too small'. Vapñarski labelled the early pattern 'immature' and argued that urban primacy could be associated with either immature or rank-size distributions.

Geographers have not paid a great deal of attention to the immature city-size distribution. But recognition of the type is of considerable importance for two reasons. First, it shows that there are four, rather than two, possible types of city-size distributions: rank size *without* primacy; rank size *with* primacy; immature *without* primacy; and immature *with* primacy. Secondly, it shows that the forces that cause urban primacy are not necessarily opposed to those that cause the rank-size distribution. Argentina's urban system became both more primate and closer to rank size over the same ninety-year period. The developmental trajectory of Argentina's cities, moreover, is not unusual. It is common to most Central American countries in the twentieth century—and I have proposed that it is the 'classic' Latin American pattern of urban development.[8]

2. Immature urban systems

The information accumulated on the immature city-size distribution (where top-ranking cities are smaller than predicted by the rank-size rule) is spotty because it has been defined as a type only quite recently.[9] All the information, however, points in a single direction: that the urban system in question is not well integrated or mature. An urban system might fail to be mature for any one of several reasons. In the middle of the nineteenth century national urban systems were immature in most Latin American countries. That is, the largest Latin American cities were simply 'too small' relative to the sizes of smaller cities. The most likely explanation is that commercial interchange between cities was limited throughout the economy.[10] Today, however, most Latin American countries contain one or two strongly primate

---

[8] C. A. Smith, 'Theories and Measures of Urban Primacy: A Critique' and 'Class Relations and Urbanization in Guatemala: Towards an Alternative Theory of Urban Primacy', in M. Timberlake (ed.), *Urbanization in the World Economy* (New York, 1985).

[9] The pattern has been discussed in detail only by Vapnarski, 'Argentine System of Cities'; G. Johnson, 'Rank Size Convexity and System Integration: A View from Archaeology', *Economic Geography*, 56 (1980), 234–47; and C. A. Smith, 'Modern and Premodern Primacy', *Comparative Urban Systems*, 9 (1982), 79–96.

[10] See A. Portes and J. Walton, *Urban Latin America* (Austin, Texas, 1976).

cities followed by urban distributions that are much closer to that predicted by the rank-size rule.

The urban economies of traditional (1843) China and modern (1959) Russia, described by G. William Skinner and Chauncy Harris, show a different pattern.[11] In both cases, the national systems show urban immaturity (the top-ranking cities are smaller than expected from an examination of the entire national urban system). But in both cases most (though not all) regional systems show rank-size regularity. Skinner argued that there was no national economy in traditional China. China's largest city, Peking, played the largest role in the national economy, but was not large enough to dominate other Chinese cities. He notes that the urban economy was mature in 1843, but its scope was limited, in part because of poor inter-regional transport and the great distances involved; in part because of peculiarities in China's economy and national political system; and in part because of its limited degree of urbanization (only 5.3 per cent of China's population lived in cities with 4,000 or more inhabitants). Hence, nineteenth-century China could not support a well-integrated *national* urban system.

The Russian case illustrates some of the complexity of determining the kind of urban system one finds. Harris's study shows that the urban distribution in the European part of Russia was 'immature' below the level of Moscow. Some fifty secondary cities in that region were much smaller than predicted by the rank-size rule. And Moscow is thus more than ten times the size of the second-ranking city in its system—in all of Russia, in fact. Thus we have an equivocal situation where Moscow is primate if the usual measure of primacy (size in relation to a few secondary cities) is used, but is of appropriate size in relation to the *smaller* cities in its region (i.e. by the rank-size rule), and is 'too small' as the national capital or primary city of all Russia. Obviously, then, to determine whether or not a city is primate, one must look at the situation in its proper context. Moscow is a primate city within its relevant urban system and within Russia, but it is primate because secondary cities are too small, rather than because Moscow itself is too large.

Skinner and Harris could reach these conclusions, however, only because they defined the appropriate units of analysis in their studies. Most people have simply classified China and Russia as non-primate systems.[12] Or worse still, some have assumed that China has a rank-size national urban system because it does not have a primate city, while they consider Russia to have a slightly primate (rather than immature) urban system.[13]

Immature urban distributions are also found in many smaller countries or

---

[11] G. W. Skinner, 'Regional Urbanization in Nineteenth-Century China', in G. W. Skinner (ed.), *The City in Late Imperial China* (Stanford, 1977); C. Harris, *Cities of the Soviet Union* (Chicago, 1970).
[12] Cf. e.g. S. El Shakhs, 'Development, Primacy and Systems of Cities', *The Journal of Developing Areas*, 7 (1972), 11–16.
[13] Cf. Berry, 'City Size Distributions and Geonomic Development'.

regions. Russell examined the city-size distributions of twenty-one regions of Europe for the years immediately before 1348, when the first major population devastation from plague occurred. All these urban systems were immature, most of them exceedingly so. Russell himself argues that a rank-size relationship obtained in these cases. But he changed the usual rank-size formula by a square-root reduction (to a slope of -0.5 rather than one of -1.0) because he found empirically that the larger cities in these systems were too small. Russell's explanation for the 'over-small' medieval cities is that 'the pre-industrial society did not provide as much means for keeping up the larger city's size'.[14]

Jan de Vries, who looked at European city-size distributions in a later period (1500–1800), found the same phenomenon on a larger scale (when grouping European countries into larger regional systems) and agrees with Russell's explanation for it.[15] By plotting all the cities of Europe above a certain population threshold between 1500 and 1800, de Vries showed that the very shallow European city-size distribution of 1500 (-0.63) was moving towards a steeper slope; it reached maximum steepness in 1700 (-0.8) and maintained it until 1800. When de Vries separated northern and southern Europe, he observed that northern Europe had moved substantially towards a rank-size distribution by 1700, while southern Europe retained a flatter upper distribution. He summarized his findings as follows:

From 1500 to 1750 urban growth in Europe as a whole can be summarized by a process of selective city-growth which step-by-step converts a strikingly 'concave' rank-size distribution (one of low slope and of flat top) to one approaching lognormality and with a much steeper slope. . . . This is a rather abstract way of saying that urban growth was concentrated in the larger cities, and in those whose growth persisted long enough for them to become large, and that urbanization was not characterized by the 'birth' of numerous small cities.[16]

De Vries's observation that the development of urban systems in early modern Europe involved the growth of the largest cities in the system rather than the growth or birth of smaller cities is important and directs attention to the fact that top-ranking cities in most 'pre-modern' urban systems are rather small. In almost every historical study of urban systems I could find (which are admittedly few in number), as well as in my own study of Central America, the same general growth pattern emerges. In the early system there is a 'long' flat top (major cities are too small) and a very shallow slope; later, the system loses its flat top (occasionally to develop a primate city) and fits a

---

[14] J. C. Russell, *Medieval Regions and their Cities* (Bloomington, Ind., 1972), 24.
[15] J. de Vries, *European Urbanization, 1500–1800* (London and Cambridge, Mass., 1984). De Vries's data consist of the 378 cities that contained at least 10,000 inhabitants at some point between 1500 and 1800, located in Iberia, Italy, France, Germany, Switzerland, Scandinavia, the British Isles, the Netherlands, and Belgium; Poland and the Austrian lands are included for only part of the analysis.
[16] Ibid. 101.

steeper slope. When a slope of −1 is achieved, cities in the top and middle range of the distribution grow proportionately, maintaining the same slope.[17]

The United States provides the classic case of a national urban system developing from an earlier immature form to a later 'mature' form (a rank-size distribution with a slope of −1). Many people have described the urban growth pattern of the United States,[18] but most have been intrigued by the short period during which urban primacy was found (1830–50) rather than the earlier period when the system was immature (1750–1850). Only G. A Johnson has looked specifically at the immature phase and argued that it resulted from poor commercial integration of the United States economy during that period.[19] He shows that as intra-systemic trade volume increased between US cities, the urban system grew to approximate the rank-size rule. His argument about the causes of urban immaturity closely resembles Vapñarski's, whose study of Argentina was discussed above. Both Johnson and Vapñarski used a systems approach and suggested that urban immaturity resulted from the lack of systemic integration in the urban economy, more specifically from poor commercial interchange between cities.

The overall empirical evidence which links the immature distribution to poor urban-system integration is so compelling that I conclude that it is, indeed, a major factor. In other words, an immature system can result from improper specification of the appropriate urban system (Russia's national system in 1959, China's national system in 1843, Europe's macro-regional system in 1800). Or it can result from a related phenomenon, poorly developed commercial interchange between a group of cities that one might expect to be related (various medieval urban systems, China's several less commercialized regional systems, the United States' eighteenth-century urban system, Latin America's nineteenth-century national urban systems). These are not, however, the only factors that can produce an immature system. We must also consider the level of urbanization that can be supported by an agrarian economy.

De Vries has argued that the urban systems in early modern Europe were well integrated commercially, but that the agricultural economy of the period was not productive enough to allow the growth of very large cities characteristic of a well-defined urban hierarchy. Hence, urban systems in early modern Europe were 'immature', but they were neither poorly

[17] Cf. Smith, 'Theories and Measures of Urban Primacy'.

[18] Cf. e.g. C. H. Madden, 'On Some Indications of Stability in the Growth of Cities in the United States', *Economic Development and Cultural Change*, 4 (1956), 236–52; El Shakhs, 'Development, Primacy and Systems of Cities'; B. T. Robson, *Urban Growth: An Approach* (London, 1973).

[19] Johnson, 'Rank Size Convexity and System Integration'. Johnson does not use the term 'immature', but rather describes a 'convex' pattern. This term is somewhat confusing, however, since by other measurement conventions 'convexity' would be called 'concavity'. (Cf. C. A. Smith, 'Placing Formal Geographical Models into Cultural Contexts: The Anthropological Study of Urban Systems', *Comparative Urban Systems*, 9 (1982), 50–9.) Because the system Johnson describes resembles the 'immature' system, I retain that term for it.

integrated nor commercially undeveloped. Russell used the same argument about Europe's medieval cities and Skinner agrees that it was a factor relevant to urban development in traditional China. Low rural productivity, then, is a third possible cause of the immature urban system.

Urban hierarchies are not produced by numbers of people but by numbers of urban functions. Thus we cannot simply assume that an immature city-size distribution indicates lack of hierarchy. We must assume that if an urban system contains a large primate city together with underdeveloped secondary cities (like Argentina), failure of the agricultural economy cannot account for the small sizes of secondary cities. Nor is there a failure in hierarchical organization. Other factors can lead to low growth rates in secondary or even primary cities. My own research suggests an explanation for such cases.

In the 1970s, western Guatemala contained a well-defined and well-developed commercial system. I have independent evidence to show that it had an integrated system, and that commercial interchange between cities was strong. Nearly half the population in western Guatemala was in non-agricultural occupations. Not only was the area's agricultural productivity sufficient to support these people; it even made it possible for the greatest part of the agricultural product to be exported. Yet the city-size distribution of western Guatemala was extremely immature. Not only the secondary cities, but also the primary city of the region, Quezaltenango, were much smaller than the rank-size rule predicted. We must develop a fourth explanation of immaturity to account for this case. My explanation is that urban labour markets in western Guatemala virtually did not exist. Few rural people were allowed permanent residence in western Guatemala's cities, although they were allowed to engage in trade between cities. To explain this phenomenon we must consider the social factors that underlie urban growth and development, a neglected aspect of urban sociology. Elsewhere, I have developed a sociological theory of urban primacy.[20] For the present, I simply note that the absence of urban labour markets can also produce an immature city-size distribution.

In summary, at least four factors can lead to an urban system with small top-ranking cities: improper specification of the relevant urban system; lack of commercial interchange between contiguous cities; inadequate agricultural productivity to support large cities; and poorly developed urban labour markets. Many cases of urban immaturity result from all four factors, but we cannot assume that all four factors are present if we find an immature urban system. On the other hand, all four of these explanations do assume that there is something 'immature' about the distribution, which is why I have retained Vapñarski's term. We must now enquire whether it is reasonable to assume that a rank-size distribution indicates maturity with respect to these four factors.

[20] Smith, 'Theories and Measures of Urban Primacy'.

3. Mature urban systems

Most theories of the rank-size distribution seem logically consistent, but they are highly abstract, if not downright vague, and thus of little interest to those interested in trying to understand rather than model the empirical regularities. Thus, I approach the issue by examining the empirical regularities between economic variables and urban forms rather than by assessing the theoretical postulates on their own, or, in mathematical terms. I concentrate on economic variables here because geographers have done so. Later, I will consider some relevant sociological factors.

First, let me dispose of a non-economic theory, the allometric growth model, which is based on a biological analogy. This theory is perhaps the most widely cited explanation of the rank-size rule.[21] But while it can explain (vaguely) the persistence of rank-size regularity, it cannot explain how the distribution comes about. The allometric growth model, or the law of proportionate growth, merely asserts a truism: that if there are many growth forces in equilibrium with each other, no one dominating the other, all related growing things (such as cities) will grow at the same relative rate. Thus, an existing rank-size distribution, will retain its form under these conditions. Richardson has pointed out that such an equilibrium is highly unlikely to be sustained during urbanization, because the forces affecting the urban system are distinct and selective, rather than random or balanced.[22] De Vries has observed that the historical development of rank-size regularity empirically contradicts the allometric growth model.[23] Immature urban systems grow differentially rather than proportionately as they mature. The previous section illustrates de Vries's contention: virtually all historical studies of urban growth show that large cities grow faster than small cities at first; then smaller cities grow faster than large cities. In fact, only through disproportionate growth can an immature system become rank size. The law of proportionate growth, then, can be used to explain the persistence of rank-size distributions, but not how they came about.

Various economic theories provide explanations for the stability of urban systems that are more helpful than the allometric growth model. One theory stresses the relative durability of urban capital. Large cities which have considerable capital invested in their structures are unlikely to wither away,

---

[21] The allometric growth system, also known as Gibrat's Law of Proportionate Effect, has been used as an explanation for rank-size regularity by H. Simon, 'On a Class of Skew Distribution Functions', *Biometrika*, 42 (1955), 425–40; Berry, 'City Size Distributions and Economic Development'; and Johnson, 'Rank Size Convexity and System Integration', among others. What this theory explains, mathematically, is how stability can be achieved in a growing system. What it does not explain is why a particular hierarchical form should be achieved.

[22] See H. W. Richardson, 'Theory of the Distribution of City Sizes: Review and Prospects', *Regional Studies*, 7 (1973), 239–51.

[23] De Vries, *European Urbanization*.

even as economic conditions change.[24] Another theory emphasizes how urban productivity affects urban demography. Large cities, which contain more urban capital and a higher level of productivity, will attract more people to them, and thus grow faster than small cities which will grow, proportionately, less.[25] Yet another theory looks at the centralizing forces brought about by economies of scale and how these are balanced by the decentralizing forces of transport costs.[26] A fourth theory suggests that coalitions of existing urban firms allow growth when the potential for market expansion makes growth profitable, and constrain growth where competitors would be redundant and ruinous to the local coalition.[27]

All these theories, however, concentrate on factors that bring about an equilibrium. None really explains why, empirically, systems in equilibrium take on a rank-size distribution with a slope of -1. The only theories that begin to explain this phenomenon are those that emphasize the functions of hierarchy in urban systems. Most hierarchical models are based on central-place theory.[28] Though central-place theory has been widely criticized because of its restrictive assumptions, it remains the most powerful explanation of urban hierarchy. Thus demonstrations by Beckman and McPherson as well as by Berry and Garrison that central-place theory and rank-size distributions are compatible help to explain why 'maturing' urban systems take on a hierarchical form, which stabilizes at a certain point.[29]

Perhaps the best economic theory to explain both the growth and stability of urban systems would link several theories into a single process as follows: (*a*) competition for metropolitan functions that will attract industry and workers, as well as the advantages of decentralization, lead to a diffusion of urban functions over a landscape; (*b*) the limited number of rewards that can be given to successful competitors, together with the limited number of places that can support high-level urban functions, will lead to a hierarchy of cities;

[24] Richardson, 'Theory of the Distribution of City Sizes'.

[25] See B. Ward, 'City Structure and Independence', *Papers of the Proceedings of the Regional Science Association*, 22, 159–193.

[26] This is my rendering of Zipf's thesis 'Human Behavior'. Many people have ridiculed Zipf's explanation for rank-size regularity, especially when it is presented as a balancing act between forces of unification and forces of diversification. Richardson 'Theory of the Distribution of City Sizes' has pointed out that Zipf's particular explanation for city-size distributions can be cast in more acceptable economic terms, and is consistent with the basic principles of central-place theory.

[27] A. M. Evans, 'The Pure Theory of City Size in an Industrial Economy', *Urban Studies*, 9 (1972), 49–77.

[28] Cf. e.g. M. J. Beckman and J. McPherson, 'City Size Distributions in a Central-Place Hierarchy: An Alternative Approach', *Journal of Regional Science*, 10 (1970), 25–33. They argue that cities of different sizes perform different functions, because it is more efficient for some goods and services to be provided by many small cities, and others by a few larger centres. Here, we merely assume that the production of certain goods for which there is a wide and heavy demand (e.g. bread) will be distributed among many small centres as well as large ones, whilst that of other goods for which the demand is more limited (e.g. antiquarian bookshops) will be concentrated in a few large centres.

[29] Cf. Richardson, 'Theory of the Distribution of City Sizes'; Beckman and McPherson, 'City Size Distributions'; Berry and Garrison, 'Central-Place Theory'.

(c) inter-urban capital flows based on market expansion will regulate urban wage levels; (d) urban wage levels will attract migrants (urban population growth) to those places where the market is expanding, and thus where it is most efficient to have many people; finally, (e) investment in durable urban capital and the emergence of a competitive urban labour market will lead to the relative stability of the mature urban system over time. This is not an implausible model of urban growth, but it clearly rests on the assumptions that the urban economy is (a) competitive, (b) commercially developed, (c) growing, (d) uses free (non-servile) labour, and (e) reaches equilibrium. It virtually assumes, in other words, a mature capitalist economy. This should not surprise us, since empirically rank-size distributions are almost always found in mature capitalist economies. Brian Berry, in fact, used the *sine qua non* of a capitalist economy, competitive urban labour markets, in his most recent explanations of the rank-size rule.[30]

One might immediately object that approximations of rank-size regularity are found in pre-capitalist economies as well. On this point, however, the evidence is equivocal. China provides the only clear-cut example of a pre-modern or pre-capitalist economy supporting a rank-size urban distribution.[31] What distinguishes the Chinese economy from other pre-capitalist economies is not its degree or level of commercialization: one would be hard pressed to demonstrate that China was any more commercialized during the nineteenth century than was much of Latin America—and urban distributions in Latin America during this period were uniformly immature. What does distinguish China is the high level of peasant commercialization and the high level of artisan or worker mobility. Thus it seems clear that it is not commerce *per se* which is the relevant factor, but the *kind* of commerce.[32] It also seems clear that it is not the existence of well-integrated urban (wage) labour markets that produces lognormal distributions, but rather the lack of restriction on urban mobility or the ability of people to move in response to openings in the urban economy.

We may now proceed to review the places (countries and regions) in the modern world where the rank-size rule can be said to characterize the upper end of the city-size distribution. I cannot use the usual cross-national studies for these purposes, because they either contrast lognormal systems with primate systems on the basis of an inadequate index (considering only a few top-ranking cities), or they count all non-primate distributions as rank size, ignoring immaturity.[33] I can only use particular national or regional studies,

---

[30] Berry, 'City Size and Economic Development'.
[31] Skinner, 'Regional Urbanization'.
[32] Cf. C. A. Smith, 'Exchange Systems and the Spatial Distribution of Élites: The Organization of Stratification in Agrarian Societies', in C. A. Smith (ed.), *Regional Analysis,* ii *Social Systems* (New York, 1976).
[33] The most frequently cited cross-national studies are those by Berry, 'City Size Distributions and Economic Developments'; El Shakhs, 'Development, Primacy and Systems of Cities'; and S. K. Mehta, 'Some Economic and Demographic Correlates of Primate Cities: A Case for

which cover only a small portion of the modern world. But from these studies a general picture emerges.

As mentioned earlier, many authors have shown that urban systems in the United States and Great Britain have long closely conformed to the rank-size rule. Hall and Hay's study of contemporary European economic regions (urban systems larger than countries) showed that many of them approximated to lognormal systems—all of them, if irregularities among the top ten or so cities are disregarded.[34] In all these countries commercial economies are highly developed and their factor markets, based on the mobility of both capital and wage labour, well integrated—i.e. based on capitalism. The same could be said of the several other countries now moving towards a rank-size distribution: Israel, Brazil, Taiwan.[35]

The same cannot be said of the second large set of countries with rank-size systems: the Eastern European countries (Poland, Hungary, Czechoslovakia, Yugoslavia). Here it seems that state policies rather than free markets brought about the achievement of lognormalcy.[36] But while state efforts to decentralize urban functions were crucial to achieving a lognormal pattern, so was the relative freedom of urban mobility—made possible, perhaps, by the very high rate of urbanization in these countries following the Second World War.[37] Once again, then, a certain freedom of movement to cities in accord with urban labour needs created the rank-size urban pattern.

A third group of countries, including Canada, Japan, Australia, New Zealand, Brazil, and Argentina, show rank-size regularity below the level of one or two primate cities.[38] There are probably many more such cases, but since most scholars have assumed that primacy and lognormality are opposed to one another, many such countries are usually described as simply primate. I would guess that urban size distributions of this sort, if they are not simply

Re-evaluation', in G. Breese (ed.), *The City in Newly Developing Countries* (Englewood Cliffs, 1969). In all these studies, rank-size systems are contrasted with primate systems, and immature systems are not distinguished from others. These studies show that primacy is concentrated in less developed countries, but give equivocal results for the rank-size distribution—as would be expected, given that all immature systems are classed with rank-size distributions.

[34] Cf. P. Hall and D. Hay, *Growth Centers in the European Urban System* (Berkeley, Calif., 1980). Hall and Hay defined the following urban regions for modern Europe: Atlantic Europe (the British Isles); Northern Europe (Scandinavian countries); Western Europe (the Netherlands, Belgium, and France); Southern Europe (Spain, Italy, Portugal); and Central Europe (Austria, Switzerland, West Germany).

[35] These particular urban systems are described in the following studies: Israel: E. Brutzkus, 'Centralized Versus Decentralized Patterns of Urbanization in Developing Countries: An Attempt to Elucidate a Guideline Principle', *Economic Development and Cultural Change*, 23 (1975), 633–52; Taiwan: C. W. Pannell, 'Development and the Middle City in Taiwan', *Growth and Change*, 5 (1974), 21–9; Brazil: Portes and Walton, *Urban Latin America*. Brazil is usually identified as a country with dual primacy, but my data indicate that it is the only Latin American country which is moving towards a rank-size distribution.

[36] Brutzkus, 'Centralized Versus Decentralized Patterns'; cf. also B. J. L. Berry and J. D. Kasarda, *Contemporary Urban Ecology* (New York, 1977).

[37] Berry and Kasarda, *Contemporary Urban Ecology*.

[38] Cf. C. Clark, *Population Growth and Land Use* (London, 1967).

rank size, are found in most mature (heavily urbanized and well developed) capitalist countries. The extreme primate pattern, by contrast, is usually associated with an otherwise immature urban distribution—of the sort characterizing Guatemala. These economies still contain large numbers of peasants whose labour continues to be tied to agricultural production, whether capitalist or not. In such economies, as I suggest below, rural labour mobility is often highly restricted.

To sum up, rank-size urban systems develop in economies that contrast with those that give rise to immature urban systems, not primate urban systems. In a properly defined urban system, an economy that can support a fairly large number of people outside agriculture, well-developed commerce that involves country-dwellers as well as townspeople, and free labour mobility, the urban system will probably be found to approximate closely to the rank-size distribution. In the absence of any one of these characteristics, one is more likely to find an immature distribution. Primate urban systems, however, can be found in both developed and undeveloped economies, and are associated with both mature and immature urban distributions.

4. Primate urban systems

As was noted above, urban primacy was the phenomenon that drew general attention to the variability of urban forms. Yet we still lack a satisfactory theory of urban primacy. Specialists agree that urban primacy is most often found in Third World countries or in small industrial countries, where urban systems are not coterminous with the nation. Yet in only three of the five small countries of Central America, for example, is a significant degree of urban primacy found at present, even though all five countries can be depicted as extremely dependent upon trade (inter-urban exchange) with cities outside the region and thus 'incomplete' urban systems. On the basis of the Central American (and other Latin American) cases, I have recently criticized most existing theories of urban primacy and offered an alternative theory.[39] Here I briefly summarize those arguments and attempt to generalize beyond Latin America.

Most explanations for the high incidence of urban primacy in the Third World (i.e. that it is caused by colonialism or neo-colonialism, economic dualism, export dependency, or peasant marginalization) boil down to 'transition' theories. In other words, they assume that the urban system with a primate city is in the process of transformation from pre-modern to modern—or from pre-capitalist to fully capitalist relations of production. Theorists differ mainly in the assumptions they make about the uniformity or duration of the transition process, especially for 'late' modernizers. Modernization

---

[39] Smith, 'Theories and Measures of Urban Primacy'.

theorists expect late modernizers ultimately to achieve the patterns characteristic of early modernizers, whereas dependency theorists do not. Thus modernization theorists expect that primate urban systems will become rank-size as the national economy matures and becomes integrated,[40] whereas dependency theorists argue that the dependent economy might never modernize, but rather retain the distorted structures caused by and useful to capitalist exploitation.[41]

Theorists also differ on what they identify as the particular mechanism creating one over-large 'modern' city in the midst of small pre-modern ones. Some consider the primate city to be the effect of the colonial infrastructure concentrated in the colonial capital of a Third World country along with the bulk of the colonial population.[42] Others point to 'modern' or industrial infrastructure in general which, for reasons not clearly identified, tends to develop in one city at the expense of others.[43] Dependency theorists usually point to the link between export centres (whether national capitals or ports) and the external world, which leads to the agglomeration of export infrastructure in a single place.[44] And yet others describe the neglect of subsistence regions in export-oriented economies.[45] It should be noted that all these theories assume that growth in urban infrastructure causes growth in urban population.

Most non-specialists have assumed that urban primacy was linked to colonialism in some way and to the dual economic structures associated with colonialism. But this theory was discredited in the early 1970s by Richard Morse, who found no urban primacy in most of Latin America during the colonial period; and suggested that it developed only with the growth of export dependency, mostly during the middle and late nineteenth century.[46] After Morse's demonstration that colonialism *per se* was insufficient to cause urban primacy, attention shifted from political to economic mechanisms as causes of urban primacy; export dependency was the particular mechanism most often singled out.[47]

My own theory of urban primacy is based upon a reconsideration of the political mechanisms which promote urban primacy in the light of the

[40] Berry, 'City Size and Economic Development'; El Shakhs, 'Development, Primacy and Systems of Cities'.
[41] E. A. J. Johnson, *The Organization of Space in Developing Countries* (Cambridge, Mass., 1970); Vapñarski, 'Argentine System of Cities'; Portes and Walton, *Urban Latin America*; G. Appleby, 'Exportation and its Aftermath: The Spatioeconomic Evolution of the Regional Marketing System in Highland Puno, Peru', Ph.D. diss., Stanford University (1978).
[42] Berry, 'City Size Distributions and Economic Development'.
[43] El Shakhs, 'Development, Primacy and Systems of Cities'.
[44] Johnson, *Organization of Space*; Vapñarski, 'Argentine System of Cities'.
[45] Portes and Walton, *Urban Latin America*; Appleby, 'Exportation and its Aftermath'.
[46] R. Morse, 'Latin American Cities in the Nineteenth Century: Approaches and Tentative Generalizations', in R. Morse (ed.), *The Urban Development of Latin America, 1750–1920* (Stanford, Calif., 1971).
[47] Portes and Walton, *Urban Latin America*; B. Roberts, *Cities of Peasants* (Beverly Hills, Calif., 1978).

particular example of colonial Latin America, where (as noted earlier) virtually all urban systems were immature. It also rested on empirical information in my possession on one particular 'pre-modern' urban system that included direct (rather than imputed) information on urban infrastructure as well as on urban population. Western Guatemala's urban system appears to be extremely immature, when city size is plotted against city rank.[48] But when the same system is plotted on the basis of information on urban infrastructure from approximately the same date, it takes very different forms. When city size is measured by number of urban establishments (rather than by urban population), the distribution of city sizes is nearly rank size. And when city size is measured by number of important urban functions, the distribution is one of extreme primacy, in which there are far more commercial services in all *administrative* towns than in non-administrative towns.[49]

Other urban patterns in the 'backward' regions of Latin America are quite similar to that of western Guatemala.[50] The major towns in colonial Latin America, as depicted in travellers' accounts, also appeared to be over-small in population in comparison to their commerical importance.[51] That is, virtually the whole of the commercial infrastructure was situated in administrative towns, so that administrative towns dominated their administrative hinterlands completely, even when their populations were not much larger than those of non-administrative towns. Thus, Guatemala City, the colonial headquarters for the kingdom of Guatemala (most of modern Central America), was not much larger than other administrative cities in the region, but dwarfed other places in terms of urban amenities.[52] Administrative towns in such regimes were, essentially, over-small in urban population but over-large in urban infrastructure.

Why should this be so? I argue that the nature of urban infrastructure and labour markets in most pre-capitalist economies makes it so. The urban infrastructure required to run the various pre-modern bureaucracies (political, religious, military) and to organize the economy (both production and commerce) requires relatively few people. In particular, it demands relatively little labour. In addition, workers in most pre-capitalist economies, whether rural or urban, are not free to move to different places or to change occupations. Rural peasants are tied to particular landlords and communities, urban craftsmen and merchants (especially petty merchants) are tied to particular guilds and clients. The pre-capitalist state, moreover, enforces the

---

[48] Cf. Smith, 'Theories and Measures of Urban Primacy'.
[49] Ibid.
[50] Cf. R. D. F. Bromley, 'Urban Growth and Decline in the Central Sierra of Ecuador, 1698–1940', Ph.D. diss., University of Wales (1977).
[51] Cf. S. Socolow, 'Introduction', L. S. Hoberman and S. M. Socolow (eds.), *Cities and Society in Colonial Latin America* (Albuquerque, 1986).
[52] C. H. Lutz, *Historia sociodemográfica de Santiago de Guatemala, 1541–1773* (La Antigua, Guatemala, 1982).

immobility of labour and constricts the mobility of commerce.[53] The urban centres that existed under these circumstances, therefore, grow mainly by natural increase rather than migration, and commercial interchange depends upon the mobility of traders who move goods between different places, rather than upon the mobility of production that follows demand in the way of capital and labour movements. Under these conditions one cannot expect a normal 'hierarchy' of cities, even when commercial interchange is well developed and a regional economy fully integrated. Wherever there are restrictions upon labour mobility, therefore, we may expect to find an 'immature' urban system as measured by urban population figures. But it is not possible to assume from data on population that the urban system is immature or non-hierarchical with respect to the distribution of urban, commercial (or administrative) infrastructure.

How does this explain population primacy as it presently exists in much of the Third World and virtually all Latin America? My argument, in a nutshell, is as follows. Infrastructural urban primacy results from close ties between economic and political power in certain social formations (most pre-capitalist systems but most 'transitional' colonial regimes as well), which leads to the growth of administrative centres at the expense of commercial towns. In colonial Latin America, for example, it was simply impossible to do business without having strong ties to the colonial bureaucrats, which normally meant living near the seat(s) of political power.[54] And in colonial Latin America, administrative centres were almost universally primate cities in terms of general urban infrastructure. This feature of commerce and industrial development continues to exist in modern Latin America—i.e. the direct relationship between political and economic power—even as the nature of Latin American economies has changed. Now, major cities need free rather than tied labour to work their industries, but not all cities need free labour equally. The usual pattern is for national capitals or chief ports to develop capitalist relations of production while pre-capitalist relations are retained in the countryside and in provincial towns. Thus labour that is 'freed' in rural areas cannot move anywhere: it can find employment only in those places and areas in which wage labour is used and is often prevented from settling elsewhere. It follows, then, that *population* primacy, as opposed to *infrastructural* primacy, is associated with export-dependent economies, in as far as export dependency in Latin America was directly associated with the 'freeing' of considerable amounts of rural labour.[55]

In short, the pattern of population primacy cannot be equated directly with the pattern of infrastructural primacy; but it should not be dissociated from it

---

[53] Cf. S. N. Eisenstadt, *The Political Systems of Empires* (New York, 1956).
[54] Portes and Walton, *Urban Latin America*; W. D. Harris, *The Growth of Latin American Cities* (Athens, Ohio, 1971).
[55] Cf. F. H. Cardoso and E. Faletto, *Dependencia y desarrollo en América Latina* (Mexico, 1971).

either. The pre-capitalist patterns of political and economic linkage set the preconditions for the *uneven* development of capitalist relations of production in Latin America. I suspect this pattern is common to many countries in the Third World that were colonized by the West. (This pattern of 'pre-modern' political and economic linkage may also be generalized to non-colonial cases of 'late' modernizers, such as Japan, where the 'programme' of modernization was essentially led by the state rather than by an independent class of capitalists struggling against a traditional bureaucratic state and thus able to operate more independently of the state.)

The impetus toward rank-size urban systems was provided by merchant capitalists who operated beyond the confines of the nation-state and were thus untrammelled by the administrative organization of commercial centres.[56] These early capitalists often established commercial towns and production centres distant from bureaucratic control, and in so doing established the more competitive central-place patterns that resulted in rank-size urban distributions. State growth followed, rather than led, economic expansion. But where state growth led—rather than followed—economic expansion, we might expect to find the administrative city primate pattern developing along with capitalist relations of production. The evidence I have from Latin America suggests that late capitalist development may take a more uneven path, not only because of state intervention in economic growth, but also because the élites in the provincial towns which head the agrarian regions of the country may wish to preserve non-capitalist relations of production in certain urban and rural (especially plantation) sectors. Careful historical studies would be required to establish this point more generally.

The evidence from modern (post-colonial) Latin America strongly supports the proposition that administrative towns have grown at the expense of non-administrative towns wherever the primate city pattern is pronounced. Only in Mexico, Brazil, and Colombia do fewer than 80 per cent (though more than 60 per cent) of major cities fail to attain high-level administrative status—and these are precisely the four Latin American countries with the lowest levels of urban primacy.[57] (In most of the countries with rank-size urban distributions which I have been able to investigate, between 30 and 40 per cent of major cities are of high-level administrative status.)[58] It may be overbold to suggest that wherever administrative towns grow at the expense of non-administrative towns urban primacy will develop once urbanization reaches a certain level. But the contrast between Latin America and the developed world on these

---

[56] Cf. I. Wallerstein, *The Modern World-System, Part I* (New York, 1974).

[57] This information is taken from my ongoing study of the relation between infrastructural size and population size in Latin American cities. When considering the administrative status of a city, I have considered only the highest-level divisions (equivalent to 'states' in the USA). There is no Latin American country in which fewer than two-thirds of its major cities play high-level administrative roles, in contrast to the situation in the USA, where only 9 of the 30 cities with more than 1 million inhabitants in 1980 were of high- (state-) level administrative status.

[58] Ibid.

two measures (urban primacy and administrative city dominance) is striking. The logic of the argument is also compelling. For a regular central-place hierarchy of the sort that allows free commercial interchange between cities cannot develop unless non-administrative as well as administrative cities are allowed to grow.[59] In short, irregularities in the rank-size distribution that favour the disproportionate growth of some cities at the expense of others follow from an administrative, as opposed to a commercial, design of central places.

What I find most compelling about the thesis, however, is that it shows the continuities as well as the discontinuities in the urban development process of Latin America in a way that fits in with and adds to our present understanding of the historical pattern of economic growth in those countries. Economic development throughout Latin America, whether capitalist or non-capitalist, was led by the state. Economic as well as bureaucratic power was concentrated in administrative cities. The national bourgeoisie more often than not played a direct role and held positions in the state apparatus. Rarely did a landed aristocracy or merchant class, whose power was locally rather than nationally based, arise; and when it did, it was almost invariably eclipsed in power by a state-generated bourgeoisie which developed in association with export economies based on wage labour.[60] The ties of the new national bourgeoisie to the bourgeoisie of the already developed world strengthened the state and state-connected capitalists immeasurably. The particular linkage of state and economic power, then, gave enormous advantages to administrative over non-administrative cities. And we see the pattern of administrative growth continuing even at the provincial level in the more advanced capitalist economies of Latin America (e.g. Argentina, Peru, Mexico), even as national-level (administrative) primacy remains secure.[61]

The degree to which this state-led pattern of growth 'distorts' the capitalist development process remains for me an open question, however. I see no necessary connection between state-led growth, underdevelopment, or urban primacy. Late developers faced a different historical situation from early developers. In many cases, often through the direct intervention of colonialism, this led to the exploitation of one country by another, which may have delayed the capitalist growth process. It also favoured a state-led pattern of capitalist growth, which probably concentrated the benefits (and disadvantages) of growth in fewer places. But workers are exploited by capitalists whether they live in a primate city or not. As I see it, then, the connection between colonialism, underdevelopment, and urban primacy exists as a *historical* rather than a *functional* relationship, mediated by the different role of the state in the late as opposed to the early process of capitalist development.

[59] Skinner, 'Regional Urbanization'; Smith, 'Regional Economic Systems'.
[60] Cf. S. N. Eisenstadt and A. Shachar, *Society, Culture, and Urbanization* (Beverly Hills, Calif., 1987), 97–121.   [61] See n. 57.

Given that urban primacy is neither functional to underdevelopment, nor directly (functionally) associated with the transition to capitalist relations of production, we cannot expect the primate-city pattern to disappear in all economies, once capitalist relations of production have become uniformly established. Examples from Latin America (such as Chile and Argentina), as well as other fully capitalist economies (Japan) give clear evidence of this.[62] For all these reasons I would argue that the development pattern of urban primacy can only be understood historically. This is not to say that no developmental patterns exist: population primacy *is* historically associated with a pre-existing pattern of infrastructural primacy; infrastructural primacy *is* associated with a particular pattern of linkage between state and economy; and population primacy *is* historically linked to late development, to colonialism, and to state-led capitalist growth.

5. Conclusion

The conclusions we can reach on the basis of the comparisons made above are twofold. The first is methodological: that we cannot assume a one-to-one correspondence between urban population and urban infrastructure. If we want to explain variable urban forms in terms of urban infrastructure, we must look at the actual distribution of urban infrastructure. And if we want to explain variable urban forms in terms of population size, we must consider the forces that affect the distribution of population. The second conclusion has more substance: urban primacy does not fit into a functional developmental pattern, but is associated with a particular historical pattern of development. Yet there does appear to be some general developmental patterning to the forms of city-size distribution, and understanding this patterning helps us understand urban primacy. Let me begin with the methodological conclusions.

Though work on the relation between urban infrastructure and urban population is limited, it now seems clear that, in order to assert anything about the nature of the system one must provide independent evidence to show that the infrastructural patterns parallel the population patterns. One should also have evidence concerning the actual connections between the cities assumed to be part of a system. While a complete study of this sort may be difficult to carry out, especially on historical cases, some checking on the apparent development of urban functions in the largest cities (as measured by population, on which historical evidence is also rather thin) is certainly

---

[62] Koichi Mera has argued that there are few, if any, 'disproportional' costs associated with urban primacy, basing his argument on information from modern Japan. K. Mera, 'On the Urban Agglomeration and Economic Efficiency', *Economic Development and Cultural Change*, 21 (1973), 309–24. I accept this general proposition, though physical limits to the functional size of a city may be present with existing technology.

indicated. My work on the infrastructural urban patterns in Latin America is still incomplete. But what evidence I have suggests that even at relatively high levels of urbanization it is not possible to assume that urban size in functions parallels size in population. Nor can we assume that cities may only be more (rather than less) functionally important than urban population size indicates. Modern Guatemala City, for example, contains proportionately far *less* urban infrastructure than is indicated by its present urban population.[63] If this is widely true of primate cities in the Third World, we must be even more concerned about the development of labour markets (rather than urban amenities) in relation to urban population growth. The *relation* between urban infrastructure and urban population and its changes over time and during the urbanization process, therefore, remains an important theoretical as well as empirical problem.

Concern about the difference between urban population and urban infrastructure also forces us to consider the actual factors that bring about transformative rather than reproductive population growth in cities—i.e. the relation between rural migration to cities and the particular form that the urban system takes. It is now widely recognized in Latin America that stepwise migration to cities is relatively rare.[64] But few students of migration patterns in Latin America have actually sought to explain why rural people rarely move to provincial towns rather than national cities. I suspect that important differences between the labour markets in the two types of place would be found. But so far we have virtually no direct information on differences between labour market conditions in different kinds of cities in the Third World.

The broader implications of these findings about the relation between urban population and urban infrastructure is that much of our thinking about urbanization remains mechanical. Occupational differentiation does not always lead to urbanization, as my research on rural occupations in Guatemala illustrates.[65] Urbanization, moreover, can occur when there is relatively little occupational specialization. Urban hierarchies may exist that are not revealed by the population sizes of cities; and certain cities may grow in population without taking on important hierarchical functions. An adequate study of urbanization, then, requires independent measures of the processes thought to underlie the organization of the system. Few students of urbanization have developed such measures. Until they do, it will be difficult to develop any general theories about the urbanization process.

On the basis of the studies carried out so far on city-size distributions (in virtually all of which urban size is considered only in terms of population) we can still discard certain theories about the patterning of urban growth and suggest alternatives. The firm evidence is mostly negative. But the alternative

[63] Smith, 'Theories and Measures of Urban Primacy'.
[64] Roberts, *Cities of Peasants*.
[65] Smith, 'Theories and Measures of Urban Primacy'.

theories suggested by the evidence now in hand suggest that scholars take a more pluralist view of both urbanization and capitalist growth than they have done previously. Once again, the key urban form for understanding the others is the primate form—which may be associated with both 'mature' (rank-size) and 'immature' (non-hierarchical) forms.

What is most clearly established at this point is that the immature rather than primate urban form contrasts with the rank-size system. Urban (population) primacy is associated with both rank-size and immature urban distributions. With this point established, it is clear that apart from one or two top-ranking cities there is a *general* developmental progression from a non-hierarchical city-size distribution to a rank-size distribution. Virtually all historical studies have shown that with urbanization a plot of city distributions shows a progressive movement from a lower degree of hierarchy (shallower slope) to a higher level until the urban system achieves 'stability' at the 45° slope characteristic of the most mature and fully urbanized systems. I know of no historical studies that show an urban system moving in a reverse direction—from a fully 'mature' rank-size distribution to a less hierarchical or non-hierarchical distribution, or even to a primate distribution.[66]

This historical pattern suggests a general link between urban hierarchies and capitalist growth as mediated through the development of free or unrestricted labour markets. That is, the very process of urbanization helps create free labour markets, which in turn affect the nature of the urban system. As labour moves from rural areas to cities (whether local or national) on a massive scale, it presumably becomes freer to move between different kinds of employment. And this free labour ultimately provides the foundation for wage labour, or capitalist relations of production. And as capitalist relations of production become generalized, a maximal degree of urban hierarchy emerges—with or without one or two major primate cities—because of the mobility and hierarchy required for both capital (even 'fixed' urban capital) and labour in capitalist economies.

Yet it must be emphasized once again that this *general* developmental pattern from lower to higher levels of hierarchy, normally associated with a greater degree of size regularity, does not have a specific place or role for the most important (top-ranking) cities in the system. One or two 'over-large' cities may be associated with any degree of hierarchy in lower-ranking cities; and, as de Vries's study makes clear, a single major (primate) city need not emerge in the transition from non-hierarchy to hierarchy in secondary cities—

---

[66] De Vries, *European Urbanization*, has shown that size regularity (lognormality) may occur in the 'immature' pattern before the fully fledged hierarchy with a slope of -1 is achieved. Because he could find no good explanation why cities should stabilize at a slope of -1, he suggested that 'maturity' is achieved with hierarchical regularity, rather than with a particular degree of hierarchy. But his own carefully marshalled evidence shows that a gradual increase in slope accompanies urbanization in the early modern European systems which he examined. And Hall and Hay, *Growth Centers in the European Urban System*, have shown that these same European systems eventually stabilize at a slope of -1.

or in the transition to capitalism. Instead, urban primacy appears to be a particular historical phenomenon associated with a particular kind of economy. At present, the evidence suggests that population primacy, associated with capitalist growth, may be induced by a pre-existing pattern of infrastructure primacy established in the pre-capitalist economy. What makes this an especially interesting proposition is that it suggests that the first transition to capitalist relations of production may have required a break in the infrastructural primate (administrative city dominant) pattern, though later transitions to capitalist growth may not have required this break. Historical investigations of urbanization processes and their resulting urban forms in which this question is taken up would be most welcome.

In conclusion, cities and systems of cities are not just systemic responses to certain economic needs. They are aggregates of people who live in close proximity in order to engage in certain occupations that are less easily undertaken in dispersed settlements. When we think about cities in these terms, we realize that many social and political factors affect urban growth rates and the resulting urban hierarchies. No theory of urban forms can safely ignore these non-economic factors. We also realize that historical links between many variables must be disentangled from functional relations. At this point further comparative analysis of modern urban systems will yield little more information on the urbanization process. We need theoretically informed historical case studies.

3 Problems in the Measurement, Description, and Analysis of Historical Urbanization

JAN de VRIES
Department of History, University of California, Berkeley, California, USA

In this chapter I explore problems in the historical application of three related concepts: urbanization, urban systems, and the urban transition. In discussing 'urbanization' I limit myself to 'demographic urbanization' and to problems involved in performing the superficially simple task of measuring the urban portion of the total population. 'Urban systems' refers to the ways in which *cities* within a bounded territory, or *region*, fashion an organized complexity, or system.[1] The final concept, 'urban transition', goes by several names. It refers to the way in which societies pass from low to high levels of urbanization, and, more generally, to the ways in which they achieve urban growth. The urban transition consists of two component parts: a vital revolution (more familiarly, a demographic transition) and a mobility revolution.[2]

1. Urbanization

The historical study of urbanization has long been hobbled by the broad acceptance of assumptions that effectively limit the application of the term to the rapid growth of cities associated with the rise of the factory system. By tethering the concept of urbanization to a short presentist leash, the traditional, or pre-modern, city was assigned a marginal and unchanging character. These disabling assumptions are now giving way to a broader historical perspective, but to exploit the new opportunities fully it is important to refashion old concepts, develop new ones, and devise appropriate

---

[1] For further discussion of each of these three elements in an urban system see A. Pred, *Urban Growth and City-Systems in the United States, 1840–1860* (Cambridge, Mass., 1980), 2; J. de Vries, *European Urbanization, 1500–1800* (London and Cambridge, Mass., 1984), 81–4.

[2] See A. Rogers, 'Migration Patterns and Population Redistribution', *Regional Science and Urban Economics*, 9 (1979), 275–310; W. Zelinsky, 'The Hypothesis of the Mobility Transition', *Geographical Review*, 61 (1971), 219–49; N. Keyfitz, 'Do Cities Grow by Natural Increase or by Migration?', *Geographical Analysis*, 12 (1980), 143–56.

methods, so that the specific character of urbanization in each historical epoch can be made apparent. At the risk of stating the obvious, a definition of urbanization that is concerned only with the societal impact of industrial cities is certain to frustrate and mislead. Urbanization in earlier epochs can then only be evaluated as a precocious imitation, or curious precursor, of 'true' urbanization.

A definition of urbanization that offers a sound basis for further development is provided by Charles Tilly in his classic study, *The Vendée*. He describes urbanization as 'a collective term for a set of changes which generally occur with the appearance and expansion of large-scale co-ordinated activities in a society'.[3] He offers examples of such activities: the operation of a centralized state, a religion with a professional priesthood, the control of water for irrigation, the production of goods in a factory system, and the channelling of exchange through a pervasive market. These activities foster urbanization because they (*a*) give rise to the appearance of social positions devoted to co-ordination (e.g. bishops, merchants, bankers, governors), (*b*) require lines of communication (to permit co-ordinators to carry out their work), and (*c*) stimulate the proliferation of cross-cutting social relationships (i.e. relationships that cross the boundaries of kinship, locality, and traditional alliances). Cumulatively, these three phenomena constitute urbanization, for they foster differentiation, standardization, change in the quality of social relations, and the concentration of population.

Tilly's elaborate but clear exposition can be faulted for its fascination with the tradition-eroding aspects of urbanization. Cities can also confirm and bolster existing arrangements. But his definition is useful for our purposes, for it is clearly not limited to urbanization under industrialization and it calls attention to the three dimensions of the process: structural urbanization, behavioural urbanization, and demographic urbanization.[4]

Here our concern is with demographic urbanization. The first step of almost every study is to identify quantitatively the proportion of the total population that is urban. When placed in cross-sectional and/or diachronic comparison with other such measures the simple percentage urban is supposed to indicate the scope of 'large-scale co-ordinated activities' and the intensity of all that flows from their presence. In view of the heavy weight that this humble statistic is expected to bear, surprisingly little effort has been expended on standardizing its computation so that values for different regions, or different periods, are comparable. In addition, the development of supplementary measurements that might amplify information on the impact or consequences of demographic urbanization has not been standardized. Eclecticism reigns in this field.

The weaknesses of the simple urban percentage are not unknown: they can be summarized as problems of depth, breadth, entrants, and annexations.

---

[3] C. Tilly, *The Vendée* (Cambridge, Mass., 1964), 16–17.
[4] De Vries, *European Urbanization*, 11–12.

What I will call the 'depth' problem is surely the best-known obstacle to the comparative use of the percentage urban. I refer to the criterion used for the inclusion of cities in the aggregation of the urban population. In the absence of consensus on the definition of a city, each system of national statistics employs a unique criterion to distinguish urban from non-urban settlements. Even if they were uniform, scholars would have reason to use criteria that differ from those which are suitable for political and administrative purposes. And even if this were not the case, the historical study of urbanization would require the use of *ad hoc* threshold levels, constrained by the availability of data. That is, calculations of the percentage urban differ in the extent to which the populations of smaller cities are included. Even when they include all cities, defined by an administrative rather than by a population criterion, the problem is not solved, since these definitions vary between different countries and different periods within the same country.

To illustrate the sensitivity of the urban percentage to choices made concerning 'depth', consider the results achieved for Europe as a whole in the period 1500–1800 using three criteria: cities of at least 40,000 inhabitants, cities of at least 10,000 inhabitants, and a constant set of 379 cities, all those which ever attained a population of at least 10,000 during the period (see Table 3.1).

Table 3.1 Three versions of the urban percentage in Europe, 1500–1800

	1500	1550	1600	1650	1700	1750	1800	Increase 1800/1500 %
379 Cities	7.4	7.8	8.8	10.0	10.5	10.4	10.1	136
Cities of at least 10,000	5.6	6.3	7.6	8.3	9.2	9.5	10.0	179
Cities of at least 40,000	1.9	2.6	3.5	4.4	5.2	5.3	5.6	295

Source: J. de Vries, *European Urbanization, 1500–1800*, 39, 50, 76.

While the 'depth' problem is generally recognized, this is less often the case with the 'breadth' problem. By this I mean the territory included in the aggregation of urban and total populations. By expressing the urban percentage for national territories (by far the most common practice), the problem of comparisons over time is resolved, but at the expense of meaningful cross-sectional comparisons. (For simplicity, I will pass over the problem of changing national boundaries, a problem which is often daunting for the historian who considers the very long term.) The highly uneven size of nations and the intrinsically uneven spatial character of urbanization, make it difficult to avoid being misled in the interpretation of national urban percentage figures. This is simply a roundabout way of raising the issue of the appropriate unit of analysis.[5] I will return to it below, but for the present it is

---

[5] This issue has been raised in other contexts as well. See I. Wallerstein, *The Modern World-System* (New York, 1973), ch. 1; S. Pollard, *Peaceful Conquest* (Oxford, 1981). The first emphasizes the world system as the basic unit of analysis; the second emphasizes the region.

46   Jan de Vries

important to note that alternatives to the national unit can generate substantially different patterns of urbanization.

The entry problem, too, is well known, but often ignored. This problem arises whenever a threshold criterion is used to determine which settlements are to be included in the aggregate urban population. The growth of settlements, even when that growth is simply a product of overall population growth, rather than a reflection of the 'urbanization' of settlements, results in the accretion of those places to the urban category. By including the entire populations of places that pass the threshold level in subsequent measurements of the urban percentage the advance of urbanization is overestimated, and, what is at least equally important, the timing of urbanization is mis-specified. In the extreme case in which all urban growth is concentrated in small cities initially below the threshold level, a slow gradual process is registered as a sudden increase occurring at the moment that those cities cross the threshold level.

Related to this is the problem of annexation. When outlying areas are incorporated into cities, and when metropolitan areas are included in redefined urban districts, or conurbations, a previously excluded population helps to raise the percentage urban, even though no real urban growth has taken place. Whenever total population growth is rapid these factors will lead to an upward bias in the measurement of urbanization by using the urban percentage method.

These weaknesses in using the urban percentage can be mitigated by the broad acceptance of common practices, but they cannot be overcome altogether.[6] It would seem advisable to seek supplementary measures (drawn as much as possible from the same body of basic data) that could enhance and nuance the one-dimensional view of urbanization provided by the simple urban percentage. After all, we are not content to track fertility behaviour by using crude birth rates alone.

One obvious supplementary step is to add *interval measurement* to the *point measurement* of urbanization. The proportion of total population growth captured by the urban sector during a specified period is the most straightforward of these measures. It reveals the extent of the shift of population to the urban sector. At low rates of total population growth, such as often prevailed during earlier centuries, a modest advance in the urban percentage could involve a major proportion of the available population growth. This has a direct bearing on the societal impact of urban growth, and is measured by the proportion of total population growth in the urban sector.

$$(U_2 - U_1)/(P_2 - P_1) \text{ or, simply, } \triangle U / \triangle P$$

Whether the urban proportion of total population growth is sufficient to raise the urban percentage to a higher level depends on the initial value of the urban percentage. An 'urban quotient' combines both measures, the first in the numerator and the second in the denominator, to yield a quotient that conveys the relative success of the urban sector in attracting the increase of population achieved over an interval. When the quotient is 1.0 the urban proportion of total population growth equals the initial percentage urban in the total population. The larger the quotient the greater is the captured urban proportion relative to the initial percentage urban. A drawback of both the interval measures discussed here is that they cannot deal with periods when total population is decreasing.

$$Q = \frac{U_2 - U_1}{P_2 - P_1} \div \frac{U_1}{P_1}$$

Table 3.2, which relates to urbanization in the Netherlands, illustrates the application of the point and interval measures discussed above.

Table 3.2 Urbanization of the Netherlands, 1300–1980 (population in 000)

	1300	1550	1675	1815	1860	1980
Urban population (up to 2,500)	34	312	878	845	1290	9145[a]
Total population	600[b]	1300	1950	2290	3310	14100
Per cent urban	5.6	24.0	45.4	36.9	39.0	64.9
Urban Δ/Δ Total		40%	87%	−10%	44%	72%
Urban quotient		7.1	3.6	−0.2	1.2	1.9

[a] The urban population for 1980 includes all municipalities designated as urban or suburban.
[b] The population of the territory that would become the Netherlands is not known; even approximately, for this period. A figure of 600,000 is offered as a rough guess only.

Sources: 1300: J. C. Visser, *Historisch-geografisch tijdschrift*, 3 (1985), 10–21; 1550–1860: J. de Vries, *European Urbanization*, 65 and sources cited there; 1980: Centraal Bureau voor de Statistiek, *Bevolking der gemeenten van Nederland* (The Hague, 1981).

The three measures, all based on the same basic data, offer varied insights into the process of long-run urbanization. Yet they do not consider the two dimensions of the phenomenon that together constitute the best-known definition of urbanization, that of Hope Eldridge Tisdale: 'Urbanization is a process of population concentration. It proceeds in two ways: the multiplication of points concentration and the increase in size of individual concentrations.'[7]

Neither the number of 'points of concentration' (i.e. cities) nor their size play any direct role in Table 3.1. Data relating to both the number and size of cities stand behind the aggregates of Table 3.1, but have not yet been put to any direct use. This information should not be wasted, for it can add yet

[6] One proposal for improvement is offered by E. E. Arriaga, 'A New Approach to the Measurement of Urbanization', *Economic Development and Cultural Change*, 18 (1969–70), 206–18. For a criticism of his 'urbanization index' see de Vries, *European Urbanization*, 153. For further detail on techniques of measuring urbanization see E. E. Arriaga, 'Selected Measures of Urbanization', in S. Goldstein and D. F. Sly (eds.), *The Measurement of Urbanization and Projections of Urban Population* (Liège, 1975).

[7] H. E. Tisdale, 'The Process of Urbanization', *Social Forces* (1942), 311–16.

48   *Jan de Vries*

another dimension to our appreciation of the urbanization process. Consider the high level of urbanization reached around 1700 by the Dutch Republic and south-eastern England. In both territories about 40 per cent of the population lived in cities. But in the Republic that urban population was distributed over nineteen cities with more than 10,000 inhabitants and scores of smaller ones, while in England the urban population was overwhelmingly concentrated in one city, London, with all others being very much smaller.

This information is important because of our expectation (based on Tilly's definition of urbanization introduced above) that interrelationships among cities reflect the process by which societies become more complex. That is, urbanization is embodied in urban systems. Angyal observed that the difference between an aggregate and a system is that in the former the parts are added while in the latter they are arranged.[8] The measures of urban percentage, share, and quotient assume urbanization to be a question of aggregation. If, as we suspect, the arrangement of the urban units is also of importance, how can that arrangement be revealed, and what meaning can be attributed to different arrangements of cities?

2. Urban systems

Two basic approaches to the arrangement of cities into systems can be distinguished in the literature: one based on urban functions, the other based on city size.

The best-established functional approach is central-place theory. This geographical theory of how cities (central places) are distributed in space need not be described here in detail. As developed by Christaller it relies on the varying size of markets for the economic, administrative, and cultural functions carried out in central places to demonstrate that a nested hierarchy of central places produces an optimal and stable 'system' for the provision of these functions.[9]

Geographers have devoted much more attention to the properties of a mature central-place system than to its historical development. The presumption must be, as Hohenberg and Lees put it, that 'the central-place system views urbanization as an outgrowth of rural development. In it, economic activity grows from local exchange and production for local markets to the higher stages of long-distance trade and a more complex division of labor.'[10] For the historian of urbanization central-place theory is remarkably barren: most discussions present it as a static concept and its apparent historical

---

[8] Cited in B. Robson, *Urban Growth: An Approach* (London, 1973), 16.
[9] For literature on central-place theory, see P. Haggett, A. Cliff, and A. Frey, *Locational Models* (London, 1977).
[10] P. Hohenberg and L. H. Lees, *The Making of Urban Europe, 1800–1950* (Cambridge, Mass., 1985), 58–9.

implications are at variance with the chief tradition in both European and American urban history, which emphasize long-distance trade as an early, rather than a late, stimulant to the formation of central places.

Recently Gilbert Rozman has developed a stage model of urbanization that draws on central-place theory. He identifies seven levels of central places and seven stages of pre-modern urban development, each characterized by the presence of certain combinations of the seven types of central place.[11] On the basis of empirical studies of Japan, China, and Russia he regards pre-modern urbanization as passing through stages that begin with the appearance of administrative cities, forming a hierarchic pattern of governance 'from the top down'. This is followed by stages in which commercial towns and market-places are created 'from the bottom up'. The result is a hierarchic urban network designed to pass resources upwards to the administrative centres and 'commands' downwards to the grassroots.

This formulation of central-place theory is rich in insights and offers a practical method for the historical study of very large-scale social processes. But, ironically, it may not be sufficiently general to incorporate all major forms of historical urbanization. Students of North American and European urbanization have repeatedly put central-place theory aside as being either wrong or incomplete as an explanation for the structure of urban settlements in their areas of study. James Vance suggested an alternative 'mercantile model' and, more recently, Hohenberg and Lees introduced the 'network system' as either alternatives or supplements to central-place theory.[12] Both emphasize linear rather than hierarchical arrangements of space, competitive rather than administrative relationships, and flexibility rather than stability in the functional role of specific units of the system.

Both approaches are functionally based. But in the first, cities interact chiefly with their hinterlands (including, of course, subordinate cities). In the second, 'cities are implicated in a nodal manner in the larger system of society, economy, and government'.[13] Those nodes could be central places, but could also be outposts, gateways, relays, and junctions. It then becomes possible to explore the inter-urban ties that give rise to the peculiar and important 'urban archipelagos', the landscapes dense with cities that arose at widely spaced time-intervals in northern Italy, the southern and northern Netherlands, and northern England.

The size-based concept of rank-size distributions is the chief alternative to the function-based concepts discussed above. Its quantitative character makes comparisons with other places and times relatively straightforward, which

---

[11] This literature is described in G. Rozman, 'Urban Networks and Historical Stages', *Journal of Interdisciplinary History*, 9 (1978), 65–91.

[12] J. Vance, *The Merchant's World: The Geography of Wholesaling* (Englewood Cliffs, NJ, 1970); Hohenberg and Lees, *Making of Urban Europe*, 59–69.

[13] P. Abrams, 'Towns and Economic Growth: Some Theories and Problems', in P. Abrams and E. A. Wrigley (eds.), *Towns and Society: Essays in Economic History and Historical Sociology* (Cambridge, 1978), 24.

perhaps accounts for its appeal. As a descriptive tool it is well suited to display the numbers and sizes of cities that comprise a system. However, it has become more than a descriptive tool: modern scholarship has elevated it to a 'rank-size rule', a standard from which to measure deviant cases. In short, the concept has become a diagnostic method for the assessment of the health of urban systems. This literature has implications for the historical study of urbanization, but the historical dimension has only recently begun to attract attention in its own right.

The size-based study of urban systems exploits the fact that the distribution of cities by size corresponds to the general form of Pareto's distribution and the related lognormal distribution. In non-technical terms this means that when cities are arrayed in rank order according to their size (population), they form a distribution that approximates a straight line with negative slope when plotted on a double logarithmic scale. Thus we have a convenient way to display information about the sizes of a region's or nation's cities.

The rank-size rule identifies a special case of these distributions as a norm, a distribution that represents the steady-state equilibrium of an urban system. This norm is a rank-size distribution with a slope of -1. Then, the population of the city of rank R is equal to the population of the largest city divided by its rank: the tenth city is one-tenth the size of the largest, the hundredth city, one-hundredth the size of the largest, etc.

Now the question arises, how can this technique and the theory attached to it be exploited for the historical study of urbanization? Can we identify a pattern or sequence through which the rank-size distributions of a region should pass during the course of urbanization? If, for the sake of argument, we accept the rank-size rule as the goal—the stable equilibrium distribution of a modern urbanized society—by what path, or sequence, is that position reached? The geographer Berry proposed a developmental sequence, based on cross-sectional analysis, that began with primacy (where the largest city is much larger than twice the size of the second-largest city) and a slope in excess of -1, and moved gradually toward the rank-size rule.[14] The historian Russell applied a rank-size formula to medieval Europe in a way that embodied the assumption that the slope would be far less than -1. Presumably, long-term urbanization implied the gradual achievement of a steeper slope.[15]

The most sophisticated historical, or developmental application of rank-size distributions is found in the work of the anthropologist Carol Smith.[16] She distinguishes three principal types, primate, rank-size, and immature distributions. 'Stable log-normal systems', she argues, 'are restricted to the developed economic systems of the modern world, whereas [immature]

[14] B. J. L. Berry, 'City Size Distribution and Economic Development', *Economic Development and Cultural Change*, 9 (1961), 571–87.
[15] J. C. Russell, *Medieval Regions and their Cities* (Bloomington, Ind., 1972).
[16] C. A. Smith, 'Theories and Measures of Urban Primacy: A Critique' and 'Class Relations and Urbanization in Guatemala: Toward an Alternative Theory of Urban Primacy', in M. Timberlake (ed.), *Urbanization in the World-Economy* (New York, 1985), 87–167.

distributions are characteristic of the pre-modern world as well as the underdeveloped economic systems of the modern world.'[17] Primacy can arise in both the modern and pre-modern setting, although its meaning and its stability is not the same in both situations. For present purposes our interest is directed to the character of the 'immature' distribution. This is a rank-size distribution of shallow slope (less than −1) perhaps with a 'flat top', a group of the largest cities that are of similar size. Modernizing urbanization, to Smith, brings about a steeper slope of the distribution. The issue of primacy, whether in the pre-modern or modern situation, is a separable issue with contingent historical causes.

In all these studies we see the rank-size rule held up as the goal, or the definition of modernity. Immature or unbalanced urban systems are identified by measuring the deviation of their distributions from this rule. But how is this measurement to be made? The techniques used to analyse rank-size distributions vary with the interests of the investigators. The deviation of an empirical rank-size distribution from the rank-size rule will look different, depending on whether the diagonal line of a slope −1 is drawn downwards from the largest city (a common approach), upwards from the smallest, or lower threshold, city (Smith's preference), or fitted to the body of the distribution.

The analysis of rank-size distributions is sensitive not only to the technique chosen to describe it and measure its deviation from a norm; it is also bedevilled by the choice of the region whose cities are being arrayed. Consider briefly the justification for labelling the distribution of a shallow slope 'immature'. This happens when many cities are of similar size and presumably perform similar functions in relatively autarchic hinterlands. There is insufficient integration and specialization to speak of a modern urbanized society. But it can also happen when two or more regions are wrongly combined, i.e. when the system is misspecified. Unless we possess a clear set of criteria for the specification of a region that is *independent* of the attributes of the urban hierarchy itself we plunge into circular reasoning: the shallow slope that betokens insufficient system integration is prima-facie evidence for misspecification of the region. The smaller the region is made to be, the steeper the average slope of the rank-size distribution of its cities.

It may be objected that nation-states and/or 'natural regions' provide objective and independently determined entities for the analysis of urban systems. It is my view that the most useful regional entities for the study of urbanization are neither nations nor natural regions, but spatial entities that are given their coherence by the very emergence of urban systems. They are neither constant in the very long run, nor independent of the cities that organize their space.[18]

To summarize, the usefulness of the rank-size distribution as an analytical

---

[17] C. A. Smith, 'Modern and Premodern Urban Primacy', *Comparative Urban Research*, 11 (1982), 80.
[18] For further discussion, see de Vries, *European Urbanization*, 83–4.

tool in the study of urbanization is eroded by the use of a largely arbitrary norm (the rank-size rule), the confusion over measurement techniques (directly related to the unwarranted prominence of the rank-size rule), and the problem of arbitrariness in the delimitation of regions. Where the percentage urban is used to illuminate urbanization without any reference to the number and size of cities, the rank-size rule attempts to diagnose urban systems entirely in terms of the numbers and sizes of the cities contained in it, disembodied from the specific societies in which they function, that is, from such factors as geographical area, economic structure, or level of technology.

The rank-size distribution is a blunt instrument with which to evaluate the process of growth and change in urban systems. The danger is great that these beguiling arrays will not simply be misinterpreted but also over-interpreted. Misinterpretation can occur for the reasons listed above; over-interpretation is a danger because rank-size distributions can vary from each other in many details without this being of far-reaching importance to the way the system functions.

This does not mean that rank-size distributions are of no value. They can summarize effectively the process of urbanization and identify gross differences in the design of urban systems over time (and, with greater difficulty), in different societies. They should be treated as empirical findings, and allowed to reveal their own patterns as much as possible. In my book, *European Urbanization, 1500–1800*, rank-size distributions revealed a progression that formed the basis for a division of urban growth into three periods. The slopes of the distributions did, indeed, become steeper and the distributions more regular. But they never achieved the value of −1.

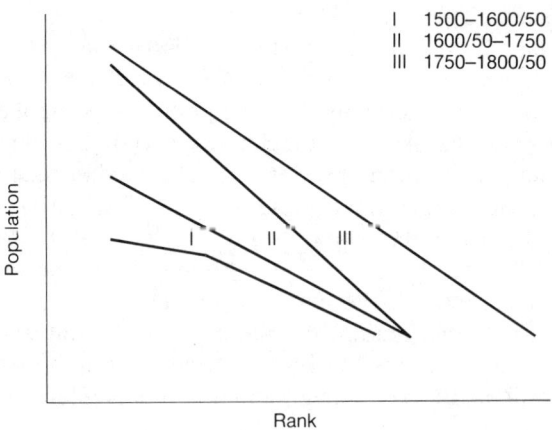

Figure 3.1. Three phases of early modern urbanization
    Source: J. de Vries, *European Urbanization, 1500–1800*, 256.

Moreover, the maximum slope was attained *before* the beginning of the modern era. During early industrialization the slope became shallower. That is, the empirical study of rank-size distributions showed urbanization to be highly selective, and revealed periods in which the basis of selectivity changed. Urbanization has more than one 'mode'.

The proper use of the rank-size distribution undermines faith in the widespread assumption that urbanization is a unitary, linear process. The issue is not simply one of timing and rate of growth, it is also one of character, or 'mode'. In other words, we must ask not only what drives urban growth,[19] but also what causes urban growth to be sometimes located in the largest cities and sometimes in smaller places, sometimes highly concentrated in a handful of locations and sometimes dispersed among many, including new urban settlements.

3. The urban transition

The percentage urban, and in particular the interval measurements based on this measure, identify the size of the shifts of population from the rural to the urban sector. The rank-size distributions show how the urban population is distributed among the points of concentration—whether it forms new cities, concentrates itself in the largest places, obeys the law of proportionate effect, etc. The two measures in combination tell us much about urbanization as a quantitative phenomenon. But they are silent about the processes that bring about the shift of population and that guide the distribution of population among urban locations. We need to supplement these descriptive measures with an account of the demographic and migration forces that, as it were, stand between the change in the urban share and the change in the rank-size distribution.[20]

The 'urban transition' concept offers an approach to this problem by relating the transition from low to high levels of urbanization to the simultaneous and presumably interacting consequences of a vital revolution (i.e. demographic transition) and a mobility revolution (or transition). The first refers, of course, to a societal transition from high to low levels of fertility and mortality; the second refers to a transition from low to high migration rates. From this perspective, urbanization can be seen, in the words of Andre Rogers, as resulting

> from a particular spatial interaction of the vital and mobility revolutions. It is characterized by distinct urban–rural differentials in fertility–mortality levels and

[19] This is taken from the title of A. C. Kelley and J. G. Williamson, *What Drives Third World City Growth?* (Princeton, 1984).
[20] This is not the 'ultimate explanation', of course, but only a proximate one. Underlying the demographic and migratory movements discussed here are technological change, capital accumulation and investment, and institutional and organizational changes. By better understanding the proximate factors, the deeper causes may be discussed more fruitfully.

patterns of decline, and by a massive largely voluntary net transfer of population from rural to urban areas through internal migration.[21]

He is strengthened in this portrayal by Wilbur Zelinsky's assertion that 'the course of the mobility transition closely parallels that of the demographic transition'.[22]

From our perspective this presentation of the 'human accounting' of urbanization has serious weaknesses. It provides no explicit justification for linking the mobility and the demographic transitions. The implicit assumption seems to be that the modernization driving the demographic transition also loosens the constraints that immobilize labour, unleashing rural-to-urban migration for reasons unrelated to urban labour markets. The urban transition concept is too closely tied to the sociological convention of bundling urbanization, modernization, and industrialization as a single package. As a consequence it is designed to explain a one-time phenomenon, occurring in Europe during the course of the nineteenth century, and implies that the modern urban hierarchy is a creation of the specific forces released during that era.

The concept is seriously flawed, but by using it we can see more clearly how historical urban transitions really occur. In this sense it can serve a useful function despite its shortcomings. Fig. 3.2 portrays the 'stylized' urban

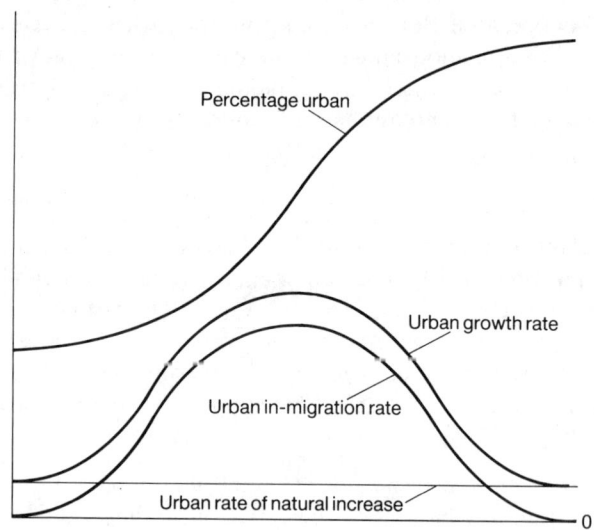

Figure 3.2. The stylized urban transition

[21] Rogers, 'Migration Patterns', 302.
[22] Zelinsky, 'Hypothesis of the Mobility Redistribution', 222.

transition. The transition from low to high levels of urbanization proceeds through a phase of accelerating followed by one of decelerating urban growth which, following Zelinsky, is dominated by a mobility transition. Urban immigration rates drive urban growth in the acceleration phase. Thereafter, the urban population's own natural increase dominates the process. Immigration as a percentage of the (much enlarged) urban population falls off, although it remains large as a percentage of the (shrunken) rural population from which it is recruited.

Now, what is wrong with this description? The answer may be obtained by returning to Rogers's definition, cited above. How, specifically, does the urban demographic transition differ from its rural counterpart? And what are the specific, quantitative dimensions of the 'massive net transfer of population from rural to urban areas'?

The demographic transition is usually represented and analysed as a societal process. It is generally understood that the factors which brought about lower fertility were diffused gradually among social classes, but the possibility that a spatial diffusion process may have generated urban–rural differentials both in the levels and the time-paths of fertility and mortality rates has rarely been examined.

Here it is important to distinguish between two types of urban–rural differentials. One is general; it applies to rapid urban growth at all times. The second is specific; it applies only to the era of the demographic transition. The general differential is the product of rural–urban migration. The young-adult selectivity bias characteristic of migration results in different age distributions in the towns and the country which in turn raise urban birth rates and reduce urban death rates compared to rural levels. This occurs independently of changes in age-specific rates in either sector; it is a compositional effect. A related, but not necessarily universal, phenomenon is the sex ratio of migrants. Where strong urban demand for labour is 'pulling' migrants, the proportion of men among migrants is likely to be greater, bringing overall urban sex ratios more nearly into balance and encouraging earlier and more universal marriage.

Nathan Keyfitz and Dimiter Philipov modelled the compositional effects of rural–urban migration.[23] By using the concept of 'reproductive value' they demonstrated that migrants had not only an immediate, short-term effect on population growth, but also a substantial longer-term effect based on their superior reproductive value. Migration alters crude birth and death rates so as to give the urban population momentum—'a built-in demographic mechanism whereby present immigration serves to diminish the need for future immigration'.[24]

---

[23] N. Keyfitz and D. Philipov, 'Migration and Natural Increase in the Growth of Cities', *Geographical Analysis*, 13 (1981), 288–9.

[24] The words are those of J. G. Williamson, 'The Urban Transition during the First Industrial Revolution: England, 1776–1871', Harvard Institute of Economic Research Discussion Paper Series, no. 1146 (Apr. 1985), 45.

Jeffrey Williamson has sought to measure the importance of this phenomenon for English cities as their growth accelerated during the late eighteenth and early nineteenth centuries. Comparing crude birth and death rates during the mid-nineteenth century with 'counterfactual' rates (those that would have existed if the age and sex distributions of the cities had been the same as in England as a whole), he found that the effect of age–sex specific migration doubled the urban rate of natural increase. He calculated the counterfactual urban rate of natural increase at 5.82 per thousand; the actual rate stood at 11.12.[25]

The specific process whereby a strong urban labour market can increase urban fertility through its impact on the sex ratio of migrants has been described by van der Woude.[26] His argument is based on changes in the sex ratio of first marriages in Amsterdam during the seventeenth and eighteenth centuries. During the first half of the seventeenth century, when the city grew vigorously, only 95 brides married for the first time for every 100 first-marrying grooms. Between 1676 and 1800 (an era of stability or stagnation) there were always 104 to 108 such brides for every 100 grooms. Clearly, the total ratio of brides to grooms did not budge from 100. When the number of women marrying for the first time fell below the number of men, as it did before 1650, this implied that the city attracted many more men seeking brides than could be accommodated by the available supply of never-married women. Some of these men married widows. When the ratio exceeded 100, from 1676 onwards, the opposite was true: eligible bachelors were relatively scarce, forcing many women to marry widowers as their first husbands. From this measure of relative scarcity in the urban marriage market van der Woude goes on to reason that before 1650 most urban women must have married, and married at relatively young ages. As the city ceased to grow and the changing economic structure lost its appeal to migratory men, the mean age at marriage rose and spinsterhood became more common. On this basis van der Woude argues that Amsterdam, before 1650, contained a surplus of men eager to marry, a large number of children, and that its age structure was relatively young. The crude birth rate must have been higher than during later periods.

We have here a process that can generate urban–rural fertility and mortality differentials which give momentum to urban growth, once it has been initiated by migration. However, this momentum is exhausted soon after the initiating migration stream disappears. It is not self-sustaining.[27]

---

[25] Williamson, 'The Urban Transition . . . 1776–1871', Harvard Institute of Economic Research Discussion Paper Series, no. 1146 (Apr. 1985), 45.

[26] A. M. van der Woude, 'Demografische ontwikkeling van de noordelijke Nederlanden, 1500–1800', in *Algemeene geschiedenis der Nederlanden*, 5 (Haarlem, 1980), 148–9. The sex ratio of first marriages is drawn from S. Hart, *Geschrift en getal*, Hollandse Studiën, 9 (Dordrecht, 1976), 136–43.

[27] None of this analysis would hold, or not with the same force, if the interpretation of A. Sharlin, in 'Natural Decrease in Early Modern Cities: A Reconsideration', *Past and Present*, 79

The historically specific urban–rural differential stimulated urbanization during the European demographic transition. It affected both fertility and mortality. At this point we can say very little about the course of urban–rural fertility differentials. Allan Sharlin's analysis of data from the European Fertility Project demonstrated (for the late nineteenth and early twentieth centuries) that fertility in urban districts was almost always lower than in rural districts. Sharlin also affirmed the general assumption that urban marital fertility began to decline earlier than rural fertility, but these differences appear to be quite subtle.[28] In general, our knowledge about urban–rural fertility differentials is still insufficient to make far-reaching claims. For this reason I shall concentrate here on urban–rural differences in mortality.

The urban mortality transition can be summarized as follows: at the beginning of the nineteenth century mortality levels varied directly with density; by the early twentieth century mortality varied inversely with density. Mortality declined for society as a whole, but more rapidly in cities, which at the beginning of the century were uniquely vulnerable to the most common causes of death, but which, by the end of the century, were the chief beneficiaries—or the first beneficiaries—of advances in medicine and improvements in public hygiene.

There are two crossing-points which are important to the role of the urban demographic transition in urbanization (see Fig. 3.3). The first is the point at which the urban mortality rate falls below the urban fertility rate. Until this occurs on a permanent basis (as opposed to the transitory, migration-driven effect described above) urban growth depends *entirely* on migration. In addition, this crossing-point must be passed in order to remove the ceiling on urbanization which prevents the urban sector from growing much beyond 40 per cent of the total population. This was shown in simulation exercises in which a variety of rural and urban rates of natural increase and a variety of initial sizes of the urban sector were used.[29] Once positive urban rates of natural increase (however small) are achieved, this ceiling no longer applies.

The second crossing-point is where the urban mortality rate falls below the rural rate. Then it becomes possible (but by no means necessary) for the urban rate of natural increase to exceed the rural rate. Whether this happens depends on the course of the urban–rural fertility differences. As noted above, urban fertility rates are usually lower than rural rates, and this ratio

(1978), 126–38, is borne out by research. He suggested that urban social and political institutions prevented most in-migrants to the cities from marrying. Their stay in the city was, in a sense, temporary. During their stay, they were at risk of dying, but not eligible for marriage and reproduction. If this were broadly true the second-order demographic effects of rural–urban migration discussed above could not occur, or not to the same degree.

[28] A. Sharlin, 'Urban–Rural Differentials in Fertility in Europe during the Demographic Transition', in A. J. Coale and S. C. Watkins (eds.), *The Decline of Fertility in Europe* (Princeton, 1986), 234–60.

[29] D. Friedlander, 'Demographic Responses and Population Change', *Demography*, 6 (1969), 359–81; Keyfitz, 'Do Cities grow by Natural Growth or by Migration?'; Williamson, 'Urban Transition'.

58   Jan de Vries

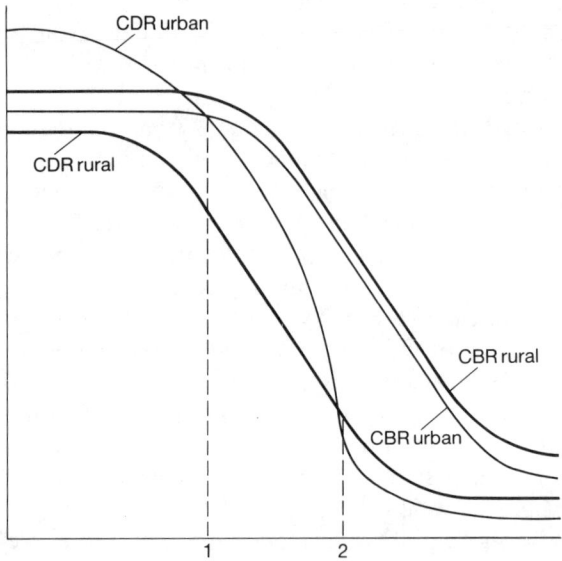

Figure 3.3. The stylized urban demographic transition

may not have changed greatly during the course of the demographic transition (once again, apart from the transitory migration-induced effects noted above). If this proves to be the case generally, then this second crossing-point marks the beginning of 'autonomous urbanization', where the demographic *capacity* exists for urbanization to be self-sustaining, independent of rural to urban migration, and very rapid.

If the urban–rural differentials in mortality and fertility followed a course broadly consistent with the above analysis, the second component of the urban transition, the 'massive net transfer of population', that is, the mobility transition, is placed in a new light. European urbanization since the mid-eighteenth century has been propelled demographically in two phases. It began, as had earlier eras of urban growth, with a typical migration-led growth phase that led to urban–rural differences in vital rates based on favourable urban age–sex distributions. Instead of ending there, it was carried forward by the historically unique consequences of the demographic transition. By generating positive and rising urban rates of natural increase the urban–rural differentials of the demographic transition allowed urbanization to reach new heights. The combined effect of these two phases was gradually to diminish the relative importance of rural–urban migration as a source of urban growth. Instead of a mobility revolution driving urbanization, urban growth came to depend, perhaps for the first time, on a secular rise in urban rates of natural increase.

Does this mean that the mobility transition is an illusion? If it is understood to imply that nineteenth-century urbanization was primarily based on a new, higher level of net migration, raising the proportion of migrants in urban populations, the answer would be 'yes'. However, there may be other senses in which the concept can be saved. The absolute volume of migration certainly rose, and measured as a percentage of the rural population, migration rates probably also rose. In addition, mobility (gross rather than net migration flows) may have risen. But for the purpose at hand net migration is most important, and here the emphasis must be on continuity rather than revolution.

High rates of migration were not new to the period of massive urbanization. What changed then (and may have been mistaken for the mobility revolution) was the destination of migrants. This, finally, brings us to the relationship between the sources of urban growth and the character of the urban hierarchy. This relationship is effectively obscured from view so long as we adhere to the tradition of examining urbanization in the context of two-sector (urban–rural) models.[30] Such models direct attention to the shift of population between two undifferentiated sectors. This can give the false impression that an absence of net migration to the urban sector is equivalent to an absence of migration. A multi-sector model can better capture the variety of options available to migrants, and thereby identify both the forms of population distribution that compete with urbanization (e.g. proto-industrialization) as well as the alternative forms of urbanization (such as primacy, large city concentration, new city creation).

A first step in this direction (but only that) is the three-sector model of migration and natural increase presented in my *European Urbanization, 1500–1800*. By separating a rural non-agricultural from an agricultural sector it proved possible to demonstrate that the varying power of attraction of cities over time did not so much signify the ebb and flow of migration (broadly defined) as the redirection of migratory flows.[31] A further step would be to distinguish between large and small cities, with a view to identifying the forces that channel migration, sometimes towards the one and sometimes towards the other—such as stepwise rather than direct migration, or the migration of single persons rather than family migration, or men rather than women.

The conclusion I wish to reach is this: urbanization is not a uniform, linear process. A single statistic cannot take its measure, nor can a model such as the urban transition adequately account for the diversity of urban hierarchies in which urbanization is embodied. Similarly, rural–urban migration is not

---

[30] De Vries, *European Urbanization*, 221–33.
[31] Ibid. 231–40. See also E. A. Wrigley, 'Urban Growth and Agricultural Change: England and the Continent in the Early Modern Period', *Journal of Interdisciplinary History*, 15 (1985), 683–728.

something new to the era of 'modern urbanization', with a uniform, predictable impact. Rather, it is historically an ongoing phenomenon with a selective and changeable impact. It drove urbanization and de-urbanization, hierarchy formation and city creation. In contrast, urban natural increase, once it became structural rather than transitory, has been more uniform in its impact. It gives modern urbanization a stability and an autonomy that it did not have when migration dominated both the growth of the urban sector and differential growth among cities.

4 East Asian Urbanization in the Nineteenth Century
Comparisons with Europe

GILBERT ROZMAN
Department of Sociology, Princeton University, Princeton, New Jersey, USA

In the 1970s, led by the innovative studies of Akira Hayami[1] and G. William Skinner,[2] quantitative research on nineteenth-century East Asian cities developed rapidly. For the first time detailed statistics on local and regional urbanization in pre-modern East Asia were being systematically evaluated. Through the analysis of correlations between urbanization and prefectural population growth rates, and through comparisons of city-size distributions to ideal rank-size ordering, new insights were gained about the patterns of urbanization in this region. At the beginning of the 1970s,[3] I was also engaged in assembling aggregate urban data to study the development of an urban hierarchy and to determine the spatial patterns of urbanization in China and Japan. Although I found the data sufficient to estimate levels of urbanization, to compare urban hierarchies across regions and countries, and to make some general statements about changes over time, I ran up against two primary obstacles: (*a*) the dearth of urban data for periods before the eighteenth century, which created difficulty in making quantitative comparisons over time; and (*b*) the dearth of studies of pre-modern urbanization in other countries, which meant that there was an absence of models for research methods and of cases for comparative study. Europe, the one region in the world with superior data and substantial urbanization, surprisingly remained without appropriate analytical studies and even without data surveys that could serve as a guide for comparisons. Later I extended my analysis to the Russian Empire and found data for a single period in England and France, but these steps were not a substitute for a comprehensive study of European urbanization.[4]

---

[1] A. Hayami, 'Tokugawa kōki jinkō hendo no chiikiteki tokusei', *Mita gakkai zasshi*, 64: 8 (1971); 'Kinsei kōki chiikibetsu jinkō hendo to toshi jinkō hiritsu no kanren', *Tokugawa Rinseishi Kenkyūsho Kenkyū Kiyō* (Mar. 1975).
[2] G. W. Skinner, *The City in Late Imperial China* (Stanford, Calif., 1977).
[3] G. Rozman, *Urban Networks in Ch'ing China and Tokugawa Japan* (Princeton, 1973).
[4] G. Rozman, *Urban Networks in Russia, 1750–1800, and Premodern Periodization* (Princeton, 1976).

62 *Gilbert Rozman*

With the publication of Jan de Vries's *European Urbanization, 1500–1800* (1984), there is now available a work on Europe that can inspire those interested in East Asia to take a fresh look at cities in their region of study. In the light of de Vries's findings, the two central themes of research on pre-modern urbanization should be re-examined: (*a*) how does the urban hierarchy develop, and (*b*) what are the spatial patterns of urbanization? These two themes should remind us that quantitative evidence is of interest, in part, for the light it sheds on pre-modern social change more generally and on a country's readiness for modernization. De Vries carried his analysis forward to the transition to modern city systems, while this Chapter only takes us to the starting-point of that transition.[5]

1. The data base

The data for China are scanty in comparison with those for Japan, and the data for Japanese cities before the 1870s are meagre in comparison with European urban data for all periods between 1500 and 1800. Whereas de Vries found sufficient data to assign size categories to over 60 per cent of cities with a population in excess of 10,000 in 1500, over 80 per cent in 1600, 90 per cent in 1700, and 99 per cent in 1800, East Asian specialists have not found population data for even as many as 10 per cent of cases for most of these periods. Japanese data from 1750 to 1850 become more numerous than for earlier periods and make possible estimates based on more than half of all cities with populations of 10,000 or more for 1800 (with interpolations for cities for which there are no figures for 1775–1825, but earlier data from the period 1700–74 and a later figure from 1825 to 1860). Over 80 per cent of the total urban population resided in these cities for which estimates are available. Data from 1875[6] provide a complete survey of urban populations; from the mid-1880s, continuous, comprehensive coverage is possible.[7] In the case of China, there is no prospect of exceeding 10 per cent of cities in our data search before 1800. Then, by loosely grouping data from the late eighteenth century to the 1860s–70s (with interpolations possible in only a minority of cases), we can arrive at an estimate which applies to either 1800 or 1850 (or some date in between). The estimate is based on more than half of all cities with populations of 10,000 or more only if we use a time span of close to a century. Around 1900, with some cities not recorded until the 1910s,[8] data again become sufficient to give hope to the researcher who would study the distribution of urban populations. Even so, the data for the late nineteenth

---

[5] J. de Vries, *European Urbanization, 1500–1800* (London and Cambridge, Mass., 1984), 146–50, 258–66.
[6] *Kyōbuseihyō* (Tokyo, 1875).
[7] S. Ito, 'Kenkyū nōto: senzenki Nihon no toshi seichō', *Nihon rōdō kyōkai zasshi*, 24: 7, 8 (1982).
[8] *Shina shōbetsu zenshi* (Tokyo, 1917–20).

century (1870s–1910s) show little if any improvement over the previous urban population data.

In contrast to de Vries's calculations,[9] for seven points at fifty-year intervals from 1500 to 1800, the East Asian specialist interested in conditions that precede modernization is probably limited to two points separated by between fifty and seventy years—one in the early and the other in the late nineteenth century. More unknowns must be assigned to East Asian city-size categories in three of the four periods—the exception being the 1870s in Japan. Obviously, the more limited data base places more restrictions on the types of analysis that are possible.

2. The contours of East Asian urbanization

Although no substantial sample of city populations before 1800 is available, scattered statistical records and descriptive evidence[10] make possible some general observations about earlier periods. Japan's long seventeenth century (from about 1580 to 1720) brought vigorous economic expansion, population growth, and demographic urbanization. The number of cities with at least 10,000 inhabitants appears to have increased by 400 per cent or more, outpacing population growth by a wide margin. China's long eighteenth century (from about 1680 to 1850) brought economic expansion, population growth, and urban growth without demographic urbanization (apart from a possible recovery from short-term decline in the mid-century). The number of cities with at least 10,000 inhabitants may have increased by 150 per cent, roughly keeping pace with population growth. This is a guess based on information in Chinese local gazetteers (*difang zhi*), which cannot be supported by firm statistical evidence. The evidence for Japan is firmer, and has been assembled in hundreds of *kenshi* (prefectural histories), but also does not constitute a proper sample.

Urban growth in each country was well distributed, but some regional variations can be observed. Starting well below west Japan, east Japan led by Edo (modern Tokyo) urbanized more rapidly and pulled even in urbanization by the early nineteenth century. South-east China (Lingnan and the south-east coast), which was restricted for a time by efforts to close coastal trade, re-established itself during the eighteenth century as a leader in urbanization. The Lower Yangzi region (east-central China) retained its pivotal role for interregional trade and continued to be relatively urbanized. Whereas in Tokugawa Japan (1600–1868) a strikingly new distribution of cities (both regionally and by size levels) had emerged, in China the basic patterns of the Ming dynasty (1368–1644) continued in the Qing.

Tables 4.1 and 4.2 divide Japan into two regions, and China into six and

---

[9] De Vries, *European Urbanization*, 27.
[10] Rozman, *Urban Networks in Ch'ing China and Tokugawa Japan*.

64 Gilbert Rozman

Table 4.1a Cities with at least 10,000 inhabitants in Japan, 1825–1875

	Number of cities		Total population (mill.)	
	1825	1875	1825	1875
East Japan	39	38	1.93	1.75
West Japan	43	42	1.74	1.57
Total	82	80	3.67	3.32

Table 4.1b Cities with at least 10,000 inhabitants in China, 1840s–1890s

	Number of cities		Total population (mill.)	
	1840s	1890s	1840s	1890s
China divided administratively:				
North China	70		3.20	
North-west China	23		0.85	
East-central China	69		4.15	
Central China	54		2.80	
South-east China	55		2.70	
South-west China	40		1.85	
Total	311		15.55	
China divided into macro-regions:				
North China	78		3.24	3.95
North-west China	22		1.00	0.92
Lower Yangzi	60		3.91	3.71
Middle Yangzi	56		2.68	2.77
Lingnan	26		1.45	2.03
South-east China	23		1.08	1.19
Upper Yangzi	31		1.38	1.78
Yun-Kwei	10		0.32	0.51
Total	306[a]	330[b]	15.06[c]	16.86[c]

[a] There is no way to calculate the number of cities with at least 10,000 inhabitants directly from the data in Skinner's book. For the Lower Yangzi and north China regions, where he provides a breakdown of cities by population size, I include all cities with 16,000 or more inhabitants plus two-thirds of the number of cities with 8,000–15,999 inhabitants. For the Lower Yangzi the result is that 18.2% of urban central places with 2,000 or more inhabitants are included, while for north China the figure is 18.7%. For other regions I have used the multiplier of 18.5% to estimate from the total number of urban central places given by Skinner (p. 229) the number of cities with 10,000 or more inhabitants. The fact that he asserts (p. 248) that there were 292 cities above this threshold, reveals that the resulting calculation of 306 exceeds his own by 5%.

[b] Skinner (p. 229) estimates the number of urban central places (over 2,000 population) in 1893 as being 8% greater than in 1843. This is the basis for my calculation of 330 cities with 10,000 or more in 1893, compared with a total of 306 in 1843. Although Skinner divides China into different boundaries, his urban data for 1843 (the sources for which are not given) are virtually identical to mine.

[c] Skinner gives the overall urban population of the Lower Yangzi in 1843 as 4,930,000 and the population of cities with at least 16,000 inhabitants as 3,391,000. To obtain the population of cities of 10,000–15,999 inhabitants I have multiplied his population in cities of 8,000–15,999 by 80%. The result is 516,000, which, when added to 3,391,000, yields 3,907,000, or 78% of the urban total. Skinner gives similar statistics for only one other region, north China, which indicates that 68% of the urban total, 3,237,000 of 4,651,000, lived in cities of this size. On the assumption that the high percentage of city residents in large cities in the Lower Yangzi region is

atypical and that north China is somewhat below other regions in this regard, I have chosen 71% as the multiplier for other regions in order to convert Skinner's figures for 1843 and 1893 for the overall urban population to estimates for the population in cities with 10,000 or more inhabitants.

Sources: The figures in Table 4.1 are derived from urban data given by Rozman, *Urban Networks in Ch'ing China and Tokugawa Japan* and 'Castle Towns in Transition', 323, 329–30, and, where macro-regions are the unit of analysis, by Skinner, *City in Late Imperial China*, 229, 244–5.

Table 4.2a Percentage of total population urban in Japan 1800–1875

	1800–1825	1875
East Japan	11.7	12.1
West Japan	11.6	9.4
Total	11.7	10.4

Table 4.2b Percentage of total population urban in China, 1840s–1890s

	1840s	1890s
China divided administratively		
North China	3.3	
North-west China	3.3	
East-central China	4.0	
Central China	3.5	
South-east China	4.9	
South-west China	3.4	
Total	3.7	
China divided into macro-regions:		
North China	2.9	3.3
North-west China	3.6	4.0
Lower Yangzi	5.8	8.3
Middle Yangzi	3.2	3.7
Lingnan	5.3	6.6
South-east China	4.2	4.6
Upper Yangzi	2.8	3.2
Yun-Kwei	2.2	2.5
Total	3.7[a]	4.4[a]

[a] Skinner (p. 229) estimates that the percentage of China's population in cities rose from 5.1 to 6.0 between 1843 and 1893. Following his example, I have used the growth rate of 17.6% to calculate the increase for cities with 10,000 or more residents. The result is 17.47 million in cities of this size, rather than the figure of 16.86 million calculated in Table 4.1. The population in cities with at least 10,000 inhabitants was estimated from Skinner's charts as follows. For the Lower Yangzi and north China regions, the overall urban percentage he gives on p. 229 was multiplied by his index for each region given on p. 240 for the percentage of population in large cities, and by a multiplier for the additional percentage in middle-sized cities with at least 10,000 inhabitants. Skinner's data point to a multiplier of 1.269 for the Lower Yangzi, where big cities predominate, and of 1.425 in north China, which was typical of most regions. The multipliers for the Upper Yangzi and north-west China, where the index for large cities was almost identical with that in north China, is also 1.425. Multiplying their index figures of 48.0–48.9% by 1.425

gives a figure of 69%, which we then multiplied by the overall percentage of the population in cities to estimate the percentage in cities of at least 10,000 inhabitants. Other multipliers were calculated by interpolation. Only in the Yun-Kwei region, where big cities are scarce (Skinner gives an index of 29.8% of the total urban population) was a larger multiplier warranted. By extrapolation I have estimated that if the multiplier for the Lower Yangzi with an index of 61.8 is 1.269 and for north China with an index of 48.4 is 1.425, then the multiplier in the Yun-Kwei region should be 1.617. The same multipliers were applied to 1893.

eight, separately presenting data that I have calculated according to administrative divisions,[11] and that Skinner presents on the basis of macro-regions.[12] Sharp contrasts exist between the relatively high rates of pre-modern urbanization in Japan and the low rates in China. During the first half of the nineteenth century (the dates of 1825 for Japan and the 1840s for China should be taken as indicative of this entire half-century as urban data are scattered over many decades), the percentage of Japan's population living in cities with a population of at least 10,000 was more than three times the corresponding figure for China. No Chinese macro-region contained as many cities as the eighty-two in Japan, although the population of north China was more than three times that of Japan, and the Middle Yangzi and Lower Yangzi each contained more than twice Japan's total population. Japan's 11.6 or 11.7 per cent resembles the 11.7 per cent of the Mediterranean region in 1700 or the 10.9 per cent in north and west Europe in 1650, while China's regional figures of 2.2–5.8 per cent were exceeded by these two European regions already in 1500, and by central Europe by 1650 at the latest. Only eastern Europe had not surpassed the Chinese mean in 1750, but its figure of 4.2 per cent in 1800 does show it moving ahead.

3. Nineteenth-century changes in urbanization

Our data do not permit us to distinguish between what I have argued were two stages of urban change in Japan between the early nineteenth century and 1875.[13] The first stage was under way for at least a century and involved a gradual de-urbanization in which castle towns (*jōkamachi*), including most cities with at least 10,000 inhabitants, gradually declined as did the two largest cities of west Japan, Osaka and Kyoto. Of thirty-seven cities for which scholars have found records for two dates, twenty-seven declined, six showed little change, and only four grew appreciably.[14] These were mostly castle towns of west Japan—the principal region of urban decline before the 1860s. In east Japan, the second stage of decline was more important. This was the

---

[11] Ibid.; cf. also 'Castle Towns in Transition', in M. B. Jansen and G. Rozman (eds.), *Japan in Transition: From Tokugawa to Meiji* (Princeton, 1986).
[12] Skinner, *City in Late Imperial China*.
[13] Rozman, 'Castle Towns in Transition'.
[14] T. C. Smith, 'Pre-Modern Economic Growth: Japan and the West', *Past and Present*, 60 (1973); Y. Nakabe, *Jōkamachi* (Kyoto, 1978).

impact of the Tokugawa–Meiji transition in the 1860s and 1870s, when castle cities lost their monopoly functions as domain administrative centres, *samurai* stipends were ended, and the obligatory residence of most *samurai* in segregated areas of castle towns was replaced by freedom of movement. With the end of the alternate residence system (*sankin kōtai*) in Edo and other changes affecting that city, it lost several hundred thousand people,[15] and still showed a deficit in excess of 150,000 people in 1875. The second stage of decline in the transition to the Meiji period also brought de-urbanization and redistribution from large to small cities. Our figures omit cities of 5,000–9,999, whose growth partially offset the decline of larger cities.[16]

It is necessary to relate changes in absolute urban populations to population growth and decline. Hayami Akira has demonstrated that demographic developments were different in west and east Japan between the 1720s and 1840s and again in the Tokugawa–Meiji transition.[17] In Tables 4.1 and 4.2 we see that the urban experiences of these two regions also differed. While the urban percentage in east Japan was increasing, mainly because of population decline, that in west Japan was declining from 11.6 to 9.4 per cent in cities of at least 10,000, as a result of population growth, as well as absolute urban decline.

China's urban experience from the 1840s to the 1890s was essentially the opposite of Japan's from 1825 to 1875. China's urban percentage was rising. While treaty ports (Yokohama and Kobe) had a small impact on Japan's urbanization to 1875, they led the way in China's urbanization to the 1890s. There was no sharp discontinuity in the Japanese urban distribution by region in the short-term aftermath of the arrival of foreigners, but in China two regions experienced a sudden spurt in urbanization without parallel in recent centuries. The Lingnan macro-region, and especially the Lower Yangzi, widened the already substantial gap between their levels of urbanization and the levels found in other Chinese regions.

4. The properties of the urban system

De Vries presented rank-size distributions for his analysis of the properties of the European urban system, and we can do likewise. In fact, Skinner has already done so for the macro-regions of China,[18] and for China as a whole in 1843. While I would alter the placements of some cities (Beijing, Nanjing, and Fuzhou among them), and of the lower ends of his regional distributions, the general pattern he identified for China as a whole is consistent with my data. The distribution flattens for the largest cities, and slopes quite evenly for

---

[15] H. D. Smith III, 'The Edo–Tokyo Transition: In Search of Common Ground', in Jansen and Rozman (eds.), *Japan in Transition*.
[16] Rozman, 'Castle Towns in Transition'.
[17] A. Hayami, 'Population Changes', in Jansen and Rozman (eds.), *Japan in Transition*.
[18] Skinner, *City in Late Imperial China*, 238–9, 243.

cities with 10,000 to those with more than 100,000 population. In Fig. 4.1 the distribution for China as a whole, and for Japan as a whole is presented.

If we had separated east and west Japan, we would have determined that west Japan seems to lack a single great city, while east Japan's first city, Tokyo, is much larger than would be expected from the rank-size distribution of other cities in the region. From the early seventeenth century onwards, this city's primacy exceeded what one would expect from its region. It operated as a centre for west Japan too, and extended its primacy as the major cities in the west, Osaka and Kyoto, declined. As Japan moved from many local and regional urban systems to two systems during the early seventeenth century, and then increasingly to one system over the Tokugawa period, China

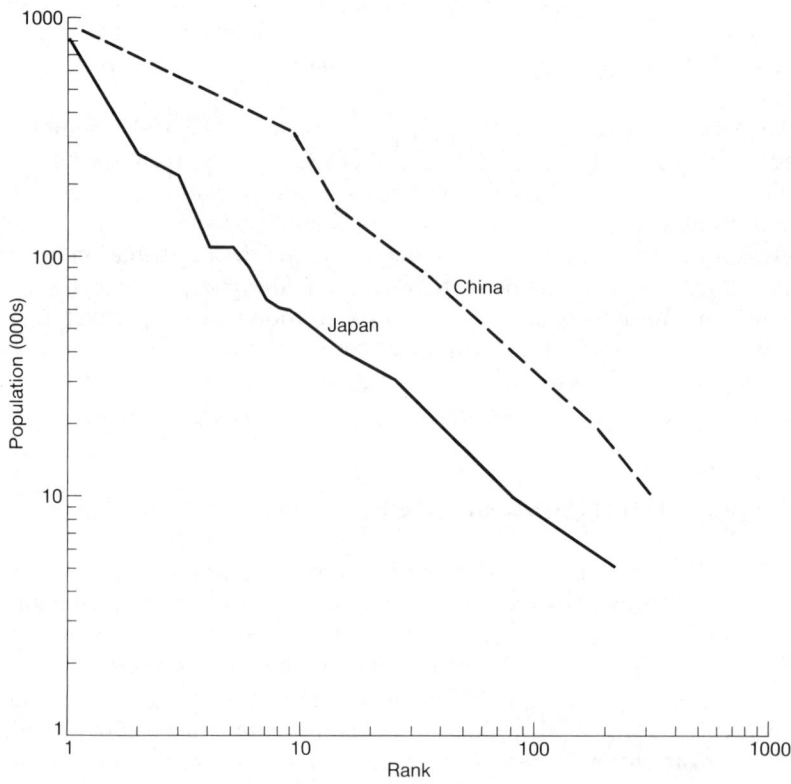

Figure 4.1. Rank-size distribution: China (1840s) and Japan (1875)

East Asian Urbanization 69

retained a pattern of many regional systems until the late nineteenth century.

It is necessary to analyse many levels of cities to appreciate the character of a country's urban network in comparative perspective. As de Vries has pointed out,[19] the rank-size rule, which assumes that knowing the size of the largest city, or of some small group of large cities, is sufficient to estimate the number and size of smaller cities, does not hold. One alternative is to carry out an empirical rank-size study, determining such things as the slope, the extent of a 'flat top' for large cities, and the point at which a 'lower limb' forms, indicating fewer cities than the slope for other cities would suggest. In Fig. 4.1, I present actual rank-size distributions for Japan in 1875 and China in the 1840s. The slope is steeper for China. This is also apparent in Table 4.3; the number of cities with 10,000 to 20,000 inhabitants in Japan was 30 per cent of that in China, the corresponding percentage for cities with 20,000 to 40,000 inhabitants was 26, with 40,000 to 80,000 inhabitants 21, and with 80,000–160,000 inhabitants 14. Only in the category with between 160,000 and 320,000 inhabitants was the pattern broken, with two Japanese cities against five Chinese. For cities with more than 320,000 inhabitants the percentage fell again to 11 per cent. Thus, with one exception, the larger the size category, the fewer Japanese cities there were relative to Chinese ones.

Examined from a different viewpoint visible on a rank-size diagram, China and Japan each produced a city of about one million residents (Edo had dropped to 860,000 in 1875 as a result of the Tokugawa–Meiji transition), but Japan did this with relatively few cities with 40,000 or more inhabitants and relatively many cities with 10,000–40,000 or 3–10,000.[20] If we distinguish local, regional, and national integration, we can make the following comparisons. Japan contained large local cities (about one-tenth the population of a domain with 10,000–1,000,000 people[21]), while China had small cities containing 2–3 per cent of the district population. In Japan, however, there were few regional cities for inter-domain exchange. Local areas were generally directly tied to the three great, central cities. Both administrative arrangements were worked out around 1600, and geographical conditions contributed to this Japanese pattern. In turn, the dearth of Chinese cities in the range with fewer than 20,000 inhabitants suggests a lack of vigour in local administration and commerce. Whether rank-size diagrams, de Vries's size categories, or some other set of size categories (such as those I used in five-country comparisons) are used, the variations all point to the need to look at the histories of the countries, as well as at the urban data in order to make comparisons meaningful. Regional variations within China or Japan do not much affect the analyses by city-size categories.

---

[19] De Vries, *European Urbanization*, 52.
[20] Rozman, *Urban Networks in Russia*, 245.
[21] J. W. Hall, 'The Castle Town and Japan's Modern Urbanization', in J. W. Hall and M. B. Jansen (eds.), *Studies in the Institutional History of Early Modern Japan* (Princeton, 1968).

Table 4.3 Number of cities by size category[a]

Number of inhabitants	1825		1875		1840s						
	East Japan	West Japan	East Japan	West Japan	North China	North-west China	East-central China	Central China	South-east China	South-west China	All of China
10,000–19,999	20	19	22	18	33	10	28	24	24	16	135
20,000–39,999	12	14	10	15	23	9	19	15	18	14	98
40,000–79,999	4	8	3	6	7	2	13	9	6	5	42
80,000–159,999	2	0	2	1	4	1	6	3	5	3	22
160,000–319,999	0	1	0	2	2	1	0	2	0	0	5
≥320,000	1	1	1	0	1	0	3	1	2	2	9
Total	39	43	38	42	70	23	69	54	55	40	311

[a] These data come from Rozman, *Urban Networks in Ch'ing China and Tokugawa Japan* and 'Castle Towns in Transition', and *Kyōbuseihyō* (1875).

5. Comparisons with urban Europe

Which region had more cities, Europe or our two countries in East Asia? If we start with de Vries's table 3.1,[22] in which the cities of Europe with at least 10,000 inhabitants are enumerated, we can compare these to the number of cities in China and Japan. The East Asian total of 391 in the 1840s surpasses the European total of 364 for 1800. If China's population was at least 20 per cent lower in 1800 than in the 1840s, it is reasonable to surmise that China's cities with 10,000 inhabitants were also 20 per cent fewer. This places the two-country total at 329—10 per cent below Europe's figure for the same date. While Europe's total had spurted from 261 to 364 during the previous fifty years, China's had also climbed, with population growth exceeding 25 per cent. The proportionate Chinese total for cities would have been below 200, and the combined total in 1750, given Japan's virtual constancy in this regard, not much more than the 261 in Europe. Japan's contribution falls off sharply for the years 1500 to 1600, while China's was depressed in 1650; therefore, together, they may have matched the 150–225 cities in Europe from 1500 to 1700. On the basis of these estimates, it would not be unreasonable to assert that available evidence supports the conclusion that the number of cities with 10,000 or more inhabitants in China and Japan was roughly the same as the number in Europe during the entire period 1500–1800.

Which region had more urban residents? With a similar number of big cities, East Asia sustained much larger urban populations. Europe's 12.2 million inhabitants in cities over 10,000 in 1800 were surpassed by East Asia's 19.2 million a few decades later. At no point between 1500 and 1800, and perhaps at no point after the fall of the Roman Empire, did Europe approach East Asia's urban population totals. Comparisons of my Table 4.3 with de Vries's Table 3.4[23] show the size categories that account for this difference. East Asia contained many more cities of 320,000 compared with two in Europe between 1650 and 1750 and three in 1800, and East Asia contained proportionately fewer cities of 10,000–20,000 (175 of 391 compared with 206 of 364). Between 1750 and 1800 there had been a spurt in cities of 10,000–20,000 inhabitants in Europe, but not in East Asia. Before 1750 there had been a progressive concentration in larger European cities, but without achieving levels of concentration long visible in East Asia.

These figures acquire new meaning when we take national and regional populations into account. Europe's population was less than half that of East Asia; though there were fewer people the number of cities was similar. In 1500 little of Europe was urbanized; however, by 1600, few countries in Europe were below the urbanization levels found in China in the nineteenth century. From 1650 to 1750, Europe's levels (primarily those in the north and

[22] De Vries, *European Urbanization*, 29.
[23] Ibid.

west and round the Mediterranean) were close to the level of urbanization in Japan. Not only in its urban percentage, but also in its distribution of cities by size, Japan was more similar to Europe than was China.

Which region in Europe did Japan most resemble? Table 4.4 indicates that

Table 4.4 Urban population by size category

Size category	Japan 1875		North and west Europe 1750–1800		Central Europe 1750		Mediterranean Europe 1750	
	No.	%	No.	%	No.	%	No.	%
10,000–19,999	600,000	18	650,000	20	629,000	20	721,000	23
20,000–39,999	625,000	19	520,000	16	908,000	30	689,000	22
40,000–79,999	450,000	14	768,000	24	670,000	22	529,000	17
80,000–159,999	220,000	7	183,000	6	204,000	7	891,000	28
160,000–319,999	498,000	15	298,000	9	0	0	305,000	10
≥320,000	860,000	26	770,000	24	576,000	19	0	0
Total	3,253,000		3,189,000		2,987,000		3,135,000	
Total population	33,000,000		22,000,000		40,000,000		26,500,000	

it was north and west Europe. By averaging the data for this region for 1750 and 1800, we obtain an urban population (3,189,000) close to that of Japan (3,253,000). Mediterranean Europe's urban population (3,135,000) in 1750 was in the same range, while central Europe's figure of 2,987,000 was somewhat smaller. I have excluded eastern Europe's 330,000 people in 1750, which reflects a much lower level of urbanization.

Japan and north and west Europe require fewest changes in percentages to produce identical results. Most of the difference is in cities of 40,000–80,000—Japan is underrepresented—and 160,000–320,000—Europe is underrepresented. On the one hand, cities of 40,000–80,000 were few in Japan, because there were not many domains of more than 400,000 population and smaller domains tended to be linked directly to the central cities. Even after the abolition of domains in 1871, this pattern did not change quickly. On the other hand, cities with populations between 160,000 and 320,000 may have been deficient in Europe, including north-west Europe, because separate national units were not fully integrated, in contrast to Japan's single state.

6. Conclusions

More remains to be done before we can have confidence in the analytical tools for pre-modern urban studies. De Vries mentions many themes: the relationship of large to small cities, the degree of integration of the urban system, the looseness or tightness of the system, the degree of dominance of cities at the head, etc. Various ways of comparing cities by size can help us to give substance to these themes.

Scarcity of data makes it more difficult to study East Asian than European urbanization. Evidence is sufficient, however, to find similar trends in progress: a rising level of urbanization in Japan, the fashioning of a single urban system over a large territory and, in the case of Japan, a nation, and, again in Japan, urban growth from below. China's level of urbanization during the nineteenth century resembles part of Europe a few centuries earlier, while Japan's level was close to eighteenth-century levels in Europe. Moreover, Japan's spatial distribution is most like that of north and west Europe. Further analysis may show in clearer detail how Japan and northwest Europe were well positioned for modernization.

5 Patterns of Settlement and Political Changes
The French Revolution and the National Urban Hierarchy

BERNARD LEPETIT

EHESS, Laboratoire de Demographie Historique, Paris, France

It is impossible to conceive of a city in abstraction from the space which surrounds it and on which it depends for subsistence and, often, for an important fraction of its population and its revenues. Each city has economic links with its surrounding countryside, links which are based on the division of labour and on the organization of markets, and which become apparent through monetary flows.[1] This description of the situation applies to the period before industrialization and shows that even though there may not have been any links between different towns, their development was, none the less, interdependent. There is a limit to the amount of provisions, people, and incomes that a town could draw from the surrounding countryside before the Industrial Revolution. The situation and the size of a city will depend on those of other cities.

Yet it had already become apparent during the eighteenth century, before the beginning of the Industrial Revolution, that the urban structure was changing. In an economy which was only growing slowly, spectacular growth of one city had to be paid for by decline or stagnation of neighbouring cities. The general pattern of the urban hierarchy could not remain rigid.[2] The problem was relatively unimportant when growth and decline were very localized and applied only to a small number of cities. But what happens when, as a result of government action, factors which are external to the urban system change, for example, when there are changes in the transport system or in the administrative system which affects towns as a whole? We shall attempt to investigate the effect of one major political event, the French Revolution, on the urban system as a whole.

---

[1] R. Cantillon, *Essai sur la nature du commerce en général* (London, 1755).

[2] É. François, 'Des républiques marchandes aux capitales politiques: remarques sur la hiérarchie urbaine de Saint Empire à l'époque moderne', *Revue d'histoire moderne et contemporaine* (1978), 587–603.

1. Standard distributions

There are two types of distribution which play the same part in the analysis of urban structures as standard populations. One of them is theoretical and is based on central-place theory, the second on the rank-size rule. The historian of the pre-industrial period needs to make some very strong assumptions to use central-place theory: a completely open spatial system, a strictly ordered hierarchical system of towns, and consumers who behave rationally in accordance with the canons of liberal economic theory.[3]

The use of the rank-size rule does not necessarily involve similar constraints. In discussing it, one must remember that if the towns of a region, state, or even of the world as a whole are classified by size of their populations, there will be a few large cities, slightly more cities of medium size, and a large number of smaller cities. There is an approximate inverse geometric relationship between the population of cities and their rank order.

Such a relationship can be described by a number of different statistical distributions,[4] and the many scholars who have attempted to discover general laws on which these regularities are based and which would give them a scientific meaning have not been conspicuously successful. In 1973, there were more than a dozen theories in which stochastic, hierarchical, or allometric models were used, even if minor variants are ignored.[5] 'If our concern is with substantial aspects of cities, rather than with probability theory *per se*, the study of size distribution appears to be an elaborate maze, which ends only in a cul-de-sac.'[6]

Economists and geographers, therefore, abandoned this ground, but it has recently been reoccupied by anthropologists and historians.[7] However, their approach, with which I find myself in agreement, differs from that of their

---

[3] C. Ponsard, *Histoire des théories économiques spatiales* (Paris, 1958). A critical view of central-place theory will be found in H. Carter, *The Study of Urban Geography* (London, 1972).

[4] F. Auerbach, 'Das Gesetz der Bevölkerungskonzentration', *Petermann's Mitteilungen* (1913), 74–6; A. J. Lotka, *Elements of Physical Biology* (Baltimore, 1924); M. Saibante, 'La Concentrazione della popolazione', *Metron* (1928), 53–99; R. Gibrat, *Les Inégalités économiques* (Paris, 1931); H. W. Singer, 'The "courbe des populations": A Parallel to Pareto's Law', *Economic Journal* (1926), 254–63; G. K. Zipf, *Human Behavior and the Principle of Least Effort* (Cambridge, Mass., 1949); The best presentation of the work relating to the rank-size law in the French language will be found in D. Pumain, *La Dynamique des villes* (Paris, 1982).

[5] H. W. Richardson, 'Theory of the Distribution of City Sizes: Review and Prospect', *Regional Studies* (1973), 239–51.

[6] B. Robson, *Urban Growth: An Approach* (London, 1973), 37.

[7] Representatives of this school of thought are: G. W. Skinner, 'Regional Urbanization in Nineteenth-Century China', in *The City in Late Traditional China* (Stanford, Calif. 1977), 211–49; G. Rozman, 'Urban Networks and Historical Stages', *Journal of Interdisciplinary History* (1978), 65–91; G. A. Johnson, 'Rank-size Convexity and System Integration', A View from Archaeology', *Economic Geography* (1980), 234–47; C. Smith, 'Placing Formal Geographical Models into Cultural Contexts: The Anthropological Study of Urban Systems', *Comparative*

predecessors. Conscious of the diversity of urban systems in different cultures and periods, scholars in these two disciplines have generally rejected the concept of an a priori law, which explains urban systems in terms of a uniform basic theory. They agree that two consequences follow from the fact that the observed distributions are empirical in their nature.

1. As a matter of priority, a list of different systems must be constructed. In drawing up such a list, those formal models are considered to be an aid to analysis which facilitate comparisons through their use of standard distributions. The rank-size rule is merely one of several such standard distributions. If we standardize the terminology, and attempt to put forward propositions systematically, we shall be able to distinguish between four standard distributions (Fig. 5.1):

(a) a convex distribution with a flat top formed by high-ranking towns of comparable sizes;
(b) a rank-size rule which is graduated by the formula $in\ P_i = in\ P_i + q\ln R_i$, where P_i and R_i stand respectively for the population and rank of the i'th city; P_1^* is the theoretical population of the largest city and q is the slope of the regression line; q is not necessarily equal to 1, as in Zipf's law;
(c) a concave distribution which corresponds to a situation in which there is a definitely superior primate city, and the remaining cities conform to the rank-size rule;
(d) a curve which is first concave and then convex, where a primate city is at the top of an otherwise convex distribution.[8]

2. If we accept an empirical approach, then in my judgement the method of graduating the distribution becomes important. Graphic methods of graduation are likely to prove inadequate and statistical techniques must be used. The most suitable would seem to be regression analysis. This means that for each of the empirical distributions, the values of the parameters P_1^* and q in the preceding equation will have to be estimated. The technique has the following advantages: no particular level of the hierarchy is regarded as more 'normal' than any other; it can provide an estimate of changes in the slope of the curve; it makes it possible to measure the goodness of fit, i.e. the extent to which the observed distribution differs from the rank-size rule; finally, because the type of distribution will depend on the population of the largest cities, it is possible to assess how the slope of the line and the goodness of fit will vary, as cities of the first rank are introduced into the calculation.

Urban Research (1982), 50, 52; S. A. Kowaleski, 'The Evolution of Primate Regional Systems', ibid. 60–78; C. Smith, 'Modern and Premodern Primacy', ibid. 79–96; J. de Vries, *European Urbanization, 1500–1800* (London and Cambridge, Mass., 1984); H. Fassmann, 'City-Size Distribution in the Austro-Hungarian Monarchy, 1857–1910: A Rank-Size Approach', University of Liverpool, international seminar (1984).

[8] Examples of each of these types will be found in the works of Johnson, Fassmann, Skinner, de Vries, and Smith quoted in n. 7.

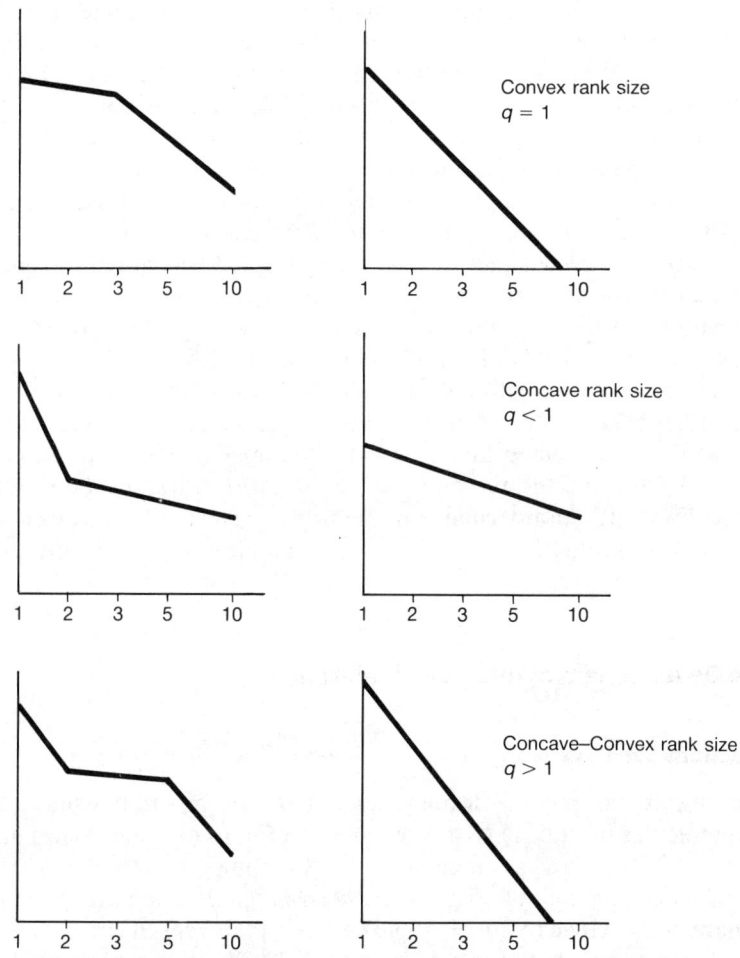

Figure 5.1. Urban hierarchies: model distributions

2. Sources and their use

Size distributions of cities have a long history. In spite of difficulties caused by having to use different sources, it will be convenient to use observations over a long period of time, if we are to appreciate the impact of the Revolution.

Data for the pre-revolutionary period are not accurate, and as our observations relate to different points in time, the information tends to be somewhat blurred. For the period between the reigns of Louis XIV and Louis XVI, I have examined three distributions that relate to periods centred about 1700, 1750, and 1780. The data for the first two periods come from library research; I have used the figures which were collected for a much wider purpose by de Vries and have limited myself to some minor geographical adjustments and a few necessary additions.[9] The data that relate to 1780 are taken from counts of baptisms in the parochial registers which were carried out by the administrative authorities towards the end of the *ancien régime*.[10] For the revolutionary and post-revolutionary periods I shall use four points: 1794, 1806, 1821, and 1836. These dates were chosen so that we should be able to trace possible changes in the system and take account of the quality of successive censuses.[11] For each of these dates I examined the distribution of towns with more than 10,000 inhabitants: there were 60 such towns in 1700, 65 in 1750, 85 in 1780, 95 in 1794, 92 in 1806, 95 in 1821, and 120 in 1836.

The information was plotted on a double logarithmic scale in the usual manner (Fig. 5.2). The gradual shift of the regression line between successive censuses gives the figures their characteristic appearance and hardly needs comment. However, the proximity of the lines for different dates indicates that there was little if any change in the urban system. I have calculated the parameters of each of the regression lines and their values are shown in Table 5.1.

3. The Development of the urban hierarchy

3.1 Medium-sized towns

In looking at the general development of the urban framework, the line relating to cities of rank 11 to n is the most useful, as this line is least affected by the size of the largest cities. We can distinguish between two different periods. The first is characteristic of the *ancien régime*, when the urban system was characterized by a relatively rapid decline in the sizes of cities. The values of the slopes ranged between -0.76 and -0.78. During that period the total size of the urban population grew; in Fig. 5.2 the lines move progressively to

---

[9] De Vries, *European Urbanization*, 272–5. Dunkirk, Lille, and Valenciennes which appeared under 'Belgium' have been incorporated into the distribution. The populations of Tarascon and of Vannes which do not appear in de Vries's list have been estimated at 10,000 in 1700. In 1750, Issoudun, Lunéville, Tarascon, Thiers, and Vannes have been estimated at 10,000. The populations of Saint Étienne and Saint Omer were not known for that date; I have taken them to be 12,000 and 17,000 inhabitants respectively.

[10] B. Lepetit, 'L'Évolution de la hiérarchie urbaine française au xviiie siècle: l'étude des rangs', *Geographie historique des villes de l'Europe occidentale* (Paris, 1984), 184–98.

[11] For 1794: *Archives nationales*, F20 298–394. For 1821: Bibliothèque municipale de Rouen, Manuscrit Montbret 299. For 1806: R. Le Mée, 'Population agglomérée, population éparse au début du xixe siècle', *Annales de démographie historique* (1971), 455–510. For 1836: *Bulletin des lois* (Jan.–Juin 1837).

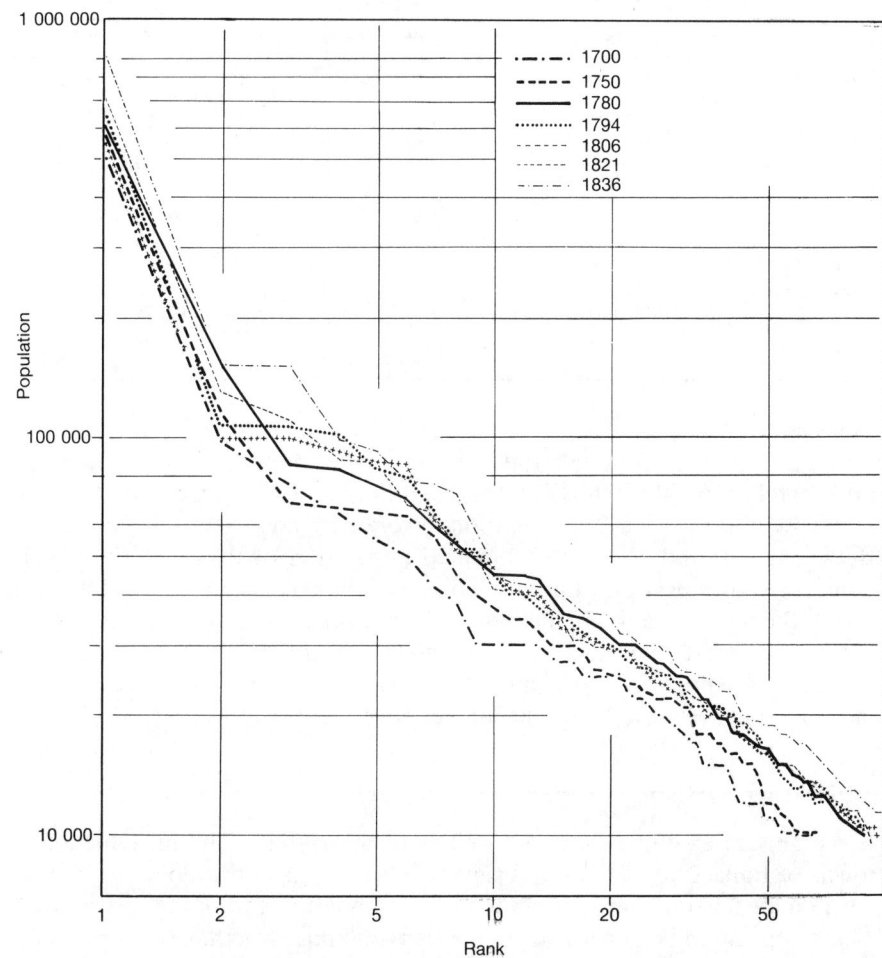

Figure 5.2. Urban hierarchies, 1700–1836

the top left-hand side of the system as time proceeds. Except for the metropolitan towns, there was no change in the urban system.

There is a similar situation towards the end of our period, after the end of the Empire. The lines again shift towards the top left-hand corner of Fig. 5.2, and their slopes are similar. But the system has changed: both in 1821 and in 1836 the slope is now −0.67. This difference, which amounts to ten points when compared with the situation during the *ancien régime*, indicates that the period of the Revolution and the Empire brought about considerable changes in the French urban system.

Table 5.1 Parameters of the rank-size lines in France, 1700–1836 (towns with 10,000 or more inhabitants)

	1836	1821	1806	1794	c.1780	c.1750	c.1700
Number of towns (n)	120	95	92	95	88	65	60
Towns ranked 1 to n							
q	−0.72	−0.73	−0.73	−0.74	−0.74	−0.76	−0.75
$\log P_1^*$	5.49	5.44	5.42	5.45	5.46	5.40	5.33
R_2	0.97	0.97	0.98	0.97	0.98	0.95	0.95
Towns ranked 2 to n							
q	−0.68	−0.68	−0.68	−0.70	−0.70	−0.70	−0.67
$\log P_1^*$	5.41	5.35	5.35	5.37	5.39	5.30	5.22
R_2	0.99	1.00	0.99	0.99	0.99	0.98	0.98
Towns ranked 11 to n							
q	−0.67	−0.67	−0.69	−0.70	−0.76	−0.78	−0.77
$\log P_1^*$	5.41	5.35	5.36	5.39	5.49	5.42	5.36
R_2	0.99	0.99	1.00	0.99	0.99	0.96	0.97

There are two aspects of this change. In the first place, urbanization receded. Between 1794 and 1806, the estimated population of the town of rank 10 fell from 49,000 to 47,000 and that of the town of rank 100 from 9,800 to 9,500. Secondly, the distribution pivoted in favour of smaller towns. Between 1780 and 1794, the estimated population of the town of rank 10 diminished by 9 per cent, that of the town of rank 50 remained constant, and that of the town of rank 100 increased by 5 per cent.

We must note that these movements began relatively early: the trend favouring smaller towns was already visible in the census of 1794, and the movement persisted well into the nineteenth century.

3.2 Metropolitan cities

It remains to examine the largest cities in the system. The introduction of towns of ranks 2 to 10 always results in a reduction of the slope of the line, which indicates the convexity of the curve at the top end of the distribution. There appears to be general agreement among those who have written on the subject that this convexity means either that the limits of the urban system have been misspecified, or that relations within the system were insufficiently developed.[12] I think that these two explanations are similar; both suggest that different adjacent subsets, which are in reality separate, are treated as belonging to the same system.

We shall pay less attention to the slope of the line than to the difference between its slope and that of the line for towns of smaller sizes. In France, this difference diminished slowly throughout the eighteenth century. The Revolution again introduced a discontinuity and after 1794 the differences

---

[12] C. D. Harris, *Cities of the Soviet Union: Studies in their Functions, Size Density and Growth* (Chicago, 1970). See also the works of Skinner, Johnson, and Kowalewski cited in n. 7. Although he admits that there is an unavoidable ambiguity in the rank-size distribution, De Vries (*European Urbanization*), is of the same opinion.

ceased to diminish. Their values varied between 0.10 and 0.06 during the period 1700–80, and remained at 0.01 or 0.02 between 1794 and 1836. This does not mean that the distribution has suddenly opened out: the change in slope is small if the larger towns are included, and the changes are really caused by changes at the bottom end of the distribution, i.e. the small towns.

There remains Paris, the enduring primate city. The change in the slope of the line when it is introduced into the calculation, and the reduction of R^2 indicate that the distribution is concave. A calculation of the primacy index by Jefferson's method,[13] in which the ratio between the populations of the town of the first and of the second rank is used, would be completely inappropriate in this case: the political and demographic upheaval in the second city, Lyons, during the period of the Revolution was too great. It is, however, possible to use other measures. I have used the ratio between the actual population of Paris and its population estimated from the distribution of the sizes of all towns with more than 10,000 inhabitants. The indices are shown below: [14]

1700	138	1794	128
1750	129	1806	121
1780	110	1821	160
1794	128	1836	194

There are two points to note in these figures. The primacy of Paris, which is clear after 1700, is reduced throughout the eighteenth century. The high rate of growth of the capital city compared with that of other towns occurred during the seventeenth century. Moreover, the change in direction of the trend during the revolution period was largely due to the effects of the crisis in provincial towns. It was only during the period of the Empire and after the Revolution that the growth of Paris took off again.

4. The impact of the Revolution

The observations in the preceding paragraphs suggest two different theoretical frameworks which characterize the urban hierarchies under the *ancien régime* and during the nineteenth century respectively. I have drawn two curves, one for 1750 and one for 1836 (Fig. 5.3), which pass through four points: the actual population of Paris; the population of the second largest town, estimated from the regression line for all agglomerations with more than 10,000 inhabitants (except Paris); the population of the towns with the tenth and the hundredth ranking, estimated from the regression line calculated for towns of rank 11 to n.

If we accept the typology suggested at the beginning of this chapter, the

[13] M. Jefferson, 'The law of the Primate City', *Geographical Review* (1939), 266–92.
[14] Our index is of the form $100 n_i/n_{i+h}$. The estimated population for the highest-ranking city is one of the parameters of the regression line.

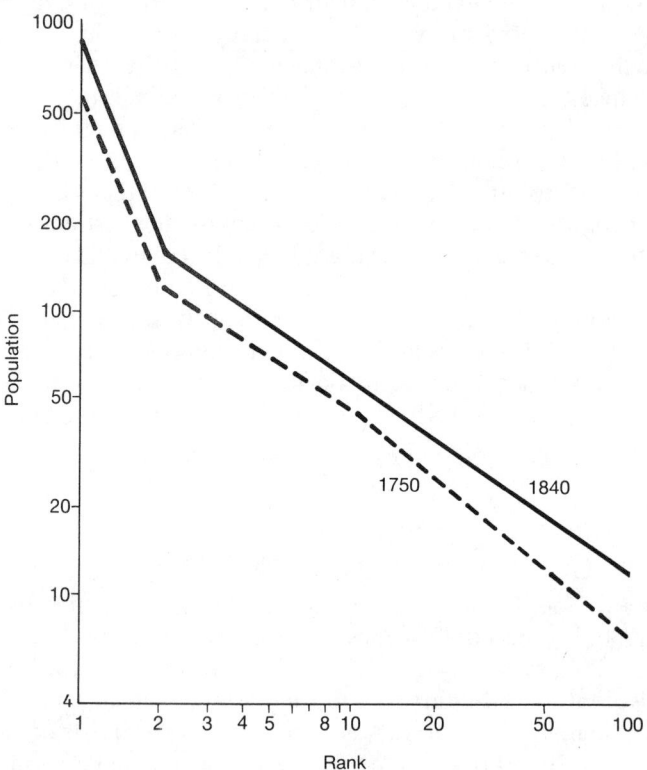

Figure 5.3. Urban hierarchies, theoretical distributions, 1750 and 1840

change is clear: the distribution of towns in France which was concave and then convex in 1750, had become concave by 1836. This is not as insignificant a result as would appear at first sight. Our attempt to formalize rank-size distributions has provided us with a clearer view of the modifications to the urban framework at the time of the Revolution. Although the reduction in urbanization was known, the change in the structure of the urban system which accompanied this reduction had not previously been recognized. The change in structure proved to be lasting: during the nineteenth century, the change in the slope of the regression line was limited and relatively slow. The Revolution marked a turning-point between two systems, each of which lasted for a relatively long time. This goes to show that political changes over a relatively short period can have lasting consequences for the urban system.

The value of the rank-size rule is not limited to description: it suggests new directions for research and hypotheses which must be tested in order to improve our explanation of the phenomena observed. We shall mention two:

1. The different histories of towns of different sizes at a period when there was a general upheaval in the urban system point to differences in their socio-economic structure. It is, therefore, desirable to pay particular attention to those towns in which, for political or economic reasons, the population was most mobile. This mobility may have occurred among the privileged groups of the population which would entail consequences for employment. Economic crises may also have been important in the emergence of a mobile proletariat.

2. If the urban system retains the same structure during a period of later growth, this means that a new equilibrium situation has been reached for the system as a whole. One aspect of the revolutionary period seems to have been particularly important here: the redistribution of administrative functions. The power which used to be concentrated in about thirty regional capitals (the seats of the *Intendants*) during the pre-revolutionary period was distributed to eighty-six departmental capitals as a result of the administrative reform. During the period of the Revolution and later of the Empire, differences in the administrative pyramid were reduced. Hierarchic explanatory models of the urban system have stressed the importance for the rank-size law of administrative functions in urban stratification, and a correlation between the slope of the regression line and the framework of power.[15] The different experience of being promoted or demoted in the hierarchy of power in different towns must be looked at.

The perspectives from which economists and geographers considered the problem during the 1950s and 1960s have changed. The object is no longer to establish a 'law'. Differences between different types of formal empirical distributions are regarded as indicators to researchers which cause them to study other indicators specific to the economic and social structure of the period, of which the towns form part. The analysis of urban structures becomes an exercise in detection. It is hardly a coincidence that historians and anthropologists have been among those who have been most ready to adopt it.

[15] Richardson, 'Distribution of City Sizes'.

6 The German Urban Network between the Sixteenth and Eighteenth Centuries
Cultural and Demographic Indicators

ÉTIENNE FRANÇOIS
Unité de Formation et de Recherche des Sciences Historiques et Geographiques, Université de Nancy II, Nancy, France

The index that is generally employed in the study of urban networks is the size of a town's population: it is simple, easily measured, and can be universally applied. However, is this index really as valuable as it would seem at first sight? Does not its very simplicity sometimes blur a proper understanding of the structures that it is designed to explain? Would it not be better if other statistical indicators could also be used to help us in appreciating the true nature of urban networks and their dynamics? If so, what indicators should be employed?

I shall use the German urban network between the sixteenth and eighteenth centuries as an example to illustrate these points. There are a number of numerical indicators for this period which can be represented both in the form of statistical tables and as maps, and which are very different in nature. There is the demographic indicator, which is generally used, i.e. the size of the population of the principal German towns in about 1600 and about 1800; there are also certain 'cultural' indicators which illustrate the dynamics of intellectual life at the time and give information about publishing activities in the same cities.

I shall begin by summarizing the changes which occurred in the urban network and the urban hierarchy between these two dates by using the demographic indicator, i.e. population size. I shall then proceed to investigate the extent to which the conclusions drawn from this analysis are confirmed by information obtained from indicators of cultural activities, and attempt to show that by employing a combination of these two indicators a better understanding of the structure of the German urban network and its transformation to modern conditions can be achieved.

I

We begin our analysis with Map 6.1 on which all German cities with a population of 10,000 or more inhabitants in about 1600 are shown. This map

The German Urban Network 85

Danzig	50	Erfurt	19	Thousands of inhabitants	
Vienna	50	Frankfurt/M.	18	•	10–19
Prague	50	Braunschweig	16	○	20–39
Augsburg	48	Elbing	15	○	40–79
Cologne	40	Regensburg	15		
Magdeburg	40	Leipzig	14		
Nuremberg	40	Frankfurt/O.	13		
Hamburg	40	Bamberg	12		
Breslau	30	Dresden	12		
Berlin	25	Stettin	12		
Lübeck	23	Münster	11		
Ulm	21	Emden	10		
Aachen	20	Freiburg/Br.	10		
Bremen	20	Salzburg	10		
Königsberg	20	Soest	10		
Mainz	20	Würzburg	10		
Munich	20				

Reichsstädte: underlined

Map 6.1. Geographical location of the 33 largest German towns about 1600 (frontiers of 1789)

has been drawn from data recently published by de Vries,[1] to which I have added my own figures for Augsburg, Aachen, Bremen, Königsberg, Regensburg, and Emden. In order to make comparisons with the situation at the end of the eighteenth century easier, I have used the frontier of the German Empire at the time as the western border of my area (this explains the absence of Strasburg at the end of the sixteenth century), and as the eastern border a line passing through Königsberg, Warsaw, and Trieste.

A glance at the map will show three principal characteristics. The first is the clear dominance within the urban network of the towns lying within the *limes* (i.e. the oldest and most densely populated area of Germany). The eighteen cities which are situated south of a line going from Emden through Bamberg to Prague and which separates south-west Germany from the north-east, account for 62 per cent of the total population of the thirty-three towns shown on the map. On the north side of this line the towns are not only fewer in number, they are also smaller (except for the port towns), and more widely dispersed. It is almost as if the line which passes through Emden, Bamberg, and Prague differentiates between two different types of urban systems.

The second main characteristic is the polycentric structure of the German urban network towards the end of the sixteenth century. In the absence of a clearly defined capital city, and with few really large towns, urban Germany contained an appreciable number of medium-sized towns with similar populations, around which were grouped regional urban networks which were largely independent of one another. The market towns and the ports were particularly important as a consequence, because they provided the links between the different subregions which made up the multipolar German urban system.

The third characteristic of urban Germany around 1600 was the dominant position occupied by the commercial and industrial cities, as well as by the ports. Of the nine towns with the largest populations, seven were characterized by their importance in the system of trade and industry (Danzig, Augsburg, Cologne, Magdeburg, Nuremberg, Hamburg, and Breslau), and the same is true of some of the smaller towns. Many of these towns, which derived their power from their wealth and economic importance, were free cities, directly subordinate to the Emperor. Ten of the thirty-three cities shown on Map 6.1 were *Reichsstädte* (free cities); they accounted for nearly half the population of all the cities shown on the map and the dynamics of German urbanism were mainly manifest in these cities.

II

On Map 6.2 I have shown the situation as it was about two hundred years later, and a comparison of the two maps will indicate the changes that

[1] J de Vries, *European Urbanization, 1500–1800* (London and Cambridge, Mass., 1984).

The German Urban Network   87

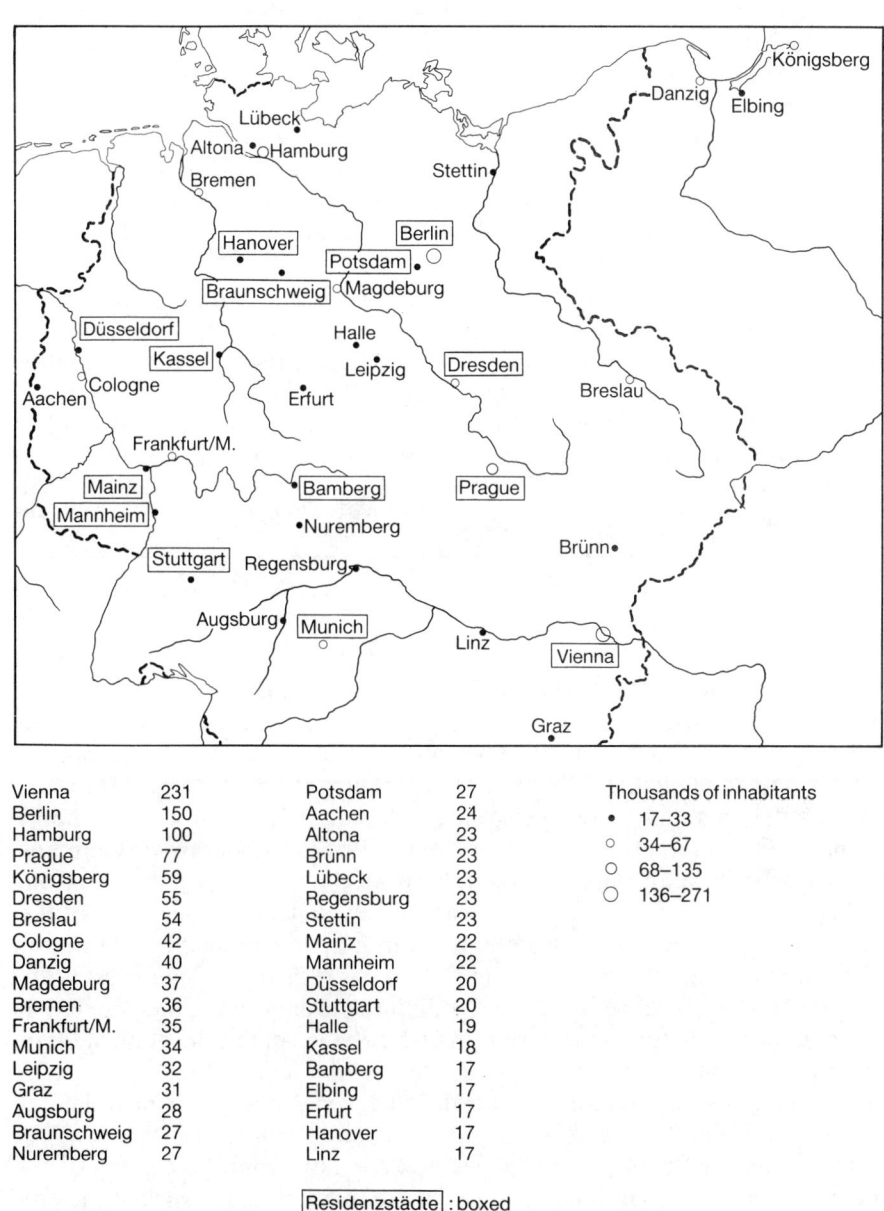

Vienna	231	Potsdam	27	Thousands of inhabitants	
Berlin	150	Aachen	24	•	17–33
Hamburg	100	Altona	23	○	34–67
Prague	77	Brünn	23	○	68–135
Königsberg	59	Lübeck	23	○	136–271
Dresden	55	Regensburg	23		
Breslau	54	Stettin	23		
Cologne	42	Mainz	22		
Danzig	40	Mannheim	22		
Magdeburg	37	Düsseldorf	20		
Bremen	36	Stuttgart	20		
Frankfurt/M.	35	Halle	19		
Munich	34	Kassel	18		
Leipzig	32	Bamberg	17		
Graz	31	Elbing	17		
Augsburg	28	Erfurt	17		
Braunschweig	27	Hanover	17		
Nuremberg	27	Linz	17		

Residenzstädte : boxed

Map 6.2. Geographical location of the 36 largest German towns about 1800

occurred between the end of the sixteenth century and the end of the eighteenth. (As the populations of some of the towns at the lower end of the hierarchy were the same, the map contains thirty-six towns, rather than the thirty-three shown on Map 6.1; the statistics have once again been taken from de Vries's study.)

The most important feature of the comparison is the extent of the urban development that occurred during these two hundred years. In about 1800, Germany contained no fewer than sixty-one towns with populations of 10,000 or more, and, in order to maintain a sample with a similar number of towns as in 1600, we had to increase the lower limit of population for inclusion in our list to 17,000.

This growth coincided with an increased dispersion in the distribution of population sizes of towns and with the emergence of metropolitan cities. In 1800 the ratio between the population of the largest town (Vienna) and that of the smallest was 14:1; in 1600 it was 5:1. In Table 6.1 we see the distribution of the towns in our sample by population size; the population figures are shown as multiples of the minimum size of the towns (m).

Table 6.1 Distribution of German towns as multiples (m) of the towns with the minimum population size

Year	1–2m.	2–4m.	4–8m.	8–16m.	All
1600	16	9	8	—	33
1800	23	9	2	2	36

The growth of population during the eighteenth century also led to a shift in the centre of gravity of urban Germany towards the north-east. In 1800 the population of the eighteen towns situated south of the Emden–Bamberg–Prague line amounted to 48.5 per cent of the total population of our towns, compared with a figure of 62 per cent two hundred years earlier. Significant changes also occurred within the two groups of cities. In south-west Germany the most significant change was the relative decline of the population of the towns of Swabia, Franconia, and Bavaria (they contained 25 per cent of the population of all our towns in 1600, but only 10 per cent in 1800). In north-east Germany the importance of the port towns declined (27 per cent of the population in 1600, 22 per cent in 1800), but the proportion of the population living in the inland towns increased. In 1800, 30 per cent of the population of our group of towns lived in the quadrilateral with Hanover, Erfurt, Breslau, and Berlin as its corners, compared with 25 per cent living in the quadrilateral with its corners at Brunswick, Erfurt, Breslau, and Berlin in 1600.

The main reason for these changes was the shift from the old trade and industrial free cities which dominated the German urban network at the end of the Middle Ages and into the sixteenth century to the new types of towns which were administrative capitals (*Haupt-und Residenzstädte*). I have already referred to the declining importance of the ports. The shift becomes even more apparent when we consider a number of commercial and industrial cities which were flourishing during the sixteenth century: in Swabia, Augsburg slipped from fourth to sixteenth place; in the Rhineland, Cologne from fifth to eighth; in the middle of Germany, Magdeburg from fifth to tenth. These shifts were partially compensated by the growth of some ports and commercial towns, especially by the growth of Hamburg (with Altona), Königsberg, Breslau, Frankfurt, and Leipzig. But, even in these towns, the population only slightly more than doubled between 1600 and 1800. The loss of influence and the relative decline of the old economic metropolitan towns is attested by three facts: the loss of population (23 per cent of the population of our group of cities lived in the free cities in 1800, compared with 43 per cent in 1600), the shrinking of their social structure (with many resulting conflicts), and their continued attachment to the architectural style of the Middle Ages and the Renaissance.

By contrast with this decline, the growth of the administrative capitals was striking. The population of Vienna grew nearly fivefold between 1600 and 1800. It was the largest city in both 1600 and 1800, but the difference between its population and that of other cities increased. The population of Berlin increased sixfold (excluding the garrison population) and the city moved from tenth to second place in rank order; the population of Dresden, too, increased nearly five times and surpassed that of Leipzig, and Dresden became easily the largest town in Saxony.[2] Among the towns which appeared in our list for 1800 for the first time (altogether eleven towns accounting for 14 per cent of the population) six were capital cities in the strict sense of the term (Stuttgart, Potsdam, Hanover, Kassel, Düsseldorf, and Mannheim). The movement towards the administrative capitals could also been seen in the regions: thus, in the Rhineland, Mannheim, Düsseldorf, and Mainz increased in importance relative to Cologne, Aachen, and Frankfurt and became serious competitors of these cities. Of the total population of our thirty-six cities in 1800, 50.2 per cent lived in these *Residenzstädte*. This spectacular demographic growth was linked with policies which encouraged immigration and contrasted with the selective and restrictionist migration policies of the older German home towns.[3] It resulted in the dominance of a new type of town, which I have already documented in previous publications.[4]

The result was a change in the structure of the German urban system from a multipolar to a dualist one, with Berlin and Vienna as the two poles. The

---

[2] H. Blaschke, *Bevölkerungsgeschichte Sachsens bis zur industriellen Revolution* (Weimar, 1967).

[3] M. Walker, *German Home Towns, Community, State, and General Estate, 1648–1871* (Ithaca, NY, 1971).

[4] É. François, 'Des républiques marchandes aux capitales politiques: remarques sur la hiérarchie urbaine du Saint-Empire à l'époque moderne', *Revue de'histoire moderne et contemporaine*, 25 (1978), 587–603; id. 'De l'uniformité à la tolérance: confession et société urbaine en Allemagne, 1650–1800', *Annales E.S.C.*, 37 (1982), 783–800; id., 'Städtische Eliten in Deutschland zwischen 1650 und 1800. Einige Beispiele, Thesen, Fragen', in H. Schilling and H. Diederiks (eds.), *Bürgerliche Eliten in den Niederlanden und in Nordwestdeutschland* (Cologne/Vienna, 1985), 65–83.

change was itself a result of the change in the political structure of the Empire (the dualism of Austria and Prussia), but it remained incomplete and did not impinge on large hierarchic and well-structured network of towns. In the different regions, there were networks such as those centred on Munich and Dresden, for example, which retained coherence and autonomy. The links between the various decentralized regional sub-systems were provided by the 'relay' towns, ports such as Hamburg, or the market towns, such as Frankfurt, Breslau, and Leipzig.

III

The value of the preceding findings is, however, limited, as it is based on only one quantitative indicator—the size of the population. I therefore propose to compare these results with results obtained from a study of 'cultural' indicators. There are two such indicators which relate to the end of the sixteenth and the beginning of the seventeenth centuries. The first is taken from the printed records of the book fairs of Frankfurt and Leipzig, and shows the total number of works listed in the catalogues of each of these fairs as being published in particular towns between 1610 and 1619.[5] However, these lists can only give approximate results, because they were not necessarily complete; some of the works listed were not, in fact, published and the Catholic towns of southern Germany were underrepresented. I have, therefore, supplemented this information by using the nominal lists of publishers in German-speaking towns (excluding Bohemia) for the sixteenth and seventeenth centuries.[6] For ease of comparison with Map 6.1 which shows the population size in 1600, I show on Map 6.3 the thirty-three towns in Germany which listed the largest number of printed publications between 1610 and 1619, and on Map 6.4 the thirty-five towns with the largest number of publishers. I have used the same geographical limits in both maps: this is necessary for purposes of comparison, but may be criticized as an inadequate representation of German intellectual life, because the towns of German-speaking parts of Switzerland have been omitted, though they obviously formed part of German culture, then as now.

When these two maps are compared with Map 6.1, a number of differences become immediately apparent. There are sixteen towns on Map 6.3, and nine towns on Map 6.4, which do not appear on the first map, and many of these towns are important. Moreover, the differences between the urban hierarchies depicted on Maps 6.3 and 6.4 and that on Map 6.1 are much more striking than the similarities. The relative differences between towns on Maps

---

[5] J. Goldfriedrich, *Geschichte des deutschen Buchhandels vom Westfälischen Frieden bis zum Beginn der klassischen Literaturperiode 1648–1740* (Leipzig, 1908).
[6] J. Benzing, 'Die deutschen Verleger des 16. und 17. Jahrhunderts: Eine Neubearbeitung', *Archiv für Geschichte des Buchwesens*, 18 (1977), cols. 1077–322.

The German Urban Network 91

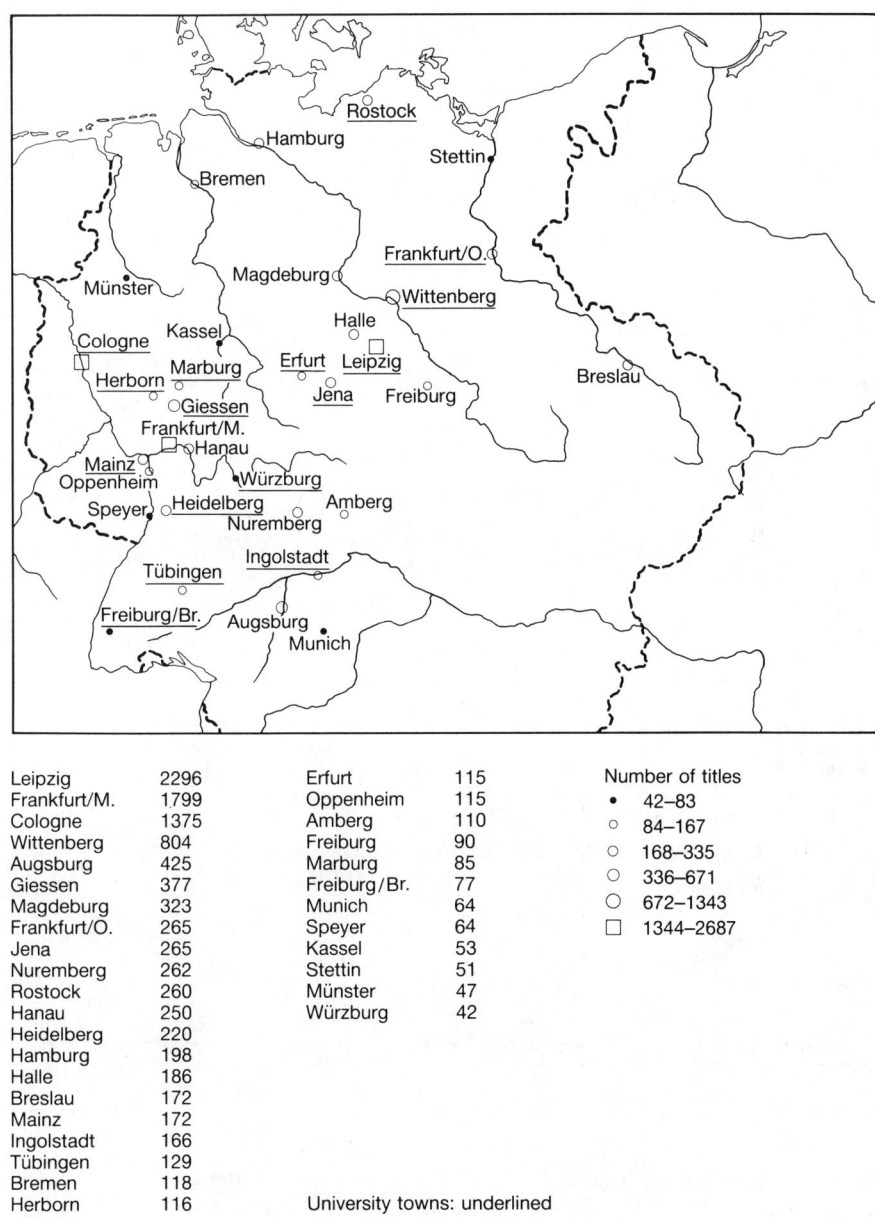

Leipzig	2296	Erfurt	115	Number of titles	
Frankfurt/M.	1799	Oppenheim	115	•	42–83
Cologne	1375	Amberg	110	○	84–167
Wittenberg	804	Freiburg	90	○	168–335
Augsburg	425	Marburg	85	○	336–671
Giessen	377	Freiburg/Br.	77	○	672–1343
Magdeburg	323	Munich	64	□	1344–2687
Frankfurt/O.	265	Speyer	64		
Jena	265	Kassel	53		
Nuremberg	262	Stettin	51		
Rostock	260	Münster	47		
Hanau	250	Würzburg	42		
Heidelberg	220				
Hamburg	198				
Halle	186				
Breslau	172				
Mainz	172				
Ingolstadt	166				
Tübingen	129				
Bremen	118				
Herborn	116	University towns: underlined			

Map 6.3. Geographical location of the 33 main publishing towns in Germany (by number of titles listed in book fairs 1610–19)

92 *Étienne François*

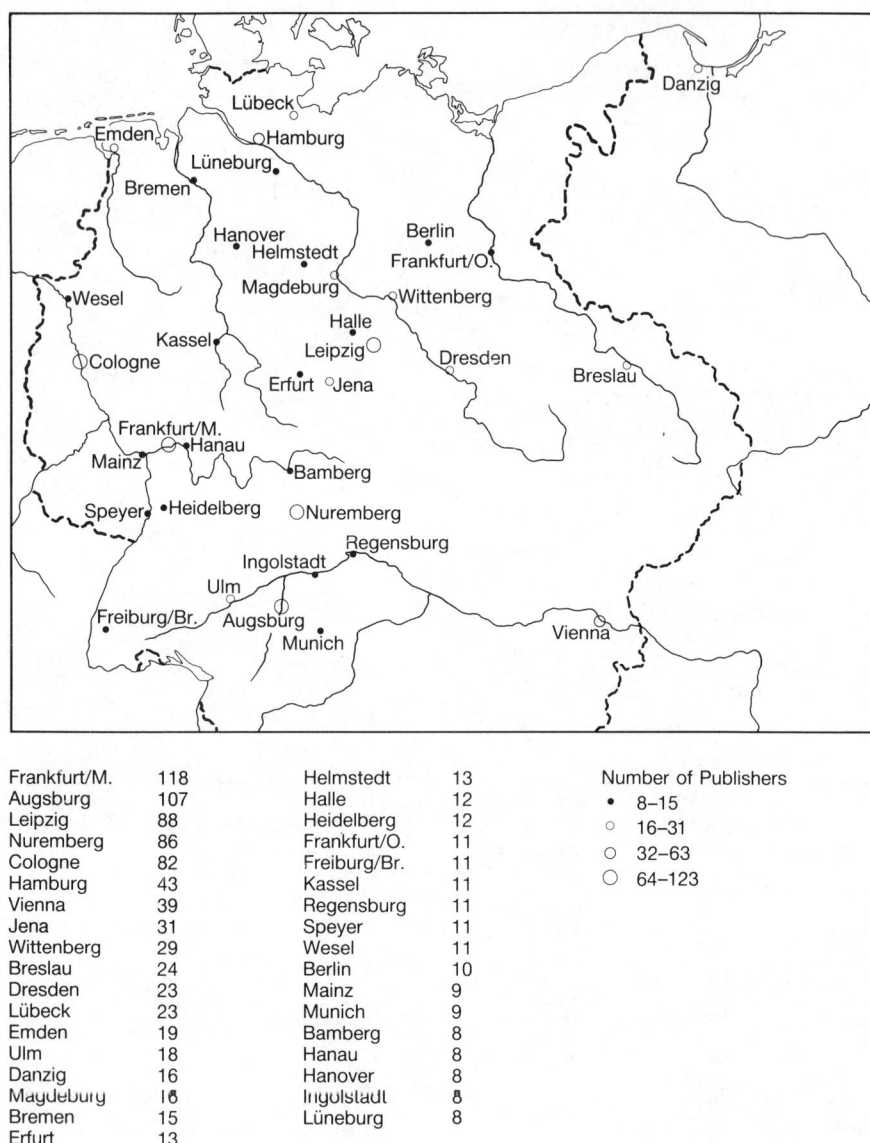

Frankfurt/M.	118	Helmstedt	13	Number of Publishers	
Augsburg	107	Halle	12	•	8–15
Leipzig	88	Heidelberg	12	○	16–31
Nuremberg	86	Frankfurt/O.	11	○	32–63
Cologne	82	Freiburg/Br.	11	○	64–123
Hamburg	43	Kassel	11		
Vienna	39	Regensburg	11		
Jena	31	Speyer	11		
Wittenberg	29	Wesel	11		
Breslau	24	Berlin	10		
Dresden	23	Mainz	9		
Lübeck	23	Munich	9		
Emden	19	Bamberg	8		
Ulm	18	Hanau	8		
Danzig	16	Hanover	8		
Magdeburg	16	Ingolstadt	8		
Bremen	15	Lüneburg	8		
Erfurt	13				

Map 6.4. Geographical location of the 35 German towns with the largest numbers of publishers during the sixteenth and seventeenth centuries

6.3 and 6.4 are much greater than those on Map 6.1; it seems as if the cultural indicators emphasize differences which seem to have been attenuated by using the demographic indicator. Part of the explanation for these differences is a phenomenon which is specific to Germany: the university towns, which account for one-quarter of the titles of the works listed in the catalogue of publications. This oddity of structure is reinforced by religious rivalries; it is not an accident that the bastions of each of the rival religions that appear at the top of the list of university towns do not figure on the list of the most populous towns: Wittenberg and Jena for the Lutherans, Heidelberg for the Calvinists, and Ingolstadt for the Roman Catholics. The hierarchy of university towns on these two maps corresponds to that of the German universities ranked by number of their students.[7]

A second reason for the differences between Maps 6.3 and 6.4 on the one hand and Map 6.1 on the other is that a substantial number of relatively large towns only occupies a relatively low rank or is completely absent from the list defined by the 'cultural' indices. This is particularly true of the ports (the eight ports between Emden and Königsberg contain 28 per cent of the population of the towns on our list, but only 12 per cent of the publishers, and are responsible for only 6 per cent of the titles published), but it also applies to a number of other, often quite large, inland towns, such as Vienna and Prague. Their situation is the converse of that of the university towns: their real vitality is less than would appear at first sight based on their size alone, for their demographic and economic potential is not matched by an equivalent cultural dynamism. The cultural indices for the eight largest towns in 1600 reveal a disparity which is hidden by the demographic indices when used alone. Thus, Danzig, Vienna, Prague, Hamburg, and Magdeburg occupy a much lower rank on the cultural index than they do on the index for population size. Augsburg, Cologne, and Nuremberg occupy similar ranks in each classification. These three towns, by reason of their equivalent ranking on the demographic, economic and cultural indices, deserve to be considered as being the foremost German towns of the period.

Lastly, in contrast to the polycentrism apparent on Map 6.1, Maps 6.3 and 6.4 show the existence of two well-defined regional subgroups, in which German cultural activities were concentrated. This bipolarity is well illustrated on Map 6.3: one of the regions is south-west Germany, bordered by the cities of Cologne, Kassel, Regensburg, Munich, and Freiburg (a region which contains 52 per cent of the publishers and accounts for 53 per cent of the titles listed), and the other a smaller middle German region, bordered by Erfurt, Magdeburg, Wittenberg, and Freiburg, which coincides with Saxony and Thuringia and contains 22 per cent of the publishers, and in which 37 per cent of the titles listed were published. Each of these subregions contains a well-defined capital city: Frankfurt in the first, and Leipzig in the second. It was in these two towns that the principal German book fairs were held. Each region

---

[7] F. Eulenburg, 'Die Frequenz der deutschen Universitäten von ihrer Gründung bis zur Gegenwart', *Abhandlungen der philologisch-historischen Klasse der königl. Sächsischen Gesellschaft der Wissenschaften*, 24: 2 (1904); W. Frijhoff, 'Surplus ou déficit? Hypothèse sur le nombre réel des étudiants en Allemagne à l'époque moderne (1576–1815)', *Francia. Forschungen zur westeuropäischen Geschichte*, 7 (1979), 173–218.

also contained a structured urban network in which these towns can be ranked in relation to exchange activities and independence. In addition to the difference in their relative importance (which confirms our previous observations on the primacy of the towns in the south-west) the form of spatial organization of the two networks is different. The south-west region, centred on Frankfurt, is itself divided into a number of partially autonomous subregions which are centred around their own capitals (Cologne, Augsburg, and, to a lesser degree, Nuremberg) and which are reminiscent of the organization which we have already noted on Map 6.1 for south-west Germany as a whole. Saxony and Thuringia, on the other hand, are much more dominated by Leipzig, the city in which 56 per cent of the titles listed in these provinces were published. The ratio of the number of titles published in Leipzig to that published in the city with the second largest number (Wittenberg) is 2.9:1, whereas the ratio between Frankfurt and Cologne is only 1.3:1.

IV

Maps 6.5 and 6.6 depict two series which relate to the end of the eighteenth and the beginning of the nineteenth centuries and may, therefore, be compared with the information on Map 6.2. Map 6.5 is the analogue of Map 6.3 and has been constructed from published catalogues of book fairs. On it are shown the thirty-three towns in Germany responsible for the largest average number of titles published in each decennium between 1765 and 1805.[8] The second map (Map 6.6) was constructed from a topographical index of a reference book published at the beginning of the nineteenth century, which contained the names of more than 10,000 men of letters (*Schriftsteller*) or intellectuals. The thirty-four German cities with the largest numbers of writers are shown.[9]

The changes that occurred between 1600 and 1800 are spectacular. When Map 6.2 is compared with Map 6.1, only eleven new towns, containing 14 per cent of the total population of all the towns shown, appear on Map 6.2. But when we compare Map 6.5 with Map 6.3, more than half the towns (nineteen in total) on the second map are newcomers. Some of these new towns have only relatively modest rankings, but the nineteen new towns were responsible for the publication of 39 per cent of all the titles in our list. These facts again point to the importance of these 'cultural' indices. As was the case with the maps for 1600, a comparison of the towns appearing on Map 6.2 and Maps 6.5 and 6.6 show a discordance between the largest towns and those with the most

---

[8] J. Goldfriedrich, *Geschichte des deutschen Buchhandels vom Beginn der klassischen Literaturperiode bis zum Beginn der Fremdenherrschaft, 1740–1804* (Leipzig, 1909).

[9] J. G. Meusel, *Das gelehrte Teutschland oder Lexikon der jetzt lebenden Schriftsteller*, xii (Lemgo, 1806).

The German Urban Network

Leipzig	5556	Stuttgart	259	Number of titles	
Berlin	2423	Gotha	257	•	178–355
Vienna	1235	Munich	240	○	356–711
Halle	1154	Mannheim	239	○	712–1423
Frankfurt/M.	1137	Ulm	237	○	1424–2847
Nuremberg	972	Giessen	228	□	2848–5695
Hamburg	890	Königsberg	227		
Göttingen	787	Dessau	224		
Breslau	569	Magdeburg	214		
Augsburg	466	Weimar	214		
Dresden	459	Erfurt	208		
Jena	445	Salzburg	207		
Prague	389	Altenburg	199		
Braunschweig	338	Lemgo	191		
Erlangen	332	Bremen	178		
Hanover	319				
Tübingen	274				
Altona	259				

University towns: underlined

Map 6.5. Geographical location of the 33 largest German publishing towns by 10-year average of titles appearing in catalogues, 1765–1805

96 *Étienne François*

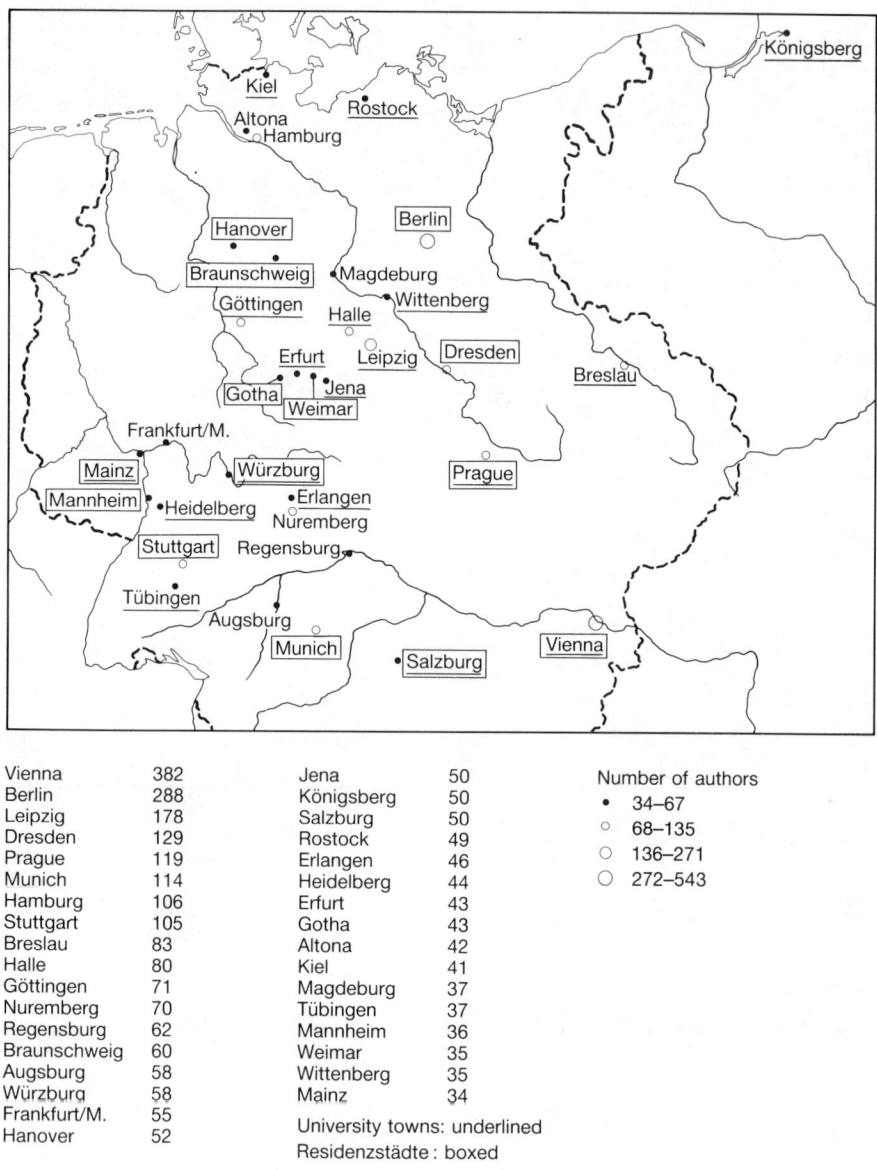

Vienna	382	Jena	50	Number of authors	
Berlin	288	Königsberg	50	•	34–67
Leipzig	178	Salzburg	50	○	68–135
Dresden	129	Rostock	49	○	136–271
Prague	119	Erlangen	46	○	272–543
Munich	114	Heidelberg	44		
Hamburg	106	Erfurt	43		
Stuttgart	105	Gotha	43		
Breslau	83	Altona	42		
Halle	80	Kiel	41		
Göttingen	71	Magdeburg	37		
Nuremberg	70	Tübingen	37		
Regensburg	62	Mannheim	36		
Braunschweig	60	Weimar	35		
Augsburg	58	Wittenberg	35		
Würzburg	58	Mainz	34		
Frankfurt/M.	55				
Hanover	52	University towns: underlined			
		Residenzstädte : boxed			

Map 6.6. Geographical location of the 34 German towns with the largest numbers of authors, 1806

vigorous intellectual activity. Twelve towns on Map 6.2 (containing 23 per cent of the total population in the group of towns altogether) do not appear on either Map 6.5 or Map 6.6.

The persistent importance of the university towns in the intellectual life of Germany provides an element of continuity between Maps 6.3 and 6.4 and Maps 6.5 and 6.6. This structural continuity becomes even more interesting when we come to consider changes in the relative importance of different university towns: the universities which were most closely involved in the religious struggles of the sixteenth and seventeenth centuries are either not represented on Maps 6.5 and 6.6, or occupy a lower rank: their places have been taken by the newly created universities of the Enlightenment (*Aufklärung*) and of German idealism, such as Halle (founded in 1694), Göttingen (founded in 1737), or Erlangen (founded in 1743). Göttingen, though only containing 9,000 inhabitants in 1800, was placed eighth among the German towns ordered by number of titles published, and eleventh if ranked by the number of intellectuals.

A second element of continuity between the end of the sixteenth and eighteenth centuries is the persistent low ranking on the cultural index of the towns defined as being important in commerce and industry. This holds particularly true of the ports. They contained 22 per cent of the population of all the towns in our group, but only 11 per cent of the intellectuals, and only 7 per cent of the titles in the list of publications originating in these towns. The only exception to this relative cultural mediocrity is provided by Hamburg. What applies to the ports also applies to inland towns, such as Magdeburg.

When the information given on Maps 6.5 and 6.6 is compared with that on Maps 6.1 and 6.2 it will be seen that the cultural indicators can be used to validate the impressions given by the demographic indices of stagnation or decline, and to provide a more differentiated account of these phenomena. The lessened importance of the free cities which was already manifest in their declining populations is now even more apparent: in 1600 they contained 42 per cent of the total population in our group and 54 per cent of the publishers, and 38 per cent of the titles listed originated in them. By 1800 these percentages had fallen to 23 per cent, 13 per cent, and 18 per cent respectively.

However, if we look at the situation in different regions, some striking discrepancies are noted. Thus the old metropolitan towns of Swabia (such as Augsburg, Nuremberg, and Ulm) maintain their position or even improve it in the hierarchy of intellectual activity, though their population decline was relatively large. Other towns in which the population was maintained between 1600 and 1800 suffered a veritable intellectual collapse. Thus Cologne fell from fifth to eighth place when the cities were ranked in order of population, but from third to fifty-third when ranked by the number of titles published. Magdeburg was in a similar position. This discrepancy is interesting, because it throws doubt on the value of reductions in population (either absolute or relative) as an index of general decline: smaller populations do not necessarily lessen the importance of towns in other areas. A declining population might mean a 'qualitative change' (such as in

Nuremberg or Augsburg); whereas a constant population could mean a complete collapse of certain urban activities which were dependent on numbers. For instance, Cologne was described by contemporary writers as being in a state of lethargy and as having been invaded by beggars.

The cultural indices also point to the increasing importance of the *Residenzstädte* and confirm that the growth of population in these towns was not brought about artificially, but implied a real transfer of urban dynamism to the political capitals. Six of the eight towns which contained the largest numbers of intellectuals in 1806 were *Residenzstädte*; 55 per cent of all the intellectuals listed lived in the capital cities, compared with only 50 per cent of the overall population. The exceptional position of Leipzig as a publishing centre means that the capital cities were relatively less important in the rank order of titles published (33 per cent of all the titles listed originated in them), but a comparison of Map 6.3 and Map 6.5 shows that, nevertheless, the capital cities made most progress: Berlin moved from thirty-sixth place to second; Vienna from seventy-fourth to third; Dresden from thirty-eighth to eleventh. And this excludes the towns which did not appear at all on the list for 1610–19, but occupied a high rank on the list for the later period, such as Hanover or Mannheim. When the capital cities are arranged in order of these cultural indices, the small capitals of Saxony and Thuringia appear in the list and exercise an influence quite disproportionate to their numbers and, indeed, rival the university towns. (This represents a change which occurred between the sixteenth and eighteenth centuries.) Thus, Weimar ranked twenty-seventh when cities are arranged in order of the number of titles published and thirty-second in the number of intellectuals (who included Goethe and Wieland), although its population amounted to only 6,000.[10] Although this is the most famous example, Weimar was not unique; Gotha contained 11,000 inhabitants and Dessau 8,000 in about 1800. However, the converse situation is also found, though less frequently; there are capital cities which rank low on the cultural indices and whose growth was much more fragile, even artificial. Among these we must mention Potsdam, Düsseldorf, and the regional capitals of Austria, Graz, Brünn, and Linz, though the statistical data for the latter probably underestimate their true importance.

Another advantage of Maps 6.5 and 6.6 is that they illustrate the changing spatial distribution between south-west and middle Germany during the two centuries much better than does Map 6.2. Relatively to Maps 6.3 and 6.4, south-west Germany loses both population (particularly in the triangle bounded by Giessen, Salzburg, and Tübingen) and also in the cultural sphere (28 per cent of intellectuals and 21 per cent of titles published), whereas middle Germany increases its size (in the area bounded by Hanover, Berlin, Dresden, Erfurt, and Göttingen), affirms its primacy in intellectual life (40

---

[10] H. Eberhardt, *Goethe's Umwelt. Forschungen zur gesellschaftlichen Struktur Thüringens* (Weimar, 1951); W. H. Bruford, *Culture and Society in Classical Weimar 1775–1806* (London, 1975).

per cent of intellectuals, 60 per cent of titles published), and gives an impression of dynamism and intellectual creativity unparalleled elsewhere in Europe. The difference between a declining south-west and a growing and increasingly dominant middle Germany is also shown in another aspect of the internal structure. In middle Germany the urban network is both dense and diversified (thus Leipzig was predominant in publishing, and Berlin in intellectual activities), but the network in south-west Germany is much more weakly structured, almost as if it were in the process of breaking up and losing its internal cohesion. It seemed unable to provide a counterweight to the middle German network and seemed to be sliding inexorably into dependency.

In the intellectual sphere proper this development remained incomplete, and an attenuated polycentrism remains. But as regards publishing, Leipzig became the clear capital among all German towns in 1763–4, relegating its old rival, Frankfurt, to being merely a regional centre, and extending its ascendancy over almost the entire German cultural scene.[11] Statistical data relating to the attendance at book fairs in Leipzig at the end of the eighteenth century, published by Wittman,[12] show this very clearly: from year to year the number of German-speaking cities which sent at least one bookseller or publisher to Leipzig grew (there were 101 in 1778, 105 in 1783, and 129 in 1785), and, even more significantly, the ranking of these towns in order of the number attending the Leipzig fairs is astonishingly similar to their ranking in the list of printed titles.

V

We can draw three conclusions from the preceding arguments. The first relates to the unification of the network of 'publishing' towns under the leadership of Leipzig, and more generally to the hegemony over intellectual life in Germany exercised by Berlin and Leipzig. This contrasts with the absence of a clear demographic capital in Germany and the continuing polycentrism of the German urban network. It was partly due to the fact that integration occurs more easily in the cultural than in the demographic area: books and ideas move more freely than do people. But it also goes to show that the cultural integration of Germany preceded her political and economic integration and that Germany was a *Kulturnation* long before becoming a *politische Nation*.

Our second conclusion bears on the value of combining different types of statistical indices in the study of urban networks. The cultural indices which I

---

[11] H. Kiesel and P. Münch, *Gesellschaft und Literatur im 18. Jahrhundert. Voraussetzungen und Entstehung des literarischen Markts in Deutschland* (Munich, 1977).

[12] R. Wittman, 'Die frühen Buchhändlerzeitschriften als Spiegel des literarischen Lebens', *Archiv für Geschichte des Buchwesens*, 13 (1973), cols. 613–931.

have used in this chapter are more sensitive than those relating only to population size in pointing to modifications of the internal structure of the urban network: they also reveal a geographical concentration and the crystallization of a process of domination which would otherwise have remained hidden, and illustrate the difference between apparent and true growth and apparent and true decline.

Thirdly, we need to examine critically the relevance of indices based on population size. Not all the activities that are carried on in towns depend on the size of their populations, and the number of inhabitants is not a sufficient indicator of a city's influence and importance, nor does it express the dynamic structure of the urban network. We must return to the intuitive beliefs that served as the beginnings of central-place theory for Christaller,[13] and follow him in using a variety of indicators (both of stocks and of flows). Without these, statistics relating to population size, even if organized according to the rank-size law, are of limited value in explaining the processes in which we are interested.

[13] W. Christaller, *Die zentralen Orte in Süddeutschland. Eine ökonomisch-geographische Untersuchung über die Gesetzmässigkeit der Verbreitung und Entwicklung der Siedlungen mit städtischen Funktionen* (Jena, 1933; repr. Darmstadt, 1968).

7 Brake or Accelerator?
Urban Growth and Population Growth before the Industrial Revolution

E. A. WRIGLEY

Cambridge Group for the History of Population and Social Structure, Cambridge, UK

No pre-industrial country could become urbanized to the degree which is now commonplace throughout the industrial world. The ultimate reason for the comparatively low levels of urbanization in pre-industrial societies is not far to seek. To live, one must eat. Only if levels of output per head in agriculture rise to the point where one man on the land can feed ten, twenty or even fifty off the land can a very high degree of urbanization be reached. Until recently, such levels of productivity were far beyond the reach of any economy. Indeed, in many pre-industrial societies levels of output per head were so modest, and so variable from year to year with the vagaries of the harvest, that there was no margin available to support any considerable proportion of the population outside agriculture. The existence of a considerable urban percentage in a country was always, amongst other things, an indication of an agriculture capable of yielding more than mere subsistence to the cultivators.

The fact that the productivity of the land, and still more the productivity of individual workers in farming, set limits to the extent of urbanization, however, conceals a complex set of relationships between urban growth, population growth, and economic attainment. Consider first the constraint represented by the Ricardian doctrine of declining marginal returns in agriculture. If it were true that, once settlement had spread across all land capable of yielding well under the methods of cultivation which represented best practice at the time, declining marginal returns to each additional unit input of capital or labour must set in, urban development would be placed under great threat. Declining marginal returns imply a fall in average output per head in agriculture, and through their effect on the relative prices of agricultural and manufacturing produce and on real wages, they further imply that a rising fraction of the average family budget would have to be devoted to food, and hence that a rising proportion of the labour force would tend to be drawn into agriculture. Eventually, in the classical model, economic growth ceases because the return to new investment, whether directed to breaking in more marginal land or to coaxing higher output from the land already in use, falls to the point where no additional capital can be attracted into agricultural improvement. The 'steady state' then supervenes. Such a situation, however, will only occur after the urban climacteric of the society has long passed. To the degree that the Ricardian paradigm is appropriate, therefore, it is reasonable to expect to find urbanization at its most extensive during what Adam Smith would have termed the 'progressive' phase in the development of an economy.[1]

It is clearly possible that there should have been cycles in the history of pre-industrial societies which exemplified the pattern of change just described. Indeed, it is not difficult to imagine a set of linkages which would produce a phase of contraction, rather than stagnation, following an urban climacteric, which might in turn be the prelude to a further phase of expansion, a chain of changes comparable to what Le Roy Ladurie had in mind when he launched the term *histoire immobile* to describe France between the thirteenth and eighteenth centuries.[2] For example, a progressive reduction in the size of the urban sector of a pre-industrial economy, enforced by changes in the structure of demand consequent upon the operation of declining marginal returns in agriculture, might well result in a reduction in agricultural efficiency and a fall in the output of agriculture. Urban demand was a powerful force making for agricultural specialization. Particular regions were induced to concentrate on, say, grain-growing by the existence of market demand on a scale which encouraged the abandonment of local self-sufficiency and the fuller exploitation of regional comparative advantage. Any weakening of such demand would have an effect on aggregate output. *Ceteris paribus*, population decline might follow and, for a time at least, further aggravate existing problems until the headroom was created, by reduction of pressure on the land, to begin the rising phase of the cycle once more.

Ricardo's formulation of the law of diminishing returns, though so powerful in logic, does not always 'save the phenomena' effectively when applied to pre-industrial economies. In the case of early modern England, for example, there is reason to think that output per head in agriculture roughly doubled between 1600 and 1800, even though only a limited area of new land was taken into farming use. Ricardo wrote only of an inevitable tendency towards declining marginal returns in agriculture, and recognized that technological advance might postpone its arrival for a long period, yet even so the scale of changes in early modern England casts doubt on the value of his principle in any but the very long run, at least for some historical instances.[3] It is no coincidence that England should have been urbanizing rapidly over the same period that productivity per

---

[1] D. Ricardo, *On the Principles of Political Economy and Taxation*, in *The Works and Correspondence of David Ricardo*, ed. P. Sraffa with the collaboration of M. H. Dobb, 11 vols. (Cambridge, 1951–73), i, Ch. 2, 'On rent'. A. Smith, *An Inquiry into the Nature and Causes of the Wealth of Nations*, ed. E. Cannan, 2 vols. (6th edn., London, 1961), i. 90–1.

[2] E. le Roy Ladurie, 'L'Histoire immobile', *Annales. Économies, Sociétés, Civilisations*, 29 (1974), 673–92.

[3] It was Ricardo's general thesis that both real wages and profits must tend to fall because of the operation of declining returns in agriculture, but he recognized that the tendency could be

head in agriculture was growing substantially and population rising fast; nor, perhaps, that over the same period none of the three variables in question was changing greatly in France. Examination of the two cases may serve to clarify further some aspects of the linkages between urban growth and population growth in the pre-industrial period.

As a preliminary to the discussion, however, it is convenient to consider first a subsidiary issue, though one which was very prominent in the lives of urban dwellers in the past. The issue constitutes a paradox in that, although there was a close relationship between urban growth and population growth in the past, urban life was often most unhealthy and urban death rates frequently so high that only constant infusions of new blood from the countryside prevented a progressive shrinkage in urban populations.

The distinguished Victorian demographic statistician, William Farr, working at the very end of the period in which mortality rates in the towns were substantially higher than in the country, suggested that, other things being equal, mortality rates varied as the twelfth root of the density of the population.[4] Thus, urban slum-dwellers were subjected to much higher mortality than equally impoverished people living in the countryside. Although Farr tried to bring a new degree of precision to the issue, an association between high density and high mortality had been observed many times previously and has been emphasized in many subsequent studies. The ease with which diseases were propagated and spread in densely packed populations; the ignorance of modes of disease transmission; the difficulty of imposing effective quarantine measures; the inadequacy of systems of sewage disposal and of drinking-water delivery; and the ineffectiveness of medical treatment of most infectious diseases, all combined to make urban life unhealthy, and tended to ensure that it was least healthy in the largest cities.

So acute were the problems arising from the development of large urban populations that it has been estimated that, during the later seventeenth and early eighteenth centuries in England, roughly half of all the surplus of births in the country was needed to offset the surplus of deaths in the capital, London, and to enable it to continue to grow relative to the country's total population. In the Dutch Republic, where urbanization had progressed still further at the same period, similar calculations led de Vries to the conclusion that the urban sector by the mid-seventeenth century was approaching the point at which it could expand no further without a reduction in the rural population, or large-scale immigration from other countries, so heavy were the demographic demands created by the unhealthiness of urban life.[5]

---

checked for long periods. See e.g. Ricardo, *Principles of Political Economy*, p. 120. The evidence for a sustained, progressive rise in output per head in English agriculture is discussed in E. A. Wrigley, 'Urban Growth and Agricultural Change: England and the Continent in the Early Modern Period', *Journal of Interdisciplinary History*, 15 (1985), 683–728.

[4] W. Farr, *Vital Statistics* (London, 1885), 173–6.
[5] E. A. Wrigley, 'A Simple Model of London's Importance in Changing English Society and Economy 1650–1750', *Past and Present*, 37 (1967), 45–9. J. de Vries, *The Dutch Rural Economy in the Golden Age, 1500–1700* (Newhaven and London, 1974), 107–18.

Dramatic though such calculations are, however, they are apt to be seriously misleading. Proximately, no doubt, urban growth and overall population growth might appear to be at odds, but in a wider setting the reverse was true. The Great Wen might absorb, at times, a large fraction of the demographic surplus of the rest of England, so that national population growth during the later seventeenth century might have been far faster if London had been removed from the national demographic accounts. But the apparent gain is spurious. The indirect benefits derived by the country from the growth of London were massive, to the point where urban growth may be regarded as one of the most important reasons for general population growth in spite of its deleterious immediate impact. General population growth was contingent upon an expanding economic base, and between the latter and urban growth there was an intimate connection.

The relationship between urban development, economic growth, and population increase is one of the major themes of the *Wealth of Nations*. Adam Smith identified trade between town and country as 'the great commerce of every civilized society'.[6] He regarded their mutual relationship as one of what today might be termed positive feedback. The existence of an urban demand for foodstuffs encouraged investment in agriculture and facilitated specialization of function, and the range of manufactures and services supplied by urban artificers and tradesmen sharpened rural appetites for 'luxuries' and so provided a spur to greater participation in the market. Equally, a productive agriculture was of vital importance to urban growth, and a great stimulus to it. It was not merely that townsmen needed to eat, so that their number was conditioned by the size of the rural surplus, but that the land was the source of virtually all the raw materials that entered into urban manufacturing production—wool, flax, silk, hides, hair, fur, and wood. The high strategic importance of good transport facilities was stressed by Adam Smith. It was the means by which the potential for mutual benefit through economic contact could be realized by town and country alike. The association between water transport and city growth was a development of this point. The location, no less than the scale of agricultural production, was heavily conditioned by the siting of towns. It is no accident that the father of locational economics, von Thünen, regarded himself as a disciple of Adam Smith. Von Thünen rings are the embodiment of the working-out of the economic ties linking town and country, a web of economic connections whose radial ties are the transport system.[7]

Adam Smith distinguished between productive and unproductive use of any surplus produced in agriculture and available to be absorbed elsewhere in the economy. Conspicuous consumption reflected in trains of servants, court

---

[6] Smith, *Wealth of Nations*, i. 401.

[7] Ibid. i, Book 3, Chs. 3, 4. J. H. von Thünen, *The Isolated State* (trans. of *Der isolirte Staat in Beziehung auf Landwirtschaft und Nationalökonomie*, 2 vols., Rostock, 1842–50), ed. P. Hall (Oxford, 1966), 225.

functionaries, prelates of the Church, the armed services, and all comparable professions or forms of employment were alike unproductive, whereas all engaged in manufacturing employment, such as those pinmakers who formed the *dramatis personae* of a famous parable in the *Wealth of Nations*, were productive.[8] The distinction is one which fell out of favour with the further development of economics as an intellectual discipline, but it is not without value in considering urban growth and the links between town and country, industry and agriculture, in a pre-industrial economy. The line of thinking which lay behind Adam Smith's distinction between productive and unproductive labour is akin to that which has given rise in the more recent past to a distinction between 'parasitic' and 'generative' cities.[9]

A politico-economic system in which the ruling élite extracted some or all of any rural surplus above what was needed for rural subsistence, and consumed the surplus in cities, since an urban setting was both more congenial and more secure, might well be regarded as creating parasitic cities if the presence of the élite in cities did little to stimulate further economic development in the countryside. A city in such a system might be regarded as a permanent 'potlatch', a place where the surplus wealth of the community as a whole was consumed in a way which constantly reiterated and reinforced the propriety of the existing institutional framework of society. The rural surplus might be regarded as the gift of nature, so to speak, the result of a particular, relatively favourable balance between production and population, but a surplus whose size was not further increased by the manner in which the surplus was expended.

In contrast, if the bulk of any rural surplus was not extracted by the ruling élite, or if the élite spent its income principally in ways which stimulated what Adam Smith termed productive industry, other possibilities existed. The scope for increasing agricultural output, both aggregate and per head, was often substantial in the past, provided that appropriate incentives existed. The sole aim of production is consumption, and in every lackadaisical producer there is a tiger of consumption waiting to be aroused. Leisure preferences are not fixed, nor do labour supply curves bend backwards inexorably in pre-industrial societies. A tantalizing array of consumer goods and services may galvanize husbandmen or peasants into different work habits, into adopting different crop combinations, even into contemplating altering the institutional arrangements of the local farming system. Perhaps no other single factor is so influential in this regard as the development of urban–rural exchange of the kind that Adam Smith deemed so beneficial. If the town contains craftsmen, artisans, and tradesmen offering secondary or tertiary products appreciated by rural producers, both the extent of

---

[8] Smith, *Wealth of Nations*, i. 351–2.
[9] B. F. Hoselitz, 'Generative and Parasitic Cities', *Economic Development and Cultural Change*, 3 (1954–5), 278–94; E. A. Wrigley, 'Parasite or Stimulus: The Town in a Pre-industrial Economy', in P. Abrams and E. A. Wrigley (eds.), *Towns in Societies. Essays in Economic History and Historical Sociology* (Cambridge, 1978), 295–309.

improvement in agricultural productivity and the scale of urban growth may be on a scale far greater than that attainable where the city is 'parasitic' in nature.[10]

It may be objected that a simple urban/rural dichotomy is too restrictive, or even actively misleading. It has become common in recent years to stress the prominence of proto-industrial development in the countryside in the early modern period.[11] Indeed, the near-stagnation in urban growth except in the largest cities in the seventeenth and eighteenth centuries in Europe as a whole has been attributed in large measure to the rapid growth of proto-industry in rural areas.[12] To the degree that this observation is accurate, it undermines the validity of one aspect of Adam Smith's model, though without affecting other features of his analysis, such as the relationship between the size of the accessible market and the existence of opportunities for specialization of function, or the significance of good transport.

England appears to have differed considerably from the general pattern in Europe as a whole. Unquestionably, there was an increased level of industrial activity in the countryside: rural non-agricultural employment grew faster than that of the national population as a whole, and very much faster than that of the rural agricultural population.[13] But urban population was growing faster still, and the growth was shared by all size categories of towns, so that urban growth and rural non-agricultural growth in England appear as complementary rather than in opposition, and it is not inappropriate, at least in the context of a lightning survey, to make use of a model which has many features in common with that of Adam Smith.

Between the mid-sixteenth and the early nineteenth centuries the population of England was rising faster than that of any other major European country for which moderately dependable estimates exist. Between 1550 and 1820, for example, the English population increased by about 280 per cent while the populations of Germany, France, the Dutch Republic, Italy, and Spain all grew by between 50 and 80 per cent, though even at the end of the period the *absolute* English population total remained substantially smaller

---

[10] Malthus took a very similar line to that of Adam Smith in all these matters. He was concerned that a natural tendency to prefer leisure to the purchase of additional goods might frustrate economic growth, remarking, memorably, that, 'It is unquestionably true that wealth produces wants; but it is a still more important truth that wants produce wealth.' In his discussion of the commerce of town and country, he laid special stress on the importance of advance in transport and communications. T. R. Malthus, *The Principles of Political Economy* (2nd edn., London, 1836), 362–3, 403.

[11] The applicability of the concept of proto-industrialization in the case of England has recently been discussed by D. C. Coleman, 'Proto-industrialization: A Concept Too Many', *Economic History Review*, 2nd ser., 36 (1983), 435–48. For a wide-ranging survey of the literature and a critical discussion of the concept, see also R. Houston and K. D. M. Snell, 'Proto-industrialization? Cottage Industry, Social Change and Industrial Revolution', *Historical Journal*, 27 (1984), 473–92.

[12] This is the view of de Vries: see n. 21 below for source references.

[13] See below.

than that of France, Germany, or Italy.[14] Over the same period, England remained very largely self-sufficient in all basic foodstuffs, which implies, of course, that the output of English agriculture must have risen roughly in line with the growth in numbers. There is, however, good reason to think that from about 1610 onwards there was very little growth in the size of the rural population engaged in farming, so that there must have been a very substantial rise in output per head in agriculture, probably a doubling between 1600 and 1800. Meanwhile urban growth was spectacular. Sixteenth-century England was less urbanized than most other European countries, and did not begin to change greatly until the seventeenth century. Indeed, setting London aside, the proportionate degree of urbanization may have fallen slightly during the sixteenth century. By 1800, however, England was more urbanized than any other European country apart from the Dutch Republic. About 25 per cent of the population lived in towns with 5,000 or more inhabitants. Furthermore, of the population living in the countryside, a higher proportion was employed outside agriculture than was the case in Continental countries.[15]

In England, therefore, growth of population and of aggregate output was rapid but lopsided. While population overall increased by 111 per cent between 1600 and 1800, urban population increased by 600 per cent (defining as urban any place with 5,000 or more inhabitants); rural non-agricultural population increased by 249 per cent; but the agricultural population by only 9 per cent. In France, in contrast, growth was far less hectic and far more balanced. The percentages comparable with those just quoted for England were 53 per cent (total); 94 per cent (urban); 108 per cent (rural non-agricultural); and 30 per cent (agricultural). As the percentages imply, the proportion of the French population living in towns was not significantly higher at the time of the Revolution than it had been two hundred years earlier. Approximately 9 per cent of the national population had been urban in 1600, a higher figure than the comparable English one, but in 1800 the percentage had edged up only slightly, to 11 per cent, and a large gap had opened up between France and England.[16]

It is a striking feature of English urban growth that, even though in aggregate it was so rapid, some types of town were barely keeping pace with national population growth. The major regional urban centres of medieval and Tudor England fall into this category. For example, Norwich, York, Salisbury, Chester, Worcester, Exeter, Cambridge, Coventry, Shrewsbury, and Gloucester, a group of ten towns which in 1600 comprised half the twenty

---

[14] E. A. Wrigley, 'The Growth of Population in Eighteenth-century England: A Conundrum Resolved', *Past and Present*, 98 (1983), 122.
[15] Wrigley, 'Urban Growth and Agricultural Change'.
[16] Ibid. 700–1, 718–20, tables 4, 9, and 10. On the virtually stationary agricultural labour force from the time when Gregory King made his estimates (1688), and the strength of the rise in labour productivity in agriculture, see also the recent econometric studies by N. F. R. Crafts, *British Economic Growth During the Industrial Revolution* (Oxford, 1985), 14–17, 62–4, 83–6.

largest towns in England, contained 73,000 people in 1600 and 153,000 in 1800, an increase of 110 per cent. National population rose by almost exactly the same percentage (111 per cent). Such towns were little different, therefore, from their Continental equivalents in that they grew broadly in step with national trends. But London, the port cities, and the new manufacturing towns were very different. The last group in particular enjoyed growth rates which were truly spectacular. The total population of Birmingham, Manchester, Leeds, and Sheffield, for example, came to only 11,000 in 1600. At that date none of them was much more than an overgrown village. By 1801, 271,000 people lived in the four towns; Manchester and Birmingham were the second and fourth largest towns in the country (Liverpool was the third largest: it, too, had been an insignificant settlement in 1600); Leeds and Sheffield stood sixth and seventh. Over the same period London became the largest city in Europe, and several port towns grew immensely: some, like Sunderland, from a tiny initial total.[17]

Urban growth in England during the early modern period, in short, was not a 'blanket' phenomenon. The old urban hierarchy, which had been maintained with only minor changes in rank order for many centuries, was radically transformed. Once again, the contrast with most of the Continent is marked. Although a few French cities grew rapidly, notably some of the port cities, the urban hierarchy was not greatly different in 1800 from what it had been two hundred, or even five hundred years earlier. It was as if French towns were all similar in function to the traditional regional centres in England, increasing broadly in step with the increase of population in their hinterlands. In England there was fundamental, structural change in the urban system as a whole, not simply an increase in its proportional size.

The measurement of urban growth is inevitably a complex matter. Many different methods may be employed, and will result in somewhat varying apparent results. If, however, urban growth is defined as an increase in the percentage of the total population living in settlements above a particular size, rather than as an increase in absolute numbers (so that if both total population and urban population double, this is regarded as zero growth), it can be shown that the share of England in the total urban growth taking place in Europe rose steadily throughout the seventeenth and eighteenth centuries, until, between 1750 and 1800, 70 per cent of all European urban growth was taking place in England, although even in 1800 less than 8 per cent of the total population of Europe was to be found in England. Unquestionably, the phenomenon of English urban growth deserves the fullest attention. It was so conspicuous in itself, and so great a contrast with experience elsewhere in Europe, that it must be regarded as one of the most strategic points of entry into the discussion of the distinctive nature of English economic, social, and demographic history of the early modern period.[18]

[17] Wrigley, 'Urban Growth and Agricultural Change', 686–7, table 1.
[18] Ibid. 709, table 7.

Description of the scale and pace of urban growth and population growth in England from Elizabethan times onwards is feasible, at least in broad outline. Explanation and analysis pose more severe difficulties. It may be taken for granted that the growth process involved complex feedback patterns between all the variables whose changing levels are capable of measurement. But data are lacking, intermittent, or unreliable for so many of the variables which are probably of most significance that it is discouragingly difficult to demonstrate which models 'save the phenomena' effectively and which do not. The phenomena themselves are seldom known with sufficient precision to be invoked as arbiters. In any case, the scope of this chapter is too limited to permit any but the briefest review of the issue.

Certain points, however, may be enumerated, if only as a basis for discussion, and as an indication of the kinds of topics which might repay further study. First, it is clear, by inference of the type sketched above, that there was a very substantial growth in output per head of those employed in agriculture, thus enabling far more of the work-force to move into non-agricultural pursuits. By 1800, only about 40 per cent of the adult male labour force worked on the land, a much lower fraction than in any other country which met the great bulk of its own food needs. This was clearly a necessary condition for the scale of urban growth which occurred, and for the movement of about half the rural population into non-agricultural occupations.[19]

It is not clear whether there was an equally impressive rise in productivity per head outside agriculture over the same period. The classical economists, following Adam Smith's lead, were inclined to expect increasing marginal returns in industrial production, brought about by specialization of function in the manner of the pinmakers. In their analysis, this process is intimately connected with the increase in the size of the accessible market, and this in turn may come about both from establishing access to more and more distant markets because of improved transport systems, and from individuals in an existing market area creating an increased demand because of the effect of rising real incomes, combined with an elasticity of demand for industrial goods greater than unity. Empirical evidence about the relative strength of these two influences, or about the scale and prevalence of productivity rises in different employments, is, however, usually slender and often indirect.

In this connection accurate evidence of changing occupational structure might prove especially illuminating. While the parable of the pinmakers has great appeal and was applicable in many industries, there were still very large numbers of workers serving strictly local markets even in the early nineteenth

---

[19] There are details of early 19th-cent. changes in the size of the agricultural labour force and rough estimates of labour productivity trends, together with some observations and data about the growth of employment elsewhere in the economy in E. A. Wrigley, 'Men on the Land and Men in the Countryside: Employment in Agriculture in Early Nineteenth-Century England', in L. Bonfield, R. M. Smith, and K. Wrightson (eds.), *The World We Have Gained* (Oxford, 1986), 295-336.

century, when, indeed, they considerably outnumbered those in occupations in which a major rise in output per head may have occurred. Shoemakers, tailors, butchers, masons, publicans, and such like formed a large part of the total labour force outside agriculture, and it is reasonable to doubt whether their methods of work and productivity were very different from those of their seventeenth-century predecessors.[20] If then annual output had increased, this may have had more to do with hours of work than with output per hour. It is not beyond the bounds of possibility that productivity per head outside agriculture in general increased less than agricultural productivity between Elizabethan and Regency times.

Secondly, it may prove important to explore further a point which emerges from de Vries's authoritative compilation and analysis of urban growth in Europe between 1500 and 1850. He shows that, in general, smaller towns and cities, those with less than 40,000 inhabitants, were treading water, if not actually in marginal decline, during the seventeenth century and the first half of the eighteenth century. He associates their plight with the growth of industry in the countryside, where cheaper labour, fewer guild controls, and access to wider markets are alleged to have resulted in the spread of proto-industrialization.[21] This structural feature is not found in England, where there was *both* a rapid rise in non-agricultural employment in the countryside *and* a steadily accelerating urban growth at all size levels, though not, as we have noted, in all classes of town. How far the contrast between English and Continental experience was due to straightforwardly economic, and how far to political or other factors, is unclear, but the contrast is striking and may prove instructive.

Thirdly, there are social and demographic matters which have yet to be explored effectively in the context of urban growth in England compared with other countries in Europe. It is plain that an exceptional scale of urban growth in England was not incompatible with unusually rapid overall population growth. Indeed, in spite of the apparent problem posed by the level of urban death-rates and the probable frequency of negative urban intrinsic growth rates,[22] it is more than likely that urban growth indirectly helped to cause the high rate of overall population growth. Nor should it be overlooked that during the seventeenth and eighteenth centuries not only was

[20] Wrigley, 'Men on the Land', 296–304. Recognition that the great bulk of the labour force outside agriculture was still in, say, the 1830s employing traditional methods of production in very small units of production is not, of course, new; see e.g. J. H. Clapham, *An Economic History of Modern Britain*, 3 vols. (2nd edn., Cambridge, 1930), i. Book 1, Ch. 5, 'Industrial Organisation'.

[21] J. de Vries, *European Urbanization 1500–1800* (London and Cambridge, Mass., 1984), 69–77, esp. 76 (table 4.14) and 257–8.

[22] The frequency of natural decrease in pre-industrial European cities is attested by innumerable studies. Its interpretation is more problematic. In this regard two recent studies are noteworthy: A. Sharlin, 'Natural Decrease in Early Modern Cities: A Reconsideration', *Past and Present*, 79 (1978), 126–38; and A. M. van der Woude, 'Population Developments in the Northern Netherlands (1500–1800) and the Validity of the "Urban Graveyard" Effect', *Annales de Démographie Historique* (1982), 55–75.

the domestic rate of population growth high in England, but that the rate of net emigration from England was also much higher than from most other European countries. Indeed, in much of the seventeenth century the net rate of emigration from England was probably higher than in any subsequent period.[23] The elucidation of this apparent paradox presents an interesting challenge. One promising point of entry into the maze is to explore the implications of the very high levels of mobility to be found in early modern England.

There is evidence drawn from a range of different sources to suggest that levels of mobility were high in England during this period. Only a minority, and often a small minority, of those born in a parish, even in deeply rural areas, also died there. This probably represents a substantial contrast with most Continental areas, though the degree and consistency of any difference is not reliably established. High mobility and extensive opportunities to find employment elsewhere are not, of course, necessarily correlated with each other. Distress migration during times of crisis and even over protracted periods of stress may also produce high mobility, but, as a permanent structural feature of a social system, an association between high migration rates and relatively good opportunities to find a living elsewhere is likely to be found. This is especially likely to be true when migration is common for both sexes, as was the case in England. Rules of exogamy may otherwise account for the phenomenon.[24]

High mobility may also be associated with relatively high intrinsic growth rates. The homeostatic features so often visible in studies of west European parish populations implicitly assume restricted local opportunities and little relief from local problems by large-scale out-migration. Homeostatic features were not, of course, absent from English populations during the period, but, equally, population growth was more rapid there than in other countries. It is plausible to suppose that urban growth, economic expansion, high rates of population mobility, a generally stationary agriculturally employed workforce, and moderately high overall population growth rates were intimately related to one another, though there is both scope and need for additional research to try to clarify the assumed relationships.

The list of topics for investigation could be extended considerably; and

---

[23] E. A. Wrigley and R. S. Schofield, *The Population History of England 1541–1871. A. Reconstruction* (London, 1981), 219–28.

[24] A systematic study of this topic would be very instructive. Some details of the level of migration into and out of two villages in England and two in France may be found in P. Laslett, 'Clayworth and Cogenhoe', in P. Laslett, *Family Life and Illicit Love in Earlier Generations* (Cambridge, 1977), 50–101. The differences are pronounced, with substantially higher levels in the English communities. Family reconstitution studies, in which data drawn from Continental parish registers were used, seem normally to show much higher percentages of cases where brides and grooms were born in the parish in which they married, than is the case in England. There is systematic information available for English parishes in D. C. Souden, 'Pre-industrial English Local Migration Fields', Ph.D. diss., University of Cambridge (1981). Comparable data for French, German, and Scandinavian reconstitutions are widely scattered through monographs and theses.

those mentioned would benefit from a less cavalier treatment than they have received, but their scale precludes any but a cursory review in a short essay. In concluding, we may return with profit to Adam Smith. In his inquiry into the nature and causes of the wealth of nations, he was concerned to try to identify the means by which the possibilities for growth could be maximized in a pre-industrial world, that is, a world in which the scope for growth was substantial, but limited. In such a world, urban growth was both a measure and a motor of success; a necessary, though not a sufficient, cause of the favourable ratio between output and consumers which was Adam Smith's definition of wealth.[25] Because of the implications of his distinction between the productive and unproductive use of any agricultural surplus, urban growth in itself was not a guarantee of economic success, of progress towards the attainment of that limited increase in the wealth of the nation which lay within the sphere of human attainment. But if this growth reflected the increasing volume of 'the great commerce', which was for him the life blood of economic success, then urban growth was indeed an accelerator rather than a brake; not in the sense that it uniquely supplied the energy to propel the system as a whole, but rather in a sense conveying the same notion as that attaching to the term positive feedback. Within limits, urban growth might galvanize an economy which was inevitably principally agricultural, by providing stimuli to the agriculture of a nation without which it must remain comparatively unspecialized and unproductive.

In writing the *Wealth of Nations*, Adam Smith was, of course, very largely reflecting on the past two centuries of English history, seen perhaps with special clarity by Scottish eyes and with the advantage of a Scottish perspective. The *Wealth of Nations* might be described as a paradigm of growth on the English model. In my view it is a just and impressive analysis of the path English development had taken. This was certainly one route by which a pre-industrial economy could realize its potential. Others had travelled a similar route, though most had discovered that the trail was easily lost. Paradoxically, however, though Adam Smith's analysis provided a particularly persuasive statesman's guide to success, so to speak, his work soon lost much of its practical relevance. It was published only a short time before the economic landscape was transformed by the Industrial Revolution. Because the nature of economic life was so greatly changed as a result, his analysis and precepts soon had only a limited applicability to the problems and opportunities of the new age. Applied to the age which was about to close, however, his writings have much to tell us about the nature and significance of urban growth.

[25] The *Wealth of Nations* opens with a definition of the subject-matter of the work which is, in effect, the same as the modern concept of average real income per head. 'The annual produce of every nation is the fund which originally supplies it with all the necessaries and conveniencies of life. . . . According therefore, as this produce, or what is purchased with it, bears a greater or smaller proportion to the number of those who are to consume it, the nation will be better or worse supplied with all the necessaries and conveniencies for which it has occasion' (Smith, *Wealth of Nations*, i. 1).

8 Agricultural Productivity, Trade, and Urban Growth during the Phase of Commercialization of the Swedish Economy, 1810–1870

GUNNAR FRIDLIZIUS
Department of Economic History, Lund University, Lund, Sweden

It has generally been considered that foreign trade was the driving force of economic growth in Sweden during the second half of the nineteenth century. A rapidly growing volume of exports of cereals and timber has been regarded as the foundation of the growth of Swedish welfare.[1]

This picture of Swedish economic growth appears to have been confirmed by estimates of the national income for different European countries presented by Bairoch. Economic growth was faster in Sweden after 1870 than in most other European countries. This is quite remarkable, considering that the figures presented by Bairoch for the period before 1870 painted a picture of an extremely poor country in which gross national product per head was growing more slowly than in any other European country.[2]

This model of backwardness was articulated further in an article by Lars G. Sandberg who wrote: 'About the best thing that can be said for the country's economic performance between 1750 and 1850 is that Sweden proper was supporting more than twice as large a population in 1850 as in 1720.'[3]

However, following recent Swedish research on this period, the validity of this view has become more doubtful. In its place has emerged a picture of a vital economy with a considerable degree of market integration.[4] Development during the latter part of the nineteenth century no longer appears as a

---

[1] Cf. e.g. G. Fridlizius, 'Sweden's Exports: 1850–1960', *Economy and History*, 6 (1963); L. Jörberg, 'Structural Change and Economic Growth: Sweden in the 19th Century', *Economy and History*, 8 (1965); B. Carlsson, 'Jordbrukets roll vid Sveriges industrialisering', in E. Dahmen and G. Eliasson, *Industriell utveckling i Sverige. Teori och verklighet under ett sekel* (Stockholm, 1980).
[2] P. Bairoch, 'Europe's Gross National Product: 1800–1975', *Journal of European Economic History*, 9 (1976).
[3] L. G. Sandberg, 'Banking and Economic Growth in Sweden before World War I', *Journal of Economic History*, 38 (1978).
[4] L. Jörberg, *A History of Prices in Sweden, 1772–1914* (Lund, 1972).

discontinuity when compared with previous periods, but rather as a continuation of growth based on internal market integration. It is, therefore, not surprising that Krantz and Schön were able to show that gross national product per head in Sweden during the first half of the nineteenth century did not differ much from the European average, a position that was maintained throughout the century.[5]

This new interpretation of Sweden's pre-industrial growth is of fundamental importance for understanding the process of urbanization in that country. Some of the main features of this process are depicted in Figs. 8.1 to 8.3. As is shown in Fig. 8.1, urbanization, in the sense that populations of towns increased faster than in the countryside, only began after the middle of the nineteenth century. Before that period the increases were roughly similar. Another characteristic was the low level of urbanization. In 1810 only 9.3 per cent of the total population lived in towns; by 1870 this figure had increased to 12.9 per cent. In addition, what towns there were were small. At the beginning of the period 35 out of a total of 82 towns contained fewer than 1,000 inhabitants; 30 contained between 1,000 and 2,999; 11 between 3,000 and 4,999, and only 5 contained between 5,000 and 14,999 persons. The only town with a metropolitan character was Stockholm, with 65,000 inhabitants or about one-third of the total urban population.

The last point of interest which is of special importance for our investigation is the growth pattern of towns in different geographical areas.

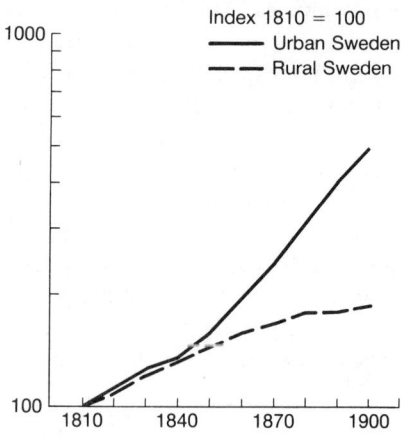

Figure 8.1. Population increase in rural and urban Sweden, 1810–1900

[5] Material taken from the project 'Structural Changes in the Swedish Economy from 1800: Construction and National Product Series' (project participants: O. Krantz, L. Schön, *et al*). Cf. also O. Krantz, *Utrikeshandel, ekonomisk tillväxt och strukturförändring efter 1850* (Malmö, 1987).

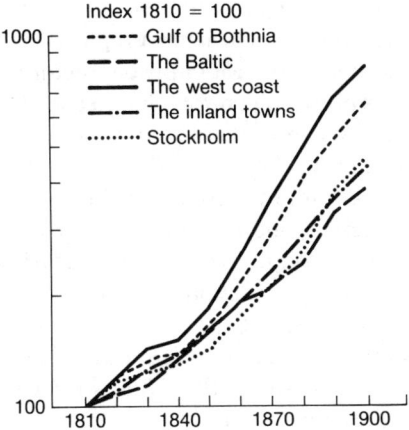

Figure 8.2. Population increase in the towns according to their geographical location

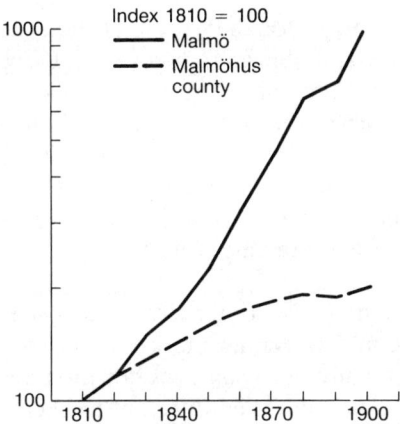

Figure 8.3. Population increase in Malmö and the county of Malmöhus

As may be seen in Fig. 8.2 the port towns on the Swedish west coast and the Gulf of Bothnia grew much more rapidly than the others. This means that towns involved in long-distance trade—at first with other Swedish regions and later with the expanding markets of Western Europe and particularly of England—grew fastest: the ports with a more local trade on the east coast and the inland towns and Stockholm lagged behind.

This period may be characterized as the phase of commercialization in Swedish urban development. The towns served primarily as centres of distribution and developed at different rates, depending on the nature and size of their surrounding markets. It was, therefore, to be expected that towns with important surplus areas (iron, timber, or grain) and with access to consumers' markets should have grown most rapidly.

However, this development did not imply a structural break with an earlier pattern of growth: towns grew, in general, within a traditional socio-economic framework. This pattern did not begin to change until the 1850s when real wages of the lower social groups in the rural population increased markedly.

This change led not only to an increase in the towns' rate of growth, but also to a change in their economic functions. Their traditional roles as commercial centres whose prime function was distribution, was extended increasingly to include the production of manufactured goods. The new industrial town had begun to take shape.

We shall study this process in greater detail by using the town of Malmö as an example in support of the suggestions that we have put forward earlier. Malmö was one of the growing towns situated on the west coast. Its population in 1810 was 5,800; by 1870 it had risen to 25,600, a rate of growth considerably in excess of that of most other Swedish towns. Its population trends began to differ from those of the countryside considerably earlier than elsewhere (Fig. 8.3).

Malmö was the chief town for the export of the Scanian surplus of grain. Exports of grain from Malmö began to increase as early as the second half of the eighteenth century, the main areas of destination being Göteborg, Stockholm, and the towns of the Gulf of Bothnia. Following the repeal of the British Corn Laws this internal trade was increasingly replaced by a growth of exports to the English market. Within a radius of about 30 km. from Malmö the land was cultivated by peasant proprietors (the peasant region); outside this circle cultivation was by tenants who belonged to different estates (the manorial region).

I shall begin by looking at the 'outer circle', i.e. the contributions made to growth by production and consumer markets, and go on to discuss the role played by transport. Finally, we shall consider the important part played by the city of Malmö as a link between different markets, stressing the mutual stimulus between urban growth and agricultural improvement.

1. The growth of agricultural productivity

A first estimate suggests that the total acreage of arable land in Sweden approximately doubled between 1800 and 1860.[6] At the same time the production of vegetables increased by about 150 per cent. This rise in productivity was probably caused by a reduction of the amount of land left lying fallow. Towards the end of the period rotation of crops was generally practised, mainly on the manorial estates. Another reason for the improve-

---

[6] On the growth of agricultural productivity in Sweden, cf. the survey by L. Schön, *Jordbrukets omvandling och konsumtionens förändringar 1800–1870* (Lund, 1985).

ment in productivity of land was the introduction of new techniques designed to improve the quality of the soil, including more effective drainage, improved methods of ploughing and harrowing, the use of fertilizers, and, during the latter part of the period, the use of improved seeds.

It has generally been assumed that this process was initiated and made possible by the enclosure movement. Enclosures began in the peasant regions of southern Scania (the Malmö hinterland) during the early years of the nineteenth century and resulted in a disintegration of the villages and the total elimination of the partitioning of land. In less than twenty years, a large part of the land originally owned by peasant proprietors was enclosed, villages were broken up, and nearly half the previous owners had left the land. Rarely can an enclosure of such dimensions have been so complete and efficient in so short a period of time.[7]

In the manorial areas, the enclosure movement became an important feature of a large-scale structural transformation. The manor was extended, marginal homesteads sold off, and organizational improvements were introduced. These included a gradual replacement of peasants by wage labourers, crofters, and modern tenants. Agricultural experts from Schleswig-Holstein were engaged and model farms set up after the English pattern. Profits which had previously been spent on private consumption were increasingly ploughed back for the maintenance and improvement of the land. All these factors constituted important steps away from the almost feudal system of agriculture that prevailed during the eighteenth century and constituted a movement towards a capitalist form of organization. On the manor, the ownership of land became 'a way of life, not a method of making a living'.

Although enclosure was a necessary condition for the improvement in agriculture during the first half of the nineteenth century, it must be regarded as an integral part of development which began during the latter half of the eighteenth century as the result of an increasing degree of market integration and commercialization.[8] This process resulted in an economy in which each region could develop so as to maximize its comparative advantage. One of the important reasons why the enclosure movement began in southern Scania was the growth of long-distance trade in grain between the Scanian area where there was a surplus, and other areas in Sweden where there was a deficit. It also resulted in increasing social and economic differentiation within the class of freeholders. A small group of mainly market-oriented farmers was created, some of whom managed to accumulate a substantial amount of capital, and whose attitudes towards changes which promoted production differed from those of the majority of subsistence farmers. The latter group continued to be concerned with self-sufficiency and the minimization of risks. The former, on the other hand, must have regrded the system of strip farming as the principal

---

[7] On the enclosure movement in Scania cf. G. Fridlizius, 'Population, Enclosure and Property Rights', *Economy and History*, 22 (1979).

[8] G. Fridlizius, 'Handel och sjöfart, 1830–1870', *Malmö stads historia*, 3 (Malmö, 1981).

118 Gunnar Fridlizius

obstacle to the efficient utilization of land during the period of high grain prices which was characteristic of the latter part of the eighteenth century. Even if the act of enclosure was in the form of an *ukaz* from an absolute government, the fact that it was effected rapidly and happily was due to the earlier expansion of the market.

The repeal of the Corn Laws in England during the 1840s radically changed the dynamics of the process of growth. The bright market opportunities in England resulted in an extremely rapid growth of external trade which was added to the growth generated by trade from internal sources. Between 1841–5 and 1866–70 grain exports from Malmö increased by 37 per cent, whilst exports to the home market decreased by 45 per cent.[9] By the end of the period, therefore, the foreign market was in a dominant position. The fact that the English demand was mainly for oats was important. The cultivation of oats did not demand soils of the same quality as were needed for other cereals, and they could be produced on reclaimed land.

Thus the agrarian economy was provided with a number of new stimuli for growth which had not been present during the period when growth depended primarily on internal sources. The rapid increase in exports made the economy more dependent on the terms of trade which, as is shown in Fig. 8.4, were remarkably favourable for Sweden, and particularly for her grain-producing regions.

These developments had a positive impact on the supply of capital for agriculture. This was important because until the mid-1860s loans were

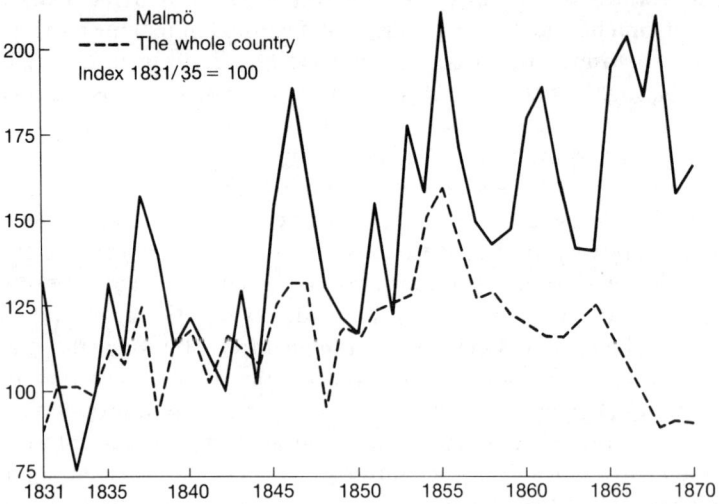

Figure 8.4. Terms of trade for Malmö and the whole country, 1831–70
        Source: G. Fridlizius, 'Malmö handel och sjöfart, 1830–1870', *Malmö stads historia* (Malmö, 1981).

[9] G. Fridlizius, 'Handel och sjöfart, 1830–1870', *Malmö stads historia*, 3 (Malmö, 1981).

largely in the form of credits exchanged between individuals, and there was little institutional credit. Although this system had functioned reasonably well until then, it had become obsolete and proved far too rigid for channelling capital from surplus to deficit areas.

The expansion of external trade also led to new ways of providing short-term capital support, the crucial point in the provision of capital. Trade also proved important in the introduction of new techniques, organizational innovations, and improved knowledge in the Swedish agrarian economy. These aspects will be discussed in greater detail in the section that deals with the merchant houses. Altogether, the timing of the market stimulus from England proved to be unusually favourable for Sweden, and particularly for the region of interest to us. A new 'vent for the surplus' was created which had a positive influence on the growth of the economy.

This approach emphasizes the dynamic role exports have played as an engine of growth from the middle of the nineteenth century. The fundamental difference between this view of events and older approaches to the problem is that we no longer assume that this process began in a country which was extremely backward, but rather in an integrated market economy in which there was a considerable degree of commercialization.

Unless we take account of this continuity of development, it becomes difficult to explain—as have the 'export economists'—how the gains from export trade could be diffused so rapidly throughout the economy by way of the multiplier, or how farmers responded so quickly to external incentives, or, for that matter, why a dual economy never developed. This growth pattern resulted in Sweden, which had been a net importer of grain during the latter half of the eighteenth and the beginning of the nineteenth centuries, achieving an equilibrium during the 1820s and the 1830s and becoming a net exporter after the 1840s, particularly of fodder grains such as oats.

Several authors have indicated that there was an increase in the production of vegetables per head between 1800 and 1860 amounting to about 0.5 per cent per year.[10] It is, however, as yet far from clear how these improvements in output occurred. In theory, they could have been achieved either by an increase in production per hour of work, or by an increase in the number of hours per worker. The introduction of the rotation of crops towards the end of our period is likely to have led to an increase in the number of hours worked per year for those with annual contracts of employment, because the working season was extended. The enormous amount of land reclamation and ditching that occurred in connection with enclosure took place during the off-season and was generally undertaken by workers who did not have annual contracts of employment, such as crofters, cotters, and lodgers. These projects could also have resulted in an increase in the number of hours worked per worker. Increases in production per hour could only have

[10] Schön, *Jordbrukets omvandling*.

depended on improvements in agricultural technology to a very limited degree. The introduction of the scythe, however, may have been of some importance in this connection.

Instead, we emphasize improvements in the organization of the labour force, from central planning by the owners to planning for the day by supervisors in the field. Attempts to reduce the time lost between different working operations must have played an important part. Time became more important than had been the case—we might mention *en passant* that the number of watchmakers in the country increased more rapidly than that of other craftsmen. Nor can we exclude the possibility that better motivation of the workers may have led to higher productivity.

Thus the contribution of structural transformation, or the Agricultural Revolution if we prefer a more expressive term, to economic growth lay not in the release of labour, but rather in making it possible to increase output per worker at a time when the input of labour was also rising, without a decline in the standard of living. But before introducing the town into this scenario, we must touch upon the strategic role played by improvements in transport in the market expansion.

2. Growth of productivity in the transport sector

In the past, the introduction of the railways in the 1850s was regarded as the decisive innovation in inland transport. The railways brought a solution to a severe transport problem and were a basic prerequisite for rapid industrialization during the latter half of the nineteenth century.

Recent studies show a somewhat more diversified picture.[11] During the second half of the eighteenth century there were considerable improvements in inland roads as well as in road vehicles. Transport by packhorse became considerably less common. Vehicles with iron wheels appeared by the middle of the century, and by the end of that century vehicles with iron axles were introduced. Improvements in roads were a necessary condition for the new technology. Transport could be distributed more evenly over the year, and trade was becoming less dependent on winter roads. Grain exports during the decades preceding the introduction of railway transport would not have been possible had roads and vehicles been of the same standard as half a century earlier.[12]

These improvements in the transport network would also have been a logical outcome of the increasing degree of market integration and commercialization during the second half of the eighteenth century: this development could hardly have occurred without an improvement in communications

---

[11] Cf. esp. G. Ahlström, *Infrastruktur och kommunikationer: Sverige under 1700- och 1800-talen* (Lund, 1985), and C. J. Gadd, *Järn och potatis* (Göteborg, 1983).

[12] Gadd, *Järn och potatis*.

resulting in lower transaction costs which made it possible for each region to develop in accordance with its comparative advantage. In addition, economies of scale could be introduced and the degree of specialization raised.

The construction of the railways should be regarded as only one of many improvements in the transport system, but it was undoubtedly the most important. In this chapter I have made no attempt to estimate the effect of railways on freight costs. However, some reflections will illustrate the importance of the railways in the continued expansion of Malmö.[13]

Before the advent of the railways a whole day was normally required to move a carriage of goods over a distance of 30 km. However, this assumed that the roads were passable, which was not always the case in the Malmö region, particularly in winter. The mild and humid climate made transport on winter roads impossible and raised difficulties for transport on ordinary roads. After the railways were built, transport over the same distance took only one hour and was generally independent of weather conditions.

The railways opened up new large production centres in the interior of the country which had previously been excluded from access to the exporting ports in the south. Production in these new areas, with their great potential for the cultivation of oats in particular, could in the new circumstances be regarded as responses to new demand. The very large increase in the exportation of grain from Malmö during the 1860s can largely be ascribed to the completion of the railway.

In the sea transport sector there were also considerable gains due to rationalization. According to my estimates, during the early 1840s the freight factor (i.e. freight rates in relation to the CIF value) of the Göteborg–London grain trade was approximately 12.[14] (For Malmö, located as it is some 300 km. further south on the coast, it is bound to have been somewhat higher.) By the end of the 1860s it had fallen to 6.4, i.e. by nearly 50 per cent as Fig. 8.5 shows. The effects of such a sharp decline could hardly be neglected.[15] Some of this decline was due to improvements in shipping that were gradually introduced during this period. The size of sailing vessels increased, thus resulting in economies of scale. The first large Malmö-owned vessel appeared during the 1850s, and this event could be taken as indicating a general trend. Efficiency was also improved in techniques of shipbuilding. Vessels were faster, could carry more cargo in relation to their tonnage, and a smaller crew was required to man them.

Probably an even more important factor in reducing cost was the smaller number of voyages made in ballast, as a result of the increase in the commodity trade. This increase became possible as a result of the increasing

---

[13] My description of Malmö trade and shipping is based on my paper, 'Malmö handel och sjöfart'.

[14] The series of freight rates is taken from O. Krantz, 'Historiska nationalräkenskaper för Sverige. Transporter och kommunikationer 1800–1910' (unpublished).

[15] D. C. North, 'Ocean Freight Rates and Economic Development 1750–1930', *Journal of Economic History*, 18 (1958).

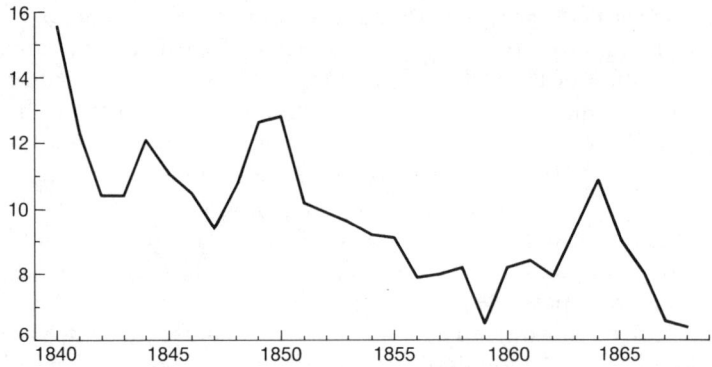

Figure 8.5. Freight factors on corn shipped from Göteborg to London, 1840–69

size of ports which made loading and unloading more efficient. The amount of time vessels had to spend in port was considerably reduced. Liberalization of the naval laws and reductions in harbour dues also contributed to the lowering of costs.

3. The town: a catalyst of growth?

In the export model the merchant houses play a central part as a growth factor, since theirs was a key position in the export trade of grain and timber; they became a catalyst for the whole growth process.[16] Although the activities of these houses appear to be less unique in the 'continuity model' that has been outlined it can hardly be denied that they were a far from passive link between producers' and consumers' markets throughout the whole period.[17] They provided the contacts between buyers and sellers and between creditors and debtors. They knew the market conditions. They often maintained personal contact with buyers in the consumer countries. They also brought information to the producers relating to the quality demanded by the buyers and to conditions of delivery. In addition they provided producers with pamphlets and handbooks which introduced them to new agricultural technologies.

In several instances successful exporters of grain invested their profits in manorial land where they tried new technologies of cultivation in order to produce high-quality grain. Some were successful and their example was imitated by others, so that manorial grain became a synonym for high quality. The substantial improvement in the quality of Swedish grain during the

[16] Cf. Carlsson, 'Jordbrukets roll'.
[17] My description of the merchant houses is based on my article, 'Malmö handel och sjöfart'.

period could to some extent be attributed to the operations of the merchant houses.

The role of the merchant houses as suppliers of credit is less well known. An important problem which was faced by agriculture during this period was difficulty in obtaining short-term credit to finance operations. This was far more difficult than the provision of long-term capital, largely because of the seasonal character of the trade, the absence of functioning credit institutions, and a notoriously strained liquidity situation among the farmers and large landlords. A small proportion of such credit had traditionally been provided by the merchant houses.

During the period of export expansion the demand for short-term credit increased considerably. To a large extent this demand could be satisfied by different forms of foreign credit. Advance drafts, bills of acceptance, and *in blanco* credits were often interwoven in a complex manner. The system was based on a complete register of credits comprising all stages of the chain of distribution. It also depended on mutual confidence between the parties involved. The various stages in the chain from producer to purchaser corresponded to an equal number of stages in the credit system. The merchant made advances to the producer. He, in his turn, was provided with credit by the dealer in the country of destination. The latter had received credit from the purchaser or a banker associated with him, or from some other intermediary.

The same pattern applied to the import trade. The foreign seller was probably given credit by the exporter, who, in turn, could count on credit from bankers in Hamburg, London, or both. In turn, the bank allowed the Swedish importer a credit *in blanco*, so that the latter was enabled to pay for transport and give credit to Swedish buyers.

A precondition for transferring economic growth to the countryside by increasing market integration in different sectors was a continuous increase in the productivity of commerce, which lowered transaction costs. One such change was the transition from general to specialized merchanting firms. This did not occur particularly quickly, but it was reflected in the large expansion of grain exports during the 1840s. This was logical since the expansion was most pronounced in the grain trade, so that the conditions which favoured specialization were to be found particularly in this trade.

By taking advantage of economies of scale the new firms could more easily lower prices or provide more favourable discounts. Furthermore, the cost of holding stocks was reduced because of faster turnover. Operations became more standardized and could be organized more cheaply and easily. This change appears to have been general. In all branches in which there was a new technology together with a previously unknown type of mass production, general merchants were increasingly replaced by specialized firms.

Within the distribution system, costs were reduced by a transition from consignment trade to various forms of trading in futures. The former implied that grain was left unsold to the dealer, who had to sell for the exporter's account. Consignment trade was a risky form of enterprise. The grain delivered could not always be sold immediately the ships arrived in the ports of destination. This resulted in increasing costs because large amounts of capital were tied up for prolonged periods. Studies of merchants' accounts have shown that a large part of the total stocks held by merchants at the time were in the form of consignments.

The shift to trading in futures was dependent on a number of necessary conditions. The first was the improvement in the quality of the grain. Another was that the purchaser could make his decisions after having received a sample in advance. Thus, in contrast to the consignment trader, he did not need access to the entire cargo in order to examine its quality. This made it possible for merchants to use the enormous advantages in the method of distribution brought about by the invention of the telegraph.

Another important necessary condition for a rapid increase in productivity was that trade could develop without restrictions in the form of cartels, etc. Strong competition certainly succeeded in neutralizing different attempts in that direction.

This also puts in question a common suggestion that merchants determined prices by giving large credits or advances to the farmers. This pattern of credit was largely the result of different income and expenditure periods for the farmers. They found this time-lag difficult to reconcile, partly because liquidity among the farmers was notoriously bad, and partly because the institutional credit system was underdeveloped. If the merchants wanted to retain the farmers as customers, they were obliged to give credit. An analysis of their gains does not suggest that they profited at the expense of the farmers.

The suggestion which has often been put forward that Swedish merchants were dependent on the Hamburg merchant bankers may be questioned for the same reasons. Competition among the Hamburg merchants was too fierce for this to happen. The income pattern of the Hamburg merchants points in the same direction. Thus Soetbeer writes: 'It is noteworthy . . . how in comparison to other large cities, Hamburg contains a large number of wealthy, but only very few rich merchants.'[18]

It seems that changing conditions of trade contributed to the appearance of a new and more modern type of merchant, capable of responding to the demands of the market and more inclined to think in terms of expansion and of profit maximization. For the older type of merchant his business was often a means of reaching a higher position in the social scale. Consequently, he tended to be cautious in his operations, attempting to maximize safety and investing in secure assets, often in real estate and land outside the range of true mercantile activities. All in all, we can see a pattern of trade with great

---

[18] A. Soetbeer, *Ueber Hamburgs Handel* (Hamburg, 1840), 80, quoted by S. Tveite, 'Hamburg og norsk naeringsliv, 1814–1860', *Historisk tidsskrift*, 42 (1963).

possibilities for stimulating economic growth in Malmö and its hinterland.

4. A dual labour market

In discussing the economic interdependence between town and country we must also consider labour-force problems. In the previous sections we have frequently used the term 'integration' to characterize important aspects of economic development during the period under consideration. However, this term is less applicable to the labour market in Malmö. Instead, we need to emphasize a dual pattern, with a marked dividing line between the city and its traditional small hinterland on the one hand and a more distant region, which in this case was particularly manorial, on the other. We have not been able to verify from our material that agricultural transformation resulted in 'push' migration into the city. However, this pattern is not illogical, given the picture of urban and rural economic development which we have painted. The main function of the town was to act as a centre of distribution, with limited possibilities for capital investment that would provide employment opportunities. The construction of the grand harbour was to a large extent undertaken by prison labour and by soldiers. At the same time the rural sector was in a position to absorb a rapidly increasing population without, or with only a small, decline in the level of real wages. This is particularly remarkable in view of changes in the age structure; thus numbers in the age-group 20–25, the most mobile section of the population, increased by 40 per cent between 1830 and 1845 in the country surrounding Malmö.[19]

Figs. 8.6 and 8.7 illustrate different aspects of my argument. Fig. 8.6 shows a relatively stable rate of natural increase of the population of Malmö of between six and seven per thousand up to the middle of the century. Thereafter, the rate of growth changed rapidly and nearly doubled. The pattern is similar, though at a lower level, for all towns, but Stockholm diverges from the general pattern. This increase was caused in part by an increase in crude birth-rates, but mainly by a fall in mortality. Here, too, the pattern for Malmö reflects the general development (see Fig. 8.7). It is interesting that the decline in the crude death-rate after the 1840s was, apart from the reduction in infant and child mortality, due also to a reduction in mortality of those aged between 25 and 50 years. This is also true of the other towns and of the rural sector (see Fig. 8.8).

The decline is surprising, for there are no apparent causes to be found in the socio-economic environment. Large-scale improvements in sewerage and water supply only began some thirty or forty years later. It may be more

---

[19] For the whole country the increase amounted to 48%. In some counties the increase was between 60 and 80%. See G. Fridlizius, 'Sweden', in W. R. Lee (ed.), *European Demography and Economic Growth* (London, 1979).

126 *Gunnar Fridlizius*

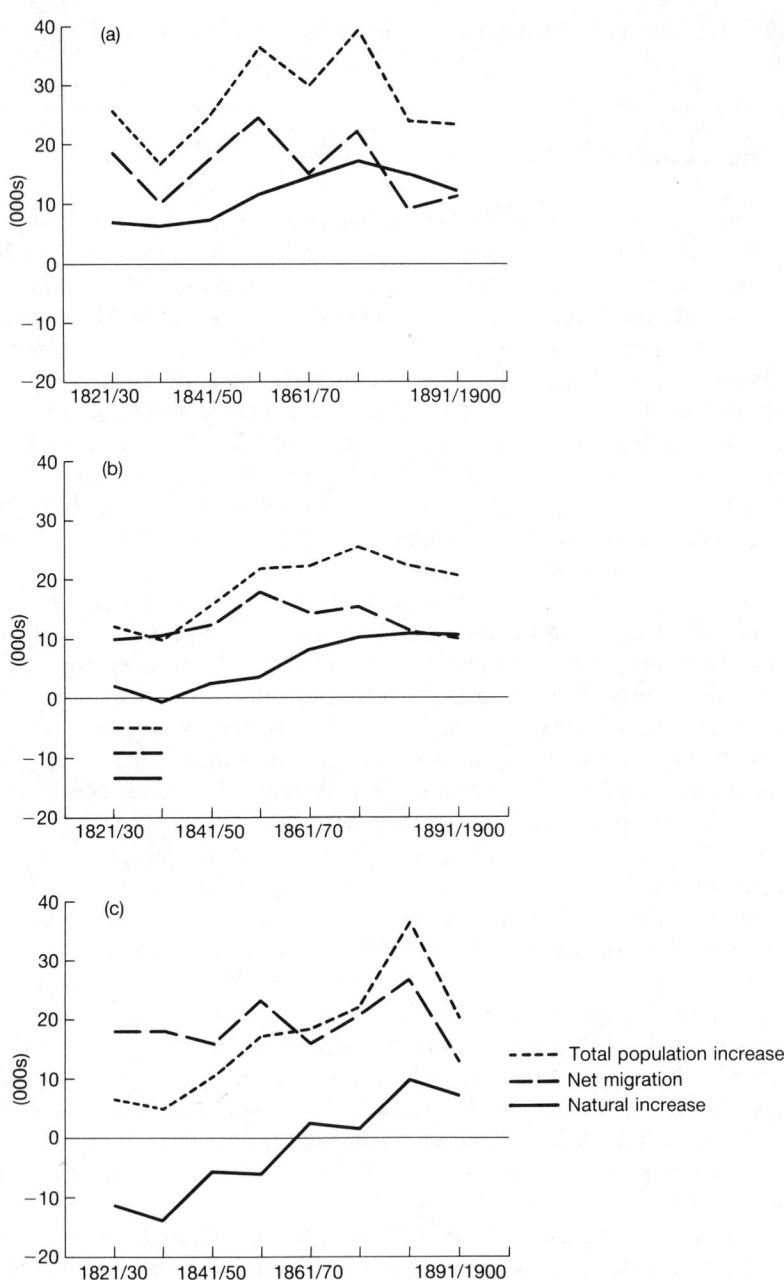

Figure 8.6. Total population increase, net migration, and natural increase in Malmö (*a*), urban Sweden excluding Stockholm (*b*), and Stockholm (*c*), 1821/30–1891/1900

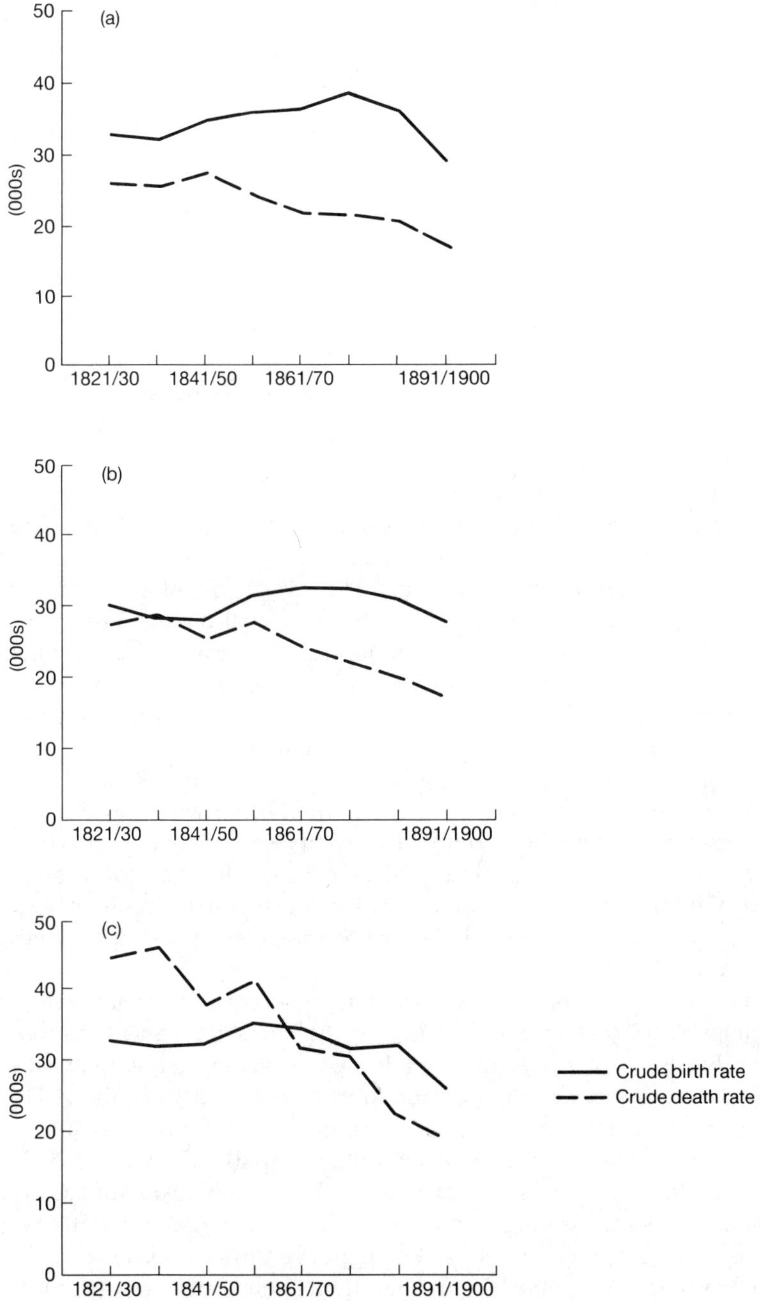

Figure 8.7. Crude birth and death rates in Malmö (*a*), urban Sweden (*b*), and Stockholm (*c*), 1821/30–1891/1900

128 *Gunnar Fridlizius*

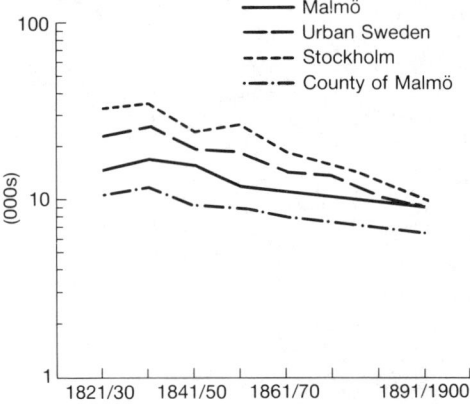

Figure 8.8. Age-specific mortality rates 1821/30–1891/1900 in the age-group 25–50

valuable to relate this fall to changes in the long-term patterns of disease. If this suggestion were adopted, the simultaneous increase in the birth rate can be related to the same phenomenon.[20] However, a detailed discussion of this topic goes beyond the bounds of this chapter. In such a discussion the excess mortality of men of working age—amounting to nearly 100 per cent in Malmö and to twice as much in Stockholm—and its implications for natural increase and for migration would be of considerable interest, as would the differences between the mortality of the married and the unmarried.

To conclude, the figures imply that, up to the middle of the century, migration was the most important component of growth, and that after that time growth was about equally due to natural increase and to net in-migration. During this period, therefore, Malmö did not replace itself through in-migration. Its position was more fortunate than that of other towns, not to mention Stockholm, whose population did not replace itself until the 1850s.

Some of the principal trends in the migration pattern of Malmö are shown in Tables 8.1–8.4. The figures relate to the years 1835 and 1855, and show generally similar patterns. In-migration was concentrated among those aged 20–29 and among this group lone migrants were prevalent (Table 8.1). About one-third of the male migrants were craftsmen, predominantly journeymen. The other two-thirds were mainly farmhands, particularly in 1835. In 1855, however, the number of servants is reduced and a new group of day labourers becomes evident. Among female in-migrants domestic servants were the predominant group (Table 8.2). The high proportion of craftsmen indicates that there was an important in-migration from other towns, and this is

[20] G. Fridlizius, 'Sex Differential Mortality and Socio-Economic Change: Sweden 1750–1914', in A. Brändström and L. G. Tedebrand (eds.), *Society, Health and Population during the Demographic Transition* (Umeå, 1988).

Table 8.1 In-migration to Malmö by age and sex, 1835 and 1855 (%)

Age	1835			1855		
	Male	Female	Total	Male	Female	Total
15–20	16.1	13.7	15.0	32.5	12.4	23.4
20–24	41.9	35.3	38.9	29.1	32.6	30.4
25–29	22.6	27.5	24.8	13.7	24.7	18.7
30–34	9.8	9.7	9.7	12.8	18.6	15.4
35–39	9.7	5.9	8.0	4.3	5.2	4.7
Over 40	—	7.8	3.5	7.7	7.2	7.5

Table 8.2 In-migration to Malmö by occupation and sex, 1835 and 1855 (%)

Occupation	1835		1855	
	Male	Female	Male	Female
Craftsmen	34.3		35.8	
Farmhands	41.8		24.9	
Domestics		75.2		81.5
Youths	13.4	12.9	13.1	4.9
Day labourers	—	—	15.0	—
Others	10.5	11.8	11.2	13.5

Table 8.3 In-migration to Malmö from other towns as percentage of total in-migration

	Craftsmen	Farmhands	Domestics	Total
1835	82.6	17.0	35.4	38.1
1855	52.7	6.9	32.8	30.7

Table 8.4 Out-migrants, 1835 and 1855, by year of in-migration (%)

	1835				1855			
	Craftsmen	Farmhands	Domestics	Total	Craftsmen	Farmhands	Domestics	Total
Same year	18.2	—	—	6.6	6.9	—	3.2	3.8
After 1 year	54.6	41.7	57.9	52.6	29.7	41.9	33.7	37.1
After 2 years	4.5	25.0	21.1	14.7	18.1	25.8	13.7	20.5
After 3 years	9.1	16.7	5.3	9.3	12.5	6.5	8.7	11.9
After more than 4 years	13.6	16.8	15.8	17.4	32.8	25.8	40.1	26.7

confirmed by the figures in Table 8.3, which show that 83 per cent of members of this group originated in the surrounding or more distant towns. Most of the other in-migrants, however, tended to be recruited from a limited area in the surrounding countryside. A rough calculation shows that most came from parishes within a distance of 20 km. from the town.

My investigations of the relations between out-migration and birthplace are not yet complete, but the preliminary results indicate no stepwise migration movement to the town. Thus, Malmö's labour demands from the countryside during the period of commercial expansion were satisfied from a very narrow hinterland, traditionally integrated with the town and related to it by a set of different networks. The pattern is one of traditional circular movement with an increasing proportion of people remaining in the town.

This hypothesis is strengthened when we look at net in-migration in relation to total in-migration and to the time that the in-migrants spent in the town. During the period as a whole net in-migration amounted to about 26 per cent of total in-migration, a little more during the years between 1840 and 1860, a little less during the previous and later periods. The figures in Table 8.4 show that 58 and 41 per cent respectively of the in-migrants remained in the town for periods of one year or less.[21] In particular, many craftsmen left the town after remaining there for a short time only. In contrast to many servants, they were not bound by one-year contracts of service. The mobility of craftsmen may have been even higher than is shown in the record books: some journeymen who unsuccessfully looked for employment in the city remained there for so short a period that they did not register as inhabitants.

This pattern of migration makes it difficult to separate 'pull' and 'push' factors in short-term migration. Journeymen were motivated by different considerations from those of farmhands, and to some degree this was also true of female domestic servants. Economic development in the neighbouring towns must be taken into account, as well as wages and harvests in the countryside. Employment opportunities were associated with a high income elasticity of demand for services and this made the labour market sensitive to changes in trade. During years when profits were high the demand for services and handicraft products increased, and this stimulated employment opportunities in the handicraft sector.

Bengtsson has obtained different results for different towns when correlating rye prices with in-migration.[22] For Malmö he finds that until the end of the 1840s in-migration was particularly high during years of high prices. He understands this to mean that short-term factors must have determined the timing of migration. After that period the pattern was broken and higher urban wages acted as a structural 'pull' factor. This is possibly reflected by a marked increase in total migration during the 1850s which occurred simultaneously with an increase in net migration.

Out-migration from the towns does not appear to have been determined by harvests. The absence of 'push' migration from the more distant manorial regions to the towns is also in agreement with the economic development pattern that we have outlined. What happened in the first place was a social and economic stratification within rural society. There was no push from the soil; those who were forced to migrate to a large extent obtained employment in the same or an adjacent parish.[23] Possibly the network of different

---

[21] Calculated on the basis of out-migrants, the figures give only a rough estimate.

[22] T. Bengtsson, 'Migration, Wages, and Urbanization in the Nineteenth Century', ch. 12 in this vol.

[23] During the last part of this period, however, there was a small net out-migration from these regions, possibly to Denmark.

connections which was so important a condition for migration to the town had not yet developed. The urban environment seemed too strange to a potential out-migrant from the countryside to be a realistic alternative.

5. Inequalities in income and urbanization

Having discussed briefly the different ways in which the development of towns was able to stimulate agricultural modernization we can now explore how these improvements in their turn influenced urban growth and in a more long-term perspective gave way to the industrial town. The increase in production per head in agriculture which we noted earlier generated agricultural incomes which resulted in an increase in income per head. But in order to analyse economic growth we need to know what groups of people benefited from these higher incomes. The effect would vary depending on whether the increases were equally spread or whether the incidence of these increases was unequal; whether there was an income distribution which left the masses with a constant low income or one which allowed the lower social groups to enjoy a rise in incomes.

In this context it should be noted that the period we are considering was one of extensive social change. The number of farmers remained nearly constant, though there were certain regional differences. On the other hand, the numbers of landless labourers, cotters, and crofters increased dramatically. At the beginning of the period the number of farmers was double that of the landless; by the end of the period the two groups were almost equal in size.

It is commonly believed that the lower social groups were adversely affected by these changes, and that their standard of living fell between 1820 and 1850. It was at this time that the large number of people born during the ten years following the Napoleonic wars joined the labour market. Jörberg's estimates of real wages indicate, however, only a slight fall in the lower social groups.[24] Lennart Schön arrived at a similar conclusion using different estimates of consumption, though he thinks that there was stagnation, rather than an actual decline.[25]

A major change occurred after 1850. Both Jörberg's estimates of real wages and Schön's estimates of consumption indicate that there was a rapid improvement in the income of the lower social groups (see Fig. 8.9). The reasons for this rapid change are far from clear. However, we can point to one or two important factors. The fast growth in the numbers of persons between the ages of 15 and 25 stopped at a time when the demand for labour in agriculture increased because of the favourable cycle for exports and the

---

[24] Jörberg, *History of Prices in Sweden*. However, Jörberg himself has admitted that his estimates do not take account of the possibility that a growth in production per head may have been the result of increased working hours.

[25] Schön, *Jordbrukets omvandling*.

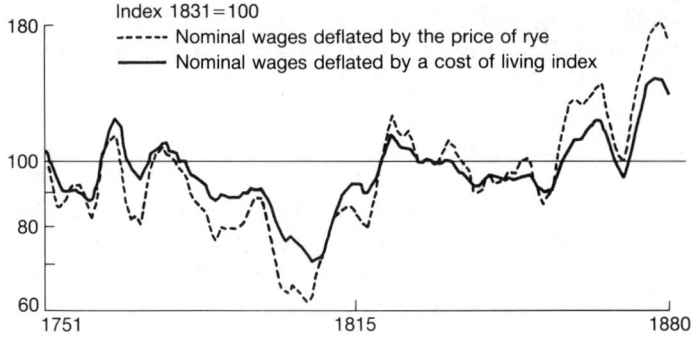

Figure 8.9. Real wages for agricultural workers, 1751–1880 (5-year moving average)
   Sources: Calculated from L. Jörberg, *A History of Prices in Sweden 1732–1914* (Lund, 1972)

boom created by the Crimean War. Labour-saving threshing machines and harvesters were not introduced until some decades later. In addition, there was increasing competition for labour from the large projects for railway construction which began during the mid-1850s.

This income pattern must have been of fundamental importance for the process of urbanization in Sweden. The unequal distribution of incomes meant that, until the end of the 1840s, the purchasing power of the lower social groups was insufficient to create a market for the large-scale production of cheap consumption goods. As a consequence there were few incentives in the towns to establish mass production plants. The town functioned as a distribution centre for the export of surplus grain to expanding markets and for the import of consumption goods which were supplied to market-oriented farmers, landlords, and the urban bourgeoisie. What production there was was in the form of handicrafts for consumption in the town itself.

However, the rise in real wages which began during the 1850s paved the way for a new pattern of urbanization. For the first time in Swedish history there was a market for the large-scale production of cheap consumer goods. This created the necessary conditions for the emergence of factory production, particularly at first in textiles. The new mechanized factories, with their competitive power enhanced by growing markets as well as rising wages and improved looms, began to compete with the system of household production.[26] In this process the towns, rather than the old proto-industrial regions

[26] L. Schön, 'Market Development and Structural Change in the Mid-Nineteenth Century with Special Reference to Sweden', in W. Fischer, M. McInnis, and J. Schneider (eds.), *The Emergence of a World Economy, 1500–1914* (Wiesbaden, 1986). In this article Schön formalized the development of markets in terms of widening and deepening at the same time, and distinguished between internal and external developments of this process. His thesis is that both the widening and the deepening effects of the internal factor have been neglected to the detriment of our knowledge of the intricate relations between trade and economic growth. His thesis was, however, published too late to be discussed in this chapter.

of the countryside, attracted the new factories. Thus it was at the end of this period that the first textile mill was established in Malmö, and that the description 'factory worker' first appears in the statistics of occupations. The role of the town as a centre of distribution was beginning to be eroded and the commercial *and* industrial phase was beginning to take shape.

9 The Impact of Crop Yields, Agricultural Productivity, and Transport Costs on Urban Growth between 1800 and 1910

PAUL BAIROCH
Département d'Histoire Économique, Université de Genève, Genève, Switzerland

In this chapter I shall attempt to evaluate the impact of three factors on urbanization which, while operating outside the towns, nevertheless exercised considerable influence. There is no doubt that crop yields, agricultural productivity, and transport costs each influenced the process of urbanization, and I shall estimate the relative importance of each of these factors for urbanization, particularly during the period when urbanization in the developed countries underwent the most profound changes, i.e. during the nineteenth century.

I had originally hoped to be able to carry this study further back in time, but scarcity of data on crop yields and agricultural productivity means that we can discuss the situation only in very general terms. For instance, it is likely that during the pre-industrial period the higher yield of rice compared with that of wheat was one (but not the only) factor which helps to explain the higher levels of urbanization in civilizations in which the basic staple was rice.[1] The difference is substantial: it has been estimated that before the eighteenth century the yield of (paddy) rice was of the order of 13 to 16 quintals per hectare, compared with only about 6 to 7 quintals per hectare for wheat. In addition, less had to be put aside as seed for the following year: between 5 and 7 per cent of the rice crop, compared with between 18 and 20 per cent of the wheat crop. However, the non-edible fraction of paddy rice is some 33 per cent, compared with some 15 per cent for wheat. Altogether, therefore, one hectare of rice yielded more than twice as much nutritional value as one hectare of wheat, particularly when we take into account that the calorific value of rice exceeds that of wheat by some 10 per cent. One hectare of rice could, therefore, feed a population at least twice as

---

[1] P. Bairoch, *De Jéricho à Mexico. Villes et économie dans l'histoire* (Paris, 1985), esp., 21, 270, and chs. 22 and 23 of part c (451–89). An English trans. has been published, *Cities and Economic Development From the Dawn of History to the Present* (Chicago, 988).

large as one hectare of wheat. However, in order to estimate the surplus available which could be used to feed the towns, it would be necessary to have valid and comparable series of data relating to the productivity of labour in the production of these two cereals. Note also that both maize and potatoes in pre-Columbian civilizations yielded more food per unit of cultivated land than did wheat. I shall return to discuss the case of rice in Section 3.1.

The chapter falls into three parts. In the first and shortest, I summarize some results obtained in an econometric study of urbanization in developed countries during the nineteenth century, and concentrate on the factors I have mentioned above. In the second part I provide information on changes in crop yields during the nineteenth century, as well as on changes in agricultural productivity and transport costs. Finally, in the third and most important section, I attempt to assess the impact of each of these three variables on urbanization.

In order to make the analysis, especially one that relates to crop yields and agricultural productivity, more valid, we shall study a geographical area in Europe from which Russia and the United Kingdom have been excluded. I shall call this area the 'study region' and shall justify its parameters at the beginning of Section 2. By contrast, in Section 1 I shall include some areas outside Europe, including developed countries with the exception, for obvious reasons, of Japan.

1. The results of an econometric study

To some extent this chapter is the result of our awareness of both the strengths and the limitations of econometric analysis. Its strength lies in making it possible to take account of a number of different variables simultaneously; its limitations are due to the difficulty of isolating the influence of specific factors, and the need for a continuous series of statistical data which are suitable for this purpose.

The work of Gary Goertz in the Department of Economic History at the University of Geneva has been of great value here. His familiarity with the application of mathematical methods to the social sciences made it possible to carry out an econometric investigation of the factors which influenced urbanization in the developed countries (other than Japan) between 1800 and 1910.[2] Fourteen variables were used, including the productivity of agricultural labour, wheat imports, and the development of railway transport, and I shall summarize here our main conclusions and concentrate on these three factors and on Europe.

---

[2] P. Bairoch and G. Goertz, 'Factors of Urbanization in the Nineteenth Century Developed Countries: A Descriptive and Econometric Analysis', *Urban Studies*, 23: 4 (1986), 285–305.

We begin with the principal conclusions. Analysis showed that the totality of fourteen variables included in the study explained 94 per cent of the variation in the proportions of the urban population in twenty-two European countries. This figure was reduced to 87 per cent, when all twenty-six developed countries were included in the analysis. Secondly, economic variables, such as industrialization, income per head (excluding from this the effects of other factors), productivity of agricultural labour, and the importance of exports could explain the main differences between levels of urbanization.

A regression analysis showed, however, that the level of industrialization had a greater impact than the productivity of agricultural labour. It is one of the weaknesses of this type of analysis that it cannot demonstrate that an increase in the productivity of agricultural labour is a precondition for industrialization, and this is the justification for the type of analysis discussed in Sections 2 and 3 of this chapter. It should be noted, however, that if other countries with European populations are included in the econometric analysis the importance of the productivity of agricultural labour is increased.

As would be expected, there is also a fairly strong relation between the level of cereal imports and urbanization. The correlation coefficient between the level of urbanization and self-sufficiency in cereals comes to -0.55. This suggests that the more self-sufficient a country is in cereals, the smaller will be the proportion of its population who live in towns, or, to put it another way, the more a country depends on others for its cereals, the more urbanized it is likely to be. However, when we used multiple regression techniques, the importance of this factor diminishes.

Contrary to what we expected, the econometric analysis suggested that there is no significant relationship between the size of the railway network and urbanization. This, at first sight paradoxical, result can at least partially be explained by two considerations. First, the extension of the railway network was stimulated by international investment and has been relatively uniform, so that it tended not to be directly related to economic or urban factors. For example, in 1913, the size of the Latin American network per head of population was 63 per cent higher than that of Europe (excluding Russia). The development of railways was, of course, one major reason for the drop in transport costs, and this had stronger direct consequences on the siting than on the size of the populations of new towns. Secondly, the size of the railway network is not related linearly to the evolution of transport costs. Sometimes, a short line which links two water routes can have a much greater impact on costs than a longer one which follows the route of a river or canal. This suggests the need for different types of analysis (see Section 3.3).

2. Trends in crop yields, productivity of agricultural labour, and transport costs during the nineteenth century

Contrary to what might be expected, it was changes in the cost of transport that were largest during the nineteenth century. This does not, of course, imply that there were not also very important changes in agriculture. We shall consider trends in these three variables, all of which had an important impact on the development of towns, one at a time.

2.1 Crop yields

Changes in crop yields were not uniform throughout the developed world. Leaving aside national and micro-regional differences, we look in the first place at specific developments in countries outside Europe, inhabited mainly by populations of European origin, which played an increasing part in the supply of cereals.[3] In these countries, where land was plentiful, yields tended to be low and did not improve significantly during the nineteenth century. In the United States, the country for which statistics are most complete, wheat yields were in fact somewhat lower in 1913 (and even in 1939) than they had been at the beginning of the nineteenth century (between 8.5 and 9.5 quintals per hectare and 8.5 to 10.5 quintals per hectare respectively). These low yields did not prevent the rapid urbanization of regions in which the proportion of the population living in towns was low towards the beginning of the nineteenth century.

Developments in Europe were obviously different. Table 9.1 shows some statistics for the principal countries. In our study region which covers Europe, except for the United Kingdom and Russia,[4] it has been estimated that wheat yields were of the order of 8 quintals per hectare in about 1800, 8.7 quintals per hectare in about 1850, and 12.3 quintals per hectare in about 1910, i.e. the yield increased by between 50 and 60 per cent between 1800 and 1910, a rise of about 0.4 per cent per year. The rate of increase was relatively low (about 0.2 per cent per year) during the first half of the nineteenth century, but accelerated to 0.6 per cent per year between 1850 and 1913. When statistics for ten-year periods are considered, it is seen that this acceleration occurred mainly between 1880 and 1910; the 1870s were—probably for climatic

---

[3] The seven countries in this category are: Argentina, Australia, Canada, Chile, New Zealand, the United States, and Uruguay. All were countries with a temperate climate in which people of European origin came to predominate. Cereal exports from these seven countries were of the order of 1.2 m. tons per year in 1856–9; they reached 7.2 m. tons between 1878 and 1882, and 14.7 m. tons between 1898 and 1902. This led to a rapid decline in self-sufficiency in cereals, particularly in Western Europe. Cf. P. Bairoch, *Commerce extérieur et développement économique de l'Europe au xixe siècle* (Paris, 1976), 334.

[4] Russia was excluded because of her late development and also on account of her rapid population increase agricultural production (with low yields and low productivity) became relatively more important. The United Kingdom was excluded because of its early development.

Table 9.1 Yields of wheat (quintals per hectare) in Europe and some selected developed countries

	About 1800[a]	1848–52	1878–82	1908–12
Whole of Europe	6.9	7.4	7.5	9.4
Study region[b]	8.0	8.7	10.0	12.3
Germany	10.0	10.3	13.1	20.7
Belgium	13.5	14.3	15.8	25.1
United States	(10.0)	(9.9)	8.6	9.7
France	8.5	10.9	10.9	13.2
Italy	(7.3)	(7.0)	8.0	9.6
United Kingdom	13.6	17.5	16.7	21.4
Russia	(5.4)	(5.4)	(5.0)	6.6
Switzerland	11.0	13.0	—	21.4

[a] Approximate figures.
[b] Europe, except Russia and the United Kingdom.
Figures in parentheses are less reliable than others for the same period. The fact that these figures have been slightly rounded off does not imply a correspondingly small margin of error.

Source: P. Bairoch, *L'Agriculture des pays développés, 1800–1990. Productivité, production, facteurs de production et rendements agricoles* (Geneva, 1990).

reasons—a period of very low growth. Note also that yields increased more slowly during the period between the two World Wars; they only rose to 13.9 quintals per hectare during the period immediately preceding the Second World War (1934–8), whereas today they stand at 40.9 quintals per hectare.[5] The annual rate of growth between 1934–8 and 1982–6 has, therefore, risen to 2.3 per cent.

The growth in the yield of other cereals and of potatoes has been greater than that of wheat, and it can be estimated that between 1800 and 1910 the yield of all basic food crops increased by an amount of the order of 60 per cent, compared with an increase of between 50 and 60 per cent only for wheat. It is probable that other agricultural yields (viticulture, vegetables, oils, etc.) increased by similar amounts in aggregate. However, information on the yield of vegetables and oils is very rudimentary, and the yield of vines has fluctuated considerably over time.

In contrast, increases in the yield of animal products were even greater. Statistics that we have collected show that the mean annual production of milk per cow in Europe (outside Russia) was of the order of 900 litres in 1800, and 2,100 litres in 1910, an increase of 130 per cent.[6] Yields of meat products probably doubled during the same period.[7]

---

[5] FAO, *Annuaire des statistiques agricoles et alimentaires* (Rome, 1955), 21, and ibid. (Rome, 1983), 108–9. Also FAO, *Bulletin mensuel de statistique*, 6 (1987), 16. The data relate to practically the same area as our study region, i.e. Europe without the USSR, Poland, Great Britain, and Ireland.

[6] The variation here is very large. The minimum figure may be as low as 500–600 litres, the maximum 1900–2200 litres, a ratio of 3.8:1, compared with one of 2.5:1 for wheat. Cf. Bairoch, *L'Agriculture des pays développés* . . .

[7] Ibid.

If we attempt to combine these measures by calculating a weighted mean, we come to the conclusion that yields of agricultural foodstuffs increased by a figure of the order of between 75 and 80 per cent during these 110 years.

2.2 The productivity of agricultural labour

Estimates of the productivity of agricultural labour during the nineteenth century are—to the best of my knowledge—relatively rare, and the only published estimates that relate to a large group of countries so far are my own. Some twenty years ago, I first published estimates relating to eleven countries and six different periods between 1810 and 1910.[8] I have recently revised these estimates completely and have extended their geographical coverage to twenty-four countries and ten periods between 1800 and 1910.[9] I have also used improved methods and better data. It goes without saying that this work owes much to the improvement in agricultural and labour statistics in the different countries. The figures in Table 9.2 relate to the productivity in the production of foodcrops in agriculture. No allowance has been made for eventual changes in the annual number of days worked during the period. The figures are based on net rather than on gross agricultural product, i.e. seeds and food consumed by farm animals have been deducted. They are expressed in millions of calories per male agricultural worker. The omission of agricultural products other than foodstuffs makes very little difference, for industrial agriculture during the nineteenth century accounted for only about 1 or 2 per cent of total agricultural production.

[8] P. Bairoch, 'Niveaux de développement économique au xixe, siècle', *Annales E.S.C.*, 20:6 (1965), 1091–117.

[9] Bairoch, *L'Agriculture des pays développés* . . .

Table 9.2 Productivity of labour in the production of agricultural foodstuffs in Europe and some selected countries[a]

	About 1800[b]	1848–52	1878–82	1908–12
Whole of Europe	6.0	7.5	8.7	11.1
Study region[c]	5.6	7.5	9.9	14.0
Germany	6.5	10.4	16.0	30.6
Belgium	(7.0)	9.5	12.6	21.2
United States	15.4	22.8	35.0	47.0
France	6.5	11.0	13.7	17.6
Italy	(5.0)	(5.1)	5.4	6.8
United Kingdom	13.2	17.3	18.7	24.1
Russia	(5.6)	5.9	6.0	7.4
Switzerland	(5.8)	8.2	10.6	15.7

[a] The figures show the total production of agricultural foodstuffs expressed in millions of calories per male agricultural worker.
[b] Approximate figures.
[c] Europe, except Russia and the United Kingdom.
Figures in parentheses are less reliable than others for the same period. The fact that these figures have been slightly rounded off does not imply a correspondingly small margin of error.
Source: As in Table 9.1.

140 *Paul Bairoch*

The figures in Table 9.2 show that the productivity of agricultural labour increased much faster than did crop yields. In our study region productivity increased by 150 per cent between 1800 and 1910, equivalent to a growth rate of 0.8 per cent per year. Between 1800 and 1850 this rate was 0.6 per cent per year, compared with 0.9 per cent between 1850 and 1880 and over 1.2 per cent between 1880 and 1910. The lower rate of growth shown for the whole of Europe (less than 0.6 per cent per year between 1800 and 1910) is explained by the increasing importance of the Russian peasantry in the total. They amounted to about 30 per cent of the agricultural labour force in 1800 and 48 per cent in 1910.

2.3 Transport costs

Two series of data are given. The first is designed to show the levels of transport costs in Western societies at the beginning of the Industrial Revolution, expressed in kilograms of cereals per km./ton. The second series depicts changes in different types of transport costs during the nineteenth century. The study of transport costs is still in its infancy; for this reason, older studies, such as that by Avenel,[10] still retain their value.

We begin with the situation as it was before the changes caused by the Industrial Revolution, i.e. before 1730–50 in the United Kingdom, and before 1810–20 on the Continent of Europe. At that time transport costs were even less uniform than today. It is necessary to distinguish between the costs of land transport and transport by water, the second being much the cheaper. Even when the same type of transport is considered, there are differences that depend on distance, form of organization, and on security. Finally (and this does not exhaust all the variables), international comparisons between different traditional societies suggest that transport costs varied with the standard of living, because their most important component was the cost of labour.

We begin by considering land transport. The most expensive method was porterage. It is estimated that a man can move a load of between 35–40 kg. per day over a distance of 30–35 km. As this work demands considerable physical effort and requires numerous rest days for recuperation, wages seem to have been nearly double the minimum wage, which, in traditional societies, came to the equivalent of between 5 and 6 kg. of cereals per day.[11] On these assumptions we would arrive at an estimate of between 8.5 and 11.5 kg. of cereals per km./ton. Other estimates, in which lower performance figures, but also lower wages are used, yield similar results.

We mention these estimates to show that before the changes brought about

---

[10] G. d'Avenel, *L'Évolution des moyens de transport* (Paris, 1919).
[11] Some years ago I did some research on short-cut methods of estimating the gross national product per head. This suggested that the wage of an urban unskilled worker amounted to at least 6 or 7 kg. of cereals per day. Cf. P. Bairoch, 'Estimation du revenu national dans les sociétés occidentales pré-industrielles au xıxe siècle', *Revue économique*, 28:2 (1977), 177–208.

by the Industrial Revolution, progress made by the use of pack animals and wheeled transport did not result in a significant reduction of transport costs. Clark and Haswell have collected extensive data, relating mainly to developing countries,[12] which suggest that during the twentieth century the average cost of transport per km./ton expressed in kilograms of cereals amounted to 8.8 kg. for porters, 4.8 kg. for transport by pack animals, and 3.9 kg. for transport by cart. In these estimates we have in each case omitted four observations at the extreme end of the range in order to make the average more significant. However, even if traditional means of transport were used, the greater availability of cereals resulting from international trade resulted in an increase in the price expressed in cereals.

We have been able to use a number of rather diverse series to estimate the orders of magnitude of costs of different kinds of transport during the period immediately preceding the Industrial Revolution.[13] As regards transport by land, the average cost (including associated costs such as profit, wastage, etc.) turns out to have been about 4 or 5 kg. of cereals per km./ton. Water transport was considerably cheaper, but costs varied with the type of water transport used and were, therefore, much more variable than the costs of land transport. The estimated transport cost by river or canal was of the order of 0.9 kg. per km./ton; for sea transport (following the progress made in this type of transport in the Western world between the end of the fifteenth century and about 1750) the figure was between 0.3 and 0.4 kg. Transport by coaster was even cheaper, though the information available about this form of transport is even more scarce.

We next consider the reductions that were achieved during the nineteenth

---

[12] C. Clark and M. Haswell, *The Economics of Subsistence Agriculture* (London, 1970) 196–201.

[13] These estimates are based on sources which were used by Clark and Haswell or in my own earlier study (P. Bairoch, 'La Baisse des coûts de transports et le développement économique' *Revue de l'Institut de Sociologie*, 2 (1965), 307–32), or on studies published later. See particularly D. H. Aldcroft and W. J. Freeman (eds.), *Transport in the Industrial Revolution* (Manchester, 1983); P. S. Bagwell, *Transport Revolution from 1770* (London, 1974); J. Crofts, *Packhorse, Waggon and Posts* (London, 1967); J. Deloche, *La Circulation en Inde avant la révolution des transports*, 2 vols. (Paris, 1980); A. C. Leighton, *Transport and Communication in Early Mediaeval Europe AD 500–1100* (Newton Abbot, 1972); W. P. McGreevey, *An Economic History of Colombia, 1845–1930* (Cambridge, 1971); B. H. Meyer, *History of Transportation in the United States Before 1860* (Washington, 1917); L. Mottu-Weber, 'Contrats de voiture et comptes des blés et du sel. Contribution à l'étude des coûts de transports (1550–1630)', in P. Bairoch and A. M. Piuz (eds.), *Des Économies traditionnelles aux sociétés industrielles* (Geneva, 1985), 431–77; A. Rémond, *Études sur la circulation marchande en France aux xviiie et xixe siècles*, i. *Les prix des transports marchands de la révolution au premier empire* (Paris, 1956); D. Renouard, *Les transports de marchandises par fer, route et eau depuis 1850* (Paris, 1960); J. L. Ringwalt, *Development of Transportation Systems in the United States* (Philadelphia, 1888); C. White, 'The Impact of Russian Railway Construction for Grain in the 1860s and 1870s', in L. Symons and C. White (eds.), *Russian Transport. An Historical and Geographical Survey* (London, 1972), 1–45. It goes without saying that the costs of transport for provisioning any particular town will depend on its siting within the transport network. See the very interesting calculations by Lepetit on the accessibility of large French towns in 1835, B. Lepetit, *Chemins de terre et voies d'eau. Réseaux de transports et organisation de l'espace en France, 1740–1840* (Paris, 1984).

century. A number of studies have been published since I made my own estimate in 1976,[14] the results of which support my own figures. In the case of land transport, the real reduction in costs (taking the general movement of prices into account) was of the order of 15:1 if transport other than by railway was included. (In 1910 the cost of transport by railway waggon over long distances amounted to less than 0.1 kg. of cereals per km./ton, a reduction of 50:1 over previous levels.) The reduction in the cost of sea transport was of the order of 7:1. Reductions in the cost of river transport were lower, but the development of canals led to important changes and is estimated to have lowered the level to one-third of its previous value. As regards the coastal trade it is impossible to reach a definite conclusion. Overall, between 1800 and 1910, we estimate that the reduction in transport costs amounted to about 90 per cent, a reduction of the order of 10:1.

3. Attempts to measure the impact of higher yields, higher productivity, and lower transport costs on urbanization

As in the previous sections of this chapter, we begin by considering crop yields before discussing the impact of the other two variables. But before doing so, it will be useful to present some recently published data relating to the development of urbanization in Europe and in our study region, as well as in a number of other selected countries. The figures are shown in Table 9.3. As will be seen, any place with a population of 5,000 or more inhabitants is considered as 'urban' in the table. Although this criterion is arbitrary, it is the only one which is operationally available, and it is in any case appropriate to the conditions of the period.[15]

3.1 The effect of increased crop yields

To estimate the extent of the impact of increased crop yields on urbanization, other things being equal, we begin with a somewhat negative proposition. I have already shown in the preceding section that an increase in yields is not a necessary precondition for the development of towns. The best example of this is provided by the United States, a country in which cereal yields were actually declining during the nineteenth century, and where it seems likely that the yield of agriculture as a whole remained constant.[16] Moreover, the United States was not a country in which there was a deficit of agricultural products, indeed it had an excess, nor was it an export economy, for the

[14] Cf. Aldcroft and Freeman, *Transport in the Industrial Revolution*; P. K. O'Brien, *Railways and the Economic Development of Europe, 1830–1914* (Oxford, 1983). For my own estimate, cf. my *Commerce extérieur et développement économique*, 34–6.
[15] Cf. Bairoch, *De Jéricho à Mexico*, 281–6.
[16] During the 19th cent. the yield of wheat declined. (see Table 9.1). It remained stable for other cereals, particularly for maize. The yield of potatoes and animal products increased.

Table 9.3 Percentage of population urban[a] in Europe and some selected countries

	About 1800[c]	1848–52	1878–82	1908–12
Whole of Europe	10.9	15.8	23.5	32.8
Study region[b]	11.9	16.5	24.5	37.4
Germany	8.9	(15.0)	29.1	48.8
Belgium	20.5	33.5	43.1	56.6
United States	5.3	13.9	25.0	41.6
France	12.2	19.5	27.6	38.5
Italy	18.0	(23.0)	(28.0)	(40.0)
United Kingdom	19.2	39.6	56.2	69.2
Russia	5.9	(7.2)	10.6	14.3
Switzerland	7.0	11.9	20.4	37.1

[a] The urban population is defined as those living in agglomerations with 5,000 or more inhabitants.
[b] Europe, excluding Russia and the United Kingdom.
[c] Approximate figures.
Figures in parentheses are less reliable than others relating to the same period. The fact that these figures have been slightly rounded off does not imply a correspondingly small margin of error.
Source: Bairoch and Goertz, 'Factors of Urbanization'.

proportion of exports to gross domestic product during the nineteenth century was only one-third of the European average. In spite of the absence of an increase in crop yields, the expansion of towns in the United States was more rapid than in Europe. The proportion urban rose from 5.2 per cent in 1800 to 41.6 per cent in 1910. Our proposition must not, of course, be taken to mean that *ceteris paribus* increases in crop yields do not have a favourable impact on urbanization: the opposite is true.

To return to our study region, the increase in yields between 1800 and 1910 was of the order of 75 to 80 per cent. This figure could be called a gross increase, since it does not take any account of the need for seed. This exclusion of seed results in the estimated improvement in the yield being slightly higher than it would otherwise have been, but the difference is not significant in a large set of data. I would estimate that demand for seed accounted for 15.5 per cent of the wheat crop when the yield was 8 quintals per hectare (as in about 1800), and to 10.9 per cent when the yield was 12.3 quintals per hectare, as in 1910. The proportion needed for seed is lower for the other principal cereals, and much lower for maize and potatoes. I therefore estimate that the net gain was of the order of 83 to 88 per cent.

When the productivity of agricultural labour does not change, this increase in yields has no repercussions on urbanization, except in so far as it reduces the cultivated areas necessary for the provisioning of towns. This means a reduction in the cost of bringing the agricultural surplus to the towns and of moving manufactured goods, that originate in the towns, into the country. The situation remains the same, even if one of the principal objects of raising crop yields is to increase the productivity of agricultural labour. My estimate, of course, can only provide a very rough and approximate figure which gives an indication of the theoretical order of magnitude. This approach is similar to what are called 'direct social savings', i.e. the direct gain in economic resources that results from technological progress. This method of analysis was first employed by Robert Fogel in his studies of the development of railways in the United States.[17]

We shall need to define or recall a number of parameters for our study region which will make it possible to construct estimates. We have already seen that 11.9 per cent of the population were classified as urban. We have calculated the mean population density by excluding from our region some very thinly populated areas, particularly those situated in the north of Scandinavia.[18] These calculations yielded a mean density of 36 persons per square km. The average population of towns has been taken to be 10,000.[19]

By using these parameters we obtained a unit consisting of 'town and associated countryside' with a total population of 84,030 persons (of whom 10,000 lived in the town) and an area of 2,330 square km. The optimum configuration would be a perfectly circular and completely homogeneous area, with the town situated at the centre of the circle. This would mean that the maximum distance from the centre would be equal to the circle's radius, or 27.3 km. However, even if this optimum spatial configuration were used, the average length of journey from town to countryside, or conversely, would exceed half the radius, because the largest part of the territory is situated near the periphery. Mathematically, the mean distance will be the radius of the circle divided by $\sqrt{2}$, or 19.3 km. In practice, the configurations of many units will not be optimal, but, on the other hand, the spatial distribution of cultivated land may be such that the length of the journey would be optimized.[20] For these reasons our model probably does not differ from reality by more than 20 to 30 per cent.

When crop yields increase by between 83 and 88 per cent, the area of

---

[17] R. W. Fogel, *Railroads and American Economic Growth: Essays in Econometric History* (Baltimore, 1964).

[18] I have excluded all regions in the different countries, where the population density in about 1905 was below five persons per sq. km. This information was taken from G. Sundbärg, *Aperçus statistiques internationaux* (Stockholm, 1908). In this work, the author divides Europe (excluding Russia and the United Kingdom) into some 350 regions or districts.

[19] Clearly the concept of average size of a town is arbitrary and will depend on the criteria used to define a town. If we use a statistical definition which regards an agglomeration of more than 2,000 persons as a town, the mean populations of towns in Europe (outside Russia) in about 1800 was 7,500. If the minimum were taken as 5,000 inhabitants, the mean increases to 16,700. Cf. Bairoch, *De Jéricho à Mexico*, 296.

[20] The study of the spatial distribution of agricultural production in the neighbourhood of towns has been an interest of geographers for a long time. A pioneer was J. H. von Thünen, *Die isolierte Stadt in Beziehung auf Landwirtschaft und Nationalökonomie* (Hamburg, 1826). He suggested that land use outside towns could be characterized by a series of concentric circles, specializing in particular forms of production, depending on their distance from the town. The first was devoted to intensive agriculture, market gardening, and intensive rearing for milk production. The last was used mainly for animal husbandry, as the cost of transporting live animals is very low. For a discussion of developments following von Thünen's law, cf. A. Bailly and H. Béguin, *Introduction à la géographie humaine* (Paris, 1982), 101–8; P. Haggett, *L'Analyse spatiale en géographie humaine* (Paris, 1973), 189–206; P. Merlin, *Méthodes quantitatives et espace urbain* (Paris, 1973), 132–40.

cultivated land on which a town is dependent will be reduced to some 1,260 square km., which would imply a radius of 20 km. and a mean distance of 14.1 square km., a gain of 5.2 km. compared with the previous situation. Each of the 10,000 urban inhabitants is estimated to consume some 500 kg. of agricultural products (excluding timber) produced in the country,[21] and each of the 74,030 country dwellers will consume some 8 to 9 kg. of manufactured products originating in the town.[22] On these assumptions, improvements in yields will result in a reduction of 29,300 km./tons of movement, of which only 3,300 are accounted for by the transport of manufactured products.

We have seen in Section 3.3 that at the beginning of the nineteenth century, as in previous centuries, the cost of moving a ton over a distance of 1 km. by land was equivalent to between 4 and 5 kg. of cereals, and that of transporting the same amount over the same distance by water was 0.9 kg. In practice, attempts were always made to optimize returns by using water transport as much as possible. But this meant that the distance over which the products were moved, both by land and especially by water, was longer. We therefore estimate that the average cost of transporting one ton of products over a distance of 1 km. by road or river was equivalent to 3 kg. of cereals. The reduction in the average distance over which goods were moved, that resulted from increased crop yields, would reduce the cost of transport by some 88 tons of cereals, a quantity sufficient to feed 290 people. This figure is reduced to 230 when account is taken of the higher costs of non-cereal foods. These 230 additional people would raise the percentage urban by 0.3 percentage points from 11.9 to 12.2 per cent, compared with an observed value of 37.4 per cent (Table 9.3). In other words, the absolute number of city dwellers would rise by 2.3 per cent.

Our estimate takes no account of the cost of transporting fuel to the town. Though this is not properly an agricultural product, it is closely related to agriculture and must, therefore, be considered. It has been estimated that in pre-industrial Europe each city dweller consumed between 1.0 and 1.6 tons of firewood each year.[23] It is not, therefore, unreasonable to suggest that a reduction in the area used for agricultural production would imply a parallel reduction in the distance of the area used for the production of firewood. However, the cost of transporting firewood is lower than that of transporting

---

[21] Thus in France, which may be taken as representative of our study region, we can estimate from the data collected by J. Toutain, *La Consommation alimentaire en France de 1789 à 1964*, Cahiers de l'ISEA, 5:11 (Nov. 1971), that the average consumption per head in about 1800 was 400 kg. (net weight). Taking account of gross weight which was used in moving some of these products to the towns, a figure of 500 kg. appears reasonable.

[22] I have estimated (P. Bairoch, 'International Industrialization Levels from 1750 to 1980', *Journal of European Economic History*, 2:11 (1982), 269–333) that at the beginning of the Industrial Revolution the average consumption of manufactured goods in European traditional societies was of the order of 9 kg. per head, of which 2.5 kg. were textiles and 3.1 kg. metal products.

[23] P. Bairoch, *Production et Consommation d'énergie des sociétés traditionnelles du xviiie siècle au monde actuel* (forthcoming).

agricultural products. Because the value of firewood is lower, the risk of damage smaller, and the need for rapid deliveries less urgent, firewood generally came from areas where water transport could be used. We therefore estimate that the cost of transporting firewood was of the order of 0.9 kg. of cereals per km./ton. This would result in a gain of some 48 tons of cereals and permit an additional 125 city dwellers or 1.3 per cent of the total, and raise the proportion urban by 0.1 percentage points. Altogether, therefore, improved yields would raise the proportion of the population living in towns from 11.9 to 12.3 per cent, or raise the total numbers living in cities by 3.6 per cent, an amount which is not insignificant.

Before presenting the results of a brief statistical exercise, I return for a moment to the case mentioned at the beginning of this chapter: the difference between agricultural systems based on rice and those based on wheat. As we have seen, in terms of net yields rice implies an advantage of some 125 per cent compared with wheat. On the assumption that there are no significant differences in the yields of other agricultural products, rice-based systems would have an advantage of 140 to 150 per cent over those based on wheat. In our study region, this would mean that there would be a gain of some 7 km. in the distance over which goods had to be moved, which would allow an additional 320 town dwellers to be fed. If we were to include firewood in these calculations (but assume a lower consumption), the figure is increased to 420, which would raise the proportion of the population urban by 0.4 percentage points, i.e. from 11.9 to 12.3 per cent. Again, this is not an insignificant increase, particularly in the context of traditional societies, where in the absence of agricultural imports, the maximum possible proportion of the population that could live in towns (with a criterion of 5,000 inhabitants for a town) was of the order of between 13 and 15 per cent.

The impact of higher crop yields on the sizes of towns is even greater and deserves mention, even though it is not the main focus of this paper. We return to this subject in Section 3.3 where we consider the effects of a reduction in transport costs.

Since we did not include crop yields in our econometric analysis, because complete series of decennial data were not available, I have, as a matter of interest, calculated correlation coefficients between the proportion of the population living in towns and wheat yields in nineteen European countries at three points in time: 1800, 1850, and 1910. The values came to 0.55, 0.67, and 0.62 respectively. Thus the correlations were positive, but neither very large nor statistically very significant. If Italy and Spain were excluded from these calculations, because their urban systems in the past were largely based on commerce, the values of the correlations would rise to 0.69, 0.77, and 0.65.

3.2 The effect of increased productivity of agricultural labour

To estimate the possible effects of increases in the productivity of agricultural labour on urbanization is at the same time more simple and more complex than to estimate the effects of increased crop yields. It is simpler because the calculations are relatively easy; more complex because more theoretical assumptions are needed. It should be remembered that our calculations are based on a *ceteris paribus* assumption. When this assumption is applied to the estimation of labour productivity, three further and somewhat unrealistic hypotheses are needed. To mention them in decreasing order of importance, the first postulates that there is no increase in the consumption of foodstuffs per head either in the town or in the countryside. The second hypothesis is that crop yields are constant. This would imply a significant increase in the amount of cultivated land, an increase which is feasible in overseas countries with populations of European stock, but not in our study region. An increase in the area of cultivated land would, of course, also raise the average cost of transport. The third unrealistic hypothesis is that the number of workers in agriculture remains constant at a time when their productivity is rapidly increasing.

Consider the first hypothesis that people in the countryside do not increase their consumption of foodstuffs, but exchange their larger surplus for goods and services that are produced in the town, where the town dwellers will not increase their food consumption either. An increase of 150 per cent in the productivity of agricultural labour would then make it possible for the proportion of the population living in towns to increase from 11.9 per cent in about 1800 to an estimated 64.8 per cent by 1910. It will be recalled that the actual proportion of the urban population in 1910 was 37.4 per cent.

Given that the assumption underlying our estimate is *inter alia* one of unchanged food consumption by town dwellers and country dwellers alike and that there is an implicit assumption that the economic system is closed, it is to be expected that our estimate would be larger than the actual increase in urbanization. Of course, our study region was not a closed economy; in fact the opposite was true. During the period studied, reliance on imports of foodstuffs and agricultural products in general increased. Our calculations show that whilst our study region was self-sufficient in cereals until the beginning of the 1860s, by 1910 nearly 13 per cent of its consumption consisted of imports, a figure which was equivalent to 15 per cent of its total production of cereals. To this, we must add imports of other agricultural products, such as meat and tropical products, as well as other primary commodities of agricultural origin, such as cotton and wool. Altogether, imports of agricultural products in 1910 could have amounted to almost 20 per cent of domestic production. If imports had been included in our calculations, the theoretical proportion of the population living in towns would have risen to 76.8 per cent, an even larger difference from the observed proportion of 37.4 per cent.

We must, therefore, refine our analysis in order to incorporate the most important factor: the increase in the consumption of foodstuffs. Quantification of the second factor, the decline in the agricultural labour force, is less important given the rapid increase in the total population of our study region.

I have used the information collected by J. C. Toutain for France,[24] to estimate the order of magnitude of the increase in food consumption. Not only is France reasonably representative of the countries of our study region; similar information is lacking for other countries. By converting animal into vegetable calories we reach a figure of 85 per cent for the estimated increase in food consumption between 1800 and 1910. Incorporating this figure into our estimate of the rise in agricultural productivity suggests that the proportion of the population in our study region who lived in towns could have increased from 11.9 per cent in 1800 to about 35.8 per cent in 1910. Recall that the proportion actually observed was 37.4 per cent, and that previously estimated was 76.8 per cent.

Thus this exercise confirms that improvements in the productivity of agricultural labour played an important part in the increase in urbanization. Moreover, a simple deduction would show that in a closed economy in which the level of food consumption is similar to that found in traditional societies, the proportion of town dwellers cannot be increased significantly without an increase in the surplus of food in the countryside. The only way of achieving such an increase is through an increase in the productivity of agricultural labour.

3.3 The effect of reduced transport costs

In the study of urban phenomena transport has played an important part for a long time. However, the main emphasis in the study of transport was put on location. In addition to Kohl's study published in 1841,[25] we must refer to the more systematic analyses of the geographers Ratzel and Cooley.[26] Like Kohl, Ratzel assigns an important part to transport, but he provides a more precise analysis of the factors which have determined the siting of towns. According to him, towns are established or grow, provided they are situated at either end of a transport route, the junction of two transport routes of the same type, or the junction of two transport routes of different types. Three years after the publication of Ratzel's work, Cooley advanced his theory which has some points in common with Ratzel's. Cooley suggested that population and resources tended to accumulate at points where there was a break in the means of transport. These theories were later extended, but their basic principles continued to be regarded as valid: the important factor that influenced the siting of towns was transport routes. This held true of towns in traditional societies, as well as of those which grew after the Industrial Revolution.

[24] Toutain, *La Consommation alimentaire*.
[25] J. G. Kohl, *Der Verkehr und die Ansiedlungen der Menschen in ihrer Abhängigkeit von der Gestaltung der Erdoberfläche* (Leipzig, 1841).
[26] F. Ratzel, *Anthropogeographie*, ii. *Die geographische Verbreitung des Menschen* (Stuttgart, 1891); C. H. Cooley, 'The Theory of Transportation', *Publications of the American Association*, IX. (1894), 1–148.

However, our problem is quite different. We are concerned with estimating the effect of a reduction in transport costs on urbanization during the nineteenth century, other things being equal. The reduction in transport costs can be estimated fairly easily by studying the factors noted in Section 3.1 on crop yields. At the beginning of our period the mean distance over which goods had to be transported between country and town was 19.3 km. This implied a need for the transport of agricultural products equivalent to 109,000 km./tons, the cost of which was equivalent to 325 tons of cereals. In Section 2.3 I suggested that transport costs were reduced by 90 per cent during our period. This is equivalent to 300 tons of cereals, sufficient to maintain an additional 800 town dwellers (or more than 8 per cent of the original population of towns). This would increase the proportion urban by one percentage point, in our case from 11.9 to 12.9 per cent. This is double the increase that was attributed to changes in crop yields.

Although this point is marginal to our present discussion, we may note that the reduction in transport costs played a predominant part in the possibility of very large towns emerging. Before the Industrial Revolution, the largest town in the world certainly did not exceed two million inhabitants, and probably contained no more than one and a half million. It is unlikely that there ever existed in the world more than one city with one million inhabitants at the same time. However, since 1860 London has contained more than three million inhabitants, and its population exceeded ten million before 1910. Before the outbreak of the First World War, there were altogether eight cities in the developed world with more than one million inhabitants.[27] Given the conditions prevailing in our study region, a city with a population of ten million inhabitants would have needed an area of cultivated land extending over 2.33 million square km. to sustain it, an area four times that of France, six times that of Japan, and fifty-six times that of Switzerland. On the most favourable assumptions, the mean distance over which food would have to be transported to sustain this city would have come to 610 km. Therefore, it was impossible for such cities to exist before the reduction in transport costs which was brought about by progress during the Industrial Revolution.

4. Omissions and simplification: an inventory in the form of a conclusion

As was to be expected, of the three factors that we considered, the productivity of agricultural labour turned out to be the variable with the most important effect on urbanization. Progress in this area between 1800 and 1910 would have been sufficient by itself to make possible the increase in the proportion of the population living in towns that was experienced in Europe. The next most important factor was the reduction in transport costs: the

[27] Cf. Bairoch, *De Jéricho à Mexico*.

effects of this factor were twice as important as those brought about by increased crop yields. Thus, together, these three factors played an extremely important part in the process of urbanization during this period.

In our analysis we were forced to use a much simpler economic and social model of the process of modern economic and social development than reality. In order to make our model operational, we were forced to omit a number of factors which help in explaining the process of urbanization and we also had to leave out of account some of the mechanisms of operation of the three factors that we did consider. Thus in the following paragraphs I will give a schematic and incomplete inventory of the factors that have been omitted and the simplifications that have been used.

The list of factors that could help explain the process of urbanization is very lengthy, even if the three factors used in the present study were omitted. In our econometric analysis we used the following thirteen additional variables besides the productivity of agricultural labour:[28] gross national product per head, the level of industrialization, the form taken by industrialization, export rates, imports of cereals, international migration, population density, population size, the date when modernization began, the proportion of the population living in towns before modernization, the form of government, topography, and the importance of railways in the economy. Without attempting to be exhaustive, the following could be added to this list: mineral resources, the attitude of the dominant culture to cities, climate, the importance of navigable waterways, the politics of the redistribution of income, the quality of agricultural land, the nature of exports, the forms of consumption, etc.

The main simplifications introduced into our analysis of the three factors are as follows: we begin with transport costs, but the simplifications also apply to our study of crop yields. We neglected the possibility that the goods might have been transported by the farmers themselves with their own means of transport during periods when they were not busy in the fields. But, even in this case, a reduction in the distance over which the goods had to be transported could have been valued in terms of purely agricultural activities. In the study of crop yields, we did not take any account of the effect of a reduction in transport costs on regional specialization of agricultural activities. Such specialization could have had a positive effect on crop yields and, indeed, in many cases also on the productivity of agricultural labour. Moreover, if population density were affected by yields, the type of diet is also an important factor: a diet that contains relatively little meat makes higher population densities possible. We also neglected the effect of differences between the diets of town and country dwellers as regards quantity, quality, and structure, and the effect of such differences on crop yields and agricultural productivity. Finally, and even this does not exhaust all

[28] Cf. Bairoch and Goertz, 'Factors of Urbanization'.

the possibilities, in our model we assumed that the average population of towns did not change.

The interactions between the city and the countryside, and especially between agriculture and industry, were even more important. Technology that was developed in the towns played an important part in raising crop yields and productivity in the country. We need only mention the introduction of chemical fertilizers and agricultural machinery. Moreover, we cannot neglect the rural components of these changes, especially the development of agricultural machines during the second agricultural revolution, particularly harvesters. The mechanization of the textile industry increased the productivity of agricultural labour by removing textile production from the countryside. This led to an increase in the quantity of labour which could be used on the most productive farms, and to a reduction in the number of less productive farms. On its side, agricultural demand stimulated the modernization of industry. Thus, fundamental changes in the method of producing iron during the beginning of the nineteenth century owed much to the rural demand for agricultural implements and tools and for other consumption goods, demand for which was increased by agricultural progress.

Other aspects that could be mentioned would take us beyond the confines of this chapter. At the beginning I pointed to some of the limitations of econometric methods of analysis, but it is clear that the more traditional method also has limitations. Both approaches are necessary and will prove to be mutually enriching.

10 Migration into and out of the Danish City of Odense

HANS CHRISTIAN JOHANSEN
Department of Economic History, University of Odense, Odense, Denmark

In most countries the direct registration of migration started much later than the registration of births, deaths, and marriages. Studies of migration in earlier centuries must, therefore, make use of indirect measures. The information most commonly used is information on birthplace, collected in censuses (this is not normally available for periods preceding the middle of the nineteenth century), or the difference between actual population growth between censuses and the excess of births over deaths during the same period.

Both these measures are subject to serious limitations. The former records only two areas—birthplace and place of actual residence—in what could be a long chain of migratory movements. The second measure only yields net migration, which may differ considerably from the gross figures, and the net figures are very sensitive to even small errors in the basic data.

Thus, in any attempt to discover more about gross migration during periods before direct registration started, it is necessary to begin at the micro-level and look at individual life histories which give information about changes in place of residence, or, if this is impossible, to study the extent to which people are 'lost' from different areas over time. The following exercise is an example of this type of analysis in which material relating to the city of Odense—a city which until the late nineteenth century was the largest Danish provincial city—will be used.[1]

1. Sources

Parish registers exist for all city parishes in Denmark from 1706 and are of good quality. Census-taking began in 1769. The first census contains only the names of heads of households; other members are mentioned only by their

---
[1] The 18-cent. material is taken from the parish registers, census schedules, tax lists, guild information on apprentices, journeymen, and masters, municipal lists of trade licences, lists of those in receipt of poor relief, and probate records. Cf. H. C. Johansen, *Næring og bystyre, Odense, 1700–1789* (Odense, 1983). The machine-readable version of the Census of 1850 was prepared by Poul Thestrup, of the Fünen provincial archives, Odense.

status, sex, and age, so that family members can normally be identified by family reconstitution. In the later censuses of 1787, 1801, 1834, 1840, and thereafter at five- or ten-year intervals, the names and occupations of all individuals are listed, together with their relation to the head of household, age, and civil status. From 1845 onwards place of birth, and, later in the century, date of birth, are also given, as is year of marriage and year of migration to the city. It is normally assumed that all censuses from 1787 onwards are complete, though in the first censuses ages may be incorrect by one or two years. In 1812, the clergy were ordered to keep registers of in-migrants and out-migrants for their parishes. The government's principal aim was to control the movement of servants, but the system did not work well even for that section of the population, and, especially in the cities, we have little or no information about the way in which these registers were kept. An efficient registration system which covered all movements was not established until 1924.

However, a sample study of the population—such as is described below—requires more than parish register material and census enumerations. Even in a relatively small city, the number of registrations is so large that use of the original sources would take too much time and leave the possibility of errors, when information about individuals is sought. It is very helpful if alphabetical indices to the sources are kept, or if the material is in computer-readable form.

In Odense, data exist with complete demographic information for the period 1741–90, sorted by families and individuals. There is also a machine-readable version of the Census of 1850, and in the provincial archives there are alphabetical indices to the Census of 1845, the marriage registers for the years 1720–1891, and to persons who have died after their fifteenth birthday during the same period.

The existence of this material makes it easier to study developments between the period 1740–90 and the middle of the nineteenth century. However, before deciding which method to use, it is worth looking at the general demographic history of the city over a longer period.

2. Odense in the eighteenth and nineteenth centuries

In the first Census of 1769, 5,209 people were enumerated in Odense. However, the true population was larger by between 100 and 200 persons since enumerators were instructed not to count mercenaries living in the town, so that enemies should be unable to obtain information from the figures about the true strength of the Danish army. At the next census, in 1787, 5,536 persons were enumerated, a very modest rate of growth over a period of eighteen years. The numbers of births recorded in the parish registers indicate that the size of the population had been roughly constant since the early eighteenth century, and it is also interesting to note that the number of houses in the city had remained nearly the same. Economically, there seems to have been some progress until about 1760, but after that year a period of stagnation, or even of decline, set in. The principal reason was probably that during that period economic development in Denmark was concentrated either in the capital or in agriculture, and little, if any, of the additional purchasing power generated reached Odense, with its unfavourable situation at the head of a shallow firth. The expansion of grain exports from agriculture and of overseas trade with the colonies took place in other cities in which port facilities were better.

About the end of the century, a canal was dug from the northern suburbs to the deep sea, and this ended the period of stagnation. Between 1801 and 1850 the population doubled to 11,122. Growth began during the first ten years of the nineteenth century, but, according to the birth figures, seems to have been fastest during the 1820s. The prime factor responsible for this expansion was commerce, but there was also some growth in handicrafts.

The second half of the nineteenth century was a period of continued growth, and the city became industrialized. In 1901 the number of inhabitants was 40,138, and Odense contained the largest number of industrial workers of any Danish city outside Copenhagen. Large-scale production was particularly marked in the textile and engineering industries. Growth was fastest during the final two decades of the century.

In order to obtain a more detailed picture, the increase will first be split into natural increase and migration. This separation is shown in Table 10.1. The most remarkable development is seen in natural increase. During the eighteenth century, numbers of births and deaths remained nearly constant. In normal years births would exceed deaths, but frequently there were years of high mortality which tended to wipe out the increase (see Fig. 10.1).

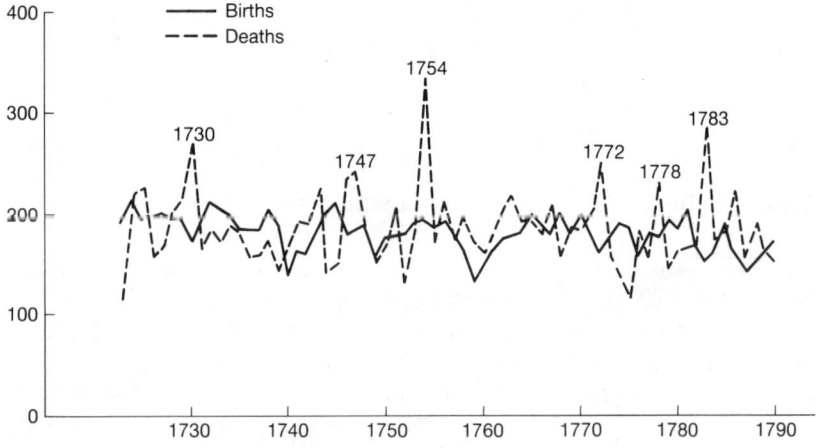

Figure 10.1. Births and deaths in Odense, 1723–90

After the turn of the century, there were few bad years—1814 was the last year in which deaths were more numerous than births—and the general level of mortality began to fall, with a resulting substantial increase in total numbers. The contribution made by migration was more volatile. During the eighteenth century, net migration was close to zero; during the nineteenth century it was—not unexpectedly—largest during those decades when population grew most rapidly, but it played a minor part during intervening periods.

However, these figures tell us nothing about either in-migration or out-migration, and in order to throw some light on this situation, we shall use a different approach.

3. Out-migration from Odense

People leaving Odense could have been born in the city or been in-migrants. The former group can be identified from studies of cohorts of children born in

Table 10.1 The population of Odense, 1720–1901

Period	Population growth	Natural increase	Boundary changes	Net migration	Annual growth %	Natural increase per 1,000	Net migration per 1,000
1720–87	0	−219	—	(219)	0	−0.6	(0.6)
1787–1801	419	−119	—	538	0.5	−1.5	6.9
1801–40	3,416	1,950	—	1,466	1.2	6.7	5.0
1840–60	5,057	2,561	—	2,496	2.2	10.9	10.6
1860–80	6,549	3,933	1,766	850	1.9	11.2	2.4
1880–1901	19,334	9,407	1,000	8,927	3.2	14.7	14.0

Until 1850, the administrative area for the census population was somewhat smaller than that covered by the parish registers.

Odense. We shall trace what happened to three cohorts: one born during the period of stagnation in the eighteenth century, one born during the period of early growth during the first half of the nineteenth century, and a third from the period of industrialization.

The nature of the sources would suggest that the first cohort should be chosen from the early part of the period 1741–90. However, 1754 was the year with the highest mortality during the eighteenth century, because of an epidemic of smallpox, and if a birth cohort were chosen from an earlier period, it would have been subject to high and untypical death rates. I have, therefore, chosen the cohort of children born in 1757–9, and have studied it for the years up to 1787, when the children were 30 years old and had passed the age at which migration rates were highest. The census of that year makes it possible to determine how many of them were still living in Odense at the time.

Similar studies were made of children born in 1821, who were followed up to the Census of 1850, and for those born in 1872, for whom the Census of 1901 marks the terminal stage. For the last cohort, all the linkages were made manually.

The overall results are shown in Table 10.2. The periods of observation for each cohort have been divided into two, as it proved possible to find a status list for each of them at the time of transition from childhood to youth. For the first cohort, this point is the Census of 1769, when the children were on average 11 years old, for the other two cohorts I used the age at confirmation which normally took place when the children were 14 years old.

Table 10.2 Experience of three birth cohorts in Odense during the eighteenth and nineteenth centuries

Cohort	1757–9		1821		1872	
	Boys	Girls	Boys	Girls	Boys	Girls
Total number	238	241	131	130	334	313
Percentage who						
Died in Odense in childhood	45	40	22	12	28	29
Moved as children	22	24	21	21	22	21
Resided in Odense at end of childhood	33	36	57	67	50	50
Died in Odense in youth	3	1	3	2	4	2
Moved away as young people	19	20	42	47	34	32
Resided in Odense at age 29	11	15	12	18	12	16

A first index of the ability of the city to provide its native inhabitants with a living is given by the proportion of members of each cohort who remained living in the city at the age of 29. This percentage has remained almost constant over time, ranging from 11 to 12 per cent among young men, and 15 to 18 per cent for young women. The objection might be raised that 29 is not a suitable age for this purpose, since travelling journeymen might marry and settle later in their lives, but comparisons of the alphabetical lists with the death registers for the two oldest cohorts show that practically no one who had disappeared from the list by the age of 29 was buried in the city at a later date: on the contrary, there appears to have been some more out-migration at later ages. It would, therefore, seem that the effect of stagnation or growth was not very important in determining the possibility of making a living in one's native town.

The differences become apparent when we look at the fate of those who disappeared from the sample. During childhood, the largest difference is found in mortality. The first cohort exhibits the characteristically high childhood mortality of the eighteenth century, both in infancy and at slightly older ages, and comparisons with rural mortality rates show that there was an excess mortality of nearly 50 per cent in the town.

The mortality figures for the second cohort are almost incredibly low. However, mortality was very low during the 1820s, probably as a result of low food prices and the introduction of compulsory vaccination against smallpox.

Members of this cohort were in their childhood during years when the number of births was increasing and that of deaths falling (see Table 10.3). Another possible explanation of the low mortality is that illegitimacy was highest in this cohort, and many unmarried mothers left the city immediately after giving birth, so that some of the members of this cohort who died as infants will have been among the out-migrants, and their deaths registered in parishes outside Odense. Even so, the number of children who appear in the confirmation lists is high. Mortality of the third cohort returns to the expected pattern of the late nineteenth century.

Table 10.3 Births and deaths in Odense, 1810–1839

Period	Births	Deaths	Difference	Ratio
1810–14	1,015	1,006	9	1.01
1815–19	1,115	892	223	1.25
1820–4	1,291	991	300	1.30
1825–9	1,438	943	495	1.52
1830–4	1,419	1,095	324	1.30
1835–9	1,484	1,158	326	1.28

The proportion of those who moved out of Odense during their childhood remains relatively constant in the three cohorts. The net result of the two factors is that there existed considerable differences between the proportions of children in the three cohorts who remained in Odense at the end of their childhood.

After childhood, the largest differences between the cohorts are found in the out-migration patterns. In general, the larger the proportion of children who survived childhood in the city, the larger was the proportion of those who left later during their lives. This resulted in constant proportions of those who remained in the city at the end of their youth. It would be natural to conclude from these figures that out-migration was due to a 'push' effect—the city could only provide an acceptable livelihood for a proportion of the children who were born there. The surplus, whether large or small, had to emigrate.

A more detailed analysis is possible for each of the cohorts. The number of births between 1757 and 1759 amounted to about 3 per cent of the total population, and if some 40 to 50 per cent of them emigrated, this would mean an annual out-migration of 1.5 per cent, or some 75 persons per year. However, a capitation tax list for 1787, which was brought up to date each month, shows that some 300 persons left the town during that year. The majority of out-migrants must, therefore, have been people who had stayed in Odense for only a short time and who had been born outside the city. Total annual out-migration can be estimated on this basis as amounting to about 6 per cent of the total population, i.e. only slightly less than during the 1960s and 1970s.

There is no direct information about the destinations of these migrants. The best evidence can be found in the ledgers of the Probate Court, which mention the place of residence of the children of deceased persons. The parents of many of the children born in 1757–9 died during the 1780s, and in Table 10.4 we see the distribution of their places of residence taken from these ledgers. Typically, migration was over a short distance only, particularly for girls. The most favoured new places of residence seem to have been the surrounding country districts, Copenhagen, and the city of Flensburg in the duchies of Schleswig-Holstein. Only a few went abroad, or to the Danish colonies overseas. It must be remembered that the records only relate to children whose parents remained in Odense. Those who migrated as children generally left with their parents, and their migration pattern could easily have been different from the rest.

Table 10.4 Place of residence outside Odense of children mentioned in probate proceedings in Odense in the 1780s

Place of residence	Sons	Daughters
Fünen outside Odense	35	43
Copenhagen	15	22
Others on the islands	18	10
Jutland	12	4
Duchies	7	10
Norway	2	2
Germany	4	1
Other	3[a]	1[b]
Unknown	7	2
Total	103	95

[a] Frederiksnagor in India, St Croix in the Danish West Indies, and Paris.
[b] Amsterdam.

There is less information for the cohort of 1821. A larger proportion of them migrated, but, as the population was growing, their number in relation to the total population of Odense during the period up to 1850 is almost the same as for the first cohort. We have no direct information about the number of earlier in-migrants who re-migrated during this period, but comparisons at the micro-level between the populations enumerated in the censuses of 1845 and 1850 indicate that total out-migration still exceeded the number of native born, probably by the same amount as in the eighteenth century.

Little is known about the destinations of out-migrants between 1821 and 1850. The probate ledgers are too incomplete and do not provide the same information as in the eighteenth century. A record of the issue of the municipal passports provided for inland travellers and the birthplaces mentioned in the Census of 1850 for areas outside Odense suggest that the migration pattern was similar to that for the earlier period.

More than half the children of the 1872 cohort migrated. However, the city was growing so rapidly that, in relation to the total population, the annual number of out-migrating citizens during the years 1872 to 1901 dropped to less than 1 per cent. From our knowledge of in-migration and of net in-migration, we can estimate total out-migration as about 8 per cent, a little higher than during previous periods. Those members of the 1872 cohort who migrated tended to move further afield than their predecessors. They lived during a period when overseas migration became important. About 1,700 persons went from Odense to the United States between 1872 and 1901, among them some members of our cohort. Other out-migrants still moved over short distances to other places in Fünen. Many went to Copenhagen which was growing very rapidly during this period, but Flensburg had lost its importance as a destination, since it had become part of Germany following the Danish defeat in the war of 1864.

4. Out-migration patterns of different social groups

Micro-level information makes it possible to determine whether migrants were or were not representative of the native-born population. In Table 10.5, we see the distribution of migrants by the occupations of their fathers. Though this is not an ideal criterion to use, given the available sources, it is the best we have.

The trend is not too clear, since migration was high in all social groups, but in general the migration rate was highest among illegitimate children, and lowest among those from well-off families. The findings can be elaborated a little further. Among the lower social groups, a higher proportion of those who left did so during their childhood. In the higher social groups the typical pattern was for a son to complete part of his education before he left Odense.

Table 10.5 Social distribution of migrants in three Odense cohorts

Date of birth	Migrants as a percentage of survivors							
	Illegitimate children		Unskilled workers		Skilled and white-collar		Others[a]	
	M	F	M	F	M	F	M	F
1757–9	90	87	86	70	74	70	74	77
1821	91	89	83	89	70	94	84	62
1872	100	89	91	74	77	76	79	73

[a] Mainly master artisans and upper social groups.

Sons of master artisans are normally found in the apprentice ledgers of one of the local guilds, and after they produced the test pieces which marked the end of their apprenticeships they would leave the city at about the age of 20 for some years to earn their livings as travelling journeymen in different workshops throughout northern and central Europe. Their final place of settlement was a matter of chance. A man might fall in love with the daughter of one of his masters, or he might return to Odense to take over his father's workshop. In such cases the 'push' effect was much weaker than for members of the lower social groups. The travelling period was considered to be a continuation of the apprentice years. Much the same considerations applied to sons who went to the grammar school and who, between the ages of 17 and

20, moved to Copenhagen to attend the university there. As regards daughters, most of the girls in the lower social group who migrated left with their parents during their childhood or in early youth when they went into domestic service. Daughters of better-off families stayed at home until they were married, normally after their twenty-fifth birthday.

These social differences are most clearly apparent in the first two cohorts. Skilled workers in the 1872 cohort belong to a more mixed group. The old handicraft traditions continued in some trades, but in others, mainly the more industrialized ones, workers tended to marry earlier as their chances of becoming masters were small and they either did not migrate at all, or spent a relatively short period of time travelling.

5. In-migration to Odense

Information about in-migrants is generally much more scanty than that about out-migrants, especially for the eighteenth and early nineteenth centuries. The analysis that follows is, therefore, inevitably more superficial.

During the period of stagnation in the eighteenth century, the capitation tax list for 1787 shows that between 200 and 300 persons, or between 4 and 6 per cent of the total population, moved into the city during a single year. There is little information about the places of origin of these migrants, but their names indicate that the overwhelming majority of them were Danes, or perhaps Norwegians. There are only a few names which indicate a foreign origin, mainly German but occasionally Swedish, French, Italian, and Dutch. Master artisans and merchants who wished to settle in Odense had to obtain a licence from the city council, and, when applying, they normally stated their birthplace. Between 1741 and 1790, 45 per cent of those who were not born in Odense came from other places in the island of Fünen, 33 per cent from other parts of the kingdom, and 22 per cent from abroad, mainly from Germany.

However, the majority of in-migrants did not belong to this group. They came at a much earlier stage of their careers. Young men arrived in the city when they were only 14 or 15 years old. They attended the grammar school, or were admitted by the guilds as apprentices. Others just arrived and looked for occasional work; those who remained in the city are found as day labourers or drivers employed by the merchants. Young women tended to be older when they arrived. Typically, they would be between the ages of 18 and 20, and their objective was to obtain a place as a servant in an upper- or middle-class family in the city.

On the rare occasions when one of these young people died shortly after arrival, it can be shown from the probate ledgers that their families were nearly always living in rural parishes at a distance of up to 15 miles from Odense, or in one of the smaller towns along the coast of Fünen. Most in-migration was, therefore, short-distance migration.

The combination of a high rate of childhood mortality, a large number of out-migrating children (with their families), and of an in-migration consisting of persons who tended to be older than the out-migrants, influenced the age distribution of the city's population (see Fig. 10.2). The influx of boys was so

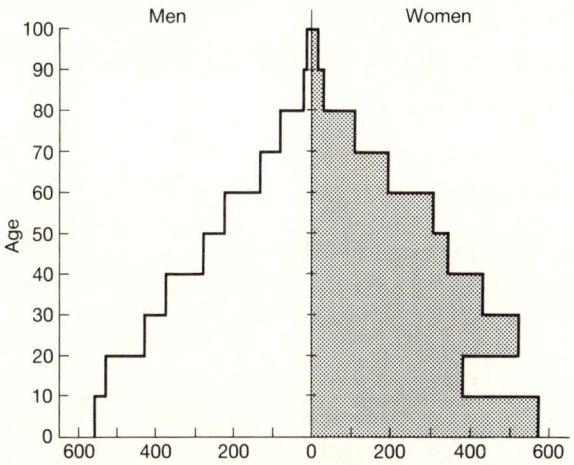

Figure 10.2. Age pyramid for the population of Odense, 1787

large that numbers in the age-groups 0–9 and 10–19 were nearly equal. For girls, on the other hand, the later arrival of in-migrant young women resulted in a disproportionately large number in the age-group 20–29.

At the Census of 1787, the cohort born between 1757 and 1759 constituted only 18 per cent of the population aged between 28 and 30. The remainder of this age group consisted of in-migrants, and, although some of them left the city again a few years later, it is clear that the vast majority of adult citizens had been born outside the city. It was rare for an individual to belong to a family which had lived in Odense for two or three generations.

The situation in 1850 can be traced from the information on birthplace given in the census of that year, and from comparisons between the censuses of 1845 and 1850. According to the latter census, 35 per cent of those aged 29—the survivors of the 1821 birth cohort—were born in the city; a much larger proportion than in 1787. However, by studying individuals in the cohort of 1821, we find that the absolute number given in the census overstates the true figure, because the census occasionally gives birthplaces which are erroneous. However, the age composition of the total urban population which is given in Table 10.6 confirms that in-migrants were less important in determining the age distribution of the population. In 1850, children accounted for a larger proportion of the population, and the large number of births during the 1820s, coupled with the low mortality of that decade, resulted in the age-group 20–29 being relatively large for both sexes.

Table 10.6 Age distribution of the Odense population, 1787–1901

Age	Men			Women		
	1787	1850	1901	1787	1850	1901
0–9	20	22	25	18	20	22
10–19	20	20	21	13	16	19
20–29	16	19	16	17	21	17
30–39	14	16	13	16	15	14
40–49	11	10	11	12	11	11
50–59	9	7	7	11	8	8
60–69	6	4	4	7	5	5
70+	4	2	3	6	4	4
Total	100	100	100	100	100	100

Information about the origins of those who migrated to Odense is given in Table 10.7. In 1850 this shows that migration was still mainly over short distances, especially among women, and that foreigners were of no numerical

Table 10.7 Birthplaces of in-migrants to Odense, 1850–1901

Birthplace	Census of 1850		Census of 1901	
	Men	Women	Men	Women
Rural Fünen	43	53	58	67
Towns in Fünen	16	25	5	5
Copenhagen	12	7	5	3
Rest of Denmark	18	3	28	18
Duchies	7	7	1	2
Foreign countries	4	5	3	5
Total	100	100	100	100

importance. Most of the short-distance in-migrants from rural areas in 1850 were employed as servants, whereas those from cities and more distant places were skilled workers or independent tradesmen, or—among the women—wives of men in these groups. Comparisons with the Census of 1845 at the micro-level indicate that the in-migration rate during this century was close to that of the eighteenth century, and that the age pattern of the migrants was also the same as during the earlier period.

Finally, the Census of 1901 can be used to study some of the characteristics of migrants during the period of industrialization. Among those born in 1872 and enumerated in the census, 25 per cent were born in Odense and 75 per cent were in-migrants. There were thus fewer native-born individuals than in 1850, but micro-analysis once again indicates that some of those who stated their birthplace as Odense were, in fact, born outside the city.

The age distribution in Table 10.6 shows that migrants now played a more modest role in the city's population. The shape of the age pyramid was more regular, both for men and for women. The distribution by birthplace shown in Table 10.7 makes it clear that short-distance migration was more predominant than in 1850, and that it was drawn mainly from the rural districts.

The majority of those who came from areas outside Fünen originated in the rural parishes of neighbouring counties.

The Census of 1901 contains information on birthplace, place of residence before arriving in Odense, and on year of arrival in that city. We can, therefore, obtain more detailed information about migration movements. A distribution by birthplace and place of last residence for those who were born in 1872 and who answered the questions relating to previous residence is given in Table 10.8. The typical situation for men and women was that they

Table 10.8 Persons born outside Odense in 1872, but resident in Odense in 1901 by birthplace and place of last residence

Birthplace	In-migrant from							
	Birthplace		Rural parish in Fünen		Rest of Denmark		Abroad	
	M	F	M	F	M	F	M	F
Rural Fünen	35	49	35	54	16	21	3	2
Fünen towns	4	6	—	—	5	3	—	—
Copenhagen	8	4	—	—	1	1	—	—
Rest of Denmark	7	5	5	2	31	25	1	1
Abroad	2	5	1	3	1	4	2	1

began as servants in rural districts on leaving school at the age of 14. In the years that followed they would move from one farm to another and finally move to the city in their twenties, often from a parish which was only a few miles distant from the parish in which they were born. Migration from one of the smaller towns in Fünen was rarer. Another possibility was to arrive in Odense at a younger age and become an apprentice, but few young people chose to do so, as after 1857 more handicrafts had been permitted to be established outside the city.

The information about the year of in-migration shows that on census day, 1 February 1901, 9 per cent of the population had arrived during the previous year, 5 per cent in 1899, and a further 5 per cent in 1898. This indicates that gross migration rates were somewhat higher than previously, and that people moved out again fairly quickly after staying in the city for a relatively short time. Though in-migration in 1900 differed from that in the 1890s the figures for net migration suggest that it was less frequent.

The occupations of in-migrants in 1901 differed from the pattern of the eighteenth and early nineteenth centuries. There were fewer servants in the city and those who were there—now almost entirely females—were younger than previously. Among in-migrants aged 29 in 1901 the unskilled men tended to be industrial workers, but many of them were in occupations which showed that they possessed some skills. Among women of that age, the main change was a lower age at marriage. In 1901 two-thirds were married, compared with 41 per cent in 1850 and even fewer in 1787.

Thus the principal conclusion of this chapter is that whilst annual net migration fluctuated between zero and 2 per cent of the total population, gross out-migration over the period was nearly constant at between 6 and 8 per cent and hardly depended on changes in the economic environment. In-migration was more volatile, but the main growth factor in the change from a small stagnating industrial town to a large industrial city was the excess of births over deaths.

11 Mobility and Migration in Pre-industrial Urban Areas
The Case of Nineteenth-Century Cuenca

DAVID S. REHER

Faculdad de Ciencias Política y Sociología, Universidad Complutense de Madrid, Madrid, Spain

One of the least known though ironically more visible aspects of past populations is their mobility. While the great migrations in history have often been extensively investigated, more local permanent and return migratory patterns have been neglected or inadequately studied.[1] Analyses based on marriage registers or municipal listings of inhabitants often portray a deceptively simple scenario of what we might suspect to be a dynamic and complex reality.[2] While this subject has received little or no attention in Spain, it cannot automatically be assumed that historical research has advanced much further elsewhere. Despite the existence of noteworthy attempts by European and American scholars,[3] it can safely be assumed that

Preliminary versions of this chapter have been given for the Graduate Group in Demography of the University of California at Berkeley and at the Population Studies Center of the University of Pennsylvania. I would like to express my gratitude to Francisco Javier Blanco Buendia for his assistance in the compiling of the data and to Eugene Hammel, Étienne van de Walle, and Benito Cachinero for their helpful comments.

[1] An important exception here is the work of urban geographers in countries like Great Britain who have made meaningful advances towards the understanding of migratory patterns within a historical context. See e.g. R. Lawton, 'Mobility in Nineteenth Century British Cities', *The Geographical Journal*, 145 (1979), 206–24, and R. Lawton, 'Population Mobility and Urbanisation: Nineteenth Century British Experience', in W. R. Lee and R. Lawton (eds.), *Comparative Urban Population Development in Western Europe c. 1750–1920* (London, 1985).

[2] For examples of this, see M. Lachiver, *La population de Meulan du XVIIe au XIXe siècle* (Paris, 1969), 339.

[3] For examples of this kind of work, see S. Akerman and A. Norberg, 'Employment Opportunities, Family-Building and Internal Migration in the Late Nineteenth Century: Some Swedish Case Studies', in A. J. Coale (ed.), *Economic Factors in Population Growth* (New York, 1976), 453–86; Y. Blayo, 'La mobilité dans un village de la Brie vers le milieu de XIXe siècle', *Population*, 25 (1970), 573–605; C. Corsini, 'La mobilità delle popolazioni nel settecento: fonti, metodi, problemi', *La Popolazione Italiana nel settecento*, ed. Società Italiana di Demografia Storica (Bologna, 1980), 401–34; G. Da Molin, 'Mobilità dei contadini pugliesi tra fine 600 a primo 800', ibid. 435–76; S. Hochstadt, 'Migration and Industrialization in Germany, 1815–1977', *Social Science History*, 5 (1981), 445–8; D. I. Kertzer and D. P. Hogan, 'On the Move: Migration in an Italian Community, 1865–1921', *Social Science History*, 9 (1985), 1–24; P. Laslett, *Family Life and Illicit Love in Earlier Generations* (Cambridge, 1977); R. S. Schofield, 'Age-Specific Mobility in an Eighteenth-Century Rural English Parish', *Annales de Démographie Historique* (1970), 261–73; P. Wilcox, 'Marriage, Mobility and Domestic Service in Victorian Cambridge', *Local Population Studies*, 29 (1982), 19–34.

dynamic analysis of mobility patterns in pre- and early-industrial societies are singularly lacking.

As a consequence, the historian is compelled to make use of the empirical and theoretical advances of modern migration research if a general framework for understanding migration is to be established. Rural–urban migrants have traditionally been seen as responding either to factors 'pushing' them from rural areas (unfavourable systems of land tenure, surplus labour supply, population pressure, etc.) or 'pulling' them to the towns (higher wages, greater opportunities, etc.). All theories of migration emphasize the importance of economic realities and decision-making in the migration process, but often differ in their emphasis on the active, more mobile risk-taking migrant, or the less mobile passive migrant, or in their macro- or micro-analytical focus.[4] In the most commonly used macro-analytical migration models movement is taken to be a function of such variables as the size of the urban areas, distance from place of origin, and the number and complexity of intervening opportunities and competing migrants.[5] In micro-analytical approaches the 'push' factors are given more weight than the 'pull' factors, and propensity to migrate has been seen as a product of the stage in an individual's life-cycle, occupational constraints, and previous migratory experience.[6] Whatever the emphasis, and despite general mention made of the potential importance of counterstream migration, little work has been done on the make-up and consequences of return migration.[7]

The most visible, though certainly not the only, consequence of migrations to both historical and contemporary urban areas is the contribution made by net migration to overall urban growth.[8] Especially in the past, cities were characterized by weak or even non-existent natural growth rates and were dependent on migratory flows for what were normally positive real growth rates.[9] In this manner, historical towns helped contribute to the maintenance

---

[4] S. Findley, *Planning for Internal Migration: A Review of Issues and Policies in Developing Countries* (Washington, DC, 1977); J. R. Harris and M. P. Todaro, 'Migration, Unemployment and Development: A Two-Sector Analysis', *The American Economic Review*, 60:1 (1970), 126–42; J. J. Zuiches, 'Migration Methods and Models: A Demographic Perspective', in R. N. Thomas and J. M. Hunter (eds.), *Internal Migration Systems in the Developing World: With Special Reference to Latin America* (Boston, Mass., 1980).

[5] E. S. Lee, 'A Theory of Migration', *Demography* 3 (1966), 47–57; S. A. Stouffer, *Social Research to Test Ideas* (New York, 1962), G. K. Zipf, 'The P_1P_2/D hypothesis: On the Intercity Movement of Persons', *American Sociological Review*, 11 (1946), 677–86.

[6] P. A. Morrison, 'Theoretical Issues in the Design of Population Mobility Models', *Environment and Behavior*, 5 (1973), 125–34.

[7] C. Goldscheider, *Population, Modernization and Social Structure* (Boston, Mass., 1971); J. Margolis, 'Internal Migration: Measurement and Models', in A. A. Brown and E. Neuberger (eds.), *Internal Migration, a Comparative Perspective* (New York, 1977), 135–44.

[8] J. Clarke, 'Patterns of Settlement and Factors affecting Population Distribution', *IUSSP International Population Conference, Florence*, 3 (1985), 63–72; Findley, *Planning for Internal Migration*, 32–4.

[9] E. A. Wrigley, 'A Simple Model of London's Importance in Changing English Society and Economy 1650–1750', *Past and Present*, 37 (1967), 44–70.

of the demographic equilibrium by acting as more or less permanent centres of attraction for excess rural populations.[10] Apart from moments of political, economic, and demographic crisis in which the migratory flow could dry up or even reverse its direction, this kind of population mobility has generally been considered permanent and almost irreversible. In this manner, a more flexible job structure, based often on domestic service or industrial and mercantile activity, assured that all urban areas would participate in these flows. Much as in present-day less developed countries, primate cities would reap the lion's share of migration, though smaller towns would also participate, at least modestly, either as permanent destinations, or as a link in stage or step-migration of unemployed or underemployed peasants from rural areas.

In macro-economic terms migration can be considered a more or less efficient adjustment mechanism whereby human resources are transferred from economically backward regions to dynamic ones, even though 'optimum migration' in which everyone seems to benefit is never achieved.[11] In the final analysis, however, migration is an integral part of the change processes, affecting not only the society as a whole but the migrant himself or herself. If the implications of migration are considered both for society as a whole and for the individuals involved, the fundamental importance of this little-known historical phenomenon not only for those populations, but for historians as well, cannot be doubted.

The lack of adequate studies can be directly attributed to defects in the documentation available before the latter part of the nineteenth century. Though parish registers often show place of origin of bride and groom, as well as of parents of baptized children, as early as the seventeenth century, they tell us little about the intensity or make-up of migration or migrants. Municipal listings of inhabitants, on the other hand, afford a complete, though static, view of the place of origin of a given urban population. None the less, despite the problems inherent in source materials the historian cannot help but pose deeper and more probing questions relating to urban mobility which cannot be answered by more traditional means of document analysis. Straightforward measures of migration, such as annual or other period turnover rates of population, as well as vital information regarding the age, sex, marital status, and occupation of migrants simply cannot be gleaned from a single listing or register. This chapter is an attempt partially to fill this vacuum in historical scholarship. In view of the lack of population registers in

---

[10] W. McNeill, 'Migration in Historical Perspective', *Population and Development Review*, 10:1 (1984), 1–18.

[11] K. Davis, 'The Effect of Outmigration on Regions of Origin', in A. A. Brown and E. Neuberger (eds.), *Internal Migration, a Comparative Perspective* (New York, 1977), 147–66; E. Neuberger, 'Internal Migration: A Comparative Systematic View', ibid. 125–34; M. Todaro, 'Rural–Urban Migration, Unemployment and Job Probabilities: Recent Theoretical and Empirical Research', in A. J. Coale (ed.), *Economic Factors in Population Growth* (New York, 1976), 367–85.

168   David S. Reher

Spain this must be based on the nominative record linkage of successive listings of inhabitants, along the lines set out some time ago by Peter Laslett[12] and Yves Blayo[13] in pioneering studies.

The results will enable us to consider a number of the issues raised by contemporary migration theory within the context of a small Castilian town midway through the nineteenth century. In- and out-migration will be analysed in an effort to outline the general characteristics of these patterns, as well as the consequences of movements for migrants, the town, and the rural areas themselves. Here, turnover rates and the age, sex, and occupational status of the migrants will be calculated. Results confirm the mobile nature of urban populations and show that while all are mobile, not all age or social groups are affected equally. The predominantly or even marginally permanent nature of rural–urban migration will be challenged, and a more global view of migration will be proposed which will regard it as the mechanism that links rural and urban societies and economies.

The point of reference for this study is the town of Cuenca, a small provincial capital located on the central plateau of Spain, some 160 km. east of Madrid. During the mid-nineteenth century the population was between 5,000 and 6,000 and the town was in a state of severe economic and social depression due to an outmoded textile industry which, after a period of brilliance during the fifteenth and sixteenth centuries, had entered into a prolonged slump after 1600. A more recent destruction of ecclesiastical wealth dating from the 1830s had eliminated the Church as the major source of urban power and further contributed to Cuenca's decay. Since no new industries had grown to stimulate the local economy, by mid-century it was little more than a small centre of provincial and ecclesiastical bureaucracy where most industrial activity was for the home market. In other words, during the period in question Cuenca had little to offer potential migrants and was, for the most part, an excellent example of most Spanish towns on the central plateau.

At this time, Cuenca was blessed with a series of annual listings of inhabitants drawn up by the municipal authorities. These listings have every appearance of being complete, and contain full nominative information as well as age, sex, marital status, occupation, relation to household head, and place of origin for practically the entire population. Despite small defects, such as the lack of surname for some servants, nominative and age variability, and possible error in place of origin, subsequent checks have shown the documentation to be of excellent quality.[14] Because an analysis of listings at

---

[12] Laslett, *Family Life and Illicit Love*.
[13] Blayo, 'La mobilité dans un village'.
[14] A small test was carried out to ascertain the degree of under-registration in the municipal listings. Since a complete registration of deaths also exists for the same 5-year period (1843–7), if the listings were complete all people found to have died should also be listed as 'absent' or out-migrants in our calculations. The test was based on 279 cases during 1843 and 1844, and included all deceased, except children under 4 years of age, and those whose residence was listed as the

five-yearly or longer intervals might conceal considerable short-term movements, we used annual listings.[15] Though even annual listings of inhabitants would also tend to miss certain kinds of movement, at least they would permit a more accurate calculation of yearly rates. Our original method followed Blayo's[16] rather closely, though a number of modifications were introduced. A complete description of the method can be found in the appendix at the end of this chapter, and only a very brief summary will be given here.

The method is based on the identification of all individuals within their families, and the subsequent linkage of individuals over successive years. Once people have been completely identified, those absent or those appearing between one year and the next can be properly considered as mobile. Once this stage has been reached it is relatively simple to classify them by age-group, sex, and—at least for household heads—by occupational status. The use of five annual listings of inhabitants (1843–7) enables us to calculate movement over a four-year period. However, in order to minimize random fluctuations, most annual rates were calculated as an average of four different years. The base population used was either the average between 1844 and 1846 or, in the case of household heads, their occupational distribution in 1844. Most rates are expressed as simple percentages. Finally, it should be mentioned that out-migration caused by death has been estimated from the series of values of q_x in a life table constructed for the city at mid-century. Since deaths are estimated yearly for entire age-groups, this form of calculation is especially dubious for those less than 5 or more than 60 years old. Here, calculations of out-migration will be little more than rough estimates.

The flow of individuals into and out of towns could decisively influence the demographic growth or stagnation of any city. This movement is a social phenomenon of fundamental importance since it affects many different individuals and most social groups and, at a more general level, the overall availability of urban labour. In order to understand so complex and pervasive a situation, it is first necessary to evaluate its numerical importance. One of the more generally accepted ideas regarding migration to towns during the nineteenth century is that it tended to be a movement of young people and was mostly permanent in nature, apart from some stage-migration to other larger urban areas and a trickle of people returning to their villages of origin. This influx of people would bolster growth rates that were often negative and

Hospital of Santiago. In so doing, we endeavoured to eliminate those groups most prone to very short-term mobility. 82.1% of the deceased were also listed as 'absent'. If we take into consideration the fact that at least 10% of the town's population entered the town every year and, therefore, would not necessarily be present on the municipal listing in the year in which they died, the effective under-registration on the listings would oscillate between 5% and 10% and, therefore, the rates of in- and out-migration are possibly overestimated to the same degree.

[15] Blayo, 'La Mobilité dans un village'; Laslett, *Family Life and Illicit Love*.
[16] Blayo, 'La Mobilité dans un village', 573–82.

would be a major source of labour supply in the town itself. The initial results of our study of Cuenca have obliged us to modify many of these ideas fundamentally.

In Cuenca, as can be seen in Table 11.1, the importance of in-migration was

Table 11.1 Migration rates in Cuenca, 1844–1847

Year	Total population	In-migration (%)	Out-migration (%)	Net migration
1844	5,761	15.0	19.0	−4.0
1845	5,719	14.9	15.5	−0.7
1846	5,645	12.9	14.3	−1.3
1847	5,333	11.7	15.7	−4.0
Total		13.7	16.2	−2.5

Source: Municipal Padrones, 1843, 1844, 1845, 1846, 1847.

considerable and more than compensated by out-migration. Well over 10 per cent of the entire urban population entered the town yearly, and this rate was equalled and, in the case of Cuenca, even surpassed by the proportions of out-migrants. The fact that even a conservative estimate of movement shows that between one and two out of every ten people either arrived in the city or left it every year warrants further consideration. In the first place, it suggests that estimates made by other authors for longer intervals of time do not even begin to suggest the importance of the phenomenon.[17] Furthermore, despite the evident decline in movement over the four-year period, there is no reason to think that these proportions were abnormal. During the decade, the town did not suffer any major crisis nor was it a period of economic expansion. In fact the town was immersed in the economic stagnation which had characterized it for some time and, in the absence of any elements which might perturb migratory flows, the period under consideration would seem entirely typical. What makes these rates even more surprising is that they existed at a period of relative lack of economic dynamism in the town which would have tended to generate new job opportunities.

Net migration was clearly negative between 1843 and 1847, a period when out-migration exceeded in-migration by 2.5 per cent yearly. This negative net rate can be safely attributed to conjunctural factors, rather than to the nature of migration itself. The already small economic importance of the town had decreased even further during the late 1830s as a result of the destruction of the Church as a major economic force in the town. This led to a decline in the numerical importance of the primary employer of domestic service in the town, and thus job opportunities were at least momentarily restricted. This situation was only temporary, and during the next decade the town's

[17] e.g. the estimation of 40% non-death-related absences from Clayworth between 1676 and 1688 cannot even begin to suggest the potential annual importance of movement (Laslett, *Family Life and Illicit Love*). Akerman and Norberg, 'Employment Opportunities', show a turnover of between 15–21% per year at the peak of the sawmill industry in Sweden.

population grew once again, even though no sort of meaningful economic take-off occurred. Yet similar proportions of movement into and out of the town probably continued, though the net rates would be positive. This does not mean that these flows were not a response to economic factors, but rather that the opportunities which did materialize were not related to a growing economy.

Another conclusion to be drawn from this information is that, at least during the period under consideration, the evolution of the town's population depended almost entirely on net migration. A slightly positive natural growth rate was insufficient to overcome the effects of migration. Though this is but one instance, it seems to suggest that migration rates were the major components of urban growth or stagnation, as has been the case in Spain until quite recently. Could this hold true for other periods of Spanish history? While difficult to prove, it would certainly go a long way towards explaining the dynamics of, say, urban population loss in seventeenth-century Castilian towns which cannot convincingly be attributed to demographic crises in the affected areas.

The importance of this constant flux of people warrants deeper analysis in order to ascertain the extent to which migration selected for sex, age, marital status, and occupation. Table 11.2 contains yearly in- and out-migration rates

Table 11.2 In-migration and out-migration by age group and sex, Cuenca, 1844–1847

Age group	Annual in-migration (% of age group)		Annual out-migration (% of age group)	
	Male	Female	Male	Female
0–4	13.7	15.4	19.9	22.3
5–9	10.8	11.8	11.3	14.9
10–14	11.3	13.8	12.4	18.3
15–19	14.1	23.9	22.1	30.7
20–24	16.6	20.1	23.0	31.2
25–29	17.3	15.1	16.5	20.0
30–34	15.2	12.6	14.3	14.8
35–39	12.1	9.9	13.5	14.6
40–49	9.4	9.9	12.4	13.3
50–59	9.7	9.5	12.6	13.6
60+	8.8	13.6	10.0	11.0
Total	12.5	14.9	15.2	19.8
% single	61.4	64.4	61.5	68.8

For method of estimation, see text and Appendix.
Source: Municipal *Padrones*, 1843, 1844, 1845, 1846, 1847.

calculated by age-group and sex, and sheds further light on the question. From the data we get a glimpse of the type of people coming into or leaving the town temporarily or permanently. For men, levels of in-migration were relatively constant up to the age-group 35–39. While the rate increased for men between 20 and 29 years of age, the most noteworthy aspect of the data is that, from birth until old age, men entered the town at a fairly constant rate. Moreover, while in-migration consisted mostly of single men, the excess was less marked than might have been expected. A good proportion of in-migrants were married, thus suggesting a movement of entire families which should not be underestimated. In-migration of women was more intense, younger and more age specific than that of men, and the rate reached a maximum for women between 15 and 24 years of age.

Data for both sexes indicate that in-migration affected all ages, and rarely fell below 9 per cent of the total population in any given group. It was thus a flow that, while relatively more intense at young adult ages, could affect any stage of a person's life-cycle. While the age distribution indicates the importance of employment and marriage in stimulating migration, it is also clear that an appreciable number of established families participated in this type of movement. The emphasis on young adult age-groups, as well as the selective participation of families in migration movements, is not surprising and has been documented in numerous studies of contemporary and historical societies.[18] What is considerably more noteworthy is the fact that migration affects all age-groups because, though the very young might move as members of families, the search for job opportunities or marriage can scarcely be considered as major stimulants of movement among the elderly.

Lifelong out-migration was also a characteristic of urban life, and always affected at least 10 per cent of any given age-group. For men, however, out-migration appears to have been far more age specific than in-migration, and was especially strong between 15 and 24 years of age, a factor probably related to temporary work in rural areas. Despite its continued importance, the fact that out-migration rates declined for men after 24 years of age suggests that age brought a greater stability for men within the town. Women's out-migration, as well as in-migration, was much younger and more age specific than was men's. Up to 30 per cent of the female population of the town between 15 and 24 years of age might move out each year. The presence of an important contingent of female servants, as well as the role of nuptiality in stimulating migration, help explain both the age structure and the rates of women's migration. The relatively greater weight of migrants among women than among men, a characteristic also shown in short-distance present-day migration patterns in Latin America, belies the importance of domestic service for women in the town.[19]

One of the major components of Cuenca's population consisted of domestic servants. In 1844 this group made up 8.9 per cent of the total population, was essentially female (a sex ratio of 24), and strongly influenced

---

[18] D. W. Adams, 'Rural Migration and Agricultural Development in Colombia', *Economic Development and Cultural Change* 17:4 (1969), 527–39; Akerman and Norberg, 'Employment Opportunities', 631; J. C. Caldwell, *African Rural–Urban Migration: The Movement to Ghana's Towns* (New York, 1969); Kertzer and Hogan, 'On the Move', 121; D. R. Ringrose, *Madrid and the Spanish Economy, 1560–1850* (Berkeley, Calif., 1983).

[19] J. P. Poussou, *Bordeaux et le sud-ouest au xviiie siècle* (Paris, 1983); Ringrose, *Madrid and the Spanish Economy*, 53; Todaro, 'Rural–Urban Migration', 370.

the prevailing social make-up of the town.[20] Servants are, perhaps, the most mobile of all urban groups and their large numbers could well vitiate our idea of the nature of migration in other groups. In order to exclude the effect of servants on migration, the data in Table 11.2 have been somewhat arbitrarily reworked by removing servants both from the population at large and from the mobile groups themselves. The results are shown in Table 11.3 and show

Table 11.3 In-migration and out-migration in the absence of domestic servants, by sex and age group, Cuenca, 1844–1847

Age group	Annual in-migration (% of age group)		Annual out-migration (% of age group)	
	Male	Female	Male	Female
0–4	13.7	15.4	19.9	22.3
5–9	10.8	11.8	11.3	14.9
10–14	10.3	11.7	11.4	14.4
15–19	11.3	13.2	16.7	15.2
20–24	13.9	15.0	19.4	17.9
25–29	17.3	13.0	15.6	15.5
30–34	14.9	12.6	13.9	13.6
35–39	11.6	8.4	13.0	13.3
40–49	9.1	9.2	12.1	12.9
50–59	9.1	9.4	12.5	13.0
60+	8.4	13.7	9.7	11.1
Total	11.7	12.2	14.0	15.0
% single	58.2	51.4	57.6	54.8
% single ≥ 20	32.8	19.7	31.1	25.8

Source: Municipal *Padrones*, 1843, 1844, 1845, 1846, 1847.

that servant mobility affected women's migration patterns considerably, while leaving those of men practically unchanged. In the case of men's in-migration, there are hardly any differences worth mentioning except, perhaps, a small reduction in the proportions of in-migrants between 15 and 24 years of age. The age distribution of the female population, though, is decisively affected by the elimination of female servants. Their exclusion means that rates are similar in all age-groups (except for the group aged 20–4), where there is a peak resulting from the arrival of potential brides or newly married women. Otherwise, rates are similar in most age-groups and, overall, women's propensity to migrate no longer exceeds that of men.

Much the same holds true for out-migration where the elimination of domestic servants once again alters results significantly. First of all, the age-specific nature of out-migration changes substantially for both sexes. In fact, slight increases in out-migration rates at certain ages seem hardly noticeable except for men between 20 and 24 years of age, the key age for men to seek work elsewhere. A comparison with men's in-migration where peak activity

---

[20] In Madrid at mid-cent., domestic servants made up 11.5% of the entire population and their sex ratio was 47.0 (see Ringrose, *Madrid and the Spanish Economy*, 57).

occurs in the next age-group might also indicate that young men in their early twenties would leave the town either to seek work or to study, only to return a few years later. While the existence of this sort of return migration is only a possibility, the influence of employment, education, and marriage on the migration trends of both sexes is apparent.

When domestic servants are removed from the migration figures, it is seen that most other movers were, or had been, married. Among those aged 20 and over, between 70 and 80 per cent of all movers were either married or widowed. Women's migration at these ages is clearly related to the mobility of their husbands. In spite of the somewhat arbitrary nature of the table, the movers were not the young and almost universally single job-seeking migrants we might have expected.

One final aspect of our data warrants additional comment. During the very early stages of life, out-migration rates are much higher than those of in-migration and both are clearly higher than for other groups of children and adolescents. This could be due to two different factors. On the one hand, errors of estimation of yearly mortality (q_x) within the age-group could well lead to an overestimation of infants' and children's out-migration. None the less, even a modification of estimated mortality would still leave both in- and out-migration higher in that age group (births are *never* considered a cause of in-migration). These proportions point to the possible existence of the custom of rural wet-nursing which has drawn the attention of many French scholars, but which I have never seen mentioned in Cuenca's documents.[21] Potential return infant and child migration probably also indirectly reflects ongoing ties between the town and its own hinterland, whereby young children and perhaps even members of other age groups would leave town (or enter it) to spend time with relatives, only to return at a subsequent date.

And what about these servants who influence the make-up of migrant groups to such an extent? In order to answer this question, Table 11.4 has been constructed. In it we can see the age distribution of in- and out-migrant servants.[22] The data confirm much of what we might already have suspected. Migrant servants were almost always single, and very young. People often entered domestic service as soon as they were 12 or 13 years old, and seldom later than their twenty-fifth birthday. For both sexes, the 15–19 year age-group was by far the most important, though for women the concentration here was greater. Moreover, almost all servants were single. The migration patterns of servants influenced general migration rates, especially in the case of women, as more than 30 per cent of all female migrants were servants. This

---

[21] A. Bideau, 'L'envoi des jeunes enfants en nourrice. L'exemple d'une petite ville: Thoissey en Dombes (1710–1810)', in J. Dupâquier (ed.), *Hommage à Marcel Reinhard. Sur la population française au XVIIIe et au XIXe siècles* (Paris, 1973); J. Caniage, 'Nourrissons parisiens en Beauvaisis', ibid.

[22] The size of the samples made it unsafe to calculate the proportion of in- and out-migrant servants within each age-group.

Table 11.4 Age distribution of in- and out-migrant domestic servants, Cuenca, 1843–1847

Age group	In-migrants		Out-migrants	
	Male (%)	Female (%)	Male (%)	Female (%)
10–14	13	5	9	6
15–19	34	47	40	41
20–24	31	30	33	36
25–29	3	9	7	10
30–34	2	2	2	2
35–39	3	2	2	1
40–49	3	3	2	2
50–59	6	1	2	1
≥ 60	3	1	2	1
Total	98	100	99	100
No. per year	32	131	45	206
% total migrants	9.9	29.3	11.4	34.6
% total migrants (excl. 1847)		34.5		29.6
% total servants	32.6	32.5	45.9	51.1
% single	91.9	97.1	94.0	96.8

Source: Municipal *Padrones*, 1843, 1844, 1845, 1846, 1847

also explains the changes in the overall picture of women's migration when female servants are eliminated.[23]

The repeated similarities between the in-migration and out-migration patterns of this sector cannot help but attract our attention and point to the likelihood that entry into domestic service was simply a transitory state for those people who, after a short stay in town, would pack up and leave. The fact that every year a high percentage of servants entered or left the city gives support to this hypothesis. Migration-related turnover for both male and female domestic servants exceeded 30 per cent per year and, if the average between out- and in-migration is calculated, it turns out that this movement might well have affected between 38 and 40 per cent of the total sector every year. In addition to this, the similar age distribution of both in- and out-migrants as well as their unchanging marital status confirm the highly transitory nature of domestic service. In this way, servants literally flooded the town at very young ages, stayed for a short time, perhaps only a couple of years, only to return to their village of origin. Domestic service, then, is no more than a temporary source of population gain for the city and should perhaps more aptly be considered from the point of view of the rural economy and population pressure. In other words, rural youths would only go to the city to work for a short period, save a bit of money which might help bolster

---

[23] The municipal listing of 1847 presents important problems on this count, since during that year the number of servant and especially female servant in-migrants dropped sharply, and those of out-migrant female servants increased. This change in trend could well indicate an under-registration of female servants in that listing. Because of this, the percentage of total female servants was also calculated for 1843–6, thereby excluding the potential distorting effects of possible servant under-registration in 1847. Even so, the results which are listed in Table 11.4 do not fundamentally alter our conclusions.

the dowries of the girls or the family economy, and return to their places of origin. This feature of servant migration, involving only a very brief stay in the city, is important and might suggest that women servants would often come to the town after arrangements had already been made for their marriage in their place of origin, and would then marry immediately on their return. Unfortunately, there are no data to confirm or deny that hypothesis. Yet, it can be safely assumed that such turnover rates point to a situation in which young servants could scarcely have had any intention of remaining in Cuenca even semi-permanently when they first arrived.

It is important to point out that we are only discussing one-third of the migration of women and one-tenth of that of men. To what extent could something similar have occurred with the other migrants? The question is not easy to answer, though the data at hand would suggest that this was not generally the case, at least not for the overwhelming majority. A key point here is the fact that age distributions of in- and out-migrants of different occupations are never so clearly correlated. As will become apparent, a slight similarity does exist in the case of day labourers, though their stay in town seems to have been longer than that of female servants. If this were the case, urban migration patterns would have consisted of at least two distinct patterns: a short-term return migration of single youths, most often working in domestic service; and another that affected all social sectors and age-groups almost equally, and which could be either short or long term. It is impossible to calculate the level of permanent in-migration which has so often been considered to be typical of urban areas, though we can safely assume that it was but one of many types of migration which affected the town.

If migration flows are estimated from numbers of household heads we shall be able to isolate not only the most stable group in society, but also to measure mobility in terms of occupational status. In Table 11.5 I estimate the

Table 11.5 In- and out-migration by economic sector

Sector	In-migrants		Out-migrants		Population (1844)
	No.	%	No.	%	
Agriculture[a]	46	10.3	45	10.0	448
Industry/Artisan	13	6.2	12	5.7	209
Services	12	7.2	11	6.6	166
Professional/ Administration[b]	30	11.2	36	13.4	268
Undeclared	8	13.3	8	13.3	60
Total	109	9.4	112	9.7	1151

[a] Day labourers are included in this sector for the table.
[b] The clergy are included in this sector for the table.
The sectoral distribution refers exclusively to household heads.
Source: Municipal *Padrones*, 1843, 1844, 1845, 1846, 1847.

importance of in- and out-migration by occupational status and show that whereas Cuenca as a whole was characterized by considerable mobility independent of occupational category, the groups most likely to move were at the opposite ends of the social scale.[24] The mobility levels, though, of day labourers on the one hand and public administrators, professionals, and the wealthy on the other, while far exceeding those of other groups, were actually quite different. Both groups moved for economic reasons, but the nature of their movement was certainly not the same. First, day labourers tended to circulate between Cuenca and its hinterland in search of work which was often temporary or seasonal. In this respect, unskilled workers would be playing a role similar to that of servants, except that they would be occupied in industrial, trading, or agricultural activities, whereas servants were almost entirely 'unproductive' from an economic standpoint. Furthermore, if it had been possible to isolate all day labourers in the population, and not just household heads, their patterns of movement would probably be even more like those of servants. The professionals, on the other hand, showed a higher propensity to migrate in many parts of the world, and the Cuenca data merely re-emphasize the general idea that migration tends to be selective of the more educated, with the exception of servants who are a classic example of passive, less mobile migrants.[25] We can also assume that out-migration of professionals was urban directed, thus forming a part of the stage or stepwise migration patterns so often noted with them; whereas the day labourers would probably move freely between urban and rural areas of the province. Rates of turnover in other sectors of the economy were appreciably lower. These differences probably reflect the nature of the economic activity of each group in which, for example, employment opportunities for lawyers or day labourers would be less place specific than those available to artisans, shopkeepers, or farmers. Moreover, the willingness of certain groups to assume the risks inherent in all migration would also be a function of their relative place on the social ladder.

One final noteworthy aspect of the data is that even though out-migration was still more intense than in-migration, as was the case with the general data, the difference is much less pronounced. Evidently, poor economic conditions affected the migration patterns of more established sectors less than those of servants, relatives, and other unmarried migrants. These less stable elements

---

[24] The division into different occupational categories has been very general, because of the small numbers involved. 'Agriculture' includes all farmers and tenant farmers, all other groups involved in rural activities (fishermen, loggers, etc.). In certain instances, as in Table 11.5, it also includes day labourers. This last group in the 18th cent. was dedicated almost completely to agriculture-related activities, though in the 19th cent. labourers, more often than not, worked as unskilled urban labourers. 'Industry/artisan' includes all professions related to the production of consumer goods. 'Services' includes all merchants, transport services, innkeepers and other non-public administration services occupations. 'Professional/Administration' includes all occupations which either required some sort of education (lawyers, medical practitioners, civil servants, etc.) or were employees of the public administration. This is a mixed category which includes the wealthy, together with rather humble civil servants. Members of the clergy are also included in this category.

[25] Caldwell, *African Rural–Urban Migration*; Lee, 'Theory of Migration'; Lawton, 'Population Mobility and Urbanisation'; Todaro, 'Rural–Urban Migration'.

of urban society were more sensitive to economic fluctuations than other groups, and times of difficulty would affect them first whilst leaving other groups relatively unscathed.

If we turn to the proportions of household-head migrants in different age-groups shown in Table 11.6, it becomes clear that while rates of in-migration

Table 11.6 Yearly migration patterns of male household heads, by age

Age group	In-migrants (% of age group)	Out-migrants (% of age group)
20–24	8.9	13.3
25–29	19.3	14.9
30–34	12.3	11.7
35–39	12.1	11.2
40–44	7.5	8.1
45–49	7.1	10.6
50–54	6.9	10.1
55–59	7.1	4.7
≥ 60	5.8	6.3
Total	9.4	9.7
Number (per year)	108	112
% single	7.4	7.8

were highest for those between 25 and 39 years of age, out-migration affected all age groups almost equally. In fact, the only noticeable peak occurred for the age group 25–9. These were the young adults who were probably seeking stable employment either in Cuenca or elsewhere, and who chose their most productive age to make the change. In other words, we can suspect that these were definite or at least more prolonged migrations, and this view is supported by the fact that they tended to take their families with them. Little evidence has been found of movement by household heads independently of their families, though this must surely have existed. Outside this age-group, mobility levels remained high, though significantly below those of the population as a whole. One further indication that this was the most stable group in the town is the fact that peak mobility among household heads was reached some ten years later than in the population as a whole.

Naturally, the generally high levels of both types of migration suggest that return or cyclical migration was also a common experience for household heads. The fact that peak age groups do not strictly coincide simply raises the question of the normal length of stay. In other words, instead of the one- or two-year stint which was typical for servants, household heads may have stayed a good deal longer. Indeed, these patterns probably varied: some heads would have been in town only for a short period, probably attending to family business; others would have stayed a good deal longer though they, too, would end up as return migrants. Finally a certain percentage would be true permanent out- or in-migrants.

How then does economic activity influence the structure of migration in a town like Cuenca? In order to help clarify this matter Table 11.7 has been

Table 11.7 Yearly migration patterns for day labourer and professional household heads, by age

Age group	In-migrants		Out-migrants	
	Day labourers	Professional/Administrative	Day labourers	Professional/Administrative
20–24	7	3	6	6
25–29	26	15	18	15
30–34	17	22	18	18
35–39	12	13	11	13
40–44	8	16	9	14
45–49	8	7	10	11
50–54	10	8	16	10
55–59	5	3	4	3
≥ 60	7	13	9	9
Total	100	100	101	99
Number	144	119	138	144
% total migrants	33.4	27.6	30.4	30.9
% single	2.1	11.8	2.0	17.2

constructed. In it, the age structure of household-head migrants is given for two key sectors in society with strikingly different behaviour patterns.[26] Professional in-migrants were markedly older and spread over a wider age range than day labourers. Yet out-migration in both cases seems more uniformly distributed over the migrants' productive life. While the samples do not enable us to reach firm conclusions on the matter, once again two different patterns of household-head migration appear. Unskilled day labourers arrived in Cuenca at a relatively young age, though older than the average for the population as a whole, and generally just after marriage. The fact that out-migration was much less influenced by age suggests the likelihood that day labourers' migration was not primarily short term, because, if it had been, the age distribution would have been similar in both instances. On the other hand, in-migration patterns of professionals and employees of the public administration were less age specific and more spread out over the greater part of the productive life of the migrants. Moreover, the peak age (30–40) indicates that these people arrived in town after having completed their professional education elsewhere, and that their arrival in town was much less related to nuptiality than was that of migrants in other sectors. Most of the people in this sector will have received some specialized training which could only be acquired outside the town, in places like Madrid. Many probably left the city as single individuals and returned some time after marriage. In fact, those sons of professional families who would essentially repeat the same migration pattern as their fathers are not included in the table since they normally did not live in an autonomous household and, therefore, had no occupational status for the census-taker to note. Thus these patterns,

[26] Because the sample is small, this has been shown as a standard age distribution without bearing in mind the population of each age group.

evidenced by married professionals, probably mirrored those of unmarried children of professionals. The smoother age-spread evidenced by both in- and out-migration flows of professionals is not at all surprising, since within this sector economic productivity did not diminish with age. In other words, a physician, a civil servant, or a schoolteacher would not be nearly as tied to the physical location of his job as would a shoemaker or a shopkeeper, and could thus move more easily. This was also true of the day labourers though the location of other employment differed sharply, as naturally, did the stability of their jobs.

In the preceding paragraphs we have discussed the dynamics of migration in Cuenca. The most noteworthy conclusion was that in-migration was more than counterbalanced by out-migration and that return migration played a major part. The majority of single, young in-migrants—servants, apprentices, or day labourers—only stayed in town for brief periods. Heads of household, too, moved into and out of town very easily, but, although there was some return-migration in this group, they probably stayed in Cuenca longer than single migrants. The levels of migration and the amount of return-migration found were surprising because in a small and decadent town like Cuenca we had expected to find only a trickle of migrants, most of whom would stay and bolster its faltering population. Both 'push' and 'pull' factors were at work, though the levels of return-migration indicate that neither was strong enough to uproot the majority of the people from their rural heritage in any permanent manner. Much of the flow consisted of people whose characteristics were similar to those considered typical of passive, less mobile migrants (kin-related moves, lower occupational status, predominantly female, often temporary moves, affecting all ages, etc.); though the professionals provided a clear example of the active migrant.[27]

This multiplicity of movement can only be adequately interpreted if we bear in mind that mid-nineteenth-century Cuenca and its province were still clearly pre-industrial and showed few signs of economic dynamism. Within this context, existing social and economic structures contributed to a situation in which a free exchange of individuals was perceived to be normal. Ultimately, close ties between Cuenca and its hinterland are both the cause and the consequence of the actual situation. Despite its clearly urban nature (fewer than 15 per cent of the active population were involved in the primary sector), a radical economic and social distinction between Cuenca and its province never occurred, as was the case with larger cities. The small size of the town certainly contributed to the strength of these ties which were an ever-present conditioning factor of urban life. Moreover, small city sizes made cities multilateral. In other words, not only did Cuenca exercise control over the rural areas through political, social, religious, and economic links, but in turn it was dependent on them for more than merely basic foodstuffs. A true interrelation between the two worlds existed, in which ties of

[27] Findley, *Planning for Internal Migration*, 16–17.

dependence were mutual, and where the urban world was an integral part of the rural, just as 'rural' was an essential component of 'urban'. The exchange of individuals between town and country in both directions was at the bottom of this relationship. The basic feature of the systems was that the labour market for a young man or woman, whatever his or her origin, extended over both town and country.

In turn, this was reinforced by the system of landholding and inheritance prevailing in the province itself. Apart from the area to the south of the town known as La Mancha where large plots were the norm and from which relatively few migrated to the town, small plots and extensive land tenure were common in the majority of the province. Since inheritance was partible, levels of celibacy low, and the population growing, the peasant who could not make a living solely from his own possessions formed an important part of the population and even merited a specific term in Spanish (*pegujalero*). These people had long since learned to diversify their economic activities with livestock, lumber, resin-gathering, work on other people's land, and, of course, jobs in town. Land was inherited upon the death of either or both parents, but people continued to marry relatively young, and new households were formed shortly thereafter thanks to the ability of the peasant household to diversify income and housing in the village, in town, or in both places at once. It was, therefore, normal for a number of sons and daughters, single or married, to live away from the family household at any given time; their destination would often be the town, even though it might be for only a short period of time. Most of them returned to their village of origin, thus completing a cycle which was probably repeated in the lifetime of an individual. Their return would be expected, and marriage patterns and family economies probably came to count on it. This mobility clearly existed within a kinship system designed to support movers, much as other authors have observed.[28] What is more, both the kinship system and this type of movement-based income supplement had probably coexisted happily for centuries.

Some, however, stayed or returned to Cuenca after marriage. They would become, so to speak, family beachheads in the town, and Cuenca would become an integral rather than a transitory supplement to their family income. This type of permanent movement into town often came about through marriage and family ties, and is yet another example of the importance of the kinship system in underpinning migration.[29] So the circulation would begin again, though this time the protagonists would be entire families. Some of them, naturally, were permanent migrants, but

---

[28] E. A. Hammel, 'The Influence of Social and Geographical Mobility on the Stability of the Kinship Systems: The Serbian Case', in Brown and Neuberger (eds.), *Internal Migration*, 401–15.

[29] D. S. Reher, 'La importancia del análisis dinámico ante el análisis estático del hogar y la familia. Algunos ejemplos de la ciudad de Cuenca en el siglo XIX', *Revista española de investigaciones sociológicas*, 27 (1984), 107–35.

others would only reside in town for more or less lengthy periods. Where to from Cuenca? Well, with the exception of professionals who may well have circulated among urban centres on the peninsula, most probably returned to where they had family property. Since the great majority of these people came from the province itself, the distance travelled would seldom exceed, say, 75–100 kms., and would normally be appreciably less. This time, though, the migrants had families in tow. What is clear is that the ties between the town and the village were never cut, and both would be seen by the migrants as complementary aspects of income diversification. The potential for 'dynamic instability' in large-scale migration, as noted by some authors and disputed by others, is simply nowhere to be found in the town of Cuenca, where movement itself had long since become an integral part of the social system.[30]

The high levels of mobility in and around the town of Cuenca had a number of implications for nineteenth-century society. We can safely suppose that the intensity of movement tended to lower fertility, at least among mobile individuals, by restricting their nuptiality. Information from the town itself for the eighteenth century and the first half of the nineteenth, based on women married in Cuenca but born elsewhere, shows that age at first marriage was more than eighteen months later than for women born in the town. The fact that it is unclear whether these people were recent or long-standing residents in Cuenca does not detract from the significance of a situation which explains at least part of the more restricted nuptiality so evident in most urban areas. Its overall importance for the society, however, depends on whether or not, and to what degree, this also occurred in rural areas. We do not possess either confirming or contradictory evidence on the matter, but it seems reasonable to suppose that return or cyclical migration had similar effects everywhere. In this manner, migration would act indirectly as a deterrent to population growth. Traditionally, higher urban mortality has been viewed as a major by-product of migration to urban areas. In the case of a small town such as Cuenca, where migration was certainly not unidirectional, the reaction of nuptiality in both urban and rural areas would have equal or greater importance in controlling population size. Moreover, the more rapidly the population grew, as was the case in the province as a whole during this period, the more intensive movement would have become as families scurried to diversify their household economies in order to maintain living standards. Ultimately, of course, the importance of movement in curtailing growth in the province depended on its overall intensity. This, unfortunately, cannot be measured at the present time.

We also do not know whether or not migration could lead directly, at least among migrants, to lower levels of marital fertility. Though evidence is not

---

[30] C. Stephenson, 'A Gathering of Strangers? Mobility, Social Structure, and Political Participation in the Formation of Nineteenth-Century American Workingclass Culture', in M. Cantor (ed.), *American Working Class Culture* (Westport, Conn., 1979), 31–60.

conclusive on the matter, this situation has been documented for migrants in urban environments whose fertility is generally lower than that of rural non-migrants, though higher than that of urban non-migrants.[31] Unfortunately the effect of short-term migration is generally unknown, though seasonal migration seems to depress marital fertility levels.[32] Could this be applicable to temporary absences of household heads in Cuenca? It is impossible to be certain, though the potential importance of human exchanges for the maintenance of some sort of demographic equilibrium in the province should be evident.

Finally, it seems likely that this cyclical movement was an important component of economic and social integration in a province where the overwhelming presence of an urban centre like Madrid did not exist. Apart from the trade in certain basic food commodities, textiles, lumber, and other lesser products, Cuenca played only a marginal role as a market centre during the nineteenth century. None the less, the economic links between the city and its province were multiple and were established largely through the exchange of individuals. Not only would short-term migrants distribute 'urban' money in rural areas, but the city itself became an integral part of the social and economic world of its hinterland, and conversely. This human permeability of a small town like Cuencà probably mitigated the alien and hostile nature that cities traditionally conveyed to peasants.

These mobile groups form the true floating population in a pre-industrial city like Cuenca, and it is they who are most likely to move at time of economic duress. They are a type of barometer which is highly sensitive to economic and demographic conditions either in the town or in the surrounding rural areas. They are the ones who would fill the town at times of acute subsistence crisis, or leave it when the sources of urban employment dried up, as probably occurred in the seventeenth century; and they would fill it when incipient industrialization began, or leave it during periods of weak rural population growth in which land, jobs, and mates might be plentiful. Mostly though, it was they who had a foothold in both the urban and the rural world, and used both as an integral part of their domestic economies. These were the concrete agents who linked towns to their own hinterlands. In like manner, those people prone to move into and out of the town probably also moved within the town itself; a supposition made reasonable by the fact that

---

[31] Akerman and Norberg, 'Employment Opportunities'; S. Goldstein and A. Goldstein, 'The Impact of Migration on Fertility: An "Own Children" Analysis for Thailand', *Population Studies*, 35:2 (1981), 265–84; A. Zarate and A. Unger de Zarate, 'On the Reconciliation of Research Findings of Migrant–Nonmigrant Fertility Differentials in Urban Areas', *International Migration Review*, 9:2 (1975), 115–56.

[32] J. Bongaarts and R. G. Potter, 'Fertility Effects of Seasonal Migration and Seasonal Variation in Fecundability: Test of a Useful Approximation under more General Conditions', *Demography*, 16 (1979), 475–80; D. S. Massey and B. P. Mullan, 'A Demonstration of the Effect of Seasonal Migration on Fertility', *Demography*, 21:4 (1984). 501–17; J. A. Menken, 'Seasonal Migration and Seasonal Variation in Fecundability: Effects on Birth Rates and Birth Intervals', *Demography*, 16 (1979), 103–20.

movement seems to beget movement in Cuenca. These groups would also be the protagonists of much of the restricted nuptiality, oscillating fertility, and higher mortality so characteristic of urban areas; as well as the principal source of the unskilled labour so essential to urban economies. Once again the city looms before us as an immensely complex reality which historians have yet fully to understand.

Appendix

The method employed for most of the calculations contained in this chapter is based on an intensive utilization of the municipal listings (*padrones*) dating from the years 1843, 1844, 1845, 1846, and 1847 which are located in the Municipal Archive of Cuenca. As mentioned in the text, these listings are quite complete, and contain full nominative information as well as information on sex, age, occupation, relation to head of household, and place of origin.

Essentially, the method consisted in locating individuals within their households in 1843. A card was filled out for each family in town and contained all pertinent information, including the parish and street of residence. Subsequently these were ordered alphabetically within each parish and were given an alphanumerical identifier which itself represented the parish, street, and alphabetical order of the 'family' card. In subsequent years, a parish-by-parish and family-by-family search was carried out. Once a family was found, new information on age was registered. If there were any new members of that household, pertinent information was written down, along with a 'P' in blue ink. If someone was absent, an 'A' was written in red ink. If a family disappeared completely, they were all given an 'A' and if a new one appeared a card was filled out and all were given a 'P'. In both cases, the cards were put back into the parish file in the correct alphabetical order. This procedure was carried out for all fourteen parishes and for every year until 1847. In this manner, the number of cards for each parish increased from one listing to the next. This was done in order to 'catch' returning families and also so that cross-checking could be carried out later in order to detect those households, say, whose heads had changed (marriage, death, etc.) and were thus located elsewhere within the parish file. A number of these 'false' cards were, in fact, detected.

The next stage consisted in filling out secondary cards for all 'P's and 'A's in the file. Each contained full information about the person as well as the identifier of his 'family' card. Moreover, a different card was filled out for household heads from that for other members so as to be able to classify movement by economic sector at a later time. In all cases, different colours were used for the 'A's and 'P's. In total, some 3,000–5,000 family cards were filled out and about 10,000–12,000 individual cards drawn up. These secondary cards, then, represent the true migrants and were ordered alphabetically, independently of parish of residence.

Subsequently, all 'P's and all 'A's were systematically compared. This was done not only among household heads and among the 'other' cards, but also between household heads and 'others', and between 'others' and household heads. This comparison was carried out for every year and was done to detect not only intra-urban movement, but also to detect movement of heads due to marriage or other reasons. In other words, if a person was single and 'absent' in, say, 1846 he might be present, married, and a household head in that same year. Ultimately, three groups of cards appeared for each year: 'P's, 'A's, and 'matches'. These then became the in-migrants, the out-migrants, and the intra-urban residence changes respectively. From this point it was a comparatively simple matter to calculate age and sex distribution, occupational status, and even the origin–destination of individuals for the years 1844–7. As mentioned in the text, four-year averages have been used in order to minimize the effects of random fluctuations, and out-migration due to mortality has been estimated from life tables drawn up for Cuenca at mid-century and deducted from the 'A's of each year.

12 Migration, Wages, and Urbanization in Sweden in the Nineteenth Century

TOMMY BENGTSSON

Department of Economic History, Lund University, Lund, Sweden

During the second half of the nineteenth century the urban share of the Swedish population increased from 10 per cent to well over 20 per cent.[1] A large part of the increase was due to population growth in Stockholm, the country's largest city, but most towns grew rapidly. This rapid urbanization took place during the period of industrial breakthrough in Sweden.

During the early nineteenth century the growth of the population of Stockholm was slow, just as it had been during the latter part of the eighteenth century, whereas the population in some other towns increased substantially. These towns were seaports involved in the increase of commerce. Thus urbanization during this period seems to have been connected with commercialization rather than with industrialization.

The fastest population growth occurred in Malmö, in the very south of

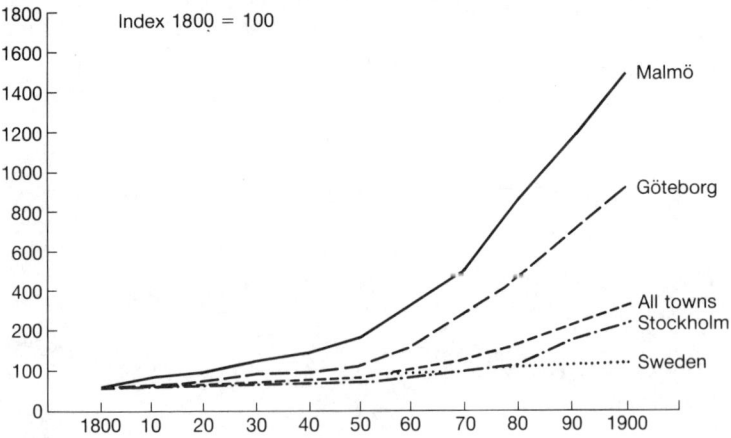

Figure 12.1. Population change in Malmö, Göteborg, Stockholm, all towns, and the whole country, 1800–1900

[1] *Historisk statistik för Sverige*, i. *Befolkning 1720–1967* (Stockholm, 1969).

Migration, Wages, and Urbanization 187

Sweden. The number of inhabitants increased fifteen times during the nineteenth century, and by the 1860s Malmö had already become the country's third largest town, having been the ninth largest at the beginning of the century. The rapid expansion of Malmö can be compared with that of Stockholm, where the population increased four times, and Göteborg, then as now the second largest town, where the size of the population increased ten times during the nineteenth century. One reason why the population increased so fast in Malmö was that it grew both during the commercial and the industrial phase.

In this chapter we shall analyse the role of migration in the urbanization process, and its causes. This will be done against the background of the two dominating theories: migration as a result of labour surplus in agriculture due to increased productivity, and migration in response to wage increases due to industrialization. Special emphasis is laid upon Malmö and other towns in the south of Sweden and their hinterland.

1. Demographic components of urbanization

The rapid growth of the urban population during the nineteenth century was mainly the result of a substantial net in-migration, although natural population increase became important during the latter half of the century. Figure 12.2 shows the actual growth of population in Malmö from 1821 to 1859. It also shows population growth on the assumption of zero net migration and zero natural increase respectively; only the direct effects have been considered. During this period the population of Malmö increased at an

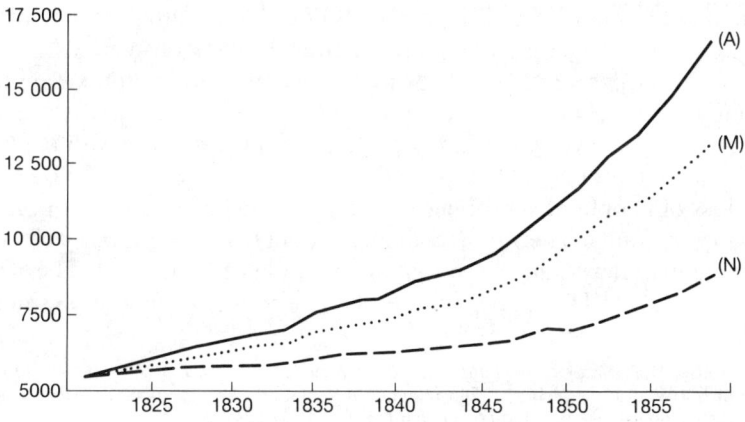

Figure 12.2. Population increase in Malmö, 1821–59: (*A*) actual increase, (*M*) increase with actual migration and zero natural increase, and (*N*) increase with actual natural increase and zero migration

average rate of 2.7 per cent a year; if net migration had been zero the increase would have been as low as 1.1 per cent. The situation is similar for many Swedish towns. In fact, in Stockholm mortality rates were higher than fertility rates, and only a constant in-migration surplus, originating mainly from the surrounding counties could prevent the population of Stockholm from declining.[2]

In the analysis which follows, the development in southern Sweden is emphasized. The investigation is based on a larger study of population growth for the period 1750–1860, i.e. until the fertility transition.[3] The main object of this larger study was to determine the causes of mortality decline. A sample was chosen consisting of about eighty parishes in Scania, the southernmost part of Sweden, representing some 20 per cent of the total population of the county. The sample also contained four towns, Malmö, Landskrona, Helsingborg, and Lund, the three first of which are seaports.

The rural parishes were divided into a number of groups according to their economic and social structure. First, they were divided geographically by separating plain regions, forest regions, and border regions from each other, the latter located on the ridges between the plains and the forests. Within each of these areas the parishes were further grouped by their social structure. Parishes dominated by landowning peasants were put in one group, and those inhabited mainly by tenants into another.

We have already seen that there was a substantial net migration from rural areas to towns during the nineteenth century, but how large was net migration in relation to gross movement and what was the age and sex composition of the migrants? It has been well established that considerable gross migration, especially over short distances, existed in agrarian society. Our results from Scania, too, although based on *Mortalitetstabellerna*, i.e. summaries that conceal movements within each parish, point to a substantial volume of gross migration. On average, gross migration in our rural regions varied between 5 and 16 per cent per year. In the towns, gross annual migration amounted to between 12 and 15 per cent (see Table 12.1). The highest gross migration recorded in a single year was 22 per cent. These figures agree with the results of studies on data relating to individuals.[4]

The loss of people in rural regions was very small compared with the total number of migrants. The average loss was about 0.2 per cent per year, which may be compared with an average gross migration of 11 per cent. The gain for the towns amounted to 1.2 per cent per year, with a gross migration similar to

---

[2] U. Jonsson, *Jordmagnater, landbönder och torpare i sydöstra Södermanland 1800–1880* (Stockholm, 1980); J. Söderberg, 'Den stagnerande staden. Stockholms tillväxtproblem i ett jämförande europeisk perspektiv', *Historisk tidskrift*, 2 (1985).

[3] G. Fridlizius, 'The mortality decline in the first phase of the demographic transition: Swedish experiences', in T. Bengtsson, G. Fridlizius, and R. Ohlsson (eds.), *Pre-Industrial Population Change—The Mortality Decline and Short-Term Population Movements* (Lund, 1984).

[4] G. Fridlizius, 'A Study of Migration in Willie Parish' (unpublished).

Table 12.1 Migration across parish borders in southern Sweden, 1821–59, as a percentage of total population

	In	Out	Net	Gross	r_{in-out}
Southern plain					
Peasant	7.9	8.6	−0.7	16.5	0.32
Manorial	5.7	6.0	−0.2	11.7	0.46
Western plain					
Peasant	6.8	7.0	−0.2	13.8	0.53
Manorial	3.9	4.1	−0.2	7.9	0.76
North-western plain					
Peasant	4.7	4.7	−0.1	9.4	0.32
Manorial	7.1	7.1	0.1	14.2	0.60
Western border area					
Manorial	5.8	6.3	−0.5	12.2	0.49
Eastern border area					
Manorial	5.2	5.6	−0.3	10.8	0.52
Northern forest					
Peasant	2.6	2.7	−0.1	5.3	0.26
Southern forest					
Peasant	4.0	4.0	0.0	8.0	0.80
Malmö	7.1	5.1	2.0	12.3	0.36
Landskrona	6.3	5.7	0.6	12.0	0.42
Helsingborg	—	—	—	—	—
Lund (1823–59)	8.0	6.9	1.1	14.9	0.48

r_{in-out} is the correlation coefficient between in- and out-migration.

Sources: Folkmängdtabellerna, Mortalitetstabellerna, and Flyttningslängderna.

that in the rural regions. Similar results have been obtained from other parts of Sweden.[5] For the period around 1900, the ratio between net and gross migration was about 1:8.[6]

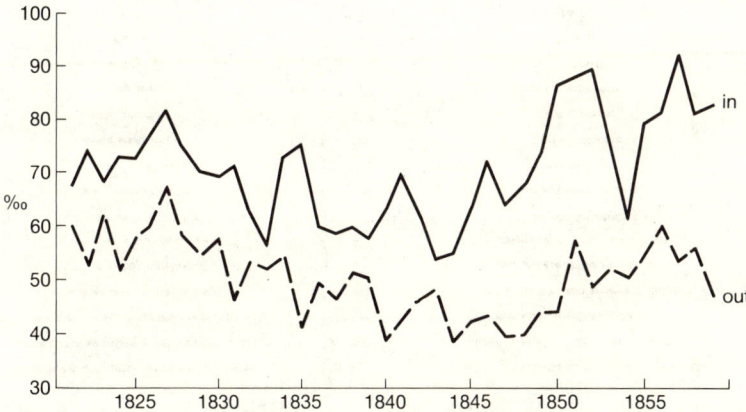

Figure 12.3. In- and out-migration from Malmö, 1821–59

[5] T. Hägerstrand, 'En landsbygdsbefolknings flyttningsrörelser. Studier över migration på grundval av Asby sockens flyttningslängder 1840–1944', in Svensk geografisk årsbok 1947 (Lund, 1947).

[6] D. S. Thomas, Social and Economic Aspects of Swedish Population Movements, 1750–1933 (New York, 1941).

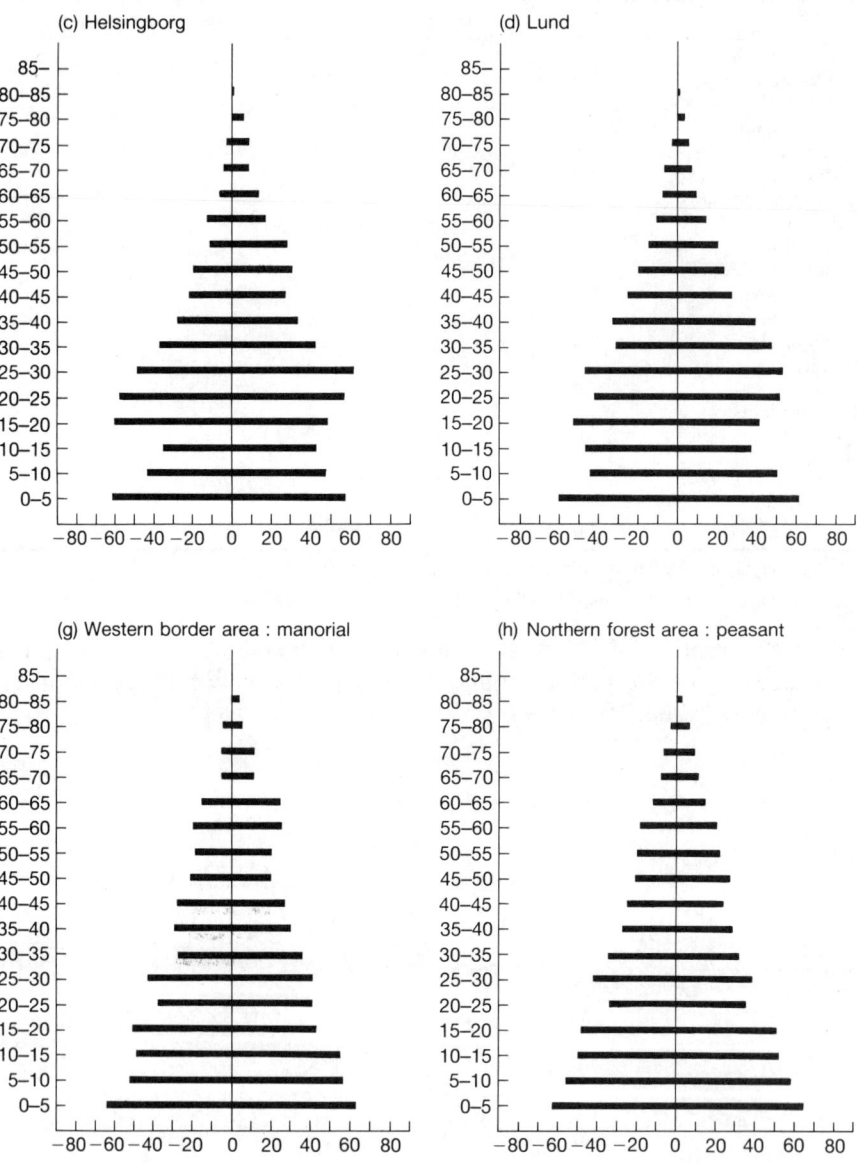

Figure 12.4. Age pyramids for the towns and some regions of Sweden, 1850

Migration, Wages, and Urbanization 191

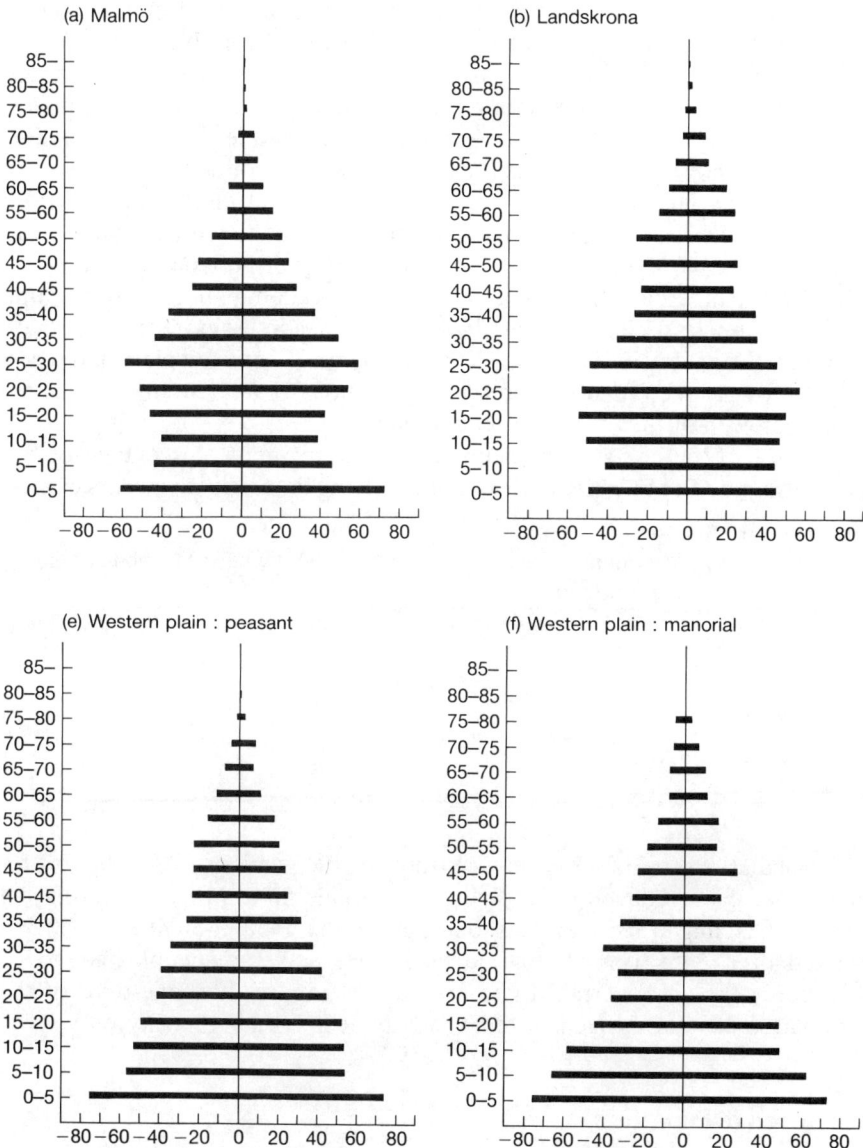

192 *Tommy Bengtsson*

The migration figures in *Mortalitetstabellerna* are given separately for each sex, but are not broken down by age. Almost as many women moved as men: the proportion of women was just below 50 per cent among both in- and outmigrants, both in rural regions and in towns. It varied very little from year to year, which means that men and women moved at almost the same time.[7] Of course, this does not mean that migration was dominated by married couples. On the contrary, we know that it was mainly unmarried servants who moved.

Fig. 12.4 shows age pyramids for towns as well as for some rural areas in 1850. As may be seen, the differences between rural and urban areas are striking. In the rural areas the pyramid takes the traditional triangular form, although in some regions there is some deficiency of population of working age. In urban areas there is a pronounced predominance of population between the ages 15 and 40 years. It is also interesting to note that there are no great differences in the shape of the age pyramid between plain and forest regions, or between manorial and peasant regions. The main differences are found between the towns and the countryside.

In Table 12.2, we see an estimate of the minimum percentage of the population in Malmö in 1850 who were not living in the city five years earlier.

Table 12.2 Minimum percentage of population not living in Malmö five years earlier, 1850

Age-group	Male %	Female%
10–14	7	16
15–19	32	28
20–24	28	34
25–29	30	25
30–34	17	15
35–39	6	3

The calculations are based on the censuses of 1845 and 1850. The figures for 1845 have been reduced by applying age-specific mortality rates during the five years ending in 1850. At least one-third of the population aged 15–30 had arrived after 1845. As gross migration was high, and many people had moved in before 1845, it is certain that, around 1850, more than one-third of the population of working age in Malmö had not been born in that city.

2. Causes of migration

Two explanations of the causes of the large-scale migration to the towns during the nineteenth century have been predominant. But the growth of

---

[7] R. Ohlsson, *Invandrarna på arbetsmarknaden* (Lund, 1975). Ohlsson analyses the immigration to Sweden after the Second World War in terms of structural and short-term 'push' and 'pull' mechanisms.

industry, more than any other factor, has been put forward as an explanation of urbanization.

Whereas the first factories were often located in rural areas, a large proportion of factories set up during the industrial breakthrough were concentrated in urban areas. According to this argument the demand for labour would tend to raise urban wages, and the towns would thus attract labour from its hinterland. This does not necessarily mean that those who actually moved did, in fact, become industrial workers.

The second explanation is based on development within agriculture. As a result of increased productivity a labour surplus was created in the rural areas. The consequent shortage of employment opportunities in the countryside led to migration to the towns. This explanation resembles a Keynesian argument; labour migration is not determined by wage differences, but by job opportunities.

Students of migration have often distinguished between 'push' and 'pull' factors. The industrial demand for labour could be regarded as a structural 'pull' factor and fairly insensitive to short-term fluctuations. Similarly, the increase of productivity in agriculture could be characterized as a structural 'push' factor.[8] The defect of both these theories, however, is that they fail to explain the dominant feature of nineteenth-century migration, namely circular migration, so that net migration is only a small fraction of gross migration. They fail to contribute to an understanding of the migration between rural parishes and from towns to countryside.

The large-scale migration of servants had been going on for a long time, and became regulated very early. The movement was organized so as to reduce the negative effects on production to a minimum. During the eighteenth century almost all migration took place on Michaelmas Day, 29 September. Servants were only allowed to seek new employment after the harvest had been brought in. The service contract could be extended, but there were several reasons why both masters and servants chose not to do so. In the first place, there was a strong seasonal variation in the agricultural demand for labour. Generally, it was largest at harvest time, when additional labour was often employed. Secondly, the demand for labour was determined by the size of the harvest. A poor harvest meant that fewer cattle could be kept through the winter—a very labour-intensive type of production, since the cattle were housed in byres. Therefore, at times of poor harvest, the farmers wished to reduce the number of workers on the farm. The converse is also true. When the harvest was good, there was often talk of a labour shortage.[9]

There are probably other explanations as well. From contemporary sources one gets the impression that servants were constantly looking around for better working and living conditions. The cost of migration must have been

[8] Ibid.
[9] G. Utterström, *Jordbrukets arbetare* (Stockholm, 1957).

very low, and they often moved to another farm, sometimes within the same parish, but just as often to some other parish, without any assurance of improvement. Dissatisfaction with their work appears to have made people move, but, on the other hand, they do not appear to have been motivated to move in order to earn enough to be able to save a little, and then return and establish themselves at home. Yet another reason for migration was movement caused by marriage, as the marriage market extended well beyond the parish.

So it can be seen that for the farm labourer the cost of migration was low, information about jobs was bad, the standard of living was not very high, and the marriage market was limited. So he or she moved time and again, sometimes to a town, but more often to another rural parish. For the landowner, costs per labourer were the same whether the labourer was bad or good, less labour was needed after a bad harvest, only limited skills were needed, and the quality of the labour might improve with new workers. So he would tend to keep the best workers and let the others go and, if necessary, hire more labour later in the hope of improving its quality.

In the next section we consider how wage levels in different parts of the country could have been influenced by industrialization. Did industrialization lead to increasing wage diffusion or not? Unless industrialization had a positive effect on the standard of living, this theory would not explain migration to the towns. In this context, we shall also look at migration between different counties. Were the flows of migrants directed towards counties with high wages? After dealing with these problems we shall return to our study of urbanization in the south of Sweden.

3. Wage differences and migration in Sweden, 1800–1900

In his well-known article on regional inequality Jeffrey Williamson analysed wage differences in a large number of countries, including Sweden,[10] and has continued to elaborate his ideas in a number of articles and in a book about England.[11] According to the classical theory, the capacity to industrialize will differ in different regions of a country. Therefore, in some regions industrialization will occur earlier than in others. The growth of productivity in industry and the demand for labour tend to raise wages in these regions. Therefore, wage differences between different regions are found during the initial phase of industrialization. In turn, this leads to a movement of labour to the regions in which wages are high. Unless there are obstacles to migration and differences in industrialization, wage differences will diminish during the second phase of industrialization. There may well be obstacles to this type of development, but we cannot discuss them here. We are primarily

[10] J. Williamson, 'Regional Inequality and the Process of National Development', *Economic Development and Cultural Change*, 13:4 (1965), Supplement.
[11] J. Williamson, *Did British Capitalism Breed Inequality?* (London and Sydney, 1985).

interested in finding out whether the first phase of industrialization leads to increasing wage differences between regions.

Williamson found that Swedish experience corresponds with his theoretical pattern. His conclusion is based on calculations of wage differences measured by the coefficient of variation, weighted by the size of the county populations. From 1930 onwards, Sweden, according to Williamson, was moving towards a less pronounced regional dualism; the weighted variation coefficient fell from 0.539 in 1930 to 0.192 in 1961. Ohlsson has shown that during the following years wage differences continued to diminish.[12] Thus, Williamson found obvious signs of reduced dualism after 1930, but what was the cause of the large wage differences in 1930? To answer this question we must study regional wage differences for the period of industrialization and the immediately preceding years.

Information about industrial workers' wages during industrialization is extremely scarce and scattered. The limited sources available do not allow calculations of coherent series of regional wage differences. Therefore, I have taken the daily wages of agricultural labourers as our point of departure. These data are useful since they refer to a homogeneous occupation. Daily wages for agricultural labourers only depend on the skills of the individual workers to a limited extent. Data are available for most counties back to the early eighteenth century. Price data for various types of necessities are also available for the same period.[13] If information on family budgets in different regions had been available, it would have been possible to calculate real wages from the beginning of the eighteenth century. However, data relating to consumption are shaky, as are those relating to the number of annual working days. Furthermore, we have little information about the extent of wage payments in kind.

Since we lack information about industrial wages we have been forced to assume that the wage level was raised throughout each region, as a result of industrialization. This assumption means that the industrial demand for labour tended to raise agricultural wages as well, although not to the same level, as a result of competition for labour. Therefore, since our study is based on wages of agricultural labourers, the size of regional wage differences is probably underestimated. Fig. 12.5 shows the unweighted coefficient of variation for wages of agricultural day labourers in five-year periods. The result is almost the same when the regional wages are weighted by the size of the population in each region. In the same figure, the coefficients of variation for cost of living and real wages are shown. The regional cost of living has been calculated by using a national subsistence budget. Regional differences in the cost of subsistence were probably smaller than is indicated by our estimates, since there was an adjustment to the regional supply of goods.[14]

[12] Ohlsson, *Invandrarna*.
[13] L. Jörberg, *A History of Prices in Sweden, 1732–1914* (Lund, 1972).
[14] L. Jörberg, and T. Bengtsson, 'Regional Wages in Sweden during the Nineteenth Century', in P. Bairoch and M. Lévy Leboyer (eds.), *Disparities in Economic Development since the Industrial Revolution* (London, 1981).

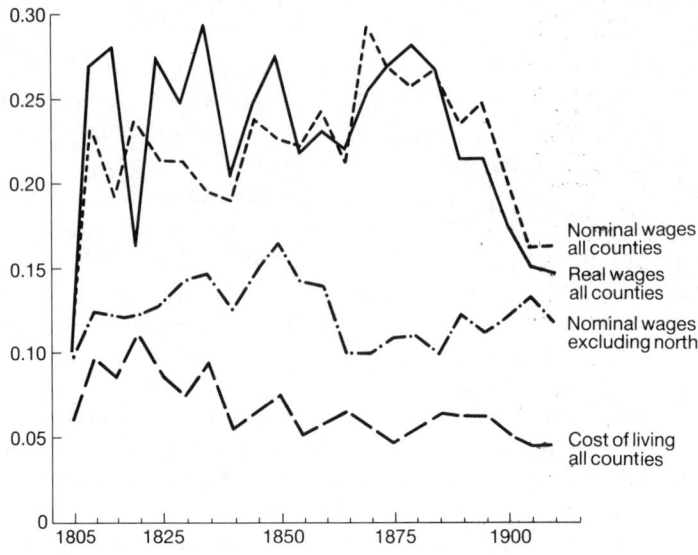

Figure 12.5. Diffusion of real wages in Sweden 1805/9–1910/14: coefficients of variation for nominal wages, cost of living, and average real wages for all counties based on 5-year averages; coefficient of variation for nominal wages for all counties, excluding the four northernmost

First, we find that the coefficient of variation for wages decreased towards the end of the nineteenth century, indicating a reduction of wage differences. As we shall see below, this was due to the spread of industrialization and also to internal migration. Furthermore, we find considerable differences between wage levels before the industrial breakthrough. We would expect a period of increasing wage differences during the 1850s, 1860s, and 1870s caused by industrialization, but wage differences seem to have been stable during this period. To clarify this, the coefficients of variation for nominal wages and rye prices have been calculated as far back as there are data available. In Fig. 12.6 we observe, first, that there were large differences between wage levels long before industrialization, and secondly, looking at the coefficient of variation for rye prices, that there were clear indications of a gradual progress towards market integration. Thus, Williamson's underlying assumption that wage differences were small before industrialization appears to be incorrect.

In order to find reasons why wage differences during the actual process of industrialization were not increasing, we must look at regional wages more closely. We find that daily wages in the counties of the far north were much higher than in other parts of the country (in Fig. 12.5 the coefficient of variation for real wages, after exclusion of these high-wage counties in the north, is also shown). Much of the variation in wages was due to the very high level of wages in the northern counties. When these extreme values were

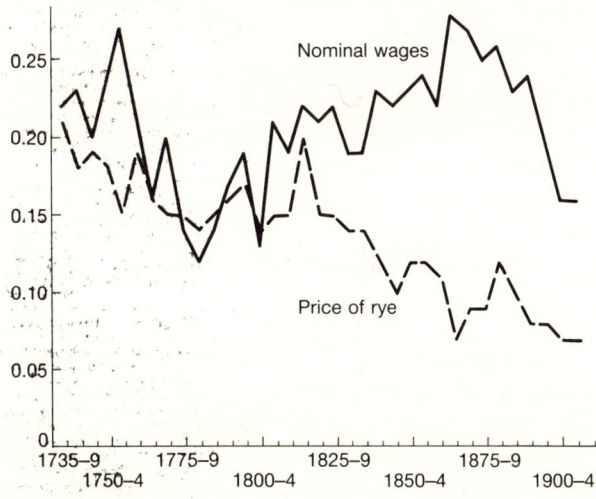

Figure 12.6. Dispersion of nominal wages and prices of rye in Sweden 1735/9–1910/14: coefficients of variation for all counties based on 5-year averages

excluded the size of the coefficient of variation was reduced by about half. A second conclusion is that the reduction of wage differences for the country as a whole during the last decades of the nineteenth century, as shown in Fig. 12.5, could be explained entirely by the closure of the wage gap between the northern counties and other parts of the country. After excluding the northern counties we find a stable, or perhaps somewhat increasing, dualism during this period.

An equally interesting finding is that a period of growing dualism already existed before the middle of the nineteenth century. This was followed by a period of rapid integration during the 1850s. It is true that industrialization had already begun during the first half of the century. However, it is not likely to have been sufficiently universal to have had so strong an impact on wages for agricultural labourers. Thus, before the middle of the nineteenth century, something appears to have happened in agriculture and commerce that led to increasing wage differences between different regions. Furthermore, in an earlier study we have shown that there was a certain correlation between migration between counties and wage levels from the mid-nineteenth century onwards.[15] Thus we find evidence for decreasing wage differences after the phase of industrial breakthrough and of migration to counties in which real wages were higher. However, there appear to be reasons other than industrialization for wage differences before the middle of the nineteenth century.

The next section deals with the relationship between towns and countryside in Scania and emphasizes urbanization before industrialization. The first real

[15] Ibid.

factories in Malmö were established during the 1850s, but the actual breakthrough did not occur until some decades later, just as in the country as a whole. We have already seen that there was massive migration to Malmö as early as the first half of the nineteenth century. What were the causes of this migration? Was it a consequence of an agrarian transformation, or were there other forces at work?

4. Urbanization in southern Sweden, 1820–1860

Industrialization cannot have been the cause of the wage differences which stimulated migration in the towns during this period. Labour still migrated to areas in which wages were high, but factors other than industrialization must have caused the wage differences. One possible factor is commerce, which was concentrated in the seaports.[16] The growth of foreign trade in Malmö and other Scanian seaports might well have stimulated economic activity in the towns, and this, in turn, could explain a rapid increase in urban wages. As is shown in Fig. 12.7, urban nominal wages did increase faster than rural wages.

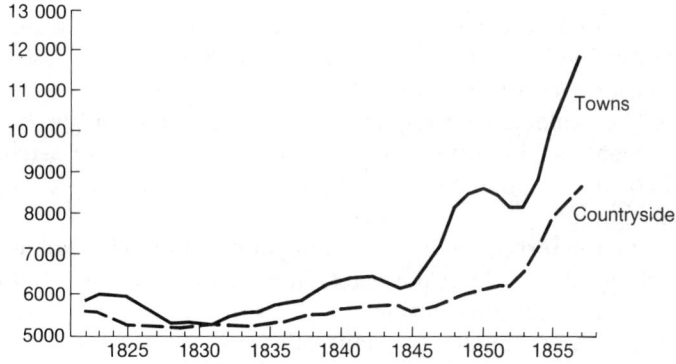

Figure 12.7. Nominal wages in the towns and in the countryside of Scania, 1821–59

These wage data also refer to agricultural daily wages. Wages for this type of manual labour are relevant, since those who moved to urban areas were often employed as outdoor labourers. Unfortunately, data for the number of days of employment are not available. We also lack data concerning the composition of consumption, and price data for certain items, such as housing.

However, the nature and conditions of work in the Scanian towns could hardly have differed much from those prevailing in rural areas. The price of certain commodities, such as rye, increased somewhat faster in the towns than

[16] G. Fridlizius, 'Från spannmålstullar till smördrittlar. Malmös handel och sjöfart, 1870–1913', in *Malmö stadshistoria* (Malmö, 1985).

in the countryside during the 1850s. However, the increased costs are not likely to have been large enough to counterbalance the entire difference in wages. There are almost no wage data for Malmö. However, since the differences between Lund, Landskrona, and Helsingborg are small, an average for these towns has been used as an indicator of wages in all four towns. The trend towards increasing wage differences between urban and rural areas could have been a result of expanding commercial activity leading to an increase in the demand for labour. This could, therefore, be characterized as a structural 'pull' factor.

The structural transformation of agriculture in the manorial regions occurred in two different ways. In some cases, farms were tied directly to the manor as part of the process of making production more rational and efficient. As a consequence, some people were forced to leave their farms. This is the type of change normally referred to when it is argued that structural transformation tends to create a labour surplus. However, in some cases the change proceeded quite differently. The land was first divided into smaller parcels and then sold. A large population could be supported on these small plots of land by labour-intensive production which led to increasing returns. Whereas the first type could be characterized as a structural 'push' factor, the second must be described as a structural 'pull' factor. Although the first alternative is often assumed to have been dominant, this is far from being self-evident.[17]

The decision to move and the choice of destination could be explained by these structural factors. Yet the timing of the movement depended on short-term factors. The tendency of landowners to reduce the size of their labour force in times of poor harvests can be regarded as a short-term 'push' factor which could explain the large variations in migration from the rural areas. Is there, then, a short-term 'pull' factor that can explain the large annual changes in in-migration to the towns? Obviously, a potential migrant would choose to move at a time when conditions were as favourable as possible at the place of destination.[18] However, what is less certain is whether he was responding solely to high wages or primarily to the supply of jobs. Once he had arrived in the town, he could look for a job with higher wages. Job opportunities could thus be a short-term 'pull' factor, as could the variations in wage differences between urban and rural areas. Since we have no direct indicator of job opportunities in the towns, we must use the wage difference as a short-term 'pull' factor. In so doing, we align ourselves with the neo-classical approach.

In discussing the influence of short-term 'push' and 'pull' factors on migration within the country, a difficulty arises, because short-term variations in prices are similar everywhere. The difference between real wages in the

[17] G. Fridlizius, 'Population, Enclosure and Property Rights', *Economy and History*, 22:1 (1979).
[18] Ohlsson, *Invandrarna*.

town and in the countryside strongly depends on the level of rural real wages, which, in their turn, are determined by food prices. Thus the size of the harvest will affect both rural job opportunities and differences in real wages, and, thereby, the attractiveness of the towns. For instance, a poor harvest leads to fewer job opportunities in the country and to a rise in food prices, thus reducing wage differences. If out-migration from rural areas increases in years of poor harvests we can, therefore, safely assume that the decision to move is determined by the short-term 'push' factor. If, on the other hand, the movement takes place in the year after a poor harvest, i.e. in a year of good harvest, short-term 'pull' factors could be assumed to dominate.

The large out-migration from the towns in relation to net migration makes it difficult to determine the influence of short-term factors. The towns appear to be part of the local labour market for agricultural workers. While some of them move to towns, others move to other rural parishes in this large-scale circular migration.

The following model has been constructed to investigate whether poor harvests led to increasing out-migration:

$$(1)\ E_t = a + b_1 E_{t-1} + c_0 R_t + c_1 R_{t-1} + d_0 D_t + d_1 D_{t-1} + e_1$$

where E is the out-migration rate, R is the price of rye, and D is the nominal wage difference between the towns and the rural region studied. The series has been detrended by calculating the first differences of the logarithms of the values. Since there is reason to assume an inherent correlation in this, as in most other demographic series, the model contains an autoregressive term. The reason for including rye prices for the previous year is that we wish to see whether any effects of a poor harvest in that year remain. This model enables us to see whether there are short-term 'push' and 'pull' factors.

In addition to our study of out-migration from different regions and towns, we may also study in-migration by means of a similar model:

$$(2)\ I_t = a + b_1 I_{t-1} + c_0 E_t + c_1 E_{t-1} + d_0 R_t + d_1 R_{t-1} + f_0 D_t + f_1 D_{t-1} + e_2$$

where I is the the in-migration rate and the other variables are as shown above. The only difference is that out-migration is included in the model as an explanatory factor. The idea behind this model is that when out-migration is particularly large as a result of structural and short-term 'pull' factors, a labour deficit could occur in a given region. This deficit is reduced by in-migration from other regions or by re-migration from the towns, either during the year of out-migration or in the following year. A model in which nuptiality is included as an additional explanatory variable has also been constructed in order to test the hypothesis that some migration occurred in connection with marriages. However, no evidence has been found to support this hypothesis. F-values have been calculated in order to test whether the model is significant and q-values have been calculated to test for autocorrelation in the residuals. Where autocorrelation was found it was reduced by an extension of the model with a two-year time-lag in the dependent variable.

For the whole period 1821–59 we find practically no correlation at all between price fluctuations and migration. A closer study of the migration series shows that the 1850s differed markedly from previous decades, in that very large annual fluctuations in migration suddenly appear. Despite the fact that the movement of corn prices was similar in different regions, migration waves did not occur in all regions at the same time. Thus the causes of migration are not to be found in economizing in connection with poor harvests. In fact, migration appears to be a result of a planned structural change. We also know from other sources that rationalizations were taking place during the 1850s.[19]

If the period is shortened to cover the years 1821–50 only, the results are quite different (see Tables 12.3 and 12.4). In many regions we find a significant correlation between rye prices and out-migration. In most cases our simple model 'explains' about 40 per cent of the variation in out-migration. However, out-migration is not affected by rye prices in all regions. The correlation is strongest in the western and north-western plains in the eastern border region. In these areas out-migration increased in years of high rye prices. Since the response is strongest when there is no time-lag, short-term 'push' factors must have dominated the timing of migration to towns and other regions. Furthermore, the correlation between wage differences and prices, as discussed earlier, is not strong enough to cause any problems of multicollinearity.

There are no signs of short-term 'push' mechanisms at work in the southern plain peasant region, today one of the most fertile areas of Europe. In this case, our results are more uncertain. First, the random variation in the data for this region is stronger since the population is much smaller. Secondly, this area is economically and geographically oriented towards Ystad, a seaport on the south coast not included in our sample. Thus, we cannot draw any safe conclusions about the results for this region. The pattern is also somewhat varied as regards in-migration to the towns. In-migration to the university town of Lund appears not to have been influenced by the harvests in its hinterland, but for the two seaports and commercial centres of Malmö and Landskrona, for which we have migration data, we find in-migration to have been particularly large in years of high rye prices. Thus, the results of our analysis of in-migration to the towns support our analysis of out-migration from the rural regions. We also find that out-migration from both manorial and peasant regions is sensitive to rye prices. Thus, quite obviously, landlords as well as peasants tended to economize by reducing the size of the labour force during times of poor harvests. In-migration and re-migration to the

---

[19] Fridlizius, 'Population, Enclosure and Property Rights'.

Table 12.3 Estimates of the out-migration model for 1821–1850

	a	b_1 (E_{t-1})	c_0 (R_t)	c_1 (R_{t-1})	d_0 (D_t)	d_1 (D_{t-1})	R_a^2	F	Q_{10}
Southern plain									
Peasant	0.03(33.3)	−0.34(6.0)	—	0.20(4.4)	—	—	0.22	4.6	5.3
Manorial	0.02(61.0)	−0.56(0.2)	—	—	—	—	0.29	11.5	4.8
Western plain									
Peasant	0.01(67.4)	−0.64(0.0)	0.15(6.7)	—	—	—	0.37	8.9	6.0
Manorial	−0.01(74.5)	−0.69(0.0)	0.25(7.3)	—	—	—	0.43	10.8	6.9
North-western plain									
Peasant	0.02(45.6)	−0.52(0.3)	0.39(0.1)	—	—	—	0.41	10.0	9.0
Manorial	0.01(72.4)	—	0.28(6.8)	—	—	—	0.09	2.3[N]	6.8
Western border area									
Manorial	0.03(48.9)	—	—	−0.28(10.1)	−0.01(13.4)	—	0.23	4.8	5.1
Eastern border area									
Manorial	0.02(60.0)	−0.48(2.6)	0.38(3.8)	—	0.02(2.1)	−0.02(5.6)	0.25	3.8	4.7
Northern forest									
Peasant	0.04(6.1)	−0.23(14.3)	—	−0.36(0.0)	—	—	0.42	10.3	6.2
Southern forest									
Peasant	0.01(87.1)	−0.30(5.2)	−0.35(0.2)	−0.60(1.0)	—	—	0.26	3.3	3.7
Malmö	0.02(28.0)	−0.43(1.1)	—	0.17(6.0)	—	0.17(6.0)	0.34	5.5	2.5
Landskrona	0.01(79.1)	−0.35(7.3)	—	—	—	—	0.08	3.5	4.2
Lund (1823–59)	0.02(59.2)	−0.59(0.2)	—	—	—	0.02(5.7)	0.36	7.8	4.1

Figures in parentheses show the probability (per cent) that the true coefficient is zero. Q is calculated for 10 lags. The 5% significance level is 18.3.
[N] means not significant at the 5% level. R_a^2 is the adjusted determination coefficient.

Table 12.4 Estimates of the in-migration model for 1821–1850

	a	b_1 (I_{t-1})	c_0 (E_t)	c_1 (E_{t-1})	d_0 (R_t)	d_1 (R_{t-1})	f_0 (D_t)	f_1 (D_{t-1})	R_a^2	F	Q_{10}
Southern plain											
Peasant	0.01(70.0)	−0.84(0.0)	—	0.42(2.6)	—	—	—	—	0.52	15.0	2.7
Manorial	0.04(30.3)	−0.40(5.0)	—	—	—	—	−0.02(3.2)	−0.02(10.3)	0.26	4.0	4.7
Western plain											
Peasant	−0.20(5.8)	−0.29(4.7)	—	0.53(0.0)	—	—	−0.01(2.4)	—	0.48	7.0	7.3
Manorial	0.01(83.7)	—	—	0.29(2.6)	—	—	—	—	0.15	5.6	3.4
North-western plain											
Peasant	0.02(66.0)	−0.40(4.2)	—	—	—	0.32(4.4)	—	—	0.18	3.9	16.8
Manorial	0.03(41.7)	−0.52(0.6)	—	—	−0.48(1.2)^A	0.32(2.3)	—	—	0.35	5.8	6.7
Western border area											
Manorial	0.01(70.1)	—	—	0.27(2.5)	—	—	—	−0.01(10.4)	0.14	3.1^N	4.3
Eastern border area											
Manorial	0.02(59.2)	−0.53(1.1)	0.66(0.3)	0.43(5.2)	−0.51(1.3)^A	0.49(2.8)^B	—	—	0.35	3.9	5.3
Northern forest											
Peasant	0.05(10.8)	−0.36(3.5)	−0.56(1.4)	—	—	—	—	0.02(3.1)	0.36	5.9	3.8
Southern forest											
Peasant	0.01(85.3)	−0.13(34.9)	—	—	−0.52(1.7)	—	—	−0.10(0.2)	0.44	7.9	2.1
Malmö	0.02(11.7)	—	—	—	0.25(0.4)	—	0.02(0.7)	0.01(3.8)	0.38	6.3	3.3
Landskrona	0.01(80.1)	—	0.28(4.7)	—	0.22(8.7)	—	—	—	0.26	5.5	5.9
Land (1823–59)	0.00(87.4)	—	—	—	—	—	0.01(9.5)	—	0.08	3.0^N	8.1

A is the coefficient for in$_{t-2}$. It has been included to reduce autocorrelation in the residuals. B is the coefficient for out$_{t-2}$. It has been included for the same reason.
Figures in parentheses show the probability (per cent) that the true coefficient is zero. Q is calculated for 10 lags. The 5% significance level for Q is 18.3.
N means not significant at the 5% level. R_a^2 is the adjusted determination coefficient.

rural regions, however, do not appear to be correlated as strongly with variations in the harvest as does out-migration. Several factors seem to work as determinants: out-migration during the previous year and—though to a lesser extent—wage differences and rye prices. Nor does out-migration from the towns appear to have been determined by the harvest.

To summarize our preliminary study of the period 1821–59, it can be seen that higher urban wages could have functioned as a structural 'pull' factor. However, these high wages were connected with commercial rather than industrial activity. The structural changes in agriculture during the 1850s appear to have led to an increase in out-migration from rural areas. Until about 1850, short-term 'push' factors appear to have been decisive for the timing of out-migration from rural areas. Thereafter, structural factors appear also to have determined short-run migration for some time. There are no signs to indicate that the social structure was an influential cause of out-migration. In manorial as well as in peasant regions out-migration increased during years of poor harvests. When it comes to economic structure we find that the differences between plain and border regions were not particularly pronounced, while migration in the forest regions does not seem to have been affected by harvests. One might perhaps discern a pattern that it was largely in the plain region that out-migration was influenced by harvests. In turn, this would be due to the more specialized nature of production in the plain region compared with other regions. Finally, there was a large re-migration which cannot be explained by either structural 'push' or 'pull' factors.

13 The Changing Structure of Urban Employment and its Effects on Migration Patterns in Eighteenth- and Nineteenth-Century Japan

OSAMU SAITO
The Institute of Economic Research, Hitotsubashi University, Kunitachi, Tokyo, Japan

The labour market may be divided into two parts. The first consists of jobs in which people are employed for longish periods, sometimes for the whole of their lives, which provide opportunities for promotion and higher wages, and where employment is relatively secure. The second part consists of jobs which last a short time only, and where labour turnover is, therefore, high. The work-force in the first part of the market is 'internalized' in the firm, but that in the second part is not. A similar distinction existed in pre-modern times, the former type of employment being live-in service, and the latter casual labour. Apprentices in merchants' and craftmen's households tended to serve longer than farm servants, and, since casual work was available mainly in the towns, this distinction was more pronounced in urban than in rural employment. Of course, there are marked differences, as well as similarities, between the work-forces of modern corporations, and service and apprenticeships in pre-modern trades and crafts. In Europe, for instance, servants and apprentices were traditionally unmarried, and lived in households other than their parents'. Indeed, as Peter Laslett has stressed, a majority were 'life-cycle' servants.[1] Thus the numbers of servants and apprentices, the proportion they formed of the urban work-force, and changes in the composition of this work-force over time must have affected migration from the countryside to the towns. Particularly relevant in this respect is recent criticism of the 'urban graveyard' model by Allan Sharlin and Ad van der Woude; calling attention to the status of servants and apprentices and to migrants' marriage behaviour, they have questioned the conventional view on

---

The research on which this chapter is based was supported by a grant from the Japan Economic Research Foundation.

[1] P. Laslett, 'Characteristics of the Western Family considered over time', *Family Life and Illicit Love in Earlier Generations* (Cambridge, 1977), ch. 1, p. 34.

the functions of rural–urban migration in pre-industrial urbanization and de-urbanization.[2]

In this chapter we ask similar questions about traditional Japan. We begin by considering the numbers of servants and apprentices listed in urban population records and seeing what changes occurred in their status. We shall see that there were two divergent trends in the urban labour markets of the eighteenth and nineteenth centuries: 'internalization of a labour market' and 'casualization of employment'. We continue by considering how such contrasting trends affected migration patterns during the latter half of the old Tokugawa regime, and, in the final section, consider some wider implications.[3]

I

How many servants were recorded in the towns and cities of pre-industrial Japan? What proportions did they form of the urban population? What proportions of all households employed servants? These are simple questions, but little effort has been made to answer them; there has been virtually no systematic survey of evidence. The figures in Table 13.1 constitute the first attempt to assess the relative importance of servants and apprentices in the urban population of the old Tokugawa regime. They summarize the evidence I have collected from either secondary sources or original registers for Edo (later Tokyo), Kyoto, Osaka, and other towns during the 1860s, i.e. the transition period from the Tokugawa to the new Meiji era. All the registers cover *chōnin* (townsmen) only; *samurai* (warriors) and their families and servants—who also lived in towns—were excluded. The term 'servant' (*hōkōnin*) which was used in contemporary documents often relates to apprentices as well as 'domestic servants', although it is not, unfortunately, possible to distinguish between these two categories from the registers.

A close look at the figures in Table 13.1 shows a surprisingly wide variation in the employment of servants. In two of the boroughs at the centre of Osaka, the great commercial city of the period, as many as half the population were servants and four out of five households employed at least one servant.[4] At the other end of the spectrum, only one male servant was listed in three

---

[2] A. Sharlin, 'Natural Decrease in Early Modern Cities: A Reconsideration', *Past and Present*, 79 (1978); A. M. van der Woude, 'Population Developments in the Northern Netherlands (1500–1800) and the Validity of the "Urban Graveyard" Effect', *Annales de démographie historique* (1982). See also J. de Vries, *European Urbanization, 1500–1800* (London and Cambridge, Mass., 1984), 179–198.

[3] Sections I–III rely heavily on my own article published in Japanese, 'Shōka hōkōnin to zatsugyōsha: kinsei toshi rōdōshijō ni okeru ninjūkōzō no keisei', *Keizai kenkyū*, 36:3 (1985). See this article for source materials and detailed bibliographical information about books and articles in Japanese not cited in this chapter.

[4] For a comparison with Europe in terms of these measures, see Laslett, *Family Life and Illicit Love*, table 1.6, pp. 32–3. It is interesting to note that the highest figures so far known for Europe

Table 13.1 Servants in towns, 1860s

Town	Year	Mean household size	Servants per household	Proportion of households with servants %	Proportion of servants in population %	Sex ratio of servants (male per 100 females)
Edo						
Nihonbashi Hongokuchō ni-chōme	1869	6.06	2.14	41.7	35.2	n.a.
Kanda Matsudachō	1870	4.50	0.17	6.0	3.8	n.a.
Yotsuya Denmachō Shin-itchōme	1865	3.94	0.09	5.2	2.4	All male
Kōjimachi jūni-chōme	1865	4.01	0.03	2.8	0.7	All male
Shibuya, 3 boroughs	1867	4.03	0.004	0.4	0.1	One male
Kyoto						
Shijō Tachiuri Naka-no-machi[a]	1863	4.06	0.77	33.3	18.9	178.9
Gojōbashi Higashi ni-chōme Higashibori	1863	6.37	2.10	57.9	33.1	233.3
Hakurakuten-chō	1868	4.64	1.00	36.4	21.6	450.0
Kameya-machi	1868	3.90	0.67	20.5	17.1	420.0
Osaka						
Amagasaki itchōme	1866	6.20	3.06	83.5	49.3	87.1
Kōraibashi san-chōme	1869	4.80	1.59	48.6	33.2	93.4
Kajikichō	1864	4.98	1.48	79.2	29.6	65.5
Shichirōemonchō itchōme	1870	4.67	1.21	41.4	26.0	97.7
Shōninmachi	1870	4.54	1.13	44.4	24.8	153.1
Dōshōmachi san-chōme[a]	1860	6.09	2.89	83.3	47.4	134.2
Hiranomachi ni-chōme	1860	5.67	2.45	68.1	42.5	71.6
Kikuyamachi[a]	1860	5.33	1.88	59.5	35.3	192.6
Kobikichō Minami-no-chō	1860	4.35	1.24	58.7	28.5	106.7
Miike-dōri go-chōme[a]	1861	4.31	1.15	50.0	26.6	169.3
Tennōji, 2 boroughs	1858	3.42	0.04	3.8	1.1	150.0
Castle Town						
Kawagoe Kitamachi	1859	5.00	0.48	16.7	9.7	211.1
Iwamurada[a]	1858	4.41	0.05	—	1.2	375.0
Kōfu Mikkamachi[a]	1858	3.96	0.04	—	0.9	400.0
Takayama, 2 boroughs	1858	4.08	0.03	1.0	0.7	392.3
Hikone Demachō[a]	1860	4.00	0.16	—	4.0	116.7
Hikone Kawaramachi[a]	1861	5.72	0.05	—	0.9	25.0
Other						
Kōriyama Kamimachi[a]	1867–8	n.a.	n.a.	n.a.	6.2	8.5
Hirano-gō-machi	1853	4.58	0.01	n.a.	0.2	216.7
Nishinomiya, 4 boroughs	1871	3.99	0.41	16.3	10.2	56.3

[a] denotes that this entry also appears in Table 13.2.

Source: O. Saito, 'Shōka hōkōnin to zatsugyōsha: kinsei toshi rōdōshijō ni okeru ninjukōzō no keisei', *Keizai kenkyū*, 36:(1985), Table 1, 252.

Shibuya boroughs on the outskirts of Edo, the *de facto* capital city during the Tokugawa period. But the shape rather than the range of the distribution is more important. In all boroughs in Kyoto and Osaka, except two Tennōji towns which were officially regarded as 'villages', the proportion of servants exceeded 15 per cent of the population, and in a majority of this group the proportion was well over 20 per cent. In all the Osaka boroughs in this group, the proportion of servants exceeded 25 per cent of the population. When the percentages are broken down by ownership of residence the figures are even higher; there was at least one servant in every household of the propertied class in Osaka boroughs, and the average number of servants per household exceeded four. In Amagasaki itchōme and Doshōmachi san-chōme, where a particularly large number of wealthy merchants lived, the average exceeded ten servants per household. Although the figures in Table 13.1 do not show clearly that there was always an excess of male servants, the ratios in all the Osaka boroughs were higher for the propertied class than for the unpropertied. As all apprentices were male, this suggests that the larger the business, the greater was the number of apprentices, rather than of domestic servants, who were employed. For instance, in Amagasaki itchōme, where overall there were more female than male servants, the sex ratio for the propertied class was 110.0 compared with 66.7 for the unpropertied; in Doshōmachi san-chōme where male servants were more numerous, the ratios were 190.9, and 97.0 respectively. On the other hand, for all the boroughs in Edo, except one in Nihonbashi, and in all the other categories, the proportion of servants in the population hardly reached 10 per cent, and in most of the towns in this group the proportion of households with servants was below 10 per cent. Even those townsmen who owned their residences, the upper class in the urban hierarchy, rarely employed servants. The distribution of towns in Table 13.1 by proportion of servants is, therefore, bimodal.

However, such a clear demarcation is not found for earlier periods. In Table 13.2 we see a similar, but smaller set of examples for the period around 1700. No borough of Edo appears in this table. But the result is unmistakable: a continuous, unimodal distribution. In other words, there was a substantial servant population in most towns, cities, and castle towns alike during the late seventeenth and early eighteenth centuries. Thus the proportion of servants in the population was very similar in Kikuyamachi, Osaka, and Iwamurada, a small castle town in the province of Shinano. Similarly the figures for Kōfu's Mikkamachi and a Kyoto borough are roughly the same. Although quantitative data are not available, Edo presumably was no exception. Recent work on the records of drop-outs in several boroughs in the city centre suggests that servants, especially those with a long-term contract, were numerous during the early eighteenth century.

are found for medieval towns: 46 and 49% for the proportion of servant-keeping households in two parishes of Rheims, 1422, and 25% for the proportion of servants in the population of Coventry, 1523. See C. Phythian-Adams, *Desolation of a City* (Cambridge, 1979), 204.

Table 13.2 Servants in towns, c. 1700

Town	Year	Mean household size	Servants per household	Proportion of households with servants %	Proportion of servants in population %	Sex ratio of servants (male per 100 females)
Kyoto						
Shijō Tachiuri Naka-no-machi[a]	1697	5.58	2.09	74.4	37.5	145.9
Osaka						
Whole city	1689	4.70	0.83	n.a.	17.6	176.3
Doshōmachi san-chōme[a]	1684	4.28	0.97	33.2	22.8	231.4
Kikuyamachi[a]	1682	3.84	0.78	39.6	20.4	186.2
Mike-dōri go-chōme[a]	1700	n.a.	n.a.	n.a.	13.7	n.a.
Castle Town						
Iwamurada[a]	1689	5.67	1.12	n.a.	19.7	138.3
Kōfu Mikkamachi[a]	1694	5.07	1.76	—	34.7	82.6
Okazaki Renjakuchō	1698	6.39	2.99	65.3	46.8	104.5
Hikone, 30 boroughs	1695	3.64	0.37	n.a.	10.1	190.7
Hikone Denmachō[a]	1695	4.29	0.50	—	11.8	147.6
Hikone Kawaramachi[a]	1695	4.03	0.54	—	13.4	197.2
Okayama	1707	n.a.	n.a.	n.a.	9.3	154.9
Other						
Kōriyama Kamimachi[a]	1729	7.91	1.57	—	19.8	84.7
Jōhanamachi	1693	5.60	1.13	36.8	20.2	24.8
Nishinomiya Hama-issaichō	1713	4.95	0.20	12.9	4.0	333.3

[a] denotes that this entry also appears in Table 13.1.

Source: O. Saito, 'Shōka hōkōnin', Table 3, 255.

Clearly, two different types of change occurred during the eighteenth and early nineteenth centuries. There was a trend towards employing more servants. This was typically so in Osaka, where on average every household ended up by employing one additional servant. The other change was a dramatic decrease in the number of listed servants. This seems to have occurred in all the Edo boroughs, except those in Nihonbashi, and in a number of castle towns. By the end of the Tokugawa period, servants had virtually disappeared from the population registers of these towns.

II

We must next ask why such divergent trends occurred. The hypothesis which immediately suggests itself is that the expansion or contraction of the employment of servants can be accounted for by growth or decline in the urban economy. Certainly, in Osaka, increased prosperity seems to have led to an increase in the proportion of servants in the population. In the city centre, where many of the wealthiest merchants had their shops, such changes were registered during the first quarter of the eighteenth century or even earlier, whereas in towns outside the centre the increase in the servant population began during the latter half of the century or even later, as prosperity spread from the centre area. But many towns, especially castle towns, diminished in size during the eighteenth and early nineteenth centuries,[5] and in most of them, the number of registered servants decreased as well.

Nevertheless, the hypothesis is not tenable. It might well be true that an increase in the employment of servants could be attributed to the expansion of urban trade and the growth of business organization. As we shall see later, this was true of Osaka's business community. However, it does not follow that the converse is also true. In many castle towns, there were considerable losses of population, especially in their central business areas. But this was not always due to urban decay. In some cases, population losses in the centre were more than compensated by increases in the outer areas, which might well be a sign of growth, rather than of decline, of urban economy. Moreover, the experience of Edo suggests an association between the decrease in the number of listed servants and economic prosperity. During the period between 1780 and 1820 when servants started to disappear from the registers, there was a flowering of popular culture such as *kabuki* and *yose* (variety shows), which was, indeed, enabled by rising levels of living among town dwellers. Clearly prosperity or decline in the urban economy could not be the only explanation for the divergent trends in the employment of servants.

---

[5] For an excellent account of the phenomenon of de-urbanization, see T. C. Smith, 'Premodern Economic Growth, Japan and the West', *Past and Present*, 60 (1973).

It is revealing to look at the occupational structure of towns in relation to the expansion and disappearance of urban resident servants. We can use the early Meiji statistics relating to occupations in the boroughs of Tokyo and Osaka for this purpose, as they are representative of the two groups of towns. While the statistics for Tokyo in 1873 cover the whole of the city's areas, the figures for Osaka, taken from a manuscript belonging to an official, relate to only one of the three city wards. But judging by its location and economic and social characteristics, the ratios obtained from these figures seem to have been close to the average for other wards. Persons listed as 'occupied' are supposed to be family heads only. A comparison of the population of the two cities in five occupational categories shows that tradesmen formed the largest group in Osaka (41 per cent), whereas in Tokyo the largest group were *zatsugyō* (41 per cent), literally 'miscellaneous occupations' which included waste-pickers and street entertainers, as well as petty stallholders, but which consisted chiefly of hawkers and day labourers. However, if we single out one area in Ward I which ran through the main street from Nihonbashi to the Ginza and where many branch shops belonging to Osaka and Kyoto merchants were situated, the occupational structure turns out to be quite different from that of all the other Tokyo areas, and is, indeed, more like that of Osaka. It is interesting to note, moreover, that the same official statistics show that the proportion of servants in this area was exceptionally high, compared with other Tokyo wards.

These results suggest that it was among tradesmen, and particularly among those trading on a large scale, that the employment of servants expanded. It is also likely that the abundance of work opportunities for day labourers and hawkers was connected with the disappearance of living-in servants from the population registers. Indeed, in contemporary comparisons between Osaka and Edo, it was pointed out that large businesses belonging to wealthy wholesalers and money-changers were characteristic of Osaka. One such merchant, Mitsui's Echigoya (now Mitsukoshi Department Store), for instance, owned nine drapery shops in Kyoto, Osaka, and Edo, and, according to an 1840 document, employed a total of 1,020 servants, all of whom were male. In contrast, there were few tradesmen in Edo rich enough to be compared to their counterparts in Osaka. The most numerous occupations in Edo were men in the catering industry, and agents acting as 'go-between' (*kuchiire*) in labour markets for unskilled jobs, such as casual workers in construction work, domestic servants living-in on a seasonal (or monthly) basis, and charwomen. Contemporary observations, therefore, support our conclusion. They also suggest that those who vanished from Edo's population registers were servants who lived in their master's household for a year or more, and that the distinction between 'servants' (*hōkōnin*) and those working for others on a short-term basis had become fluid. In these sectors of urban society, therefore, servants and apprentices were replaced by workers employed from the pool of casual labour, and for the latter *kuchiire* business grew in clusters. To put it differently, while large-scale establishments in the trading sector 'internalized' a labour-market, small- and medium-size merchants and craftsmen, and even *samurai* estates, tended to 'casualize' employment.

III

This difference between large trading establishments and other urban employers has so far attracted little attention. Virtually no effort has been made to identify factors associated with this interesting phenomenon. Yet it seems plausible that differences in the training system were crucial. In trades such as petty retailing and catering, much lower skills and expertise were required, and these could be acquired within a relatively short period. Employers liked to be able to hire and fire totally unskilled workers, such as cleaners and other domestic servants, *whenever* they wanted, unless there were abundant supplies of living-in servants at wages low enough to counterbalance the disadvantage of long-term contracts. Indeed, since real wages for agricultural labourers and, perhaps, for those in the lower strata of urban society rose gradually during the eighteenth century, resulting in a contraction of wage differentials between the skilled and the unskilled,[6] it was likely that workers engaged by the day of the month would be substituted during the late eighteenth and early nineteenth centuries for those living-in and engaged for the year. Moreover, it was noted that the number of living-in servants in Edo declined because both *samurai* and merchants became 'calculating' (*soroban-zuku*, which literally means 'reckoning on the abacus'). If such changes in attitude actually occurred, they would support our argument.

On the other hand, increased skill and expertise were required for clerical work in trading, as the size of business and hence the scale of organization grew. This seems to have been the case in the houses of Mitsui and Kōnoike, two of the best-known merchants of the Tokugawa period. Of course, trading was not the only occupation for which some form of systematic training was necessary. In various crafts, apprenticeships, usually extending over ten years, had become institutionalized; and both clerks and apprentices were exclusively male. There was a clear trend for retaining apprentices and shop assistants for longer periods than craftsmen. The case of Mitsui is instructive. Its standard form of indenture was for ten years' service, but there was a proviso which allowed the master to renew it, whenever he thought it necessary. This proviso appeared during the early eighteenth century; and during the early nineteenth century it became common for an apprentice (*detchi*) in an established merchant house to serve for, at least, twenty years

[6] For the evidence, see O. Saito, 'The Labor Market in Tokugawa Japan: Wage Differentials and the Real Wage Level, 1727–1830', *Explorations in Economic History*, 15:1 (1978).

before he would be allowed to join the management or open his own shop (*bekke*) with a substantial bonus from the master. Of course, this does not imply that he had to remain as an 'apprentice' throughout this long period of service. Recruited at the age of, say, 12, the *detchi* would be promoted to *tedai* (shop assistant) at the age of 18. It was a salient feature of this system of employment and promotion, first established among the big Osaka merchants such as Mitsui and Kōnoike at the turn of the seventeenth century, and adopted by others during the course of the eighteenth, that even the *tedai* was considered a 'servant'; he remained unmarried, and lived in his master's household. Within the rank of *tedai*, there were several subdivisions. The successful *tedai* climbed this ladder by moving from one department to another. Before he was appointed to *bantō* (head clerk), or allowed to establish his own business, he would perform almost all the tasks in the business, so that he would possess the necessary expertise to run that business on his own. The system was not designed to train specialists. Indeed, this was its major difference from craft apprenticeship. A qualified craftsman needed to have a specific skill, whereas a qualified *bantō* required all-round training. Thus, as the merchant house developed a multi-departmental organization, the length of on-the-job training inevitably increased.[7]

Table 13.3 captures the essence of this system as exemplified by the house

Table 13.3 Life-cycle of Kōnoike male 'servants', 1691–1848

	1691–1736				1801–48			
	Mean age	Standard deviation	Mode	(N)	Mean age	Standard deviation	Mode	(N)
Entry								
All	19.9	10.53	11	(80)	14.6	7.36	12	(119)
Apprentices only	12.3	1.70	11	(47)	11.6	1.30	12	(98)
Promoted to clerk	n.a.	n.a.	n.a.	n.a.	18.1	1.49	18	(98)
Quitting	29.3	9.73	23; 24	(32)	26.3	5.47	20; 23; 25; 29; 31	(45)
Living out	35.1	4.17	34	(14)	37.0	2.57	36	(47)
Own business set up[a]	41.6	4.06	42; 43	(11)	—	—	—	—

[a] Between 1801 and 1848, no one was allowed to set up his own business.

Source: Saito, 'Shōka hōkōnin', table 7, p. 262.

of Kōnoike. The mean ages and standard deviations reported for apprentices, shop assistants, and head clerks suggest how institutionalized Kōnoike's employment and promotion practices were. The table also shows that over the whole period studied most were recruited as apprentices at the ages of 11 or 12 (59 per cent [= 47 ÷ 80] to 82 per cent [= 98 ÷ 119]), and that the mean length of service as unmarried, living-in employees became even longer

---

[7] For a brief account of this distinct system of employment and promotion, see J. Hirschmeier and R. Yui, *The Development of Japanese Business 1600–1980* (London, 1981), 38–40. No mention is made there, however, on how employment and promotion practices were linked with training and skill formation. In fact, direct evidence is scarce on this matter. For a review of scattered, indirect evidence, see Saito, 'Shōka hōkōnin'.

(from 22.8 years [= 35.1 − 12.3] to 25.4 years [= 37.0 − 11.6]). The institutionalization of this system thus meant not only employing larger numbers of 'servants', but also lengthening their service to an unusual extent.

It is not surprising, therefore, that the trend to retain more 'servants' was found in a limited number of places, i.e. Osaka and Kyoto, and a small area of Edo where many Osaka and other *Kamigata* merchants had their branch shops (Kamigata is the region surrounding Kyoto and Osaka, including the provinces of Ōmi and Ise from which many large merchants originated). In these places the trend to casualization which must have been operating was no doubt overshadowed by the expansion of the apprentice–clerk population. In the next section, by focusing on the two great, contrasting cities, Edo and Osaka, we turn to the question of the effects of those trends on migration patterns.

IV

It could be argued that while townsmen with families were a stable element in the urban population, servants and apprentices—usually migrants—were mobile and unstable. The sex ratio of migrants was likely to be unbalanced, and the institutions of service and apprenticeship tended to result in their marrying later than members of more stable population groups. It is further argued that, as a result, towns and cities with substantial numbers of temporary inhabitants needed to accept more in-migrants to maintain their population.[8] This may have been the case for Edo and Osaka during the seventeenth and early eighteenth centuries. In fact, as Table 13.4 shows, the sex ratio was unbalanced for the seventeenth-century servant population in Osaka and for the eighteenth-century population of Edo (although, in contrast to pre-industrial European cities, there were more men than women). Moreover, Akira Hayami, in his study of a village population, suggests that those who were sent into service, whether urban or not, married later than others.[9] However, we need here to assess the effects of the two divergent changes that took place *later*. Did the increased demand for shop apprentices and clerks in Osaka's trading sector favour more and more migrants? On the other hand did casualization in the Edo labour-market lead to further weakening of the city's reproductive ability?

The answers to both questions seem to be 'no'. A glance at Table 13.4 shows that, beginning with the latter half of the eighteenth century, Osaka lost a substantial number of inhabitants, whereas Edo's population increased at a modest rate from the mid-eighteenth century to the mid-1850s.

---

[8] H. Kito, *Nihon nisennen no jinkōshi* (Tokyo, 1983), 153–61. See also G. Rozman, 'Edo's Importance in the Changing Tokugawa Society', *Journal of Japanese Studies*, 1:1 (1974), 101.
[9] A. Hayami, 'Labor Migration in a Pre-industrial Society: A Study Tracing the Life Histories of the Inhabitants of a Village', *Keio Economic Studies*, 10:2 (1973), 15.

Table 13.4 Population change and the sex ratio: Edo and Osaka

	Population ('000)	Sex ratio (males per 100 females)		Natives ('000)	Migrants ('000)
Edo					
1743	501	171		—	—
1832	546	120		415	131
1855	574	105		432	142
1867	540	102		422	118
Osaka					
		Non-servant	Servant		
1689	382	109[a]	176[a]	—	—
1765	420	—	—	—	—
1860s	301[b]	100[c]	117[d]	—	—

[a] Excluding those aged 8 and under.
[b] 1862.
[c] c.1870. Minami Ōgumi only.
[d] Average of 10 boroughs (excluding 2 Tennōji places) in Table 13.1.

Sources: Edo: Kōda, 'Edo no chōnin no jinkō', *Shakai keizaishigaku*, 8: 1 (1938). 1743 was a trough and 1855 a peak year in the total population series. Osaka: for 1689, E. Honjō and M. Kuroban (eds.), *Osaka hennenshi*, 6 (Osaka, 1969), vi. 278–9. For 1765 and 1862 population figures, Osaka-shi, *Osaka shi-shi, 1* (1913), 880, and *2* (1914), 759. Sex ratios for the 1860s are calculated from a MS book in the Mitsui Bunko and Table 13.1 above. 1765 was a peak year in the population series.

Admittedly, changes in numbers could occur as a result of many different factors; in this case in particular, the different economic performances of the two cities and their hinterlands could account for much of the difference in the direction of population movements.

Nevertheless, it is not entirely implausible that it was the *Kamigata* merchants' distinct employment system that undermined the city's reproductive capacity, while casualization might well be favourable for quickening the pace of family formation. Theoretically, casualization meant a removal of varied restrictions, formal and informal, on the marriage of servants and apprentices. Other things remaining equal, this must have resulted in lowering the mean age at marriage among the working poor, as suggested by advocates of the thesis of European proto-industrialization in relation to proletarianization in the countryside. In Japan, this tendency to proletarianize the peasantry was very weak; instead, it was in urban areas that *de facto* proletarianization was taking place in the form of an expanding *zatsugyō* class. Needless to say, mortality was likely to remain high among the urban poor. In particular, higher levels of infant and child mortality, and greater possibilities of marriage being disrupted by the death of one of the spouses, may well have more than compensated for the positive effect of increased family formation, so that the consequence could still have been a natural decrease. But the possibility that casualization in the urban labour-market improved migrants' chances of settlement and raising a family cannot be dismissed. This, with an increase in work opportunities, may in turn have attracted more migrants from the countryside. It is interesting to note that this was the point made in passing by a late eighteenth-century *bakufu* official in relation to the proposed repatriation of urban in-migrants to their places of origin. Moreover, Table 13.4 indicates a steady fall in the sex ratio from the unusually high figure of 171 in 1743 to a normal level during the 1850s and 1860s. By redressing the imbalance in the Edo marriage market, this must have favoured the modest increase in overall population observed for the period up to the mid-1850s.

It should be remembered, on the other hand, that the *Kamigata* system of employment and promotion did not merely require a higher intake of apprentices, but necessitated their serving for longer than ever. As is shown in Table 13.3 above, this resulted in the mean age at first marriage for the successful Kōnoike *tedai* during the early nineteenth century becoming as high as 37. Of course, there were a number of drop-outs who probably married somewhat earlier; and the successful *tedai* may well have chosen very young brides when they left their master's house. Nevertheless, the deterrent effect on family formation and, consequently, on reproduction, of a system which resulted in about half the apprentices recruited remaining unmarried until their late thirties cannot be underestimated.

Moreover, the way in which apprentices were hired changed as the institution took root in the *Kamigata* merchants' circle. It became less and less likely for their apprentices to be sons of farm families. Instead, most of them came from the families of urban merchants. Indeed, of all the Kōnoike *detchi* shown in Table 13.3 for the period 1801–48, as many as 52, or 43 per cent, were sons of Kōnoike's branch families and former *tedai* (i.e. *bekke*). Of the remainder, 44, or 37 per cent, came from Osaka and Kyoto (with Fushimi). Only 21, or 18 per cent, came from rural areas. Even in Kikuyamachi, where the businesses were not particularly large by Osaka standards, two-thirds of two big merchants' male servants, who came from outside Osaka, were sons of merchants and not of farmers. The *Kamigata* circle of established tradesmen thus became very exclusive; an extreme example of this exclusiveness could be seen in the Edo branch shops of such merchants. Virtually all the male employees were recruited from within that *Kamigata* circle, and then sent to Edo. The only exceptions were sons of the master's relatives, and former *tedai* who had settled in Edo.

Fortunately, evidence lending support to the foregoing argument is now available. A list of families in one Osaka borough, Kitahama ni-chōme, in 1872, was recently compiled from an imperfect list of registers, and cross-checked against other documents.[10] There are, of course, shortcomings: the list of inhabitants was incomplete; probably more than ten families are missing. Secondly, information is not always given about individuals, and that relating to children and relatives is particularly weak. Thirdly, the list sometimes included unmarried children who had already left home. What

---

[10] K. Wakabayashi (ed.), *Kitahama ni-chōme kochō monjo*, Osaka-shi shiryō, 11 (Osaka, 1984).

makes these imperfect data particularly valuable, however, is that employee families, presumably living-out *bantōs*, from other wage-earning families are listed separately, so that differences between the upper class with their living-out clerks and the rest, especially petty traders and casual workers, can be examined with respect to place of origin, average age of family head, age gap between the spouses, and number of listed children.

Table 13.5 summarizes how place of origin was distributed according to

Table 13.5 Place of origin by wealth class, Kitahama ni-chōme, Osaka, 1872

Place of origin	Wealth class							
	Upper		Middle		Lower		Unclassified	
	No.	%	No.	%	No.	%	No.	%
Males								
Urban								
Osaka	14	58	14	39	43	45	14	48
Kyoto (with Fushimi), Ōmi, Ise	3	13	4	11	1	1	2	7
Other	0	0	3	8	5	5	4	14
Subtotal	17	71	21	58	49	52	20	69
Rural	2	8	9	25	21	22	3	10
Unknown	5	21	6	17	25	26	6	21
Total	24	100	36	100	95	100	29	100
Females								
Urban								
Osaka	21	70	19	59	46	49	13	57
Kyoto (with Fushimi), Ōmi, Ise	4	13	4	13	9	10	1	4
Other	2	7	0	0	9	10	3	13
Subtotal	27	90	23	72	64	68	17	74
Rural	2	7	6	19	19	20	4	17
Unknown	1	3	3	9	11	12	2	9
Total	30	100	32	100	94	100	23	100
Number of families	26		35		97		30	

Source: See text.

family wealth. In order to increase the number of observations, I have included in this table not only heads of families, but also spouses and their parents; the calculated proportion rural may, therefore, be slightly too high. The distribution for twenty-six upper-class families (of which twenty were living-out clerks) shows exactly the same pattern as the Kōnoike sample of apprentices: very few were born in the country, and the majority were natives or came from other *Kamigata* centres of big merchants, suggesting that this class was virtually cut off from rural areas. As regards the rest, especially the lower class, two facts are of interest. First, the probability of family heads, spouses, and their parents originating in rural areas was more than double that for the upper class. This rural–urban link is not unexpected. Secondly, the proportion of Osaka-born was not as low as might be imagined, 45 and 49 per cent of lower-class males and females respectively. Admittedly, there were a substantial number of those of unknown origin in this class, but even if

218 *Osamu Saito*

all these were added to the rural category, the proportion would not reach 50 per cent.

This observation brings us to the question of reproduction. Obviously, it is impossible to obtain sophisticated demographic measures from such imperfect data; but Table 13.6 does illustrate the difference between different social

Table 13.6 Married couples and their children by wealth class, Kitahama ni-chōme, Osaka, 1872

	Wealth class		
	Upper	Middle	Lower
Number of families headed by married male	19	25	46
Mean age			
Husband	40.3(6.46)	46.5(11.2)	41.7(9.88)
Wife	29.6(5.41)	38.8(10.0)	34.3(8.28)
Mean number of unmarried children listed	1.42(1.22)	1.72(1.43)	1.83(1.68)

Figures in parentheses are standard deviations.
Source: See text.

classes. If married couples of the upper class are compared with those from lower-class families, where the average age of husbands was about the same, the age gap between the spouses in the upper class was as large as 10.7 years, and the mean number of unmarried children listed was as low as 1.24. These two phenomena are, of course, consequences of very late marriage among successful shop clerks who spent the whole period of their prolonged service in their master's household. Men in lower strata, on the other hand, had larger families: 1.83 children on average. It must be admitted that this is not a very high figure by pre-fertility transition standards, and that the number of observations is so small that the difference between 1.42 and 1.83 is not quite statistically significant. Nevertheless, given presumed class differentials in infant mortality, and very poor housing conditions in the back-alley tenements in Tokugawa cities, it is remarkable that the poor had larger families than the wealthy, a fact which suggests that completed family size may also have been (marginally) higher in that group.

V

The suggestion in the previous section, if confirmed by further research, would have far-reaching implications for the dynamics of urbanization and de-urbanization in pre-industrial times. Here, I should like to make just two points.

The first concerns de-urbanization in the process of so-called proto-industrialization. More than a decade ago, Tom Smith called our attention to population decrease in a number of towns and cities of the Tokugawa era and to the parallel process of rural industrialization, suggesting that rural industry and commerce grew at the expense of the urban economy.[11] In view of various pieces of evidence now available, it can not be denied that this was, indeed, the case for a majority of the places examined. Contraction in commercial transactions due to rural growth would certainly lead to decreases in opportunities for employment and, consequently, in the size of the urban population. However, the demographic aspects of this process are not yet clear. The interaction between employment practices in urban business, marriage behaviour, and reproduction has not yet been explored. In this chapter I have suggested that urban population decline was further reinforced, in the case of Osaka and other *Kamigata* cities, by the lowered reproductive potentials of stable population groups, resulting from the organizational growth of established urban merchants, rather than by competition from their rural counterparts.

Secondly, another long-term trend in the eighteenth- and nineteenth-century urban scene, i.e. casualization of employment, also had some interesting effects on urban demography. As was suggested above, while the existence of servants and apprentices tended to create an imbalance in the marriage market, casualized labour was likely to be associated with more balanced sex ratios and higher proportions married among people of child-bearing age, and consequently with higher overall birth rates. Since casualization was not a new phenomenon of the factory age, but had already begun in many pre-industrial urban places, its effects on marriage and fertility may well have diminished, as van der Woude has argued,[12] the importance of the city's postulated function as the chief graveyard in pre-industrial demography. Indeed, this was probably the way in which Edo, the largest city in the Tokugawa urban hierarchy, achieved a modest increase in population between the mid-eighteenth and the mid-nineteenth centuries, a period when de-urbanization was found in many regions. That increase, however, was not sustained. It was during the 1890s that the capital city, along with other big cities, began again to increase in size.[13] Characteristically, this was a period of new, urban-based factory industries and tertiary sector employment, neither of which tended to internalize labour-markets until the inter-war period when employment opportunities expanded for migrant workers from rural districts.

[11] Smith, 'Pre-Modern Economic Growth'.
[12] Van der Woude, 'Population Developments'.
[13] S. Itō, 'Natural Change of Urban Population in Early Modern Japan', paper presented to the IUSSP Seminar on Urbanization and Population Dynamics in History, Keio University, Tokyo (Jan. 1986).

14 Migration, Family Formation, and Choice of Marriage Partners in Stockholm, 1860–1890

MARGARETA MATOVIĆ
Stockholms Universitet, Historiska Institutionen, Stockholm, Sweden

To the best of our knowledge, Stockholm has always depended on migration to ward off population decline. Natural increase was never sufficient to maintain the population. The low rate of growth was largely due to the very high level of mortality which did not fall until the end of the nineteenth century. Without a surplus of in-migrants the population of the city would have diminished and high mortality would have made more room for an increasing number of newcomers. Stockholm's geographical position in a relatively flourishing agricultural district, in which the dominant area of migration consisted of the Mälaren valley, meant that the conditions governing internal migration were different from those in other parts of the country. Compared with other regions, migration to Stockholm was influenced more by the employment situation than by differences in real wages. The considerable amount of migration of the lower social groups from the country to the town contributed to the growth in the city of an indigent population, which was extremely sensitive to economic fluctuations.[1]

1. The pattern of pre-industrial migration

Between 1750 and 1850, Stockholm was characterized by protracted economic stagnation. The city's industries were in decline and the majority of early manufacturers went out of business. By the middle of the nineteenth century, industrial employment in Norrköping had surpassed that in Stockholm. Even in commerce Stockholm had declined, and traders had to contend with serious marketing problems. Real wages for unskilled workers fell, unemployment increased, and poverty was widespread throughout the city. This decline resulted in the development of what might be called the informal sector of Stockholm's economy. A special type of labour-market developed in which the survival strategies of the unemployed and the

---

[1] J. Söderberg, 'Real Wage Trends in Urban Europe, 1730–1850: Stockholm in a comparative perspective', Research Report no. 3, Dept. of Economic History, University of Stockholm (1984), 13–16.

destitute were expressed in various ways, which would have long-run demographic and economic consequences. The life of the city became increasingly less formal and came to be characterized by marginal employment which provided a livelihood. The latest researches on the socio-economic and demographic development of Stockholm between 1750 and 1850 suggest a similarity between conditions in the city then and today's 'poverty culture' prevalent in the Third World.[2]

Poverty was an acute problem in Stockholm at the beginning of the nineteenth century. The sharp increase in population and the proletarianization of the countryside resulted in bands of destitute persons in search of employment being attracted to the cities. Even though Stockholm depended on in-migrants for its manpower needs, contemporary commentators were afraid that in-migration would result in soaring costs for relieving the poor. In 1805, an ordinance was promulgated prohibiting further in-migration of persons without property to Stockholm. Poor families with many children, where the husband had no other income than that derived from seasonal or casual employment, were prohibited from migrating. The prohibition was also extended to impecunious persons over the age of 50, and to those who were not able-bodied. Together with the *legostadgan* of the same year, the ordinance reflected a desire for increased control over persons without property, whilst making it possible for property owners to recruit additional workers. The *legostadgan* prescribed compulsory labour for all persons over the age of 15 who did not own property, which meant that those who lost their jobs and did not find new ones relatively quickly could be considered as 'defenceless' (*försvarslösa*) and laid themselves open to police intervention.[3]

The restrictions on migration were abolished in 1847 with the passing of new laws on poor relief. The more favourable economic development of the 1840s had made it increasingly difficult to enforce them. A shortage of labour, and the Freedom of Trade Ordinance of 1846, led to increasing demands by employers for free migration. It was no longer possible to regard problems of relieving the poor as being caused solely by migration. However, the low rate of population growth in Stockholm—0.4 per cent per year during the first half of the nineteenth century—must be seen against the background of these attitudes, the restrictive measures against migration, and the regulation of trade and industry. Migration was permitted for younger unmarried members of the lower social groups in the countryside and was complemented by traditional labour migration from certain parts of the country by persons of working age who hoped to find piecework in the capital.

These migratory workers came primarily from north-west Sweden in the spring and returned home in the autumn. For them, migration did not mean

---

[2] J. Söderberg, U. Jonsson, and C. Persson, 'Stagnating Metropolis: Economy and Demography in Stockholm, 1750–1850', Research Report no. 4, Dept. of Economic History, University of Stockholm (1984), 19.

[3] A. Montgomery, *Svensk socialpolitik under 1800-talet* (Stockholm, 1934), 43–4.

an abandonment of their home in the country, in order to settle in Stockholm. Opportunities for employment in Stockholm played an important part in supporting the poorer parts of the country. The work was unskilled: sawing wood, labouring in the building trade, and street-cleaning. This also applied to women who came to dominate such occupations as working in public parks, rowing, gardening, and work in breweries. This migrant labour had entirely different characteristics from the massive in-migration which occurred during the latter part of the nineteenth century in connection with industrialization. At that time internal population movements were important in Sweden; they consisted of individuals who were looking for new places to live in permanently, where they could support themselves and improve their standard of living. The men and women who came to Stockholm were prepared to settle there for good and make a livelihood for themselves, and saw their future as being in the city.

2. The pre-industrial pattern of family formation

Demographic conditions in pre-industrial Stockholm differed from those in other Swedish or European cities. Mortality was high, even though there was an over-representation of younger men and women, the majority of whom were in-migrants. The high mortality rates of men and infants resulted in a population structure in which there was a considerable surplus of older women, whereas the surplus of females was low among children. The proportion married was unusually low. Age at marriage was high, and fertility outside marriage was between three and four times higher than in the rest of the country, and approximately twice as high as in other cities.[4] Between 1851 and 1860, Stockholm was second only to Vienna among European cities in the extent of illegitimacy.

The economic historian, Ulf Jonsson, in his work on mortality in Stockholm during the eighteenth and nineteenth centuries, concluded that men were more affected by high mortality than women between the ages of 25 and 50 years.[5] He saw the age and sex patterns of mortality as an extreme variant of the pre-industrial urban pattern, related to low standards of living, widespread sickness, and poverty, particularly among men who were crushed by unemployment and misery more than women. Stockholm's relatively limited regular labour-market was unable to absorb the male work-force during the first half of the nineteenth century, whereas women could more easily support themselves as domestic servants or housekeepers. Half the men between the ages of 20 and 29 were classified as being in poverty, compared

[4] G. Ahlberg, *Stockholm befolkningsutveckling efter 1850* (Stockholm, 1958), 60–8.
[5] U. Jonsson, 'Mortality Patterns in 18th and 19th Century Stockholm in a European Perspective', Research Report no. 2, Dept. of Economic History, University of Stockholm, (1984), 11–14.

with only 24 per cent of the women. By combining a number of different jobs women succeeded in making themselves useful, mainly within households. They could earn their livelihood as kitchen or household helps, dressmakers, or laundresses.

The marriage rate in Stockholm had been falling since the end of the eighteenth century and reached a nadir during the middle 1850s. This fall gave concern to contemporary statisticians, who regarded it as a sign of an exaggerated demand for luxuries on the part of the population. However, it was impossible to explain these low rates adequately. It was clear that marriage customs in Stockholm were very different from those in other cities or in the countryside. Another factor which gave rise to concern was that the choice of marriage partners appeared to be 'unnatural', in the sense that younger men tended to marry older women. In their report for the years 1851–5, the Official Statistical Commission commented as follows:

The capital also shows to a much greater degree than any other county that unsatisfactory state of affairs in which younger men enter into marriage with considerably older women. These circumstances, which cannot be without influence on the fertility of marriage and even reasonably can be assumed to result in greater temptation to immorality, touch upon causes which to a high degree are capable of destroying the effects of the natural inclinations and subordinate them to other, most probably economic, calculations.[6]

It was suggested that the marriage market was openly used for speculation, particularly in dowries. This should not in itself have been disapproved of, given the contemporary debates on poor relief, in which those who did not own property were accused of irresponsible behaviour by marrying early and begetting children whom they could not support. The demonstration of economic discernment on the part of Stockholm's young men should have been welcomed by those who complained about the ever-rising costs of supporting the poor. But a more detailed study of this so-called 'unnatural' choice of marriage partners would have shown that it occurred almost exclusively in the city's lowest social groups, in which the majority of children born outside marriage were also found. The difference in marriage behaviour and choice of partner between those who did and those who did not own property would have become apparent: there were two different patterns of family behaviour linked to two different urban cultures and life-styles, each with its own system of values and behaviour.[7]

The concern about low marriage rates and high ages at marriage was explicitly related to the pattern of formation of legal families in Stockholm. It was also directed implicitly against the formation of consensual unions, which were regarded as a danger to society. In the middle of the nineteenth century, almost half of all the children born in Stockholm were born outside marriage.

[6] *Contributions to Sweden's Official Statistics. Population Statistics, 1851–55*, 24.
[7] M. R. Matović, *Stockholmsäktenskap. Familjebildning och partnerval i Stockholm, 1850–1890* (Stockholm, 1984).

This was very unlikely to have been the result of casual liaisons, but rather an expression of the existence of a type of informal family. It was at that time, too, that Stockholm came to be regarded as a den of iniquity. In the country references were made to 'Stockholm marriages', or to 'being married in the Stockholm manner'. The question arises whether this term meant only that women bore children outside marriage, or whether it referred to all forms of consensual unions related to living in Stockholm.

The high illegitimacy figures for Stockholm suggest that many children were born to informal unions which closely resembled a marriage.[8] Recent researches on the economic history of Stockholm between 1750 and 1850 have confirmed this and linked the prevalence of such unions to the special lifestyle of the capital.

While this might indicate some change in customs and mentalities since the middle of the century, a change contributing to the rise of bastardy, it is likely that a major part of this rise is due to an increase in the proportion of more stable extramarital unions within lower strata. As is clear from an inspection of Figure 3, the year-to-year fluctuations in bastardy are very close to those in the marital fertility rate, implying that both were affected by largely the same mechanism. Over time, and disregarding the trends, extramarital fertility behaved very much like the marital one.[9]

The relative unresponsiveness of nuptiality to economic and other vital rates changes rather suggests differences in life styles. Stockholm marriages evidently were less restricted by considerations regarding a certain material basis for marriage. Correlations between nuptiality on the one hand and real wages and bankruptcies on the other, have the expected signs, but are remarkably weak (0.33 and − 0.17 respectively).[10]

The formation of consensual unions in Stockholm's pre-industrial urban economy was closely related to the low levels of living and to the nature of the local labour-market for both men and women. The significance of the economic contribution made by women even for the maintenance of men made for a more equal relationship between the sexes. The woman often became the breadwinner and so further increased her opportunities for independence and rational action. At the same time, her interest in getting married came to depend upon her support situation. The chance of being employed in the labour-market hardly encouraged women who were supporting themselves to enter into marriage ties. In all probability, the reverse was true. An unemployed man without property had very little security which he could offer to a woman in marriage. Moreover, Swedish law placed the wife under her husband's domination and gave him legal rights over her wages and even her private property. Women often managed better without legalizing their union and, in these circumstances, could themselves provide for their children. A woman living in a consensual union could leave

---

[8] Matović, *Stockholmsäktenskap*, 170–2.
[9] Söderberg, Jonsson, and C. Persson, 'Stagnating Metropolis', 10.
[10] Ibid. 12.

and take her children with her, if her partner maltreated her or was a drunkard, for alcohol abuse among men was the married woman's greatest fear. But, at the time, consensual unions were strongly disapproved of socially and were consistently opposed by the Church. In this form of cohabitation, the economic and legal relations which characterized the institution of marriage no longer applied. The man and the woman were not regarded as an economic unit. Sexual relations and procreation were categorized as immoral and could entail penal sanctions. Any children of such unions were illegitimate and could lose their rights to inherit, if their parents were not betrothed. Relations between the partners differed from those between legally married husbands and wives. They were not expected to take the same economic and social responsibilities for each other or for their children as were legally married persons.[11]

Many aspects of pre-industrial Stockholm in the period before 1880 remind one of the relations which characterize a 'poverty culture' as defined by the social anthropologist Oscar Lewis. He coined this concept in connection with his studies of urban slums in Mexico and Puerto Rico. According to him, an urban subculture can emerge when a socio-economic system breaks down and is being replaced by another, as for instance during the transitional phase at the beginning of industrialization. The necessary conditions are wage labour, constant high unemployment, underemployment of unskilled workers, low wages, and overpopulation. The poor congregate within certain areas of the city and live as a group. Lewis found that consensual unions were common in such groups. Sexual mores were more permissive, there was a higher proportion of unmarried mothers with children and a tendency towards mother-centred families. Women were in a relatively strong position, often as breadwinners. Bourgeois sexual morals were not unknown, they were just not practised. Family formation and life-styles became adapted to the struggle of the poor for existence, which created its own system of norms.[12]

However, it would be difficult to maintain that consensual unions were to be found only in the towns, as a consequence of the urban life-style. Many scholars have pointed out the ubiquity of the phenomenon and the need to take socio-economic factors into account. It is not sufficient to explain it by reference to the effects on human beings of life in a large city. This is true of Stockholm at the middle of the nineteenth century. Certainly many of the results of my study point to a dominance of 'Stockholm behaviour' among men and women who did not own property, but this seems less certain when looked at in a global perspective. The large in-migration seems to have played a decisive part in the past behaviour patterns of the poor; mobility by itself seems to have made it easier for men and women to use consensual unions as part of their strategy for survival. But it is well known that a tradition of

---

[11] Matović, *Stockholmsäktenskap*, 36–9.
[12] O. Lewis, *La Vida* (London, 1968); B. Horgby, 'Den disciplinerade arbetaren', *Acta Universitatis Stockholmiensis* (Stockholm, 1986), 31–2.

pre-marital cohabitation existed in the Swedish countryside, though this was normally coupled with an engagement to marry, and that so-called 'night-courting' implied a relatively relaxed view of pre-marital sexual contacts. It is probable that certain types of behaviour and values were strengthened in Stockholm among the in-migrants and that these were connected with the special relations needed for survival in the city and with the absence of social control. The 'Stockholm marriage' can, therefore, be regarded as related to the intensive wave of in-migration and its effect on the 'poverty culture' which existed in the capital with its special pattern of family formation.[13]

How was the pattern of pre-industrial family formation in Stockholm influenced by the massive migration which occurred in connection with industrialization? We cannot treat all aspects of this question within the confines of this chapter. Unfortunately, the latest research on the socio-economic and demographic development of Stockholm does not cover the period 1850–1900, so that our knowledge about nuptiality, migration, and economic change remains very limited. We cannot consider the important problem of changes in family formation during the second half of the nineteenth century, nor what happened to the extra-legal patterns of family formation during the period of industrialization. Instead, we shall concentrate on a limited number of aspects, mainly connected with the process of integration, based on my own study of marriage banns for the period 1860–90. These will include a discussion of how family formation and choice of partner could be used as a device for assimilation and integration into the life of the capital. The strategies employed by men and women who moved into the city to achieve certain objectives and advantages through family formation will be studied by looking at the geographical origins and choices of partner of couples who registered their banns between the years 1860 and 1890. The focus will be on the individual migrant who, against the background of social group membership, possession of property, working capacity, and professional skills, adopted certain attitudes to marriage and consensual union and thereby adjusted his or her choice of partner to the contingencies of survival.

3. The wave of migration

Between 1860 and 1890 Stockholm experienced a wave of in-migration which was unparalleled in its history (see Table 14.1). The population in 1860 was 111,000 and had, by 1890, grown to about 246,000, equivalent to an annual rate of growth amounting to 2.7 per cent. Within a short period, Stockholm was transformed into one of the country's foremost industrial cities. Industrial development meant a shift towards increasingly larger firms, and the disappearance of some of the early processing industries, whereas engineer-

[13] Matović, *Stockholmsäktenskap*, 155.

Table 14.1 Population changes in Stockholm, 1851–1900

Period	Live births	Deaths	Natural increase	Migration	Population increase[a]	% due to migration
1851–60	35,213	41,187	− 5,974	+25,295	19,321	130.9
1861–70	44,615	41,638	+ 2,977	+19,976	22,953	87.0
1871–80	49,231	46,962	+ 2,269	+30,490	32,759	93.1
1881–90	68,491	47,788	+20,703	+56,976	77,679	73.3
1891–1900	71,984	52,163	+19,821	+34,349	54,170	63.4

[a] Excluding gains by incorporation of new areas.
Source: Ahlberg, Stockholms befolkningsutveckling efter 1850.

ing and other export industries were thriving. The favourable economic conditions of the 1870s stimulated enterprise and resulted in real economic growth. They also attracted substantial numbers of in-migrants. During the 1880s, moreover, migration was encouraged by increased activity in house-building.

According to Ahlberg, women outnumbered men by 25 per cent among migrants up to the turn of the century (see Table 14.2). This was true, above all, for women who migrated from the country towns. The propensity to move to the capital was greater in the towns than in the countryside. This, in itself, suggests an urban surplus of women and deteriorating conditions for their support.

Table 14.2 Women per 100 men among internal migrants, 1868–1890

Place of birth	1868	1880	1890
Outside Stockholm	123	126	123
Rural	114	121	120
Urban	151	143	135

Source: Ahlberg, Stockholms befolkningsutveckling efter 1850.

In explaining the sex ratio among migrants, fluctuations in economic conditions must be taken into account. According to Gustafson,[14] the labour-market for men was most sensitive to economic conditions in Stockholm, as it was dominated by the construction and engineering industries. A reduced demand for male labour in the city was accompanied by a parallel reduction in the number of male migrants. The labour-market for women was less sensitive. The majority were engaged as domestic servants in private households or in the consumption industries. For many of these women domestic work constituted a transition to work in industry. Therefore, the migration stream of women was less variable, because the supply of jobs did not fluctuate as much.

Who were the men and women who migrated to Stockholm during the second half of the nineteenth century? Unfortunately, no large-scale investigation of migrants, their occupations, marital status, family situation, social background, or their expectations or reasons for moving has as yet been

[14] U. Gustafson, Industrialismens storstad (Stockholm, 1976), 161–72.

undertaken. Studies carried out by Ahlberg, Gardlund, and Gustafson among others suggest that the majority of the in-migrants belonged to the lower social groups. They consisted mainly of young people looking for work who were attracted to the industrial cities. A common feature of these migrants was that their only asset consisted of their labour. They therefore needed to become part of the city's life quickly, to find connections, establish a livelihood, and acquire a roof over their heads. The last of these problems was by no means the least, as the severe housing shortage which existed in Stockholm during the 1860s and 1870s bore particularly heavily on the numerous migrants. At the beginning of the 1870s the situation was almost catastrophic with unparalleled increases in rents and in overcrowding. People took refuge in attics, sheds, and all sorts of nooks and crannies, and there were hovels in the hilly areas of the city. The terrible housing situation, which particularly affected those who did not own property, should have increased the trend toward cohabitation and a lodging system. Cohabitation with a man could provide a solution to the housing problem of an indigent newly arrived woman. Similarly, a young and newly arrived man could solve his acute problem of survival by moving in with a woman who had already established herself in the capital.

In view of the great excess of women in Stockholm, it seems reasonable that non-local men would entertain expectations of being able to 'make a good match' in the capital with a local woman. These possibilities applied mainly to well-situated men. But at the same time the surplus of women meant that Stockholm-born women from the upper and middle social groups increasingly tended to marry non-local men, even men from a lower social class, because of the stiff competition for marriage partners. For men, the marriage market in Stockholm provided an exceptionally favourable opportunity for speculation. The problem was one of supply and demand. However, for the in-migrant woman without a dowry and with her labour as her only asset, the marriage market was hardly brighter than the housing market. The influx of women from the countryside increased the already large surplus of women in the capital and further reduced their chances of marriage. Sten Carlsson has shown that there was an exceptionally large number of unmarried women without property who had moved to the capital to earn their living as domestic servants, a move which in itself implied a rise in status.[15] To have served in a Stockholm family meant that one could consider oneself 'a bit better' than others. A domestic servant who returned to her original home could count on receiving many advantageous proposals of marriage.

It is probable that the fact of having been born in the capital brought with it a certain degree of social esteem. It was not only the physical proximity to the royal palace, but also the mundane life and cultural activities which provided

---

[15] S. Carlsson, *Fröknar, mamseller, jungfrur och pigor. Ogifta kvinnor i det svenska ståndssamhället* (Uppsala, 1977), 106.

a reason for this. Differences in life-style and attitudes resulted in natives of Stockholm achieving a higher degree of economic and professional specialization. Some occupational groups and organizations achieved a special status in the city, for example craftsmen, petty officials, and the city's porters and policemen. City dwellers wished to belong to a larger cultural circle, which implied proximity to gentlefolk, not least through the city's international trade in luxury goods. Even city dwellers who did not own property copied customs and behaviour from their betters. He or she dressed differently from those in the country, spoke differently, and looked down on those who had moved into the city. Someone not born in Stockholm was contemptuously referred to as a 'clodhopper' or 'country bumpkin'. A domestic servant who had been born in the city was quite different from one born in the country and could expect better working conditions. Contact with urban life for the migrant woman meant a change in behaviour and assimilation to urban customs.

The native-born Stockholmer—irrespective of his or her social group—enjoyed an advantage over the new arrivals through contacts which had been established since childhood. All in-migrants strove to establish such contacts whether they did or did not own property, because such contacts meant access to work and housing. Relatives, neighbours, fellow workers, and acquaintances played a considerable part in this. To marry or to move in with some local person could be an effective and quick way of gaining access to such contacts. Marriage which developed family-related behaviour could open undreamed-of possibilities for a better existence to non-local persons.

In-migration meant that the native-born population of Stockholm constituted a minority. Between 1860 and 1890, relations between natives and non-natives in Stockholm remained surprisingly unchanged. According to Ahlberg,[16] the proportion of the native-born population was 42.6 per cent in 1860, 43.4 per cent in 1870, 41.3 per cent in 1880, and 40.2 per cent in 1890. But the native-born were concentrated in certain social groups. Almost half the small and extremely limited upper social class were native-born Stockholmers. The percentage in the middle class was somewhat lower (between 20 and 30 per cent), while the lowest percentage of native-born was found in the working classes, particularly among skilled and unskilled labourers, servants, and soldiers.[17]

4. Integration in the capital through family formation

Traditionally, in the Nordic countries, marriage was an economic working contract between two parties. The suitor negotiated with the woman's father, who had the right to marry off his daughter, for a mutual exchange. The man

[16] Ahlberg, *Stockholms befolkingsutveckling efter 1850*.
[17] Gustafson, *Industrialismens storstad*, 137.

negotiated for property, an economic and social position, the maintenance of the woman, her fertility, her household goods, and her labour. In my dissertation on marriage in Stockholm in which I consider family formation and partner choice between 1850 and 1890, I have used an exchange model.[18] Taking its point of departure from social psychology, the model is based on the assumption that an individual's behaviour is determined by the desire to improve his situation in life and that this leads him to balance the advantages and disadvantages of various courses of action. Since I regard family formation and entry into marriage primarily as a form of social and economic exchange, in which the parties consider their advantages and disadvantages, the model makes it possible to interpret social behaviour at the time when a partner is chosen either for formal marriage or for a consensual union.

Marriage, as a legally binding contract between a man and a woman, returns both long-term and short-term dividends. The laws of the nineteenth century gave the husband rights to his wife's dowry, her labour, and any earnings, as well as to her person as a sexual partner. On her side, the wife enjoyed an immediate change in status, in which she acquired her husband's class and economic status. She received the right to be maintained for the duration of her life, and to a sexual partner. From the long-term point of view, a marriage provided legal heirs and through them a certain degree of security in old age. For the wife, there was also the possibility of becoming a widow, a status which gave her almost full legal and economic authority over her own affairs. The exchanges that took place at the time of marriage differed between those who did and those who did not own property. Ownership of goods and size of income played a decisive part. The husband's duty to maintain his wife implied that he should have sufficient means to support not only himself, but also a wife and family. A good social position depended on a satisfactory economic status. For women, during the nineteenth century, the norms made a dowry a prerequisite for marriage. Absence of dowry for a woman, or lack of a stable income or property for a man, would have rendered the marriage non-functional. It would have made it impossible for the man to support a wife, or for the woman to bring a dowry into the marriage, and when these exchanges became too insignificant, no advantage would accrue to either party from a marriage. The alternative could be a consensual union, in which there was an exchange of labour, social contacts, and material assets, and where the expenses for food and housing were divided between the parties.

The theory of integration can be viewed as part of the exchange model, in the sense that in-migrants to Stockholm attempted to become integrated into a Stockholm family. Those who had been born in Stockholm possessed certain social and economic advantages in their struggle for survival as they had access to certain contacts, and this access was an additional commodity which they could offer in exchange on marriage.

[18] Matović, *Stockholmsäktenskap*, 88–90.

The newly arrived migrant in Stockholm met two urban worlds with different patterns of family formation. In the first place there was that of the isolated upper class in which marriage tended to be endogamous, and which was distanced from the large lower-class world and pattern of life. The majority of migrants found themselves in this latter world, where the struggle for existence was their primary concern. Choice of partner and family formation were adapted to this. The in-migrant man needed to obtain a foothold in the capital, and one way of doing this was to marry a local woman. The large surplus of women in the capital meant that marriage could give men a considerable chance of success. In 1860, there were 118 women for every 100 men in Stockholm, the corresponding ratio in Copenhagen was 109 and in Berlin 101. The surplus was particularly noticeable during the 1870s and 1880s, when women predominated among internal migrants, and when there was also a considerable emigration of men to the United States. In the older age-groups, there were approximately four women to every man.[19]

The chances of making an advantageous marriage were, therefore, much smaller for newly arrived women, particularly for those without property and who had to support themselves. But even farmers' daughters with a dowry who moved into the city found their status lowered because of their rural origins and tended to be regarded as domestic servants. Their best chance of marriage was to interest a local man who was in need of capital to start in business. Another route to marriage was by the back door: taking a post as domestic servant to some man—preferably one well situated and who had been born in Stockholm—and eventually becoming his housekeeper and mistress. If children were born to such a union, the woman was regarded as betrothed. The so-called 'Mamsell (mademoiselle) marriage' was not uncommon in Stockholm. It meant that a woman of lower-class origin, often a new arrival in the city, functioned as a common-law wife and unpaid housekeeper for an upper-class man, whilst at the same time receiving a rise in status with the title 'Mamsell'.[20]

In my study of marriage banns for the period 1860–90 I have shown that consensual unions which preceded marriages were strongly differentiated by social class. They were common among men and women who did not own property and who had recently arrived in Stockholm, but they were considerably less common among the propertied classes. For upper-class daughters it was almost unthinkable to cohabit before marriage and certainly to bear children pre-maritally. In this group the system of marriage norms was observed most closely. Parental and social control operated most effectively over women of the higher social classes, who were important as a means of transferring capital. In-migrant women without property, most of whom had to support themselves, deviated most from the norms.

Reasoning from the theories of integration and exchange, I have put

---

[19] Ahlberg, *Stockholm befolkningsutveckling efter 1850*, 35.
[20] Matović, *Stockhomsäktenskap*, 246–7.

forward the hypothesis that migrant men and women, regardless of social group, strove to become integrated into a Stockholm family, by forming unions with persons who were born in Stockholm. In my study I investigated the geographical origin of couples who registered their banns in relation to the social group of the man. The data consisted of three random samples, containing altogether 5,112 engaged couples, divided into three periods of equal length: 1860–9, 1870–9, 1880–9. The information was extracted from the Register of Published Banns and the Marriage Registers of Stockholm's eight parishes. The couples were subsequently classified by the groom's occupation and social status. The information was available for the great majority of couples.

Tables 14.3 to 14.5 show that a relatively small number of engaged couples consisted of persons both of whom were born in Stockholm. Between 1860 and 1869 such couples amounted to fewer than 7 per cent and the proportion was decreasing. At least 18 per cent of couples consisted of a Stockholm-born woman and an in-migrant man, whilst the opposite configuration, a Stockholm-born man and an in-migrant woman, amounted to barely 8 per cent. The preference for in-migrant brides was significantly less pronounced among grooms of the upper middle class, primarily entrepreneurs, master craftsmen, and lower civil servants. Among the couples belonging to the upper middle class, 46.6 per cent of the women and 27.1 per cent of the men were born in Stockholm; the corresponding figures for the lower middle class were 24.0 per cent and 19.8 per cent, and in the lower class 18.5 per cent and 11.8 per cent. Clearly, the number of Stockholm-born was much smaller in the lower social groups.

Yet a very large number of couples belonged to the lower social groups. More than 88 per cent of the men in that group were in-migrants, among women the corresponding figure was 83 per cent. The dominant tendency was to marry someone born in another county and, in rare instances, one born in Stockholm. A slightly higher proportion of in-migrant men married Stockholm-born women than conversely. Only rarely did the two partners come from the parish of origin.

Between 1870 and 1890, the pattern of partner choice changed slightly, and a tendency towards a social and geographical levelling can be discerned. The number of Stockholm-born couples announcing their banns decreased, in particular the number of Stockholm-born women. Although many Stockholm-born women continued to marry men in the two highest social classes, their numbers declined. Men from these classes tended to choose their brides increasingly from among non-local women. There was an increase in the spread, both geographical and social, of the choice of partners in the two highest social groups.

During the 1880s, more than 77 per cent of all engaged couples who were not born in Stockholm came from the lowest class and in the majority of cases the bride and groom were born in different counties. Among workers and

Table 14.3a Geographical background and partner choice by county of birth, Stockholm, 1860–1869

Groom's social group	Not born in Stockholm			Born in Stockholm				Total	
	Bride and groom born in the same county and parish %	Bride and groom born in the same county %	Bride and groom born in different counties %	Bride born in Stockholm city %	Groom born in Stockholm city %	Bride and groom born in the same Stockholm parish %	Bride and groom born in Stockholm city %	Number of banns	%
Large entrepreneurs	—	—	20.5	41.0	10.3	5.1	20.5	39	3.1
Large landowners	—	16.7	58.3	8.3	8.3	—	8.3	24	1.9
Higher administrative and liberal professions									
Smaller entrepreneurs	4.0	6.3	29.3	51.2	4.9	4.9	9.8	41	3.3
Smaller landowners	—	—	37.3	29.4	9.5	1.6	11.9	126	10.1
Lower administrative, foremen	—	—	—	—	—	—	—	—	—
Shop assistants, clerks	4.8	2.7	39.1	26.4	7.3	0.9	23.6	110	8.8
Porters and personal servants	2.0	9.5	42.9	14.3	9.5	—	19.0	21	1.7
Lower professionals	—	7.2	58.6	15.2	11.1	2.0	4.0	99	7.9
	—	—	—	—	—	—	100.0	1	0.1
Craftsmen	1.4	4.3	55.1	21.7	8.7	1.4	7.2	69	5.5
Skilled labourers	2.0	8.6	64.4	12.3	8.0	1.0	3.7	489	39.2
Unskilled labourers	3.4	12.5	66.3	10.6	5.3	—	1.9	208	16.2
Landless farmers, farmhands, former servants and soldiers	—	—	66.7	20.0	—	—	16.7	6	0.5
Domestic servants	—	10.0	50.0	25.0	20.0	—	—	10	0.5
Soldiers	—	—	75.0	25.0	—	—	—	4	0.8
Total number	26	97	694	224	99	15	92	1247	
%	2.1	7.8	55.6	17.9	7.9	1.2	7.4		100.0
Unknown								2	
Grand total								1249	

Table 14.3b Geographical background and partner choice by groom's social group, Stockholm, 1860–1869

Groom's social group	Not born in Stockholm			Born in Stockholm				Total	
	Bride and groom born in the same county and parish %	Bride and groom born in the same county %	Bride and groom born in different counties %	Bride born in Stockholm city %	Groom born in Stockholm city %	Bride and groom born in the same Stockholm parish %	Bride and groom born in Stockholm city %	Number of banns	%
Large entrepreneurs	—	1.0	1.2	7.1	4.0	13.3	8.7	39	3.1
Large landowners	—	4.1	2.0	0.9	2.0	—	2.2	24	1.9
Higher administrative and liberal professions	19.2	—	1.7	9.4	2.0	13.3	4.3	41	3.3
Smaller entrepreneurs	—	8.2	6.8	16.5	12.1	13.3	16.3	126	10.1
Smaller landowners	—	—	—	—	—	—	—	—	—
Lower administrative, foremen	—	3.1	6.2	12.9	8.1	6.7	28.3	110	8.8
Shop assistants, clerks	3.8	2.1	1.3	1.3	2.0	—	4.3	21	1.7
Porters and personal servants	7.7	7.2	8.4	6.7	11.1	13.3	4.3	99	7.9
Lower professionals	—	—	—	—	—	—	1.1	1	0.1
Craftsmen	3.8	3.1	5.5	6.7	6.1	6.7	5.4	69	5.5
Skilled labourers	38.5	43.3	45.4	26.8	39.4	33.3	19.6	489	39.2
Unskilled labourers	26.9	26.8	19.9	9.8	11.1	—	4.3	208	16.2
Landless farmers, farmhands, former servants and soldiers	—	—	0.4	—	—	—	1.1	6	0.5
Domestic servants	—	1.0	0.7	0.9	2.0	—	—	10	0.5
Soldiers	—	—	0.4	0.4	—	—	—	4	0.8
Total number	26	97	694	224	99	15	92	1247	100.0
%	2.1	7.8	55.6	17.9	7.9	1.2	7.4		
Unknown								2	
Grand total								1249	

Table 14.4a Geographical background and partner choice by county of birth, Stockholm, 1870–1879

Groom's social group	Not born in Stockholm			Born in Stockholm				Total	
	Bride and groom born in the same county and parish %	Bride and groom born in the same county %	Bride and groom born in different counties %	Bride born in Stockholm city %	Groom born in Stockholm city %	Bride and groom born in the same Stockholm parish %	Bride and groom born in Stockholm city %	Number of banns	%
Large entrepreneurs	2.3	4.5	15.9	31.8	13.6	2.3	29.5	44	2.7
Large landowners	4.0	16.0	56.0	8.0	—	4.0	12.0	25	1.5
Higher administrative and liberal professions	—	2.2	33.3	35.6	17.8	2.2	8.9	45	2.8
Smaller entrepreneurs	2.1	6.4	38.6	26.4	10.0	—	16.4	140	8.6
Smaller landowners	—	33.3	66.7	—	—	—	—	3	0.2
Lower administrative, foremen	0.7	5.9	46.3	17.6	16.9	0.7	11.8	136	8.4
Shop assistants, clerks	—	2.7	18.9	29.7	10.8	2.7	35.1	37	2.3
Porters and personal servants	1.0	7.8	66.7	11.8	9.8	—	2.9	102	6.3
Lower professionals	—	—	50.0	25.0	—	25.0	—	4	0.2
Craftsmen	0.7	8.0	55.8	16.7	13.8	1.4	3.6	138	8.5
Skilled labourers	2.3	10.9	59.2	12.5	9.1	0.8	5.1	606	37.4
Unskilled labourers	1.9	10.4	70.4	9.7	6.0	0.6	0.9	318	19.6
Landless farmers, farmhands, former servants and soldiers	—	20.0	60.0	20.0	20.0	—	—	5	0.3
Domestic servants	—	12.5	75.0	12.5	—	—	—	8	0.5
Soldiers	—	12.5	62.5	25.0	—	—	—	8	0.5
Total number	28	147	906	251	159	15	114	1620	
%	1.7	9.1	55.9	15.5	9.8	0.9	7.0		100.0
Unknown								2	
Grand total								1622	

Table 14.4b Geographical background and partner choice by groom's social group, Stockholm, 1870–1879

Groom's social group	Not born in Stockholm			Born in Stockholm				Total	
	Bride and groom born in the same county and parish %	Bride and groom born in the same county %	Bride and groom born in different counties %	Bride born in Stockholm city %	Groom born in Stockholm city %	Bride and groom born in the same Stockholm parish %	Bride and groom born in Stockholm city %	Number of banns	%
Large entrepreneurs	3.6	1.4	0.8	5.6	3.8	6.7	11.4	44	2.7
Large landowners	3.6	2.7	1.5	0.8	—	6.7	2.6	25	1.5
Higher administrative and liberal professions	—	0.7	1.7	6.4	5.0	6.7	3.5	45	2.8
Smaller entrepreneurs	10.7	6.1	5.9	14.7	8.8	—	20.2	140	8.6
Smaller landowners	—	0.7	0.2	—	—	—	—	3	0.2
Lower administrative, foremen	3.6	5.4	6.9	9.6	14.5	6.7	14.0	136	8.4
Shop assistants, clerks	—	0.7	0.8	4.4	2.5	6.7	11.4	37	2.3
Porters and personal servants	3.6	5.4	7.5	4.8	6.3	—	2.6	102	6.3
Lower professionals	—	—	0.2	6.7	—	6.7	—	4	0.2
Craftsmen	3.6	7.5	8.5	9.2	11.9	13.3	4.4	138	8.5
Skilled labourers	50.0	44.9	39.5	30.3	34.6	33.3	27.2	606	37.4
Unskilled labourers	21.4	22.4	24.7	12.4	11.9	13.3	2.6	318	19.6
Landless farmers, farmhands, former servants and soldiers	—	0.7	0.3	0.4	0.6	—	—	5	0.3
Domestic servants	—	0.7	0.7	0.4	—	—	—	8	0.5
Soldiers	—	0.7	0.6	0.8	—	—	—	8	0.5
Total number	28	147	906	251	159	15	114	1620	
%	1.7	9.1	55.9	15.5	9.8	0.9	7.0		100.0
Unknown								2	
Grand total								1622	

Table 14.5a Geographical background and partner choice by county of birth, Stockholm, 1880–1889

Groom's social group	Not born in Stockholm			Born in Stockholm				Total	
	Bride and groom born in the same county and parish %	Bride and groom born in the same county %	Bride and groom born in different counties %	Bride born in Stockholm city %	Groom born in Stockholm city %	Bride and groom born in the same Stockholm parish %	Bride and groom born in Stockholm city %	Number of banns	%
Large entrepreneurs	—	4.8	23.8	38.1	19.0	—	14.3	42	1.9
Large landowners	3.4	10.3	79.3	3.4	—	3.4	—	29	1.3
Higher administrative and liberal professions	—	6.2	26.1	40.0	13.8	—	13.8	65	2.9
Smaller entrepreneurs	3.4	5.6	39.0	26.6	14.1	1.7	9.6	177	7.9
Smaller landowners	12.5	25.0	50.0	12.5	—	—	—	8	0.4
Lower administrative, foremen	3.4	8.9	37.4	25.1	12.3	2.8	10.1	179	8.0
Shop assistants, clerks	5.7	5.7	48.6	22.9	2.9	—	14.3	35	1.6
Porters and personal servants	2.5	8.3	58.7	19.0	8.3	—	3.3	121	5.4
Lower professionals	20.0	—	40.0	20.0	20.0	—	—	5	0.2
Craftsmen	2.2	13.1	59.4	12.7	7.4	0.9	4.4	229	10.2
Skilled labourers	2.5	11.6	58.7	12.1	9.9	1.1	4.1	751	33.5
Unskilled labourers	3.8	12.0	70.7	5.8	6.2	—	1.5	583	26.0
Landless farmers, farmhands, former servants and soldiers	—	—	100.0	—	—	—	—	4	0.2
Domestic servants	—	—	66.7	33.3	—	—	—	3	0.1
Soldiers	—	—	50.0	25.0	12.5	—	12.5	8	0.4
Total number	66	236	1279	325	204	19	110	2239	
%	2.9	10.6	57.1	14.5	9.1	0.8	5.0		100.0
Unknown								2	
Grand total								2241	

Table 14.5b Geographical background and partner choice by groom's social group, Stockholm, 1880–1889

Groom's social group	Not born in Stockholm			Born in Stockholm				Total	
	Bride and groom born in the same county and parish %	Bride and groom born in the same county %	Bride and groom born in different counties %	Bride born in Stockholm city %	Groom born in Stockholm city %	Bride and groom born in the same Stockholm parish %	Bride and groom born in Stockholm city %	Number of banns	%
Large entrepreneurs	—	0.8	0.8	4.9	3.9	—	5.4	42	1.9
Large landowners	1.5	1.2	1.8	0.3	—	5.3	—	29	1.3
Higher administrative and liberal professions	—	1.7	1.3	8.0	4.4	—	8.1	65	2.9
Smaller entrepreneurs	9.1	4.2	5.4	14.5	12.3	15.8	15.4	177	7.9
Smaller landowners	1.5	0.8	0.3	0.3	—	—	—	8	0.4
Lower administrative, foremen	9.1	6.7	5.2	13.8	10.8	26.3	16.4	179	8.0
Shop assistants, clerks	3.0	0.8	1.3	2.4	0.5	—	4.5	35	1.6
Porters and personal servants	4.5	4.2	5.5	7.1	4.9	—	3.6	121	5.4
Lower professionals	1.5	—	0.1	0.3	0.5	—	—	5	0.2
Craftsmen	7.6	12.7	10.6	8.9	8.3	10.5	9.1	229	10.2
Skilled labourers	28.8	36.9	34.5	28.0	36.3	42.1	28.2	751	33.5
Unskilled labourers	33.3	29.6	32.2	10.5	17.6	—	8.2	583	26.0
Landless farmers, farmhands, former servants and soldiers	—	—	0.3	—	—	—	—	4	0.2
Domestic servants	—	—	0.1	0.3	—	—	—	3	0.1
Soldiers	—	—	0.3	0.6	0.5	—	0.9	8	0.4
Total number	66	236	1279	325	204	19	110	2239	
%	2.9	10.6	57.1	14.5	9.1	0.8	5.0		100.0
Unknown								2	
Grand total								2241	

craftsmen there was a positive association between the degree of training they had received and the proportion of marriages with Stockholm-born women. The proportion of such marriages declined during the 1880s. Of the brides of unskilled labourers, more than 70 per cent were born in a different county from that of their groom, and about 15 per cent shared a birthplace with their groom.

A higher proportion of men from the upper classes tended to marry Stockholm-born women than in other social groups. This behaviour can be interpreted to mean that the principal goal for men in this class—both new arrivals and Stockholm-born—was to make an advantageous marriage. It again emphasizes the special status which was attached to having been born in the capital. This meant that Stockholm-born women's chances of marriage were greater than those of in-migrant women. The couple consisting of a Stockholm-born bride and an in-migrant groom was so common in the upper and middle classes as to suggest that it was primarily in these groups that those newly arrived could 'make a good match' in the sense of obtaining dowries and career possibilities in the capital. The choice of partners can be seen as governed by a careful consideration of socio-economic advantages. From an economic point of view, the surplus of women was probably most attractive in the upper two social groups. Competition for grooms forced many Stockholm families to accept a partner for their daughters who was not born locally. Among the propertied classes there was the continuous problem of unmarried daughters living at home for whom marriage was the only suitable form of maintenance. This gave in-migrant men the chance to establish themselves quickly in the capital, provided that they were able to support a wife.

It is much more difficult to consider the factors influencing the choice of a marriage partner by women. In their case, they might have had to make do with what was possible, rather than with what was desirable. We know very little about their preferences. Tradition required the man to take the active part and the woman had to wait for proposals of marriage and choose the most advantageous among them. When there was a shortage of men born in Stockholm, a woman might not realize her ambition to marry into a Stockholm family. Significantly fewer in-migrant women succeeded in marrying into Stockholm families than their male counterparts. My hypothesis about migrants, that they strove for integration through marriage with natives of Stockholm, therefore applies primarily to men. A very high proportion of women in-migrants during the 1870s and 1880s were unmarried, particularly those who did not own property and who were thus able to support themselves. For an in-migrant woman, marriage in the capital, given the lack of a dowry and the surplus of women, would have counted as a success in itself. A domestic servant on a low wage might have to save for ten or fifteen years before she could acquire a fiancé who, most probably would be both poorer and younger than herself. Many writers have pointed to the very high proportion of unmarried women among domestic servants,[21] many

[21] Carlsson, *Fröknar, mamseller, jungfrur och pigor*, 28–9.

of whom never married. In this group, there were least chances of integration into Stockholm society by marriage, though they might be offered the possibility of assimilating and integrating through other forms of informal unions. such as cohabitation and 'Mamsell marriages'.

The formation of a legal family for those without property could be costly, dysfunctional, and, for the female partner, risky. This resulted in other strategies. One such would be an informal union where an early migrant helped a later one, and shared the cost of living and contact nets. To illustrate migration patterns and survival strategies among migrants we quote a couple of case histories. Both relate to couples who later published their banns in Stockholm.

In 1857, at the age of 17, Olof Peterson left his birthplace and his widowed father, who was a resident farmhand, to seek employment in Stockholm. He was registered in Stockholm in the parish of St Nicholas. His employment during the first four years of his stay in the capital is not known, but between 1861 and 1862 he participated in exercises for conscripts. Eventually, he found employment as a silver worker. In Stockholm he met Stina, a domestic servant, fourteen years older than himself, and they set up house together. Stina had had three positions as a maidservant in the city. She was born outside the city in the county of Södermanland, where her father was a farmhand, but had come to Stockholm in 1854, three years before Olof. Her minister describes her as a steady and irreproachable character. She and Olof published their banns in the autumn of 1862.

Frans Persson, a farmhand and son of a soldier, was born in Kalmar county in 1832. At the age of 24 he moved to Högsby to take service as a farm labourer for a period of nine years. On leaving his place he received good testimonials and recommendations and in 1865 moved to Stockholm, where he is noted in the register as a rock-blaster. His fiancée, Anna, who was six years younger than himself, was born in Högsby and was the daughter of a blacksmith. She remained there until 1863, but moved to Stockholm in that year to take up a position as a maidservant. She may have met Frans when he was working in Högsby, but she moved to Stockholm two years before him and found work. However, in 1865 she returned to Högsby, evidently to fetch Frans. In 1866, she was again in Stockholm in service in the parish of St Nicholas. It does not seem that Frans and Anna lived together, but they did maintain a stable relationship. Just before publishing their banns in 1867, Anna gave birth to a daughter whom Frans acknowledged as his child and legitimated by their marriage.

5. The effect of migration on partner choice and family formation

The massive number of in-migrants influenced the pattern of family formation both from a geographical and a social point of view. The lack of local-born acceptable grooms meant that women from the propertied classes were increasingly forced to accept men born outside Stockholm as husbands. The marriage market, therefore, became a place in which migrant men could speculate for dowries and strategically suitable alliances. Those who were born in the city possessed an extra commodity which could be offered in exchange at the time of marriage and partner choice. The preference for local women, which is characteristic of the period at the beginning of our study, may be viewed as part of the strategy of newly arrived male migrants against the background of a surplus of women in the capital. It was possible not only for migrant men who owned property 'to make a good match', but even men without property could find brides and thus reduce the numbers of unmarried daughters who had remained on the shelf, and whose dowries sufficed for the initial capital needed to start a family. Such downward mobility resulted in a diffusion of values and customs from the higher to the lower social groups, and to the adoption of more bourgeois forms of behaviour by the latter.

It is clear that, in the upper two social classes, endogamy was preferred and that this resulted in the continuation of a closed circle which outsiders found difficult to penetrate. The large influx of young women of diverse social origin during the 1870s and 1880s greatly increased freedom of choice for men in search of a bride. Stockholm-born men increasingly chose brides who had not been born in the city, and this resulted in a breakdown of the traditional marriage pattern. Far too little is known about how native-born men, who had to choose between marrying a woman from a respectable Stockholm family or a woman who had recently arrived in the capital with a considerable fortune, saw their advantages. It is possible that the fortune weighed more heavily at the moment of decision. As such marriages became more common, the prestige conferred by being born in Stockholm became less. In the long run, this led to a loosening of the traditional constraints on marriage and greater social and geographical equality.

The changes in partner choice which we have noticed towards the end of our period of study must be viewed against the background of an increasingly individualistic view of family formation and also the social and economic transformation of the city. Industrialization increased the number of jobs available which brought relative security of employment and a stable income. The large group of working men and women and servants were those mainly affected by these changes. The city's rapid growth led to an increased demand for workers in the building industry and the service sector. The growth of factories provided opportunities for unskilled younger workers. Increases in real wages made it easier to support a family and led to earlier family formation. The savings and assets of older women became less attractive for men who realized that they could now satisfy their personal preferences in the choice of a wife, for example by marrying a younger, poor girl from their home district. A common background and common customs provided some security when choosing a partner. That this was so is suggested by the increasing tendency of couples from the lower classes to choose partners from the same areas in which they were born. In-migrant women without property were now able to start family formation earlier, and no longer needed their own savings for that purpose. As living standards rose and men were increasingly able to support a family, prudence became less important as a factor in partner choice.

Geographical mobility and migration also influenced social mobility through marriage. As the city became more industrial new and economically strong occupational groups became important. With the break-up of pre-industrial marriage patterns for the upper social groups, geographical and social background became less important in choosing a marriage partner. At the same time the marriage pattern among newly arrived men and women, who were the largest component of the lower social group, increasingly diverged from the distinctive pattern of an urban poverty culture, in which the struggle for existence took precedence over the observance of social norms, and became more like the ideal pattern which had hitherto been observed only among those with property.

15 Aspects of Fertility Decline in an Urban Setting:
Rouen and Geneva

ALFRED PERRENOUD
Department d'Histoire Économique, Université de Genève, Genève, Switzerland

The importance of urbanization in the process of fertility decline remains a subject of controversy. No causal relationship between urbanization and falling fertility has yet been definitely established, though there can be no doubt that urban life-styles are conducive to lower fertility and that, in general, falls in fertility first occurred in cities. The results of the Princeton study on the decline in fertility in Europe confirm that fertility in the towns was lower than in the countryside during the immediate pre-decline period, that it was inversely related to the size of towns, that the decline began earlier in the towns than in the countryside, and that the difference between the fertility of townspeople and country dwellers increased during the period of transition.[1]

However, a lower level of fertility and a steeper rate of decline are not in themselves sufficient proof that the towns were the driving force in the process of diffusion of birth control. Nor does the lower fertility of townspeople during the immediate pre-decline period imply the existence of family planning. This could as easily have been the result of biological and cultural factors as of demographic ones. It is also possible that couples spaced their births, voluntarily or involuntarily, in response to economic or demographic conditions, without intending to limit the sizes of their completed families. This would imply that birth control in the generally accepted sense of the term—i.e. the cessation of child-bearing once the desired number of children had been attained—was not practised, but rather that couples reacted to specific conditions by altering the spacing of their births. This constitutes the subject of the debate between those who see the spread of birth control as a process of diffusion of innovative behaviour, and those who regard it as being merely an adjustment to new situations. Moreover, townspeople could have practised birth control on a significant

---

[1] A. Sharlin, 'Urban–Rural Differences in Fertility in Europe During the Demographic Transition', Working Paper no. 329, Institute of Urban and Regional Studies, University of California, Berkeley (1980).

scale well before the decline of fertility began in the countryside. Thus it is clear that members of the highest social groups—the aristocracy and some members of the upper bourgeoisie—had been practising birth control for some time. The question, therefore, arises: how did the practice of birth control become diffused throughout the population? How was it transmitted from one social group to the remainder of the population? What were the processes of diffusion and their several stages?

If lower fertility in the towns was not the result of voluntary control, but merely reflected a difference in natural fertility, the concept of the demographic transition as a diffusion process would be supported. Conversely, if townspeople had for long practised birth control, the view that the transition represented merely an adjustment to new conditions would gain greater credence. In this case, the transition from natural to controlled fertility would not necessarily imply either social or cultural changes (e.g. changes in the function of the family, a higher valuation of children, or secularization of behaviour), nor a fundamental change in outlook or ideology including more widespread acceptance of birth control, nor even easier access to techniques of contraception.

Such questions can hardly be answered by studying aggregates. The data are not sufficient even for the purpose of sketching an explanatory model. We cannot expect to find a single monolithic theory to explain these phenomena; rather there are likely to be a variety of models showing different responses to specific situations which will depend on the locality, size, and economic functions of the city, as well as on social practices.[2]

This is the hypothesis that Kingsley Davis developed in his 'theory of multiphasic response',[3] which can be seen in the theory of a homeostatic equilibrium suggested by Wrigley and Schofield. Based on the notion that no society can sustain a high rate of growth over a long period, it suggests that populations react to disturbances in demographic equilibrium by altering one or other of the components of population growth. If this point of view were accepted, the fact that some of the traditional responses to such a disturbance—changes in nuptiality or in migration—were limited in an urban setting leaves only the control of births as an alternative.

This seems to have been the case in the two towns in which the development has been studied in depth by using the techniques of family reconstitution—Rouen and Geneva. In both these towns, a rise in fertility was halted during the seventeenth century by a contraceptive revolution which had begun very early at the top of the social hierarchy, and which was extended rapidly to the remainder of the population.[4]

---

[2] A. E. Roel, 'Modèle ou modèles de démographie ancienne? Un résumé comparatif?', *La France d'ancien régime. Études réunis en l'honneur de Pierre Goubert* (Paris, 1984), ii. 249–57.

[3] K. Davis, 'The Theory of Change and Response in Modern Demographic History', *Population Index*, 29:4 (1963), 345–66.

[4] J. P. Bardet, *Rouen au xviie et xviiie siècles. Les mutations d'un espace social* (Paris, 1983).

1. Rouen and Geneva: The socio-economic environment

The population of Rouen, which had amounted to 80,000 or more inhabitants in about 1650, had fallen by nearly 30 per cent at the beginning of the eighteenth century. This long period of decline was succeeded by one of significant growth between 1720 and 1740 followed by a period of relative stagnation which lasted until the beginning of the Revolution. During the same period, the population of Geneva, which was about 12,000 in 1650, grew very rapidly until 1720, and increased by 70 per cent during these seventy years. This period was succeeded by twenty years of stagnation, which were, in their turn, followed by a period of renewed growth which resulted in the population reaching its maximum figure during the eighteenth century (29,000 in 1790) before the long ebb of the period of French rule (1798–1814). The demographic histories of these two towns were, therefore, quite different.

Economically the capital of Normandy was an important port as well as a commercial and industrial centre. It was dominated by the textile industry with its proto-industrial pattern of production, in which one-quarter of the population were employed and which extended into the countryside. From about 1750 onwards, the expansion of the cotton industry led to a re-urbanization of the labour force and to the beginning of industrialization proper. Thus, the eighteenth century was a period of economic growth for the city. The Protestant capital, Geneva, on the other hand, was essentially a city in which, throughout the period, there were a number of small industries. Its economy was outward-looking, half its population were occupied in producing for export, and the city was therefore liable to be affected by international economic fluctuations. The watchmaking industry overtook textiles in importance during the eighteenth century, with 48 per cent of the population being engaged in the manufacturing sector. Industry continued to be organized on the craft system, with small units of production that often consisted of families. However, economic development resulted in a marked division of labour, and the artisan became more dependent on the merchant and the middleman. The printed cotton industry developed, too, but did not provide a great deal of employment for the citizens. During the second half of the eighteenth century the pursuit of profit transformed the social landscape, and economic prosperity coincided with a fall in the workers' standard of living.

The environment was no doubt more pleasant on the shores of Lake Geneva, even though the population density of 420 persons per hectare exceeded that of Rouen. During the second half of the eighteenth century, life expectancy at birth in Geneva was 35 years, compared with only 28 years in Rouen. However, the contrasts between different social classes were as great, and the expectation of life on one's fifteenth birthday was the same in the two cities.

246 *Alfred Perrenoud*

Towns contain a number of different subpopulations with very different forms of behaviour. It is, therefore, necessary to consider two principal factors: the geographical origin of city dwellers and their distribution by social class. The geographical origins of the population play an important part in the differentiation of reproductive behaviour, because the social structure of the migrants which was shaped by economic conditions was different from that of those born in the city.

2. The decline of fertility: a global approach

All the indications are that birth control had been practised in Rouen since the beginning of the seventeenth century, and that it spread very rapidly throughout the population. Fertility declined particularly steeply between 1700 and 1725, and again after 1760. Total fertility, which came to about eight children per family in 1670, fell to a figure of just over four children by 1800. Thus, the population of Rouen appears to have mastered contraceptive techniques within the space of a century.

In order to ascertain the situation in Geneva we consider the theoretical size of completed families obtained by summing fertility rates (see Table 15.1). The similarity between the two cities is particularly striking for women who married between the ages of 20 and 30. Though the initial level of fertility was slightly higher in Rouen and the rhythm of decline a little out of phase, percentage declines between the first and the last of the observed cohorts were very similar: 38.2 and 39.4 per cent respectively for women married between the ages of 20 and 24; 33.3 per cent and 35.2 per cent respectively for women married between the ages of 25 and 29. The agreement is less good both for those who married at very young and at relatively old ages. Women in the latter age groups appear to have used contraception less in Geneva than in Rouen; the opposite is true for women who married in their teens. Differences in age at marriage determined by social status are important in this connection and were more clear-cut in Geneva than in Rouen.

The similarity between the two cities is confirmed when overall averages are calculated with a constant system of weights, derived from the data for Rouen, to combine the figures for different age-at-marriage groups in order to calculate an overall average. This is done in Table 15.2. The data for Geneva do not make it possible to obtain an accurate picture of changes in period fertility. However, a comparison of the figures is of some interest. I have calculated a theoretical index from the distribution of ages at marriage for Geneva, assuming that the period of active reproduction in each marriage cohort extended over ten years. The results are shown in Fig. 15.1.

The figure gives an indication of the reduction in fertility, but it also shows striking similarities in the two cities. Though there are some small

Table 15.1 Theoretical size of completed family by wife's age at marriage and period of marriage: Rouen and Geneva

Date of marriage		Wife's age at marriage										
		15–19		20–24		25–29		30–34		35–39		40–44
Rouen	Geneva	Rouen	Geneva	Rouen	Geneva	Rouen	Geneva	Rouen	Geneva	Rouen	Geneva	Rouen	Geneva
	1625–44		10.3		8.4		6.5		3.8		2.2		0.5
1640–69	1650–74	11.1	9.6	10.2	9.4	7.2	7.1	5.3	4.3	3.3	3.0	0.8	0.8
1670–99	1675–96	10.3	8.3	9.3	8.3	7.3	6.6	4.5	4.4	2.7	2.5	0.4	0.6
1700–29	1700/4–1725/7	8.3	7.4	7.8	7.6	6.3	5.8	3.8	3.8	1.9	2.5	0.5	1.3
1730–59	1745–9	8.4	6.6	7.8	5.8	5.4	4.9	3.7	3.3	1.4	1.8	0.5	0.6
1760–92	1770–2	7.7	5.3	6.3	5.7	4.8	4.6	2.8	3.6	1.5	1.8	0.3	0.5
	1800–10		4.3		3.1		3.0		2.5		1.2		0.4

Table 15.2 Theoretical size of completed families for women married between the ages of 15 and 49 in Rouen and Geneva[a]

Date of marriage		Completed family size		% Decline	
Rouen	Geneva	Rouen	Geneva	Rouen	Geneva
1640–69	1650–74	7.28	6.66		
1670–99	1675–96	6.73	6.03	7.6	9.5
1700–29	1700/4–1725/7	5.67	5.46	22.1	18.0
1730–59	1745–9	5.34	4.41	26.6	33.8
1760–89	1770–2	4.59	4.22	37.0	36.6
	1800–10		2.65		60.2

[a] Overall averages were obtained by calculating a weighted average for women married at different ages, the weights being the proportions of women married at these ages in Rouen.

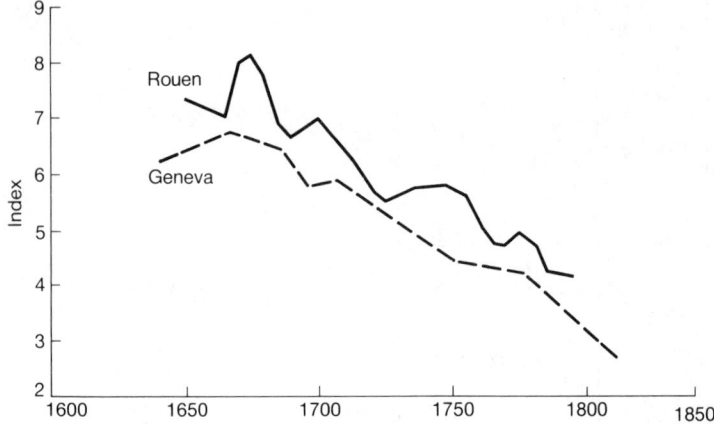

Figure 15.1. Sum of age-specific fertility rates, current (Rouen) and marriage cohorts (Geneva)

divergences, both the shape and the timing of the decline are the same. Fertility was relatively low at the beginning of the period. In Geneva at least, this low level cannot be explained by under-registration of baptisms. Fertility in the bourgeois families studied by Louis Henry[5] was lower during the sixteenth than during the seventeenth century, and this is true of the population as a whole.[6] The increase in fertility during the seventeenth century appears clearly on the graph and explains the discontinuity around 1680. Once the decline had begun, it proceeded more or less in parallel in the two towns. There is the same drop in fertility towards the end of the seventeenth century caused by economic conditions, and it is succeeded by the same weak recovery. A period of rapid decline then follows, which appears to have been more pronounced in Rouen. The rate of decline fell between 1725 and 1755, a period during which the rate was higher in Geneva. However, this state of affairs did not last long, the rate of decline in that city also fell between 1750 and 1780, preceding a very steep decline during the period of French domination, when completed family size was as low as 2.7 children per woman, a level reached in the whole of Switzerland only in 1915. If we end our observations at the end of the eighteenth century, the percentage falls for different marriage cohorts are very similar: 37.0 per cent in Rouen, 36.6 per cent in Geneva.

The fall is shown more clearly if we look at age-specific fertility rates, which are presented in Table 15.3 and plotted in Fig. 15.2. The diagrams illustrate the classical pattern which leaves no doubt about the nature of the process

---

[5] L. Henry, *Anciennes Familles genèvoises. Étude démographique, xvie-xxe siècles* (Paris, 1956).

[6] A. Perrenoud and D. Zumkeller, 'Caractères orginaux de la démographie genèvoise du xvie siècle. Structure ou conjoncture', *Annales de démographie historique* (Paris, 1980), 125-41.

Table 15.3 Adjusted age-specific fertility rates per 1,000 women in Geneva

Date of marriage	Age of woman							Total progeny	Total of families
	15–19	20–24	25–29	30–34	35–39	40–44	45–49		
Age at marriage less than 20 years									
1625–44	474	508	451	379	321	177	10	10.29	69
1650–74	404	510	436	383	320	118	25	9.63	54
1675–96	465	551	372	298	183	73	0	8.33	56
1700–4	526	476	434	324	120	29	0	8.17	27
1725–7	487	508	303	204	134	40	0	6.85	33
1745–9	437	467	302	249	122	30	0	6.58	59
1770–2	554	426	224	168	77	27	0	5.33	39
1800–10	505	405	154	96	61	0	0	4.26	41
Age at marriage: 20–24									
1625–44		530	466	405	341	186	20	8.44	101
1650–74		537	517	479	404	195	25	9.43	96
1675–96		511	519	404	321	119	5	8.24	112
1700–4		567	560	440	301	83	16	8.36	86
1725–7		574	468	333	195	82	1	6.74	81
1745–9		532	417	280	150	47	0	5.78	141
1770–2		541	414	252	145	71	5	5.73	85
1800–10		449	214	121	40	20	0	3.07	112
Age at marriage: 25–29									
1625–44			482	442	355	204	33	6.51	88
1650–74			563	491	403	226	34	7.05	71
1675–96			524	445	362	201	25	6.63	110
1700–4			528	437	298	140	10	6.00	80
1725–7			531	445	267	120	13	5.62	80
1745–9			488	397	239	93	11	4.29	147
1770–2			513	352	218	63	0	4.56	75
1800–10			418	236	116	36	0	3.03	118
Age at marriage: 30–34									
1625–44				449	362	177	0	3.79	43
1650–74				476	347	215	64	4.31	55
1675–96				472	400	211	10	4.38	67
1700–4				495	359	174	23	4.18	47
1725–7				428	340	99	44	3.48	56
1745–9				440	301	19	16	3.26	91
1770–2				505	309	124	21	3.56	59
1800–10				421	224	59	6	2.48	53
Age at marriage: 35+									
1625–44					435	164	16	1.99	42
1650–74					468	253	64	2.78	35
1675–96					479	209	41	2.45	60
1700–4					460	237	48	2.58	69
1725–7					498	204	77	2.65	61
1745–9					326	165	28	1.78	116
1770–2					355	139	40	1.78	62
1800–10					413	116	29	1.76	49

that is depicted. Fertility was high during the early years of marriage and declined ever more steeply in successive quinquennia after marriage. The shape of the curves changes from convex to concave. The decline begins by affecting women who married when they were very young and who were, therefore, exposed to the risk of childbearing for longer periods. As we pass

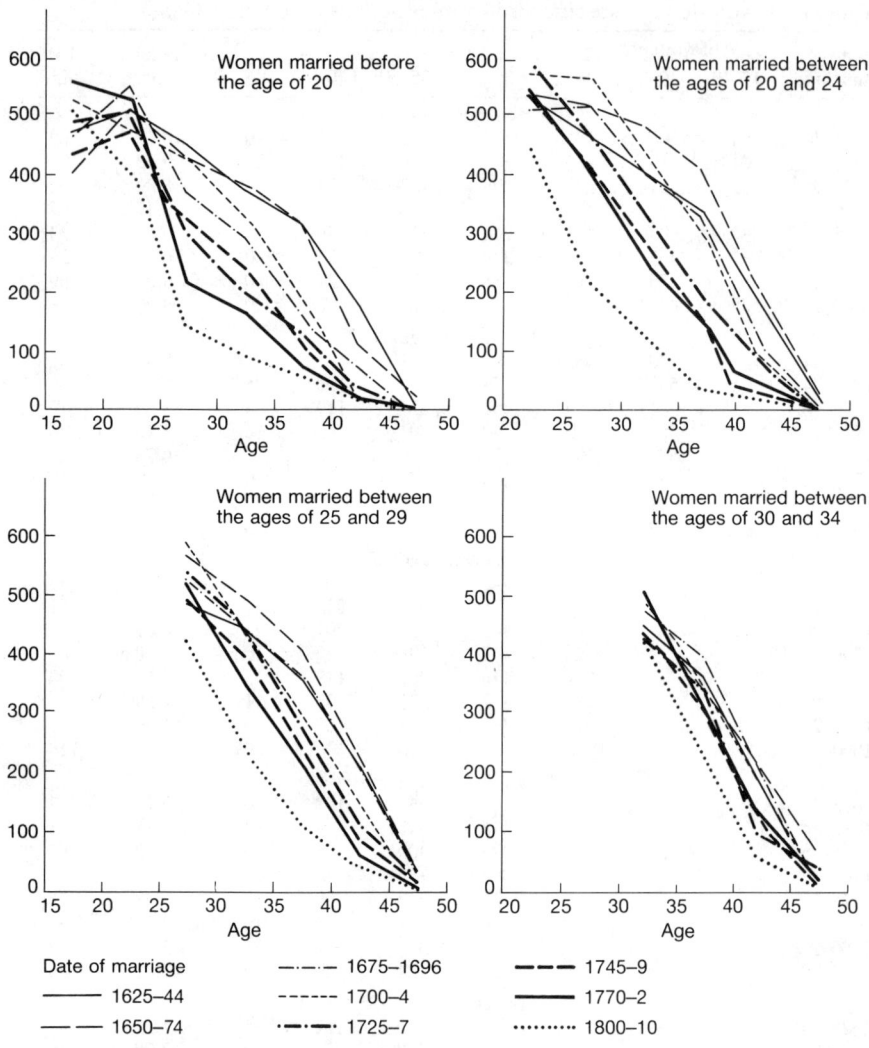

Figure 15.2. Adjusted legitimate fertility rates by age of women at marriage and date of marriage (Geneva)

from one age-at-marriage group to the next, the curves converge, the ellipse becomes narrower, so that the importance of age at marriage as a factor influencing fertility declines. A woman who married in her teens between 1650 and 1674 bore on average 9.6 children. This figure falls to 4.3 children for women who married between the ages of 30 and 34. A century later, the gap between these figures has narrowed; completed family sizes were 5.3 and 3.6 children respectively for the two groups.

The timing of the decline is strongly correlated with the age of the women. Indices calculated with the marriages of 1650–74 as a base show the connections clearly (see Table 15.4). Declines in fertility increase with the age

Table 15.4 Fertility indices by age (marriages of 1650–74 = 100)

Age of woman	Period of marriage							
	1625–44	1650–74	1675–96	1700–4	1725–7	1745–9	1770–2	1800–10
	Women married before their 20th birthday							
15–19	117	100	115	130	121	108	137	125
20–24	93	100	108	93	100	92	84	79
25–29	103	100	85	100	69	69	51	35
30–34	99	100	78	85	53	65	44	25
35–39	100	100	51	59	42	38	24	19
40–44	150	100	62	25	34	25	23	0
	Women married between the ages of 20 and 24							
20–24	99	100	95	106	107	99	101	84
25–29	90	100	100	108	91	81	80	41
30–34	85	100	84	92	70	58	53	25
35–39	84	100	79	75	48	37	36	10
40–44	95	100	61	43	42	24	36	10
	Women married between the ages of 25 and 29							
25–29	86	100	93	103	94	87	91	74
30–34	90	100	91	89	91	81	72	48
35–39	88	100	90	74	66	59	54	29
40–44	90	100	89	62	53	41	28	16
	Women married between the ages of 30 and 34							
30–34	94	100	99	104	90	92	106	88
35–39	104	100	115	103	98	87	89	65
40–44	82	100	98	81	46	55	58	27

of the woman. Thus fertility rates during the later stages of women's reproductive lives were reduced before the fall was extended progressively to earlier stages. For marriages between 1700 and 1704 the fall for women aged 40 to 44 who had been married in their teens reached 75 per cent. It was 57 per cent for those married between the ages of 20 and 24, and 38 per cent for those married between the ages of 25 and 29. Fertility declined earlier, and the fall was larger, for women who had married when they were young. The index fell by ten points after less than fifteen years of marriage for women who had married before their twenty-fifth birthday between 1675 and 1696. After 1750, the decline in fertility extended to the youngest women, and the length of the period that women actually spent in reproduction became shorter. Within one century, fertility rates after the tenth year of marriage were halved. The only period in women's lives when fertility did not fall so much was in the age group in which marriage actually occurred. Rates fell in this age group as well, but the fall differed for women who had married at different ages, particularly for those who had married between the ages of 25 and 29. The only exceptions to this rule were women who had married when they were very young and whose fertility remained high. Two compelling types of behaviour seem to be noted here. Young women waited until they had achieved the number of children that they desired, and then stopped reproducing; other women slowed down the pace of child bearing from the very beginning of their married lives. The factors that need to be considered are the choice of strategy (spacing throughout marriage, rather than stopping when desired family size has been achieved), and possibly a change in the social composition of the population.

The decline in fertility is not the only factor which leads to a concentration of fertility at the beginning of marriage. In fact, fertility increased during the early years of marriage. Thus the timing of births will depend on the level of fertility. Birth control was adopted after a prolonged period in which fertility had risen. Age-specific fertility rates for women married between 1650 and 1674 were higher than those for women married during previous decades as a result of movements which began during the early years of the seventeenth century.[7] At that time, the only exceptional group was that consisting of women who had married in their teens and who had already begun to restrict the size of their families. It is also evident that fertility rates during the early years of marriage continued to increase, even though their level was already high in our second marriage cohort. The increase was particularly marked among young married women, but it can also be discerned among those who married rather later. This increase in fertility was brought about by a reduction in the intervals between successive births (see Table 15.5).

Table 15.5 Average birth intervals in females with six or more children

Date of marriage	Intervals between successive births (months)					
	1–2	2–3	3–4	Antepenultimate	Penultimate	Last
1625–44	19.6	24.9	24.7	24.2	27.4	35.9
1650–74	19.3	20.9	22.3	25.3	25.4	30.8
1675–96	19.1	21.9	22.1	23.0	26.7	34.2
1700–4	19.8	20.5	22.1	23.5	25.9	36.8
1725–7	18.2	21.1	24.5	23.9	28.2	38.1
1745–9	16.5	19.9	21.2	23.4	26.8	37.0
1770–2	16.4	19.6	21.0	25.6	31.0	32.4
1800–10	18.3	24.2	26.1	28.9	27.1	44.1

The intervals shown are intervals for women who had large families and no account has been taken of the outcome of the previous pregnancy, so that the differences tend to be reduced. However, the average of the first three intervals is reduced from 23.1 months for the first marriage cohort to 19.0 months for the last but one, whereas the opposite trend is found for the mean of the last three intervals. This suggests that birth control was adopted as a response to increased fertility, which itself may have been caused by the practice of sending infants to be wet-nursed. However, a shorter period of lactation by the mother cannot have been the only reason for increased fertility, because shorter birth intervals are also found following the death of a child.[8]

[7] Cf. ibid. [8] Ibid.

Aspects of Fertility Decline 253

Bardet estimated the timing of the adoption of contraception by calculating the average number of children born during each quinquennium of married life for women who married between the ages of 15 and 34 years, and using a constant system of weights for different age-at-marriage groups. For the sake of comparability, I have calculated the same index which is shown in Table 15.6.

Table 15.6 Average number of children born during successive quinquennia of marriage by period of marriage for women married between the ages of 15 and 34 years

Date of marriage	Duration of marriage (years)			
	0–4	5–9	10–14	15–19
1625–44	2.33	1.99	1.50	0.96
1650–74	2.54	2.06	1.73	1.06
1675–96	2.56	1.96	1.39	0.68
1700–4	2.57	2.17	1.23	0.55
1725–7	2.56	1.66	0.82	0.45
1745–9	2.33	1.48	0.76	0.25
1770–2	2.36	1.33	0.79	0.33
1800–10	1.79	0.85	0.35	0.11

As was the case in Rouen, contraception tended to be used first by couples who had lived together for more than ten years. Among such couples use increased progressively from the end of the seventeenth century and reached a plateau among couples married between 1770 and 1772. Beginning with the second quarter of the eighteenth century, the practice spread to couples who were in their second quinquennium of marriage, among whom it showed a regular increase. Practice of contraception during the early years of marriage can be traced from the middle of the eighteenth century onwards. Fertility fell by 29.5 per cent during the first quinquennium of marriage between the second and the last marriage cohorts shown in the table; by 41.3 per cent during the second quinquennium of marriage; by 79.8 per cent during the third; and by 89.6 per cent during the fourth.

The feature of the results which I found most surprising was the astonishing efficiency with which birth control was used at a time when there were no birth control appliances, and the methods used must have been far from certain. Among fertile women who had married before their twenty-fifth birthday and whose marriage lasted until they were at least 40 years old, 33 per cent of members of the cohort married between 1745 and 1749 had no further children after their union had lasted for ten years, and this figure increased to 36 per cent, and, towards the beginning of the nineteenth century, to 56 per cent. If women who continued childbearing to the end of their reproductive lives are omitted from the analysis on the grounds that such women evidently did not wish to limit the size of their families, the percentage who were successful in controlling their fertility reached 50 per cent in the cohort of 1745–9, and 62 per cent in the cohort of 1800–10. Changes in the ages at which women in these cohorts gave birth to their last child confirm that they had achieved mastery over their reproduction (Table 15.7).

Table 15.7 Age at last birth of women with completed families by period of marriage

Date of marriage	Age at marriage								Weighted mean
	15–19		20–24		25–29		30–34		
	Mean	No.	Mean	No.	Mean	No.	Mean	No.	15–30
1625–44	39.8	23	39.7	54	40.6	45	41.4	22	40.1
1650–74	37.1	21	39.8	40	41.3	47	40.9	39	40.1
1675–96	35.0	28	36.9	58	40.3	62	40.2	47	38.1
1700–4	34.2	15	36.7	45	38.5	54	40.4	36	37.1
1725–7	30.1	14	35.8	56	37.7	53	39.0	41	35.8
1745–9	33.5	26	33.7	83	37.4	97	39.4	52	35.3
1770–2	30.0	22	34.0	54	36.5	49	38.7	41	34.5
1800–10	30.2	17	30.9	66	34.6	78	37.4	37	32.4

From the end of the seventeenth century the age at which women cease to reproduce continued to fall even faster than in Rouen. Between the cohort of 1625–44 and that of 1800–10 the fall amounted to 9.6 years for women who had married in their teens and to 8.8 years for those who had married between the ages of 20 and 24. The theoretical length of women's reproductive lives has, therefore, been reduced by nearly one-half. The figures given in Table 15.7 make it possible to trace the progress of sterility among women as a function of the ages at which they married. From the middle of the seventeenth century onwards, the pathbreakers were women who had married at very young ages, and in this group those who had married between 1725 and 1727 had already achieved complete mastery over their fertility. The mean age at the birth of their last child of women who had married between the ages of 20 and 24 begins to decline in the cohort married between 1675 and 1696, and then, after remaining steady for a while, continues to decrease throughout the remainder of the eighteenth century. Women who had married between the ages of 30 and 34, however, began to control their births much later. It would seem that there were two periods when fertility declined: the first steps were taken by women who originally had very large families; the decline later spread to middle-sized families, and this implies that it was extended to women who had married later in their lives. The movement which appears smooth at first sight is not incompatible with differences between the fertility of different social groups.

By the end of the period, however, the fall had become so large that differences between social groups became less important. It is no longer possible to maintain the view that members of the lower social groups did not have access to methods of contraception, and that fertility control remained a prerogative of the élite. Use of contraception had become so widespread that one wonders whether behaviour which had become so common in the towns could have been avoided in the countryside.

3. Fertility and origin

As in-migration was an important factor in the towns (41 per cent of married women in Geneva had been born outside the city), it is necessary to assess the effect of migration on the level and trend of fertility. In cases where no direct information about the origin of women was available, we have considered women whose date of birth was not known to have been in-migrants. It is likely that after verification some corrections to our data will become necessary, but these are unlikely to affect our main conclusions.

In Table 15.8 we see adjusted age-specific legitimate fertility rates, and in Table 15.9 synthetic indices of reproduction, for women born in Geneva and for in-migrants. The first conclusion that can be drawn from these figures is that, when birth control was not practised, the fertility of the in-migrants was lower than that of women born in Geneva. If the weighted average size of completed families is used as an index, in order to control for differences in the distribution of ages at marriage, the difference during the first half of the seventeenth century comes to 1.8 children per woman. This figure falls consistently in later marriage cohorts, and in the last two cohorts the direction of the difference is reversed. The lower fertility of in-migrant women is confirmed by figures which show that intervals between successive births are longer in that group, and that this difference is not caused by poorer quality of birth registration. In effect, fertility differences are not independent of age at marriage: the families of those in-migrant women who had married after their thirtieth birthday were consistently larger than those of a similar group of women born in Geneva. This difference may reflect differences in breastfeeding practices, particularly where the mothers were young, and social origin may also have played a part. Finally, the lower fertility of women born in Geneva may have reflected a desire to limit births from the very beginning of marriage, a trend which can also be discerned in Rouen. The fall in family size was more pronounced in that group of women than among those who had married when they were younger.

The fall in fertility began earlier and was more pronounced among women born in Geneva than among in-migrants. If a constant system of weights is used to combine the averages for women who married at different ages, family size falls from 7.0 children per woman in the second marriage cohort to 4.0 children per woman in the penultimate cohort for those born in Geneva: the corresponding figures for in-migrant women are respectively 5.9 and 4.6. However, if the different distribution of ages at marriage is taken into account, the discrepancy is reduced; it is caused largely by women born in Geneva who had married at very young ages, and whose families were particularly large during the seventeenth century.

We also note that the rise in fertility during the early years of marriage was

Table 15.8 Legitimate age-specific fertility rates by mothers' geographical origin

Date of marriage		Age of mother						Number of families
		20–24	25–29	30–34	35–39	40–44	45–49	
		Women married between the ages of 20 and 24						
1625–44	G	545	497	440	388	205	15	73
	I	484	385	305	211	141	29	28
1650–74	G	556	529	495	425	205	25	83
	I	407	446	380	257	100	0	13
1675–96	G	505	537	410	321	115	6	85
	I	529	463	384	318	130	0	27
1700–4	G	550	585	471	309	96	24	58
	I	568	513	382	284	57	0	28
1725–7	G	601	496	372	182	69	0	64
	I	411	396	320	242	122	21	17
1745–9	G	528	409	279	153	47	0	114
	I	555	452	282	133	50	0	27
1770–2	G	526	406	247	154	98	6	64
	I	589	440	271	114	100	0	21
1800–10	G	462	205	122	38	25	0	86
	I	409	243	118	47	0	0	26
		Women married between the ages of 25 and 29						
1625–44	G		491	467	366	206	25	58
	I		465	393	333	200	50	30
1650–74	G		582	498	408	221	23	58
	I		473	462	380	250	100	13
1675–96	G		554	442	350	215	33	78
	I		448	451	391	159	0	32
1700–4	G		606	424	301	159	7	48
	I		550	455	295	111	13	32
1725–7	G		560	499	318	143	15	50
	I		446	358	189	83	10	30
1745–9	G		480	377	229	78	14	101
	I		509	440	260	127	23	46
1770–2	G		509	312	178	47	0	45
	I		521	407	271	83	0	30
1800–10	G		395	226	97	25	0	79
	I		467	261	164	70	0	39
		Women married between the ages of 30 and 34						
1625–44	G			417	330	114	0	22
	I			478	400	250	0	21
1650–74	G			541	360	168	53	31
	I			351	330	300	89	24
1675–96	G			452	407	189	0	35
	I			495	393	233	23	32
1700–4	G			481	363	151	0	23
	I			511	355	201	45	24
1725–7	G			407	318	67	0	27
	I			446	358	124	75	29
1745–9	G			419	251	103	14	42
	I			458	343	133	18	50
1770–2	G			548	233	105	10	28
	I			465	372	142	31	31
1800–10	G			385	151	50	0	34
	I			506	300	91	17	19

G = Geneva-born; I = In-migrants

Table 15.9 Total fertility by mothers' age at marriage and geographical origin

Date of marriage		Mother's age at marriage						Mean
		15–19	20–24	25–29	30–34	35–39	40–44	
1625–44	G	11.1	9.2	6.7	3.1	1.6	—	7.1
	I	—	6.4	6.2	4.5	2.7	—	5.3
1650–74	G	9.8	9.8	7.1	4.3	4.0	—	6.3
	I	8.9	6.8	7.0	4.8	2.0	—	7.4
1675–96	G	9.7	8.4	6.7	4.3	3.1	—	6.9
	I	7.4	8.0	6.2	4.6	1.7	0.6	5.8
1700–4	G	7.7	8.7	6.0	4.0	3.0	1.0	5.7
	I	—	7.7	5.9	4.3	2.4	1.0	5.5
1725–7	G	7.1	7.1	6.6	2.9	1.6	—	5.0
	I	6.3	6.2	4.0	4.0	3.2	—	4.4
1745–9	G	6.3	5.8	4.7	2.9	1.8	0.5	4.7
	I	—	5.8	5.5	3.6	1.8	0.8	4.6
1770–2	G	5.1	5.8	4.2	3.2	—	0.3	4.3
	I	6.2	6.0	5.0	3.9	2.0	0.8	4.5
1800–10	G	4.3	3.1	2.8	2.2	1.7	—	2.7
	I	4.1	3.1	3.7	3.1	2.2	—	3.1

— means value not calculated, because fewer than 10 cases.
G = Geneva-born; I = In-migrants

particularly apparent among in-migrant women and continued until the beginning of the eighteenth century. It is only when the values begin to converge that a decline in fertility which parallels that of women born in Geneva becomes apparent. The two series run nearly in parallel for women who married after their thirty-fifth birthday, with the exception of an important fluctuation for the marriages between 1725 and 1727, which can be explained by a change in the composition of the population of women who were born outside Geneva.[9]

This convergence of trends after a certain level of fertility has been reached suggests that the practice of birth control extended to the migrant women as well. It would seem that married couples used the norm of family size prevalent in the city as a point of reference and modified their own fertility accordingly. Whenever one of the parameters that determined fertility changed, there was a compensating reaction the further one got away from the norm. Thus the increase of fertility among Genevan women during the seventeenth century led to a rise in the age at marriage from 23.3 years for marriages between 1625 and 1644 to 26.3 years for marriages between 1687 and 1704. However, this was not sufficient to compensate for the increase in fertility rates, and family limitation was, therefore, adopted. In the same way, during the eighteenth century the fertility of in-migrant women only began to fall after their fertility level approximated to that of women born in Geneva, and at a time when the mortality among their children fell by more than 30 per cent (from the generation of children born to couples married between 1650 and 1684 to that of children of couples married between 1725 and 1727).[10]

[9] A. Perrenoud, 'Croissance ou déclin? Les mécanismes du non-renouvellement des populations urbaines', *Histoire, Économie et Société*, 4 (1982), 581–601.
[10] Ibid.

4. Fertility differences by social origin

An analysis of differential fertility by social origin would require more space than is available in this chapter. In a town, members of different social groups will differ considerably and it is not easy to frame a definition which will capture these differences at different periods of time. In particular, it is important to avoid adopting a rigid classification based on a single factor and which would fail to take into account changes that might occur in economic conditions. A valid demographic analysis requires a fairly large number of cases, and multiple categorization might lead to results that were lacking in significance. All this suggests that the population should only be divided into a small number of groups. We have used three different groups and five marriage cohorts.

In Fig. 15.3 we show the trend of adjusted legitimate fertility rates by age at marriage and social status. The sums of age-specific fertility rates which are shown in Table 15.10 give a summary indication of these rates which are too

Table 15.10 Adjusted values of mean family size by mother's age at marriage and social origin

Date of marriage	Woman's age at marriage											
	15–19			20–4			25–9			30–4		
	1	2	3	1	2	3	1	2	3	1	2	3
1625–74	10.1	10.3	9.5	8.6	9.7	8.2	6.1	7.3	6.7	4.0	3.7	2.5
1675–04	7.2	9.1	9.4	7.3	8.9	8.0	7.5	6.4	5.8	2.8	4.2	4.5
1725–49	6.5	7.3	6.7	5.4	7.2	6.0	4.1	5.1	5.5	3.4	4.1	3.2
1770–72	3.9	5.5	5.8	4.1	5.5	5.8	2.9	3.9	4.9	1.3	2.9	2.2
1800–10	3.5	4.6	4.3	2.7	3.1	3.3	2.8	2.7	2.8	—	2.0	2.4

1 = upper social group; 2 = middle social group; 3 = lower social group.

detailed to be shown individually in this chapter. By regrouping the data we can obtain a good indication of the extent of birth control practice among women who married at different ages. It is not surprising that birth control was adopted rather earlier among the bourgeoisie than in other groups, for it has been known ever since the publication of Louis Henry's study that the patrician classes in the Genevan bourgeoisie had used contraception from the middle of the seventeenth century onwards. We have been able to pinpoint more precisely that couples married between 1650 and 1674 were already using such methods. The upper social group was the only one in which fertility rates were systematically higher in the earlier than in the later cohort. The weighted mean family size was 8.6 children per woman in the first marriage cohort, and 6.7 in the second. This practice of birth control occurred in a social group which had experienced a veritable 'demographic explosion', because a net reproduction index of 1.78 (such as was recorded for the cohort married between 1625 and 1644) would have meant that the group nearly doubled in numbers within a single generation. At the beginning of this period, women who had married relatively late in their lives did not take part in this practice, but with the passing of time contraception was universally adopted in that group soon after marriage.[11]

Members of the middle group soon followed the example set by the *haute bourgeoisie*. The youngest among them had begun practising birth control by the end of the seventeenth-century. The time grouping we have used makes it impossible to be more precise about the timing of their adoption of birth control, and I prefer to revert to the chronology which I have used earlier. This makes it possible to state that the decline in fertility began to affect women aged 30 to 34 in the marriage cohort of 1675–6, and that, in the cohort of 1725–7, 60 per cent of women who had married before their twentieth birthday, 34 per cent of those who had married between the ages of 20 and 24, and 17 per cent of those who had married between the ages of 25 and 29 were affected by the decline during the first ten years of their marriage (Table 15.11).

Table 15.11 Legitimate age-specific fertility rates by social origin: middle and lower groups

Date of marriage	Age of woman										
	15–19		20–24		25–29		30–34		35–39		40–44
	2	3	2	3	2	3	2	3	2	3	2	3
	Women married before their 20th birthday										
1625–44	504	—	514	—	450	—	354	—	255	—	125	—
1650–74	433	—	528	—	452	—	400	—	371	—	200	—
1675–96	513	—	626	—	471	—	315	—	220	—	51	—
1700–4	342	—	422	—	457	—	379	—	126	—	26	—
1725–7	550	—	488	—	317	—	159	—	58	—	0	—
	Women married between the ages of 20 and 24										
1625–44			555	506	482	455	413	385	364	306	232	128
1650–74			554	573	543	485	549	400	415	400	211	257
1675–96			537	503	506	489	457	361	340	380	137	154
1700–4			635	501	625	503	519	405	341	304	82	82
1725–7			629	526	479	442	361	329	183	248	78	92
	Women married between the ages of 25 and 29										
1625–44					534	440	504	404	336	349	224	217
1650–74					667	550	518	476	484	393	253	217
1675–96					523	545	449	413	344	340	185	209
1700–4					608	537	446	440	310	291	149	104
1725–7					509	554	430	493	285	296	94	177

2 = middle social group; 3 = lower social group.
— means not calculated as numbers too small.

Table 15.11 shows the rapid progression of rates at the beginning of marriage, and the very high levels reached towards the end of the eighteenth century. Once the practice had begun, contraception seemed to spread regularly, but not as completely as in the upper social groups. The spread of fertility control is confirmed if we look at the percentages of women married before their thirtieth birthday who bore their last child before their thirty-fifth

[11] Ibid.

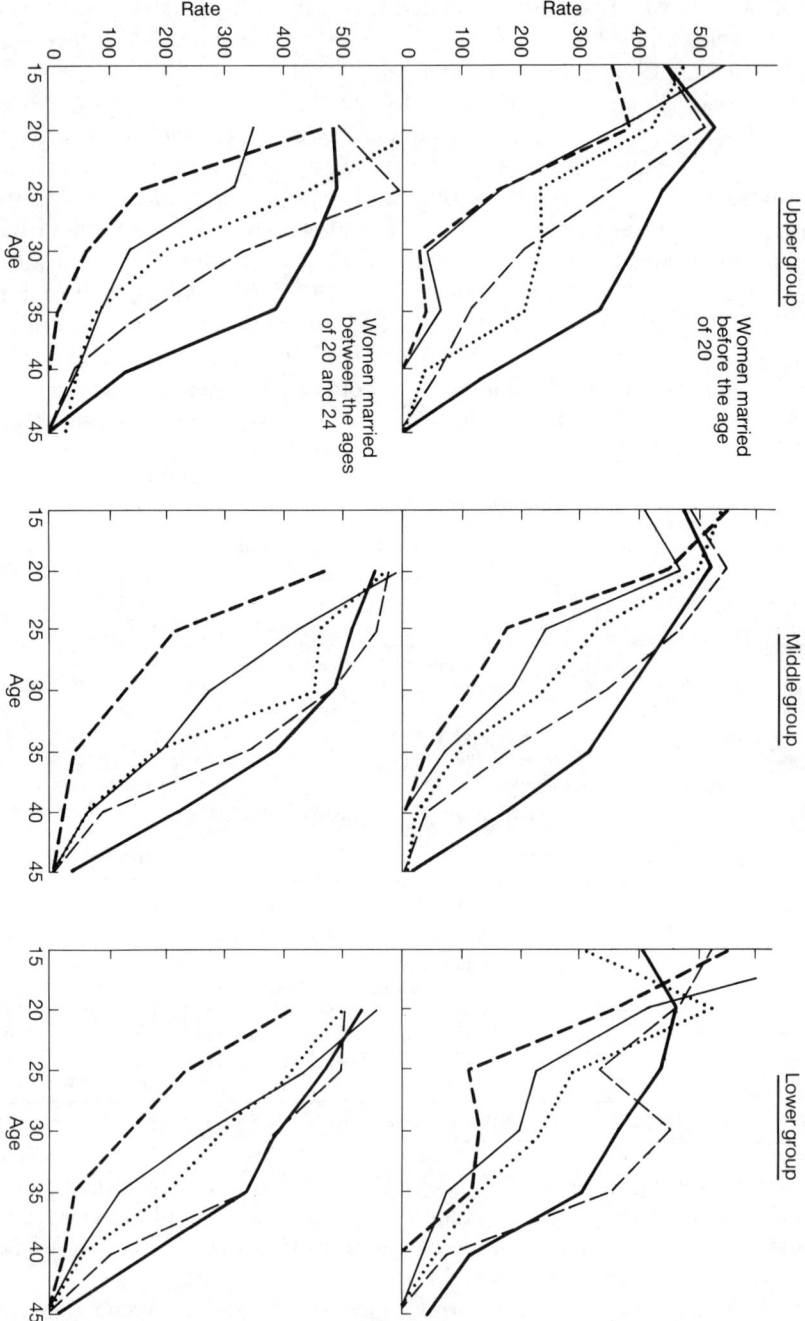

Figure 15.3. Adjusted legitimate fertility rates, by age of women at marriage and social origin, for different marriage cohorts

Aspects of Fertility Decline 261

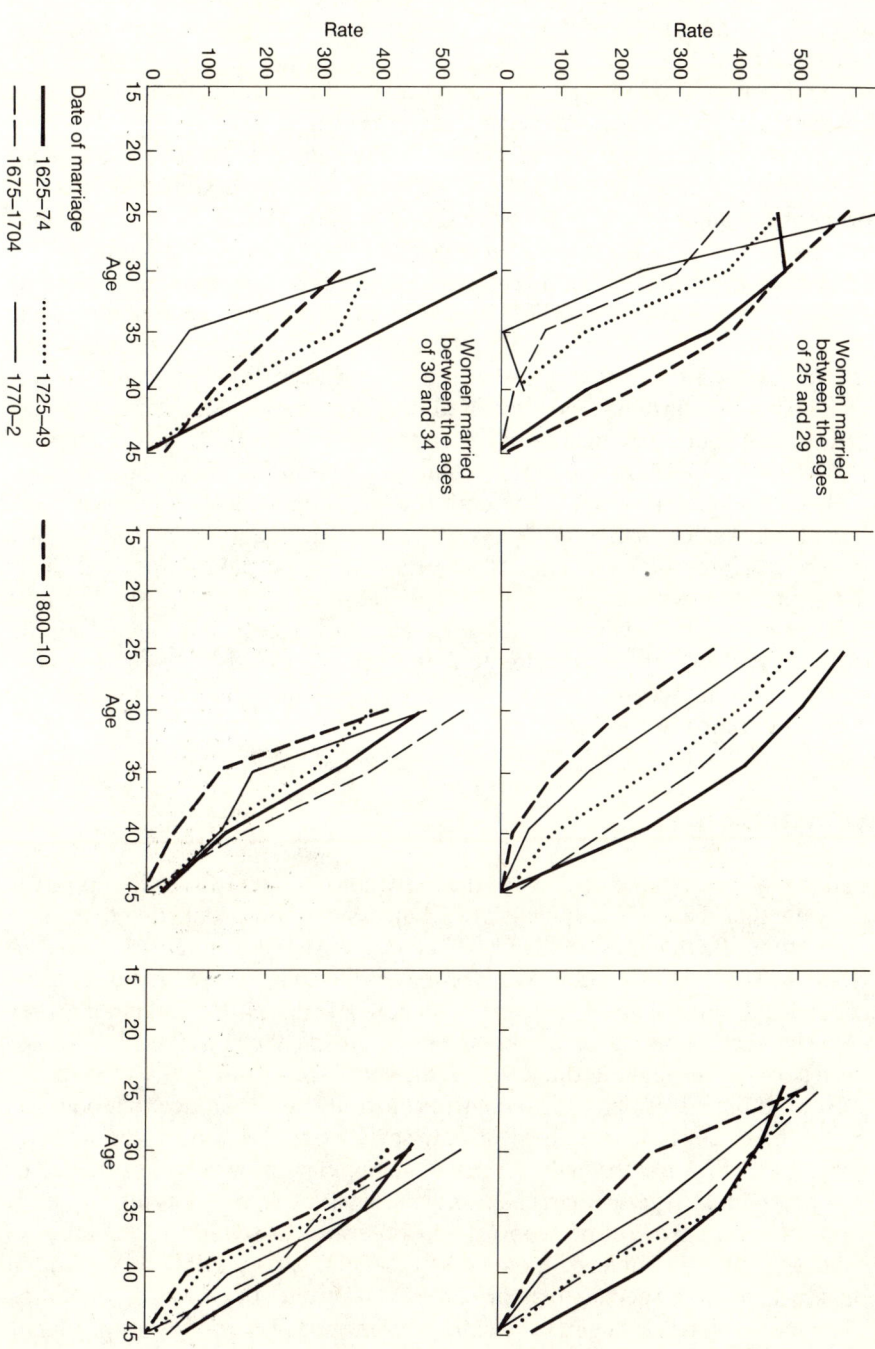

birthday; this figure comes to 10 per cent in the cohort married before 1675, and rose to 22, 30, 39, and 47 per cent in successive cohorts, and finally to 49 per cent in the cohort of 1770–2.

In the lower social groups the decline in fertility began later and was more hesitant. It was strongly affected by age at marriage. The slope of the curve did not change until the second quarter of the eighteenth century; it appears most clearly among those who married when they were young, and is less pronounced among those who married at later ages. However, among women who had married between the ages of 20 and 24 there was a pronounced fall in fertility at older ages towards the end of the seventeenth century. Fertility between the ages of 35 and 39 fell by 38 per cent among these women between the cohorts of 1650–74 and 1725–7; the fall amounted to 18 per cent between the ages of 30 and 34. The proportion of women who ceased child-bearing before their thirty-fifth birthday also increased regularly in successive cohorts from a figure of ten per cent (similar to that found for the middle group) in the cohort of 1625–74 to 17, 19, 25, 28 and 40 per cent respectively in successive cohorts.

By the beginning of the nineteenth century, behaviour had become more homogeneous. The small family system had permeated into all social groups. In these circumstances, age at marriage became less important as a determinant of the final size of the family. However, it is interesting to note that the rates fell for women of all ages, and this suggests that the practice of stopping reproduction was added to that of spacing births. The very low level of fertility is in accord with the depressed economic conditions during the period of French rule in Geneva.

5. Conclusion

Following the example of Rouen, the experience in Geneva lends support to the view that there was a specifically urban system of reproductive behaviour at the time. Birth control which had been practised by the *haute bourgeoisie* from 1650 onwards spread rapidly throughout the whole population. Fertility control did not constitute deviant behaviour on the part of members of an élite; by the beginning of the eighteenth century, the practice had already been adopted throughout the whole of the social spectrum.

Nor did the diffusion of birth control constitute an adherence to models set by the bourgeoisie to members of new social strata. It constituted rather a progressive diffusion throughout the whole population, which was affected by two parameters: age at marriage, and the level of fertility during the early years of marriage. Fertility control was determined by the total number of children a woman could be expected to produce during her lifetime, rather than by behaviour specific to a particular social group, or by a class mentality. The fact that fertility began to decline later in the lower social groups than in the higher is explained by the lower fertility rates of the first group and also by their relatively late age at marriage. This explanation also holds for women who had migrated to Geneva and who had adopted the reproductive behaviour patterns of the city once their fertility had reached a similar level.

As was the case in Rouen, the period of fertility decline followed a long period during which fertility had been rising. Decline began once fertility reached levels which were so high that they could no longer be compensated by raising the age at marriage. The process is a good example of homeostatic adjustment. The decline began in the upper social groups whose members were faced with a situation in which their numbers could double within a single generation. Given contemporary customs, these rates could not have been reduced sufficiently by raising the age at marriage, and the adoption of birth control followed quickly. This process was repeated in other social groups as fertility increased in these groups. At the beginning of the process the change in fertility was accompanied by a fall in nuptiality, but once the practice of birth control had become firmly established nuptiality ceased to be used as a regulating factor, and the age at marriage began to fall again.

The rise in fertility was brought about largely by an increase in the practice of wet-nursing, though improvements in economic conditions may also have been a contributory factor. That this is so is suggested by the low fertility of the lower social groups, either because fecundability was lower among them, or because of neo-Malthusian behaviour on their part, which was linked to economic conditions.

Relations between fertility and child mortality do not appear to have been strong. During the seventeenth century the fall in fertility preceded the fall in mortality, and it continued after the fall in the number of child deaths. However, the fertility level of the marriage cohort of 1770–2 coincided with a rise in child mortality, whereas the rapid decline in fertility towards the beginning of the nineteenth century was accompanied by a fall in mortality.

Finally, our model of urban fertility decline, which can be applied to other regions in which the practice of wet-nursing became widespread, could be used to explain the special features of the history of French fertility. Maurice Garden has suggested this: '... one of the key features of French demography is the refusal of the French urban population to produce large families.'[12] It seems surprising that the countryside should have remained unaffected by this, given that there were large movements of population in both directions between town and country. A pioneer study of a large village in the countryside near Geneva has shown clearly that women in that village began to limit their families from the marriage cohort of 1730–59 onwards, in spite of the relatively low initial level of their fertility.[13] This suggests a diffusion of behaviour from the towns, rather than a process of adjustment. Research at present under way will, no doubt, enable us to trace this phenomenon with greater precision.

[12] M. Garden, *Histoire des français xix–xxe siècles*, i. *Un peuple et son pays* (Paris, 1984).
[13] A. Perrenoud, 'La Transition démographique dans la ville et la campagne genèvoise du xviiie aux xix^E siècle', in *Mélanges d'histoire économique offerts au professeur Anne-Marie Piuz* (Geneva, 1989).

16 Innovators and Imitators in the Practice of Contraception in Town and Country

JEAN-PIERRE BARDET
EHESS, Laboratoire de Démographie Historique, Paris, France

Between 1650 and 1750, city dwellers in north-west France undoubtedly began to practise contraception earlier than those who lived in the country. This was probably also true of other regions, but it has not yet been shown to hold universally. However, town dwellers were in the van of the movement in areas which were far from the banks of the Seine, for example in the area of Lake Geneva.

The peasants of Normandy and the Île de France discovered these 'dark secrets' during the second half of the eighteenth century, and soon came to use them with zeal during the second half of the eighteenth century well before the French Revolution. By 1861, the fertility of the French rural population was lower than that of people who lived in the cities.[1]

Is it possible to improve our understanding of the changes that were observed in the villages and in the towns and to arrive at more precise estimates? What were the links, if any, between the initiatives taken by the town dwellers and the delay in the dissemination of the practice of contraception in the country? Are there two different models of the dissemination of knowledge and practice of contraception, each with its own specific rules? Or was there only a single change in attitudes which began in the more imaginative and febrile cities, and which later came to contaminate the countryside? Is a materialist or a cultural interpretation of this process more realistic?

It would be presumptuous to attempt to answer these large questions within the confines of a short chapter. My aim is less ambitious. I shall try to establish some facts, based on exact data, but it will turn out that by the end I shall have raised more new questions than provided answers. Our study area is limited, it covers only a small sector of north-west France betweeen Haute Normandie and the Île de France, both areas in which the practice of contraception began early. As the decline in fertility in these areas began before the fall in mortality, the change cannot be explained in purely

---

[1] Y. Tugault, *Fécondité et urbanisation* (Paris, 1975). Cf. particularly pp. 24 ff. Note that the difference between the fertility of the towns and the countryside varied; in 1891, for instance, the situation was the reverse of that in 1861. Paris, however, was an area in which contraception had always been widely used.

mechanistic terms. Even if it were true that population growth presented problems to the inhabitants of these areas, an explanation in terms of an automatic adjustment of reproductive behaviour is unsatisfactory, for it is possible to point to a number of other areas with much higher population densities, indeed, to some that were overpopulated, but in which the inhabitants did not react by restricting their fertility. I shall argue that these changes in behaviour need to be explained in cultural terms. First, however, it is necessary to describe the significance as well as the limitations of such an explanation.

1. The chronology of change in town and country

Our information is taken from some 12,000 family reconstitution files which have been published in a number of dissertations and research papers. My thanks are due to the authors of these studies for giving me access to the material that they have collected.

The principal city in our study is Rouen, one of the largest French towns in the eighteenth century, with a population of about 70,000. Some 6,000 files are available for this town.[2] The villages on the southern edge which adjoin the suburbs of the city, Sotteville and Petit Quevilly, are used to provide information about the transitional zone between town and country. There are 337 files for these two villages, which have been constructed by a research student studying for an M.A.[3]

Rouen can be compared with its surrounding countryside by looking at two hamlets in Haute Normandie. There are about 2,000 files which relate to three villages in Roumois,[4] about 20 km. south-west of Rouen; and at about the same distance from the town to the north-west there exist 1,563 files that relate to twenty-one communes in the canton of Barentin-Pavilly.[5] Both these were agricultural areas, though the peasants occasionally also undertook home work, producing flax and cotton for the Rouen entrepreneurs. Farmers in the Barentin basin, situated in the Caux country, were more inclined to these proto-industrial activities than those of Roumois, where the people were more traditional.

Jacques Dupâquier has kindly put at my disposal the important data file which he has constructed for in-depth study of several parishes in the Vexin region. This forms part of the Île de France, some distance from Rouen

---

[2] J.-P. Bardet, *Rouen au XVIIe et XVIIIe siècles: les mutations d'un espace social*, 2 vols. (Paris, 1983).

[3] F. Bacon, 'Étude démographique sur la banlieue rouennaise en rive gauche: Sotteville-les-Rouen et Petit Quevilly', M.A. diss. under the supervision of Professor M. Venard (Rouen, 1987).

[4] L. C. Bonnet, 'Trois Villages du Roumois', Ph.D. diss. under the supervision of J. Dupâquier (Paris, 1983).

[5] C. Renard, 'Le Canton de Pavilly au XVIIIe et XIXe siècles', Ph.D. diss. under the supervision of J.-P. Bardet (Paris, 1984).

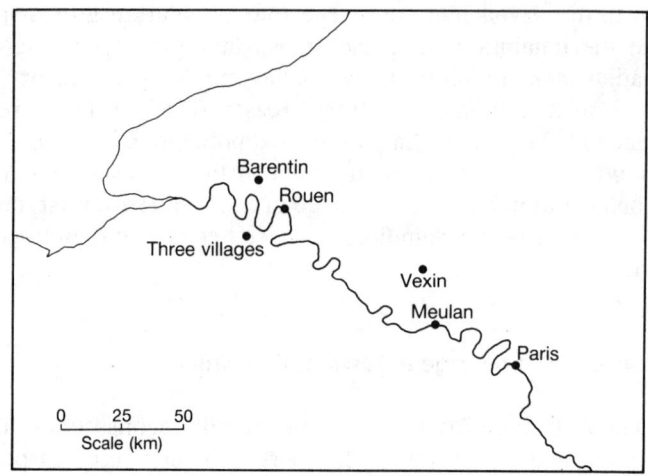

Map 16.1. Geographical location of sample

(about 60 km.), and probably maintained stronger connections with the Paris region than with the capital of Normandy. I have used these data, because their quality is remarkably good, and also because they relate to an area which was almost completely rural, without any proto-industrial activities. It would have been a pity not to attempt a comparison with this rural area which was characterized by completely different economic activities. In this study I have used only about 2,500 of the files which have been collected.

I shall also have occasion to refer to the remarkable study by Marcel Lachiver on the small town of Meulan, to the west of Paris. In spite of its distance from Rouen, it provides the best evidence about reproductive behaviour of the population of relatively small towns.[6]

2. General overview: differences in the process of change

In order to provide an overall view of the movement of fertility in different places, I have constructed an index which makes it possible to keep the number of tables to a minimum. This is a weighted average of the completed family size of women who were married at different ages. A constant system of weights was used, corresponding to the distribution of the ages of women who married in Rouen between 1660 and 1789.[7] In Table 16.1 we see a general overview of changes in time and space. Regrettably our data do not all relate to the same period. I should have liked, in particular, to have had

[6] M. Lachiver, *La Population de Meulan du xviie au xixe siècle* (Paris, 1969).
[7] The following was the system of weights used:

Age	15–19	20–24	25–29	30–34	35–39	40–44	45–49
Weight	0.09	0.31	0.27	0.15	0.09	0.06	0.03

Table 16.1 Weighted average of family size of women married between the ages of 15 and 49

Period of observation	Rouen	Suburbs	Three villages	Barentin	Vexin
1670–89	7.65				
1690–1709	6.60	6.33			5.54
1710–29	5.94	6.29	6.11		5.72
1730–49	5.69	6.00	6.04		5.56
1750–69	5.33	5.94	5.93	4.80	5.25
1770–89	4.72	4.86	5.33	4.50	4.79
1790–1809	4.20	4.81	4.76	4.16	4.08
1810–29			4.64	4.03	3.12

more information about developments before 1750 in the Barentin region. Some studies are at present in progress which will probably provide this information in the future. However, such as they are, the data confirm that control over fertility was first practised in the town. Until about 1760, townspeople reduced their fertility to a greater extent than those who lived in the country, and they appear to have started to practise birth control during the last quarter of the seventeenth century.

In the countryside the reduction in the number of births became significant between 1750 and 1769, and the process accelerated after 1770. Since that time, people in the country appear to have been at least as active in practising fertility control as their contemporaries in the towns. After 1789, the peasants of the Vexin region reduced their families even more, but it is unfortunately not possible to trace what was happening in Rouen at that time. But it would seem that, towards the end of the eighteenth century, there was a convergence of contraceptive attitudes between town and country. But there is also a remarkable heterogeneity in the behaviour of people in different parts of the countryside. We note in particular the large difference between our index for Barentin-Pavilly and that for the three villages in the Roumois. Could this difference be explained by differences in breastfeeding practices, or by a lower propensity among women in the Roumois to use contraceptive measures? The two areas were equidistant from the city, but because of proto-industrialization urban influence was undoubtedly stronger in the Barentin region than in the three villages. However, in both areas, the inhabitants received a large number of children from households in Rouen for wet-nursing, so that there were relatively frequent contacts between the villagers and the townspeople. It is interesting to note that the inhabitants of the Vexin region, whose contacts with the town were less strong, were also slower to adopt birth control.

In Table 16.2 we see some figures relating to Meulan, though these relate to marriage cohorts rather than to specific periods. A comparison of trends in that small town with those in Rouen is of some interest. During the eighteenth century the inhabitants of Meulan seemed more reluctant than those in the larger town to practise family limitation, and their behaviour was

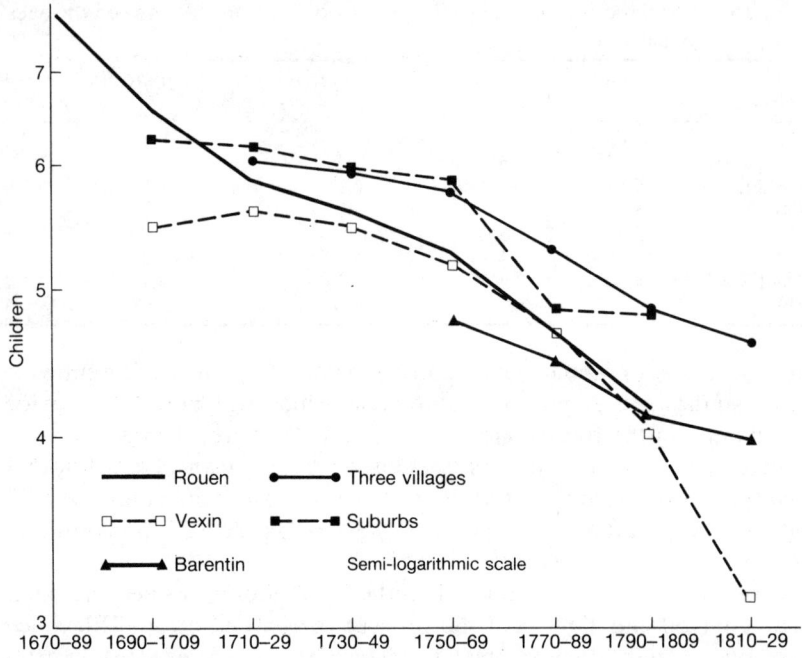

Figure 16.1. Adjusted completed family size by 20-year period of births

Table 16.2 Constructed completed family size of women married between the ages of 15 and 49

Locality	Date of marriage					
	1670–99	1700–29	1730–59	1760–89	1790–1814	1815–39
Rouen	6.73	5.67	5.34	4.59		
Meulan	6.09	6.21	5.65	5.05	3.34	3.01

more like that of the population of the rural areas of the Vexin. However, they anticipated the latter somewhat in their adoption of family limitation, and participated in the abrupt fall in family size which occurred after 1789.

Though this example is taken from a distant town, it enables us to draw up a hierarchy in the development of contraceptive attitudes during the century of the Enlightenment: in this movement the large cities were in the van, followed by the smaller towns, and the third place was taken by the countryside, though in the last group there were considerable differences between different villages. These results appear to confirm the view that the adoption of family limitation was a diffusion process which began in the urban culture. This raises the question whether it is possible to be more specific about the beginnings of this movement in Rouen, the place where at the beginning of our period of study, fertility appeared to be highest.

3. Methods of control: stopping or spacing

There are several variables which can be used to illumine the process of the adoption of fertility control which will highlight the differences in practice between the town and the countryside. It would be tempting to say that in one there was a reduction in the number of children, and in the other a lengthening of the interval between births. However, this would be an over-simplification of a complex situation. I shall suggest rather that townspeople were more radical in their choice of methods, but that the villagers were more progressive.

An examination of the figures relating to birth intervals yields results that are both interesting and surprising. We shall use two different series of measures, neither of which is entirely satisfactory. Both are averages, whereas it would have been desirable to look at complete frequency distribution of birth intervals, for the study of averages can only be regarded as a first approximation. In the second place, our calculations may be a little misleading, for I have first of all looked at the average of the first four birth intervals in families with six or more children, i.e. at large families, and these were becoming less common with the passing of time. Next, I considered the mean of the first two birth intervals in families with three or more children, when—to avoid the disturbing effect caused by the last birth interval—I should have referred to families with four or more children. It is known that the interval between the births of the last two children in a family tends to be longer than previous birth intervals and, in principle, it should have been eliminated from the analysis. However, I have been able to check from the Rouen data that the inclusion of the final birth interval does not alter any of the conclusions relating to the trend over time. In Table 16.3 the mean

Table 16.3 Mean interval between the first and second, and the second and third birth for families with three or more, and with four or more children (months)

Period of marriage	Families with three or more children	Families with four or more children
1670–99	21.05	19.90
1700–29	22.14	20.35
1730–59	22.26	20.22
1760–89	23.43	21.43

intervals are shown both for families with three or more, and for those with four or more children, and it is reassuring that the results are in broad agreement. Provisionally at least, we can use these intervals.

These figures, which are confirmed by those in Table 16.4, show how brief birth intervals were in Rouen. Apart from the anomalous result for Vexin for 1700–29, which may have been due to deficiencies in registration, the figures suggest that voluntary spacing of births became more common at the time

Table 16.4 Mean of first four inter-birth intervals in families with six or more children (months)

Locality	1670–99	1700–29	1730–59	1760–89	1790–1819
Rouen	19.85	19.95	19.76	21.53	
Barentin			24.14	25.92	26.32
Vexin	24.40	26.15	25.21	26.60	28.94

when family limitation began to be used. This trend is also apparent in Rouen, but it began there a long time after the practice of contraception started. Moreover, birth intervals in the city seem exceptionally short, even during the period just before the Revolution. Interestingly enough, the results for Meulan confirm this view, though the marriage cohorts are slightly different (Table 16.5). The study of birth intervals for families with three or

Table 16.5 Mean of the first four inter-birth intervals in families with six or more children

Period of marriage	Rouen	Meulan
1660–1739	19.87	21.37
1740–89	20.57	21.40

more children yields the same conclusion: a secular trend towards longer birth intervals, and shorter intervals in the town than in the country. In the suburbs, a transitional area between town and countryside, birth intervals were slightly longer than in Rouen, but shorter than in the country (Table 16.6).

Table 16.6 Mean of the first two inter-birth intervals in families with three or more children

| Locality | Date of marriage | | | | |
	1670–99	1700–29	1730–59	1760–89	1790–1819
Rouen	21.05	22.14	22.26	23.43	
Suburbs	22.16	22.53	22.94	24.44	
Barentin			27.71	30.52	32.90
Vexin	27.33	26.94	27.59	29.29	34.91

The statistics for birth intervals show a clear contrast between the city and the countryside. There can be little doubt that country people were more prepared to practise family limitation once the habit had begun to spread. Townspeople do not appear to have discovered this option until rather later and, instead, seemed to limit the total number of their births. Clearly, both town and country dwellers were taking steps to control their fertility; the question is whether the longer birth intervals found in the countryside are not merely the result of failure to limit the total number of births. It seems clear that townspeople were more skilled than those who lived in the country in limiting the sizes of their completed families.

We shall use two indices to assess the efficiency of the method used: the

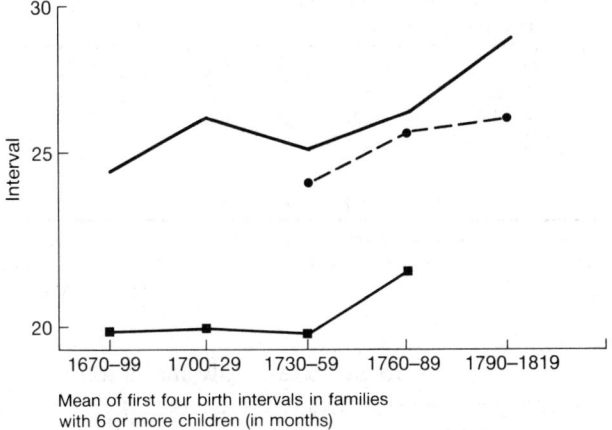

Mean of first four birth intervals in families with 6 or more children (in months)

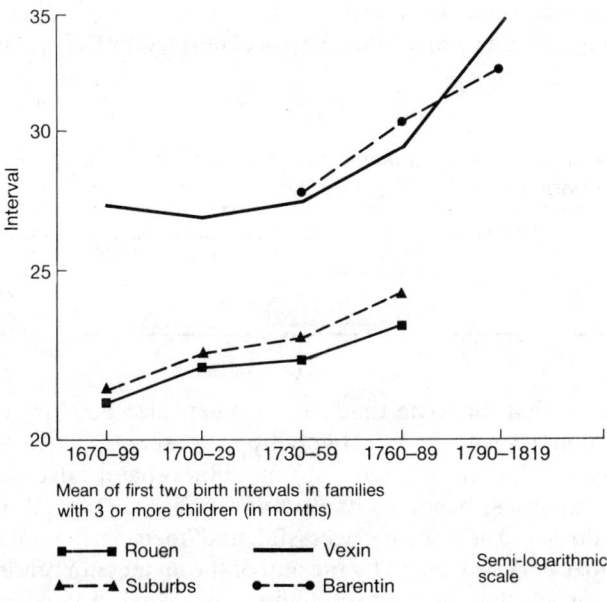

Mean of first two birth intervals in families with 3 or more children (in months)

■——■ Rouen ——— Vexin
▲——▲ Suburbs ●——● Barentin

Semi-logarithmic scale

Figure 16.2. Mean of birth intervals

proportion of women who remain childless, and the ages of mothers at the time of the birth of their last child. The figures are shown in Table 16.7. The conclusion is clear. People who lived in the country did not renounce the joys of motherhood, even though they may have limited their fertility. In their case what is difficult to decide is whether they wished to have small families,

Table 16.7 Percentage of married women aged 30 who remained childless, and mean age of married women at the birth of their last child

Locality	1670–99		1700–29		1730–59		1760–89		1790–1819	
	%[a]	Mean age[b]	%	Mean age	%	Mean age	%	Mean age	%	Mean age
Rouen	16.2	39.18	7.5	38.16	8.7	37.6	9.5	36.4		
Barentin						38.8		37.6		36.2
Vexin	2.1	39.85	0.0	39.47	3.7	38.9	3.6	37.7	5.1	35.9

[a] Percentage of married women childless at the age of 30.
[b] Mean age of married women (married before their 30th birthday) at the time of the birth of their last child.

or whether they were unable to practise family limitation during the early period of their marriages. The statistics relating to the mean age of women at the birth of their last child also show a difference, though in an attenuated form. They confirm that people in the country were slow to accept the practice of actually ceasing to reproduce. Couples in the country followed the example set by their urban counterparts, but with a significant time-lag, which amounted to at least one generation. This is confirmed by the figures shown in Table 16.8.

Table 16.8 Percentage of women married before their 30th birthday whose last child was born before their 35th birthday

Locality	Date of marriage				
	1670–99	1700–29	1730–59	1760–89	1790–1819
Rouen	19	23	26	36	
Vexin	9.5	9.5	14	27	40.5

It would seem that for some time rural women succeeded in reducing the sizes of their families sufficiently, simply by increasing the intervals between successive births. Urban women, on the other hand, overwhelmed by successive pregnancies, began to limit their families early, and used radical methods to do so. They were successful and their fertility was reduced relatively to that of rural women by the end of the eighteenth century. But did rural women, when they began to practise family limitation proper, around 1760, simply follow the example set by their urban sisters, or was the change in their behaviour caused by a change in features specific to their own situation? Before attempting to answer this question we must briefly consider the situation in the towns. This will make it possible for us to compare what happened in the two types of locality and provide a tentative answer to the question. We shall then return to consider the countryside, where a great many of the town dwellers had originated and to which many of them were later to return.

4. Wet-nursing and in-migration to towns

4.1 The importance of wet-nursing

A special feature of urban fertility was the long-established practice of sending new-born children to be wet-nursed in the surrounding country. The extent of this practice varied considerably at different periods. That it was widespread hardly needs proof. The village registers contain many hundreds of entries relating to the deaths of town children. Enquiries made towards the end of the nineteenth century show that in about 1890, a time when this practice had already become less frequent, at least 10 per cent of new-born babies were sent out to be wet-nursed.[8] We shall need to consider the effects of this practice, and Rouen can serve as an example.

In that town the Hôpital Général gave grants to women in reduced circumstances which made it possible for them either to breastfeed their children or to place them in the care of wet-nurses who lived in the country. I have been able to check the records of that institution and link them with the files of reconstituted families.[9] It proved possible to study the history of 2,000 infants born between 1750 and 1769 whose mothers were given grants. They were equally divided between those who were breastfed and those who were wet-nursed. The effect of wet-nursing is quite clear. The average interval to the next birth for women who breastfed their child was 27.2 months, that for women whose child was wet-nursed was 20.9 months. The size of the difference is similar to that which we have established between town and country dwellers. Thus the shorter birth intervals in the town can be explained by differences in the methods of child-rearing and also no doubt, in part, by the higher mortality of town children. In both localities the end of lactation led to the rapid return of ovulation.

I have constructed two distributions of birth intervals from the hospital records: one for women who breastfed their children, the second for those who sent them out to be wet-nursed. From these distributions it proved possible to estimate the proportions of infants sent out to be wet-nursed in different social groups, by adjusting the distribution of birth intervals to standard distributions (Table 16.9).[10] The method is necessarily somewhat crude, but it confirms the situation suggested by qualitative sources.

It would be interesting to determine when the practice of sending children out to be wet-nursed first began. Birth intervals in Rouen were very short from the middle of the seventeenth century. It is, of course, possible that at

---

[8] G. D. Sussman, *Selling Mother's Milk: The Wet-Nursing Business in France, 1715–1914* (Chicago, 1982).
[9] Bardet, *Rouen*.
[10] For the technique of adjustment, cf. L. Henry, *Techniques d'analyse en démographie historique* (Paris, 1980).

Table 16.9 Percentage of newborn children sent out to be wet-nursed by Rouen mothers, during the second half of the eighteenth century

Social groups	%
Professionals	71
Shopkeepers	64
Skilled workers	51
Labourers	41
Total	51

that time infant mortality was higher than during the reign of Louis XV, and that the higher frequency of infant deaths may have been one of the factors which led to shorter birth intervals. Whatever the reason, a combination of early infant deaths and the practice of wet-nursing would have resulted, in the absence of family limitation, in a high level of fertility. The same was almost certainly true in Meulan and in the Rouen suburbs, but children in these areas were less frequently sent out to be wet-nursed and, even in the absence of family limitation, this would have had the effect of lengthening birth intervals.

Clearly, wet-nursing and family limitation were connected. The high fertility of urban women led them to adopt fertility control early. This hypothesis is supported when we look at different social groups. Women in the upper classes, who were also the most fertile in about 1650, were those who began to use contraception earliest and exercised birth control most frequently. They were followed by the petty bourgeoisie which consisted mainly of shopkeepers; artisans and workers were relatively slow to avail themselves of these 'dark secrets'. We note, however, that the differences were not necessarily related to economic status; master craftsmen and artisans were often as well off as the small shopkeepers who began to practise family limitation rather earlier. In order to simplify the statistics I have used only two social groups: manual and non-manual workers (Table 16.10).

Table 16.10 Estimated family sizes of women married between the ages of 15 and 49, by husband's occupational group

Occupational group	Date of marriage						
	1670–89	1690–1709	1710–29	1730–49	1750–69	1770–89	1790–1809
Non-manual workers	7.64	6.69	5.37	4.92	4.55	3.92	3.25
Manual workers	6.63	6.61	6.39	6.15	5.55	4.91	4.65

We should not exaggerate the importance of the link which leads from wet-nursing to high fertility, and thence to contraception. But if it did affect particularly the behaviour of non-manual workers, we should remember that this social group was the most receptive to new ideas that were circulating both among the élite and the petty bourgeoisie at the time; ideas which resulted in secularization and individualism. Even though the so-called *philosophes* were pro-natalist, when their ideas became popularized and simplified, they were seen not so much as advocates of a demographic equilibrium, but as protagonists of 'happiness' and 'freedom', concepts and ideas which appealed to the bourgeoisie and shopkeepers alike.

When members of the working classes began in their turn to practise birth control, did they simply follow the precepts and example of the social group which had preceded them in adopting this form of behaviour? The problem is similar to that which we discussed earlier in relation to the urban and the rural populations, but there are some differences. Closer physical and social proximity between shopkeepers and manual workers in the cities created an atmosphere which favoured the transmission of cultural values between different social groups.

Figure 16.3. Adjusted theoretical completed family size by 20-year birth periods

However, even if cultural factors were important in this process it was the individual's appreciation of the disadvantages associated with the practice of wet-nursing that played a crucial part in encouraging the use of birth control. This can be illustrated by an example. By combining the hospital records with family reconstitution files it proved possible to distinguish between two groups of households which were given grants to help with rearing their children. The first consisted of mothers who elected to breastfeed the children for whom they were given grants, the second of those who chose to send them to the country to be wet-nursed. It is, of course, possible that the behaviour of these women towards those children for whom they did not receive public assistance was different; in our two samples about one birth in every three was given such assistance. However, the women who elected to breastfeed their assisted children themselves chose to send only 31 per cent of their other births to be wet-nursed, whereas the analogous proportion in the second group was 82 per cent. These figures suggest that there was a tendency to treat assisted and non-assisted births in the same way.

A comparison of birth intervals in the two groups confirms the important effect of the method of rearing on the length of these intervals, though the effect will have been somewhat attenuated by differences in infant mortality. The figures are shown in Table 16.11. If contraception had not been

Table 16.11 Mean birth intervals for women who received assistance from the hospital by method of child-rearing

Birth intervals	Breastfed	Wet-nursed
First two birth intervals in families with three or more children	24.18	19.94
First four birth intervals in families with six or more children	22.48	19.45
Last four birth intervals in families with six or more children	26.78	22.38

practised, we would have expected the completed family size of women who had sent their children to be wet-nursed to exceed that of women who had breastfed their own children. However, the figures turned out to be 6.8 and 6.6 children respectively, a relatively small difference, and one which can only be explained by greater recourse to contraception in the former group. Of course, both groups have been selected because the women received public assistance, often because their families were large. Contraception may have been used more widely by women for whom we do not have information, i.e. those who were not in receipt of public assistance. These considerations suggest that wet-nursing and the practice of family limitation were linked, even if the actual decision to control fertility required cultural adaptation and a modification of behaviour.

4.2 The problem of in-migration

The city of Rouen was a magnet of attraction for in-migrants, as were other towns at that time. The hospital records from the eighteenth century and vital registration figures from the beginning of the nineteenth century suggest that one-half of the husbands of women who gave birth in the city, and more than one-third of the women themselves, had been born outside the town. Unfortunately, the nominal household lists do not always give the place of birth of the household head; indeed, before the Revolution the majority of the clergy tended to omit this information when registering a marriage or a burial. Genealogical data can generally be used to ascertain whether the husband had been born in the city, but this is possible for only a fraction of the wives. We have attempted to obtain this information by investigating all husbands whose surnames began with the letter 'B', and of all wives whose maiden surnames began with the same letter. By using all available sources of information it proved possible to trace the origins of a significant number of couples (Table 16.12). These figures confirm results obtained from death

Table 16.12 Distribution of spouse's birthplace, where known

Birthplace of husband	Birthplace of wife			
	Rouen	Outside Rouen	Total	%
Rouen	726	270	996	51.6
Outside Rouen	476	457	933	48.4
Total	1202	727	1929	
%	62.3	37.7		100.0

registration in which information about the deceased person's birthplace was given. They also show that 70 per cent of in-migrants of either sex had come from the countryside, and 80 per cent from Normandy.

A number of people of rural origin were thus living in the town, and it is possible to study their behaviour. Did these migrants remain faithful to their country customs and practise family limitation less than their counterparts who were born in the city, and did they continue to care for their own children? The answers to both these questions are in the negative. As may be seen from Table 16.13, behaviour as regards fertility control of those who had

Table 16.13 Estimated family size of women married between the ages of 15 and 49, by spouse's birthplace

Period of marriage	Husband		Wife	
	Rouen-born	Migrant	Rouen-born	Migrant
1700–29	6.03	5.96	5.87	5.91
1730–59	5.39	5.70	5.50	5.20
1760–99	4.72	4.49	4.57	4.31

migrated from the country was similar to that of those who had been born in the city. There is even a suggestion that people born outside Rouen, and who had migrated there, tended to restrict their families somewhat more than those who had been born in the city. This is confirmed by the cross-tabulations in Table 16.14. The same small differences appear as in the

Table 16.14 Estimated family size of women married between the ages of 15 and 49 by birthplace of their spouses

Husband	Wife	
	Rouen-born	Migrant
Rouen-born	5.01	4.76
Migrant	4.82	4.43

previous table. However, the figures do not necessarily suggest that contraception was more prevalent among migrants; they may have breastfed their own children to a larger extent than those who were born in the city. Birth intervals tended to be somewhat longer for immigrant than for Rouen-born women, as is shown in Table 16.15. These small differences are barely significant, and could be the result of differences in the quality of registration, or of the method of adjustment used. This is corroborated by looking at the proportion of untraced births in Table 16.16, where the figures suggest that a significant number of women who had migrated to Rouen returned home for their confinements.

Table 16.15 Mean length of birth interval by spouse's birthplace

Birthplace of wife	Birthplace of husband	
	Rouen	Outside Rouen
Rouen		
First two birth intervals in families of three or more children	23.22	22.63
First four birth intervals in families of six or more children	21.03	20.05
Outside Rouen		
First two birth intervals in families of three or more children	24.15	22.68
First four birth intervals in families of six or more children	21.90	21.50

Table 16.16 Proportion of births that could not be traced by spouse's birthplace

Husband's birthplace	Wife's birthplace	
	Rouen	Outside Rouen
Rouen	3.5	7.9
Outside Rouen	4.5	8.1

5. Town and country: influence or convergence

5.1 Some reflections on the adaptation of in-migrants

The adaptation of in-migrants to the practice of fertility control and to urban behaviour appears to have been so rapid that it is tempting to ask whether the conditions that they had experienced before their move had not facilitated such adaptation. Who were the migrants? Were they mainly poor wretches who had been forced to leave the country by reason of their poverty, or were they, on the contrary, an élite group selected for their spirit of adventure? The second explanation appears to fit the situation better than the first.

The distribution of migrants by social status is similar to that of the population born in the town, though there are slightly more of them to be found in the lower social groups. They are found least frequently among master craftsmen, though even in that group a number made the grade and became masters. In-migrants can also be found among the merchants, and even more frequently among small shopkeepers. Many, however, remained journeymen or day labourers.

It would be interesting to discover something about the circumstances which led to their move and to establish criteria which would explain their assimilation to a new social environment. We begin by recalling some facts about the geographical mobility of populations in the past. People were less settled in the countryside than is commonly thought. Monographic studies of villages have sometimes been criticized for their lack of representativeness because they contained too few cases of complete families.[11] This criticism was discussed by Louis Henry,[12] who showed by means of a theoretical argument that many of those who had moved from their villages of origin could not have moved over great distances, and had, in fact, gone to live in villages which were close to the place in which they were married. Henry's theoretical argument has been confirmed by the results of empirical studies. For instance, Claude Renard studied families in twenty-one communes in the canton of Pavilly and was able to obtain complete information for nearly 70 per cent of the files that he had opened which related to a marriage, and in the Vexin region Jacques Dupâquier obtained even better results. In a village situated in the centre of a cluster of some thirty communes, between 80 and 90 per cent of files for reconstituted families could be completed. These large-scale inquiries confirm the results of smaller monographic village studies; they were generally concerned with broader issues than the measurement of fertility of those who remained in the country.

However, some 10–20 per cent of the rural population left the area of their birth. Some were vagabonds or soldiers, but the majority moved into the towns where they became successful and prospered. They certainly did not do less well on average than friends who had been born in the city.

We shall not consider the prosperity of those who were integrated into the highest social groups in the towns, mainly people who came from bourgeois families in the small cities, or from the rural gentry, and who found relatives in the city with whom they had previously been in contact for a long time. Rather we shall consider the common people who did not achieve fame and who have, therefore, tended to be neglected by historians. There is one respect in which members of this group tended to differ from those who remained in the country, and that is in literacy.

The work of Muriel Jeorger has made it possible to compare the level of literacy in the countryside with that in Rouen.[13] For men, significant differences between the two groups are noticeable up to the middle of the eighteenth century, and for women until the time of the Revolution. If the

---

[11] G. Letti, 'Problèmes de l'échantillonage statistique dans les enquêtes de démographie historique', in M. L. Marcilio and H. Charbonneau (eds.), *Démographie historique* (Paris, 1979).

[12] L. Henry, 'Comment mesurer la fécondité des couples mobiles?', *Population* (1982), 9–27.

[13] M. Jeorger, 'L'Alphabétisation dans l'ancien diocèse de Rouen au xviie et xviiie siècles', in F. Furet and J. Ozouf (eds.), *Lire et écrire* (Paris, 1977), 101–51.

migrants had really been poor wretches we would have expected the literacy level among them to have been even lower than that found among their relations who had remained in the country. But it is shown in Tables 16.17 and 16.18 that the converse is true. Surprisingly, the level of literacy among migrants is higher than that of town dwellers. The group in which literacy was lowest is that of Rouen men who married migrant women (Table 16.19); in all other groups the level of literacy was higher among the newcomers to the town than among those who had been born there. The literacy level of women who had migrated to Rouen was the same as that of women who had been born in the city.

Table 16.17 Percentage of men and women able to sign the marriage register

Locality	Grooms			Brides		
	c.1700	c.1750	c.1790	c.1700	c.1750	c.1790
Eure	37	53	76	5	16	37
Seine Maritime	41	65	73	8	23	45
Rouen	66	76	80	44	58	63

Table 16.18 Percentage of Rouen-born and migrants able to sign the marriage register

Period of marriage	Grooms		Brides	
	Rouen-born	Migrants	Rouen-born	Migrants
1700–29	65.6	68.4	45.4	47.1
1730–59	70.5	76.4	54.2	53.2
1760–89	73.5	84.1	63.6	64.6

Table 16.19 Percentage of men and women able to sign the marriage register by origin of bride and groom

Husband's birthplace	Wife's birthplace			
	Rouen		Outside Rouen	
	Husband %	Wife %	Husband %	Wife %
Rouen	71.1	56.6	71.4	50.1
Outside Rouen	79.6	61.8	77.9	61.3

These results are not biased by an over-representation of members of élite groups among the migrants. The situation is the same among workers. Among journeymen and day labourers who married in Rouen between 1690 and 1792, 54 per cent of the grooms signed the marriage register; the proportion able to do so among those born in Rouen was 48 per cent, and among those born outside Rouen it was 58 per cent.

These statistics confirm that those who migrated were different from the rest of the population. They formed a select group, and their behaviour in regard to contraception is also likely to have differed from that of their contemporaries who remained in the country. However, they were able to help in the process of diffusing contraceptive knowledge to members of their families who had remained behind.

5.2 Contacts and initiatives

There was continuous contact between people who lived in the town and those who lived in the country. Each Friday, thousands of peasant weavers came to the Rouen market to sell their wares and their pieces of cloth; hundreds of middlemen went to the villages during the period of proto-industrialization to give out work and to collect the finished material. Wet-nursing of infants resulted in contacts between the urban and rural populations which were probably even more intimate: peasant women who looked for children to wet-nurse and lived in urban households for a period, anxious parents who came to visit their offspring in the cottages. There must have been many oppportunities to exchange both views and information.

Migrants who returned to their birthplace for visits must also have acted as agents for contraceptive propaganda. There is a good deal of evidence to show that migrant women often returned to their places of origin for their confinements. Local feast days provided other opportunities to visit relatives and tell them about city life. Nor must we forget those who returned to live in the country after spending some time in the town: one-quarter of migrant heads of households in Rouen, whose children were born in the city, left it again before their deaths. Many of them will have returned to the countryside to cultivate a small property. We have been able to trace many of these returnees by linking Rouen family reconstitution files with those in the canton of Barentin–Pavilly.

These continuing exchanges and meetings must have resulted in the transmission of information which was probably passed on discreetly. After all, the techniques of fertility control are essentially simple. More decisive would have been the presence in the countryside of individuals who had dared to use these techniques in spite of their being prohibited. The area in which the proportion of migrants was highest, the canton of Pavilly, was also that in which contraception began to be practised earliest; diffusion took longer in the Roumois and Vexin regions. In these two areas, the Revolution appears to have played an important part; it led to secularization, changes in the established order of things, meetings with the protagonists of individualism, and the discovery of a new world by hundreds of conscripts.

Our conclusion which favours a cultural explanation of the diffusion process must, however, remain provisional. It could be extended by micro-analysis and the scrutiny of the fate of individuals and their families. Jacques Dupâquier has been doing just this for several years in the Vexin region. His survey of 3,000 families should yield a rich harvest which will make the laborious task of nominative studies worth while. But we must remember that fertility control is a peculiarly private matter. Very little can be gleaned from the spiritual literature of the period about the sexual lives of married couples. Into this domain of the unspoken, the historian cannot penetrate very deeply.

17 Urbanization and Demographic Behaviour in Spain, 1860–1930

DAVID S. REHER

Faculdad de Ciencias Politica y Sociologia, Universidad Complutense de Madrid, Madrid, Spain

---

The process of urbanization in Europe is certainly one of the most salient aspects of the history of the nineteenth and twentieth centuries. The growth of cities has traditionally been viewed both as a consequence of socio-economic changes within European societies, as well as a stimulant itself of further changes in human and economic behaviour. This pivotal importance of urbanization, which renders it at one and the same time a dependent and an independent variable intimately related to the dynamics of change, makes its study fundamental to the understanding of modern Europe. While increasing urbanization was common to all of Europe, it was by no means uniform in intensity or in geographical distribution. Since the growth of cities was largely a by-product of the Industrial Revolution, the largest urban growth occurred in northern Europe. The southern fringe of the Continent lagged behind, but was not immune to the contagion of growth. Whilst in 1851 there were 28 cities with 50,000 or more inhabitants in Great Britain, and another 73 such cities in Germany in 1900, there were only 18 of that size in Spain in 1900. However, urbanization was an undeniable reality in Spain during a period in which the proportion of the population living in towns doubled.

In this chapter, I examine the relationship between Spanish patterns of urbanization and demographic behaviour. Economic, demographic, and urban variables will be used to illustrate the role of urbanization as both product and catalyst of change within Spanish society. The components of urban growth, as well as the determinants and implications of urban nuptiality, fertility, and mortality will be examined. Throughout, the ever-present reality of rural Spain will be juxtaposed to urban areas to assess, at least partially, mutual influencing factors. The results will not be conclusive, but will point rather to potentially fruitful areas for further research.

The data used in this study are taken primarily from Spanish censuses and vital registration.[1] I have used a simple method to derive the rural population;

This research has been carried out with the generous help offered by IBM Spain. I would like to thank Pedro Luis Iriso Napal and Vicente Perez Moreda for their helpful comments on different parts of this chapter.

[1] Censuses were taken in Spain in 1860, 1877, 1887, 1900, 1910, 1920, and 1930. Material from

the number of inhabitants in the provincial capital was regarded as the urban population and was subtracted from the total population of the province to obtain the rural population. Whilst the population of the capitals does not represent the totality of urban populations, and 'rural' areas inevitably include some urban dwellers, especially where the process of urbanization was most diffused and advanced, the frequent dissimilarity in the structure of the data made it impossible to include all towns with more than, say, 10,000 inhabitants in the calculations. In any case, provincial capitals appear to yield a relatively representative sample of urban populations, and, despite urban pockets, our 'rural' populations will generally be truly rural in nature. I have used standard measures of demographic and urban variables (actual increase, net migration, natural increase, crude birth-rates, I_g, I_m, crude death-rates, $_1q_0$, etc.) to facilitate the comparison of Spanish data with those for other countries.[2] Finally, I have constructed a typology of cities for Spain based on the occupational distribution of the active population enumerated in the Census of 1920, which includes the following categories of towns: agricultural, heavy industry and mining, light industry and textiles, services, and garrison towns.[3]

The age distributions used in Spanish censuses present some anomalies. With some exceptions, the following groups were used: 0–4, 5–10, 11–15, 16–20, . . . etc. Adjustments have been made to the age-specific fertility rates for Hutterite women used in deriving the Princeton indices, I_g and I_m. These adjustments were based on the assumption that fertility within a given age-group was constant, and the derivation of new rates then becomes a simple matter of interpolation. The rates used were 0.35, 0.54, 0.491, 0.439, 0.369, 0.19, and 0.049. This leads to a slight overestimation of the fertility of younger age groups which can be compensated by a small underestimation in that for the older ages. Similar adjustments were made when calculating probabilities of dying for age groups, though the census data in this case were brought in line with the age distributions of deaths for five-year age groups, beginning with the group aged 5–9. This procedure is particularly questionable when calculating the probability of dying within four years of the first birthday, as the population in that group was originally aged 0–4. This was done by assuming that the age distribution was equal for each year of age, an

---

civil registration is contained in the following publications: Junta General de Estadística del Reino, *Memoria sobre el movimiento de la población de España en los años 1858, 1859, 1860 y 1861* (Madrid, 1863); Instituto Geográfico y Estadistico, *Movimiento de la población de España en el decenio de 1861 a 1870* (Madrid, 1877); *Movimiento de la población de España, septenio de 1886–1892* (Madrid, ND); *Movimiento anual de la población de España* (yearly from 1901).

[2] I_m and I_g are measures of the intensity of women's nuptiality and marital fertility which were designed by Ansley Coale for use in the European Fertility Project. For a detailed description of these indicators, cf. A. J. Coale and R. Treadway, 'A Summary of the Changing Distribution of Overall Fertility, and the Proportion Married in the Provinces of Europe', in A. J. Coale and S. Cotts Watkins, *The Decline of Fertility in Europe* (Princeton, 1986), 153–6.

[3] e.g. agricultural towns were considered to be those in which the proportion of persons engaged in agricultural activities was largest.

inaccurate procedure, but one which could not be avoided in this case. Here probabilities of death will clearly be too low. Finally, in the Census of 1860 there was no tabulation by age and marital status. The proportions married have been estimated by interpolating between the distributions for 1787 and 1887 for each city and province. Clearly, this typology has grave shortcomings, but it does break down urban areas into fairly clear-cut categories.[4]

Urbanization in Spain between 1787 and 1930 was at best an uneven process, severely conditioned by demographic and economic variables.[5] Though the populations in towns grew nearly three times as fast as in the countryside (1.14 per cent compared with 0.38 per cent per year), there were numerous ups and downs in the process. Urban growth slowed to a standstill during the first part of the nineteenth century, only to rebound sharply during the second third. A sample of twelve towns for which data are available stagnated between 1787 and 1856 (growing at 0.04 per cent per year), followed by an annual rate of 1.71 per cent between 1837 and 1857. Rapid growth continued until 1887, slowed down towards the end of the century, and picked up again afterwards. An indirect indication of slow urban growth is that rural populations never ceased to grow, albeit at a slower rate, whilst in other countries rural populations began to decline as early as the latter part of the nineteenth century.[6]

Urban areas have often been referred to as demographic drains into which surplus rural populations could be siphoned. In this way, they played an important part in maintaining an overall balance between population and resources. High urban mortality was at least partially due to the in-migration of adults, their age distribution, high densities which facilitated the spread of infection, and to deficiencies in public health and hygiene. All these factors were present in Spanish towns. Even though it would be difficult to characterize them as veritable 'devourers of men' during this period, natural increase in Spanish urban areas was low, and these rates (shown in Table 17.1) showed no signs of improvement and reached their lowest levels between 1920 and 1930.[7]

The situation in Spain in this respect differs sharply from that in other European countries where by the turn of the century natural increase was

---

[4] To supplement the general categories, we have circulated a number of bivariate correlation coefficients, based directly on the proportion of the population engaged in specific categories.

[5] D. S. Reher, 'Desarollo urbano y evolución de la población. España 1787–1930', *Revista de historia económica*, 4: 1 (1986), 39–66.

[6] R. Lawton, 'Population Mobility and Urbanization: Nineteenth Century British Experience', in W. R. Lee and R. Lawton (eds.), *Urban Population Development in Western Europe from the late 18th to the early 20th century* (London, 1985); P. Deprez and C. Vandenbroeke, 'Growth, Distribution and Urbanization of the Population in Belgium during the Period of Demographic Transition', ibid.

[7] Crude death-rates for 1920 were based on average numbers of deaths between 1919 and 1921. In both 1919 and 1920, the after-effects of the influenza epidemic were still felt in parts of the country and the total number of deaths was, therefore, higher than normal. The end effect was to push death rates upwards somewhat.

Table 17.1 Annual rates of increase in Spanish towns, 1860–1930[a]

Period	Actual increase %	Natural increase %	Net migration/ Actual increase
1860–87	1.2	0.46	0.64
1887–1900	1.2	0.02	0.99
1900–10	1.2	0.09	0.92
1910–20	1.3	0.19	0.85
1920–30	1.7	−0.03	1.00

[a] Based on provincial capitals.

Sources: Censuses and civil registration.

gradually replacing net migration as the major component of urban growth, and provides another example of the lag in Spanish urbanization and demographic development.[8] But the process of urbanization did continue at an ever-increasing rate after 1910, thanks largely to the role played by migration which, with the exception of the period 1860–87, accounted for practically all urban growth.

In Spain, therefore, towns were growing fast largely because of net migration. Their rates of natural growth were at best low, as a result both of lower fertility and higher mortality, than in the country areas surrounding them. The relationship only began to change when age structure, improved sanitary conditions and hygiene, and other related causes contributed to reduce urban mortality at a faster rate than fertility. There is evidence that this happened as early as the second decade of the present century, though the distorting effects of crude death rates calculated for 1920 tend to hide this. Before 1930, however, we can practically ignore natural growth as a major component of urban growth, and the ability of the city to attract migrants was the key to its potential growth.

This pattern of urbanization forms a necessary backcloth for the understanding of the demographic implications of urban growth. To what extent were vital behaviour patterns in towns distinct from those in the countryside, and why? Were demographic patterns uniform in towns, or were they influenced by factors such as city size, economic structure, migration patterns, or demographic variables? We may reasonably suppose that demographic behaviour did change, but to what extent and why is not clear. Within a broader context the relationship between rural and urban areas warrants close examination. Was it limited to a rather lopsided exchange of people or were there more persuasive influences at work, which might work in both directions? Consideration of some of these issues is the central theme of most of the remainder of this chapter.

---

[8] H. D. Laux, 'The Components of Population Growth in Prussian Cities (1875–1905) and their Influence on Population Structure', in Lee and Lawton, *Urban Population Development*; P. Moreda, 'La Modernización demografica 1800–1930. Sus limitaciones y cronología', in N. S. Albornoz (ed.), *La Modernización Económica de España, 1830–1930* (Madrid, 1985), 25–62; J. Nadal, *La Población Éspañola (Siglos XVI a XXI)* (Barcelona, 1984).

1. Nuptiality and fertility

Between 1887 and 1920 Spanish nuptiality behaviour became ever more restrictive, thus limiting general fertility during a period when marital fertility was almost stationary, and mortality was falling.[9] Only after 1920, when there was a pronounced drop in legitimate fertility, did women's nuptiality increase again. The trend was roughly similar in the towns and the countryside until 1920, when there were indications that nuptiality was beginning to increase in urban, but not in rural, areas.[10] In 1920 the value of I_m was everywhere significantly lower than in 1887 (by 7 per cent in the towns and 12 per cent in the country). In many ways nuptiality continued to fulfil its age-old role of limiting population growth, much as it had in France some hundred years earlier. A faster decline in rural areas would have indicated a greater population pressure there than in the towns.[11] Urban nuptiality was appreciably lower than in rural areas at all times; values of I_m in the towns were between 14 and 23 per cent lower than in the country and the rate of permanent celibacy (between 46 and 50 years of age) in towns was at times double that in the country. A closer look at the statistics shows that these differences were due mainly to differences in the proportions single at different ages, rather than to differences in the age at marriage, as well as to a greater propensity to remarry in rural areas.[12] These differences are not surprising and have been documented in a number of other studies, though the spread in Spain, and its consistency, are certainly noteworthy.[13]

Everywhere marriage patterns are strongly influenced by a number of economic, cultural, and demographic variables, and Spain is no exception. Women's nuptiality was determined not by a single but rather by many often overlapping and even contradictory factors, with no single variable standing out. This lack of clear-cut determining factors, which is also characteristic of our analysis of fertility and mortality, is an evident indicator of the complexity of urban environments. In Table 17.2, values of I_m are shown for different categories of Spanish towns. In all cases the averages shown are unweighted for each category. The results speak for themselves. At all times, nuptiality was highest in the agricultural towns and lowest in the garrison towns. In 1887, in agricultural towns it was 10 per cent higher than average, and 5 per cent lower in garrison towns; the corresponding figures for 1930 were 8 per cent above average and 6 per cent below average respectively. On the other

---

[9] B. C. Sánchez, 'La evolución de la nupcialidad en España (1887–1975)', *Revista española de investigaciones sociológicas*, 20 (1982), 81–99; J. D. Nicolás, 'Evolución y previsiones de la natalidad en España', in Centro de Estudios Sociales, *La Familia española* (Madrid, 1967).
[10] Reher, 'Desarollo urbano'.
[11] L. Henry and J. Houdaille, 'Célibat et âge au marriage aux xviiie et xixe siècles en France. I Célibat définitif; II Age au premier mariage', *Population*, 33, 34 (1978–79), 43–84, 403–442.
[12] Reher, 'Desarollo urbano', 47–50.
[13] J. Knodel, *The Decline of Fertility in Germany, 1871–1939* (Princeton, 1974), 111–12.

Table 17.2 Values of I_m for active population

Category of town	I_m								1887=100
	1887	1900	1910	1920	1930	1900	1910	1920	1930
Agricultural	531	504	483	467	472	95	91	88	89
Heavy industry/ mining	470	437	428	423	423	93	91	90	90
Light industry/ textile	486	442	437	442	451	91	90	91	93
Services	466	447	429	415	429	96	92	89	92
Garrison	458	431	426	398	412	94	93	87	90

The values of I_m are unweighted averages for each category.

Sources: Censuses.

hand in all categories I_m declined between 1910 and 1920 and rose slightly thereafter. This seems to indicate that the general pattern of development of nuptiality was similar in all categories of town, irrespective of their occupational structure.

The relationship between nuptiality and the active population warrants further analysis. Not only can certain sectors stimulate or obstruct marriage patterns directly; they can also operate through intermediate variables, such as the sex ratio, illiteracy, and migration patterns. Women's nuptiality was positively, though modestly, correlated in 1910 ($r = 0.28$) with the proportion of the urban population engaged in agricultural activities, and negatively with the proportion occupied in the services sector ($r = -0.39$). These correlations point not only to the factors that underlie different nuptiality levels in the towns, but also to one of the sources of the urban–rural differences. The influence is not necessarily direct. In 1910, I_m was strongly positively correlated with the proportion of the population that was illiterate ($r = 0.56$). That proportion was itself correlated positively with the proportion engaged in agriculture ($r = 0.57$), and negatively with the proportion employed in the services sector ($r = -0.53$). Moreover, if the proportion of working women is correlated with the level of illiteracy, the coefficient which comes to -0.39 lends further weight to the hypothesis that certain occupational activities affect educational levels which, in turn, affect nuptiality. Clearly, both illiteracy and nuptiality would be lower the higher the proportion engaged in non-agricultural activities and the numbers of women employed in the labour force, which are themselves related. Though this evidence is not conclusive it indicates the possible existence of patterns of conscious decision-making which would tend to make marriage depend on social and economic conditions that were specific to the town, the economic situation, and the individual. The rise in nuptiality after 1920 does not contradict our hypothesis, but rather suggests that the importance of the different variables that influenced decisions relating to the timing of marriage had changed.

However, the existence of conscious, socially motivated decisions which is implied by the preceding discussion can explain only part of urban nuptiality. The role of structural factors, e.g. the availability of partners, is not negligible and can affect both the timing and the incidence of marriage, but is only weakly related to certain urban activities (mainly in the services sector). Ultimately, the sex ratio will depend on the nature of migration. Marriage opportunities would be lower in towns in which the migrants were predominantly young girls entering domestic service. Urban–rural differences in nuptiality in Spain seem to depend more on the incidence than on the timing of marriage, and this reinforces our argument.[14] In other words, the likelihood that a woman would marry at what was socially considered a 'normal' age depended to a large extent on the availability of suitable partners. Once she had passed this age, her probability of marriage would diminish, even though the sex ratio was more balanced. If we correlate the sex ratio of the population aged 26–30 with I_m, the importance of both timing and availability is brought into sharper focus. Correlations of 0.63 in the town, and 0.58 in the country, in 1910 imply a significant relationship between the two variables which, in turn, are strongly mediated by age and sex-specific migration partners.

If an imbalance in the sex ratio lowered the nuptiality of women in the towns, the effect on men should have been the opposite. When there was a surplus of women of marriageable age, as was the case in most Spanish towns, marriage opportunities for men should have been enhanced. It is not our intention to affirm simplistically that sex ratios alone determine nuptiality, but rather that, if the hypothesis had some validity, rural–urban differences in nuptiality for men would be smaller. That this is so is confirmed by the fact that the urban–rural ratio of permanently celibate men was 16 per cent lower than for women in 1900, 11 per cent in 1910, and 22 per cent in 1920. However, the appreciable urban–rural differences for men also indicate that the sex ratio alone cannot explain probabilities of marriage.

A whole host of other, often unmeasurable, factors such as job stability, availability of housing, weaker social constraints on marriage, a greater acceptability of extra-marital fertility, and even inheritance patterns also seem to have constrained urban nuptiality jointly. The existence of a clearly positive correlation between the values of I_m in town and country in 1887, 1900, and 1910 ($r = 0.40, 0.60$ and 0.51 respectively) suggests that there was certainly a relationship between the rural and the urban worlds, which was often impervious to the social and economic differences that separated them. In other words, and directly relevant to the point under discussion, the prevailing attitude towards marriage in towns was at least partially a product of 'rural' attitudes of migrants, and conversely.

In the final analysis urban areas were not only affected by influences from outside, but also acted as a stimulant to nuptiality in general and to rural nuptiality in particular. To appreciate the implications of this role fully, it is

[14] Reher, 'Desarollo urbano', 47–50.

first necessary to realize that despite the fact that nuptiality was lower in the towns, migrants' chances of marrying were far greater than would have been the case had they remained in their villages of origin.[15] This escape valve is one of the reasons why rural nuptiality was invariably higher than it would have been had the weight of urban areas been less important. Even though lower urban nuptiality had the effect of reducing general national levels, in a hypothetical situation, in which there were no towns at all, national nuptiality and growth rates would probably have been far lower than they actually were.

During the period of our study, both marital fertility (I_g) and crude birth rates (CBR) moved gradually, though not uniformly, downward. As is shown in Table 17.3, the decrease in the crude birth rate was such that by 1930 it was

Table 17.3 Crude birth rates and I_g in Spain, 1860–1930

Year	Urban				Rural		Urban–rural
	CBR	Index	I_g	Index	I_g	Index	Ratio I_g
1860	36.6	100	574	100	548	100	0.95
1887	35.3	96	594	104	541	98	0.91
1900	31.3	85	604	105	544	101	0.90
1910	29.6	81	577	101	537	94	0.93
1920	27.8	76	555	97	505	92	0.91
1930	25.7	70	502	87			

CBR and I_g are based on unweighted averages.
Births for 1860 (legitimate and total) based on live births, 1860–3; births for 1887 (legitimate and total) based on live births, 1886–9; births for 1910 (legitimate and total) based on live births, 1909–12; births for 1920 (legitimate and total) based on live births, 1919–22; births for 1930 (total) based on live births, 1926–9.
Wherever figures for legitimate births were not available the percentage legitimate has been estimated. All births have been adjusted for under-registration. All sex ratios at birth above 115 were reduced to that level.

30 per cent lower than in 1860 and 17 per cent lower than in 1900. Legitimate fertility, on the other hand, increased between 1860 and 1900, and then only decreased gradually until 1920. The key variable in the containment of growth rates would seem to have been nuptiality which was able to compensate for the relatively unchanged fertility patterns of married women, and thus partially offset the effects of declining mortality. This was so, at least between 1860 and 1900, when the two fertility indices were moving in opposite directions. After that date, however, their movements were strictly parallel, each declining by 17 per cent between 1900 and 1930. Legitimate fertility in rural areas was consistently some 7 to 10 per cent higher than in towns, and though decline was universal it was not uniform. This tendency has been noted by other authors, as has the proportionately greater urban–rural difference overall in marital fertility.[16] The appreciable increase in urban areas between 1860 and 1900 was not nearly so pronounced in the countryside. Could this be the first stages of proletarianization stimulating

---

[15] It is plausible to suppose that permanent out-migrants from rural areas would be those least likely to find a suitable mate in their villages of origin.

[16] M. Livi Bacci, *A History of Italian Fertility During the Last Two Centuries* (Princeton, 1974); Knodel, *Decline of Fertility*, 89–101.

fertility, as some authors have suggested?[17] This may possibly be the case, although it should be pointed out that the process occurred in an urban context in which legitimate fertility was significantly lower than in rural areas.

It is not a simple matter to establish the determinants of fertility in urban areas, though the Spanish data make it possible to frame some tentative hypotheses. In the first place, the composition of a town's population seems to be an important factor in conditioning levels of fertility and their evolution. Evidence from Table 17.4 shows that both general and legitimate fertility were lowest in towns in which light industry and textiles were important. With some exceptions, the next lowest levels are found in towns with heavy industry or mining.[18] Moreover, the difference between the fertility of industrial towns and that of others increases with time. Thus legitimate fertility in textile towns was 3 per cent below that of agricultural towns in 1860, 8 per cent below in 1910, 12 per cent in 1920, and 17 per cent in 1930.

The development of both legitimate and total fertility in different types of town points again to the pioneering behaviour of the inhabitants of industrial towns. The crude birth rate began to decline, and the decline was greatest in the towns which contained heavy industry. In these towns it was already 9 per cent lower than in any other category in 1920, and by 1930 towns which contained both heavy and light industry were taking the lead in an atmosphere of general fertility decline. In all categories of town, fertility dropped by about 25 per cent between 1860 and 1930. A decline in nuptiality of nearly 10 per cent and a fall of approximately 14 per cent in marital fertility after 1887 point to the principal components of this evolution. Decreases in marital fertility came later, and, at least before 1920, were much less pronounced than those in the crude birth rate. Between 1860 and 1900 legitimate fertility rose in all categories of town (with the possible exception of towns with heavy industry), but there was a modest declining trend after that date. In fact, fertility decline before 1920 was only significant in the textile towns and by 1930 these towns and the towns with heavy industry clearly took the lead in declining fertility. In the other categories there was practically no downward trend before 1920, though I_g fell by between 9 and 12 per cent in all categories during the succeeding decade.

Industrialization has traditionally been included among the primary variables that influence reproductive behaviour, though multivariate analysis has often shown that it had less importance, especially at certain stages of the

---

[17] C. Tilly (ed.), *Historical Studies in Changing Fertility* (Princeton, 1978); F. F. Mendels, 'Protoindustrialization: The First Phase of the Industrialization Process', *Journal of Economic History*, 32 (1972), 241–61; N. Birdsall, 'Fertility and Economic Change in Eighteenth and Nineteenth Century Europe; A Comment', *Population and Development Review*, 9: 1 (1983), 111–23.

[18] In 1900, in six of the seven towns with heavy industry, there was a pronounced drop in fertility, and in 1910 fertility had increased again above the level of 1887. We cannot explain these oscillations. My first instinct was to suggest that the data were defective, but when the phenomenon is observed in six out of seven towns, it is impossible to be sure.

fertility transition than might have been expected.[19] The extent to which this behaviour indicates the extension of voluntary birth control within marriage is not clear from the data. However, by 1930, levels of I_g in towns with both types of industry were well below 0.500, an indication of voluntary control over fertility. This trend was followed in other types of town, but levels of fertility were higher, and the pace of decline slower.

In contrast to its negligible influence on marriage patterns, city size was strongly associated with prevailing fertility levels. In Table 17.5 are shown both crude birth rates and values of I_g, ordered by population size. The figures suggest that the contribution made by the size of the town in determining fertility levels was not negligible. In 1860, only the really large cities stood out, but later the correlation became quite strong as may be seen in Table 17.6. This suggests that there may be a threshold size of cities, and that once this has been reached fertility is closely affected by concentration of population. The levels of I_g in very large towns were always between 10 and 15 per cent, and crude birth-rates between 4 and 9 per cent below average. If we consider only those towns in which the population exceeded 100,000 inhabitants throughout our period of study (Madrid, Barcelona, Valencia, and Seville), I_g fell by 25 per cent between 1900 and 1930, compared with a fall of 17 per cent in all cities. In other words, not only was fertility lower the larger the town was, but also size became increasingly important in determining the levels of fertility.

Generally, the correlation between city size and total fertility was weaker than with legitimate fertility. General fertility levels were determined to a large extent by factors such as illegitimate fertility and nuptiality which were generally not related to city size. Thus the influence of city size on birth-rates was somewhat attenuated. Marital fertility, however, appears to be quite sensitive to city size, apparently independently of, or at least parallel to, the occupational composition of the population (many of the medium-to-large towns contained important agricultural components). This suggests that even though the working population plays an important part in defining what might be called 'urban behaviour', it is the concentration of people in a place which itself tends to influence this behaviour.

Finally, it is important to point out once again that human behaviour was not merely a response to social, economic, and demographic variables; it was a product of human and cultural attitudes as well. This point is brought home when similar demographic patterns are found in urban and rural areas, in spite of differences in social and economic structure, population density, sex ratios, nuptiality, etc. Towns were filled with migrants, who generally came from the surrounding countryside and who, at least temporarily, remained attached to the rural values upon which they acted during the better part of their lifetime as first-generation migrants to the towns. We cannot affirm

---

[19] Livi Bacci, *Italian Fertility*, 214–15; R. Lesthaeghe, *The Decline of Belgian Fertility, 1800–1970* (Princeton, 1977), 158–71; Knodel, *Decline of Fertility*, 228–36.

Table 17.4 Crude birth rates and I_g by active population in Spain, 1860–1930

Category	Crude birth rate								I_g							(1860=100)
	1860	1887	1900	1910	1920	1930			1860	1887	1900	1910	1920	1930		
Agriculture	37.5	97	89	78	76	72			573	102	109	104	102	93		
Heavy industry/mining	38.9	94	63	79	69	63			590	99	81	100	89	81		
Light industry/textile	34.5	98	82	81	77	68			560	103	103	97	91	80		
Services	36.5	97	93	85	79	76			578	104	106	102	102	92		
Garrison	36.0	100	92	83	77	70			578	108	111	101	101	89		

See notes to Table 17.3

Table 17.5 Fertility by city size, Spain, 1860–1930

City size	Crude birth rate								I_g							(1860=100)
	1860	1887	1900	1910	1920	1930			1860	1887	1900	1910	1920	1930		
100,000+	33.0	93	92	80	80	75			498	104	104	96	99	89		
50,000–99,999	34.8	97	92	81	76	74			573	98	102	95	93	85		
20,000–49,999	37.7	91	91	80	74	70			569	102	109	107	100	90		
–20,000	37.1	101	93	85	79	74			590	107	109	104	104	99		

See notes to Table 17.3 for appropriate clarifications.

Table 17.6 Bivariate correlation coefficients between city size and fertility, Spain, 1860–1930

	1860	1900	1910	1920	1930
CBR	−0.10	−0.47	−0.41	−0.46	−0.64
I_g	−0.23	−0.67	−0.36	−0.55	−0.75

explicitly, what seems implicit in this statement, that fertility was also, at least in part, influenced by cultural and conscious human attitudes. There is no solid proof for this statement when, at least before 1900, there are few indications of intentional fertility control. However, rural and urban legitimate fertility were closely correlated, and increasingly so, throughout the period (1860: 0.45; 1900: 0.55; 1910: 0.71; 1920: 0.75). Even though the reasons behind this relationship are not yet clear, the key questions which need answering are rapidly becoming apparent.

2. Mortality

Generally mortality was higher in the towns than in the countryside and this frequently resulted in negative growth rates, and has led historians to regard urbanization as an important negative restraint to general population growth.[20] In Spain, however, beyond these general notions, little is known about the components and determinants of urban mortality, nor about its evolution or its relationship to rural mortality. We shall consider a number of these points in this section, and I have chosen to look at two measures of mortality, the crude death rate and infant mortality, $_1q_0$. A more exhaustive study of mortality would have required the use of other measures of childhood and adult mortality, but the two indices that have been used have proved adequate.

The general evolution of mortality is shown in Table 17.7, and is fairly

Table 17.7 Mortality in urban and rural Spain, 1860–1930

Year	Crude death rate					Infant mortality				
	Urban		Rural		Ratio	Urban		Rural		Ratio
	CDR	Index	CDR	Index	U/R	$_1q_0$	Index	$_1q_0$	Index	U/R
1860	31.1	100	26.9	100	116	199	100	168	100	119
1887	35.3	114	30.2	112	117					
1900	30.7	99	27.9	104	110	200	101	181	108	111
1910	26.0	84	22.5	84	116	169	85	150	89	112
1920	25.7	83	22.0	82	117	162	82	151	90	108
1930	17.9	58				120	60			

All calculations are based on average numbers of deaths over a 3-year period, identical to those used for births in Table 17.3. All calculations are unweighted averages.
Sources: Census and civil registration.

straightforward. Crude death rates in towns were consistently some 15 per cent or more higher than in rural areas. Ratios for infant mortality were similar, though, in contrast to general mortality, there were signs of the

[20] E. A. Wrigley and R. S. Schofield, *The Population History of England, 1541–1871. A Reconstruction* (Cambridge, 1981); E. A. Wrigley, 'A Simple Model of London's Importance in Changing English Society and Economy, 1650–1750', *Past and Present*, 37 (1967), 44–70; A. Sharlin, 'Urban–Rural Differences in Fertility in Europe during the Demographic Transition', in Coale and Cotts Watkins, *Decline of Fertility*.

urban–rural difference lessening, at least after the beginning of the present century. This suggests that improvements in sanitation and medical care were at last beginning to alter the imbalance between town and country at its most vulnerable point—infant mortality. It has been shown that the value of $_1q_0$ in urban areas fell below that in rural areas in 1926.[21] Mortality rose between 1860 and 1887, and by 1900 was still at or above the levels of 1860. This deterioration was more pronounced and lasted longer in the countryside. After 1900, mortality fell everywhere, though not at a uniform rate. Urban and rural crude death rates declined roughly in parallel, but infant mortality fell more slowly in the country than in the towns. The real revolution in mortality did not occur until the 1920s when crude death rates in the towns fell by 30 per cent, and infant mortality by 27 per cent. This trend probably began a little earlier but was masked by the effects of the influenza epidemic of 1918–19. In this field, too, the 1920s and, more generally, the inter-war period were crucial to Spanish demographic development.

There are many factors that differentiate between urban and rural mortality and we shall only point to the more important ones. The size of the active population plays only a moderate part, though not as clearly as in the determination of nuptiality and fertility. The data in Table 17.8 show, however, that the crude death rate and infant mortality did not necessarily move in parallel, and this makes any sort of clear-cut interpretation of the figures virtually impossible.

A more thorough analysis of the determinants of mortality will depend on an examination of other variables. If size of town is introduced as an explanatory variable, some clearer patterns begin to emerge, especially in the case of very large cities. Even though the correlation between size of city and crude death-rate (or $_1q_0$) in 1910 yields modest negative coefficients (-0.25 with the crude death-rate and -0.16 with $_1q_0$) this does not mean that there was no relation between mortality and city size. The figures in Table 17.9 show that both measures were appreciably lower in towns with more than 100,000 inhabitants, whereas in 1860 levels were higher than or equal to the general average. But subsequently mortality fell sharply, and after 1887 was consistently lowest in the very large towns. Moreover, the difference between these towns and other cities increased with time, so that the development of mortality appears to have been related, at least indirectly, to population size. Expressed as a proportion of the general average the results shown in Table 17.10 are obtained. Evidently, the decline was fastest in the larger towns. But only in the very large towns did infant mortality fall faster than the crude death rate. In small towns neither index really began to fall before 1920, and in medium-sized towns (between 20,000 and 50,000 inhabitants) infant mortality was still high as late as 1920.

It is not surprising that infant mortality first declined in the very large

[21] R. G. Redondo, 'El Descenso de la mortalidad infantil en Madrid 1900–1970', *Revista española de investigaciones sociológicas* (1985).

Urbanization and Demographic Behaviour   295

Table 17.8 Mortality by active population, Spain, 1860–1930

Category of town	Crude death rate						(1860=100)	Infant mortality						(1860=100)
	1860	1887	1900	1910	1920	1930		1860	1900	1910	1920	1930		
													1920	1930
Agriculture	30.5	123	105	85	88	67		192	114	91	108	84		
Heavy industrial/mining	28.0	121	125	97	100	73		218	101	86	86	59		
Light industrial/textile	31.7	112	94	84	83	61		174	98	93	91	66		
Services	32.8	105	102	82	85	65		208	111	94	92	76		
Garrison	32.5	115	101	86	90	64		161	102	91	98	75		

Table 17.9 Mortality by city size, Spain, 1860–1930

City size	Crude death-rate						(1860=100)	Infant mortality					(1860=100)
	1860	1887	1900	1910	1920	1930		1860	1900	1910	1920	1930	
100,000+	32.1	107	94	80	79	55		220	87	79	67	50	
50,000–99,999	33.9	105	93	83	76	58		181	116	95	98	72	
20,000–49,999	31.3	113	97	84	88	67		178	116	95	106	83	
–20,000	31.4	117	111	96	100	73		199	111	103	106	75	

All rates are based on unweighted averages within each category. See Table 17.7 for additional notes.

Table 17.10 Level of mortality in large towns measured as level of general average (general average = 100)

	1860	1887	1900	1910	1920	1930
CDR	1.00	0.97	0.95	0.93	0.92	0.87
1q0	1.13		0.93	0.97	0.81	0.82

towns, since these were the first centres in which it was possible to generate the wealth and culture necessary for the appropriate innovations in education, medical care, sanitation, and hygiene which were the keys to reduction of infant mortality. Once the need for certain hygienic and sanitary measures was taken seriously—and this first occurred in the large towns and from them spread to smaller towns and eventually to the countryside—the battle against mortality was being won and the rate of decline accelerated.[22] The reduction of other forms of mortality had to await more specifically medical solutions and this advance was only beginning to gather momentum by the beginning of the present century.

A number of other variables also appeared to influence mortality in towns. First, in 1910 there was a moderate positive correlation between overall mortality and fertility (0.35 with I_g, and 0.49 with the crude birth-rate). In the first instance, this probably represented a generalized adjustment of fertility to the prevailing levels of mortality, and the directions of causality are difficult to determine, particularly in an urban context. Historical demographers have traditionally correlated fertility with infant mortality, beginning with multiple reconstitution studies and later with larger aggregates of data.[23] The low values obtained for the coefficients suggest that the influence of infant mortality on fertility was mediated by other intervening variables. Finally, regional mortality patterns also influenced mortality levels. Infant mortality in the towns and their hinterlands was appreciably correlated (1860: 0.51; 1900: 0.60; 1910: 0.43), as were crude death rates (1910: 0.50). Although the similarity has probably little to do with acquired cultural characteristics, or even with specifically economic variables which varied substantially between town and countryside, they point to the possibility that there were similar attitudes among migrants towards hygiene, breast-feeding, weaning, nutrition, and illness, and also to an as yet only hypothetical importance of climate in determining mortality levels.[24] Throughout the period studied, in urban Spain the proportion of the population aged 40 and over was positively correlated with the crude death-rate (1887: 0.30; 1900: 0.36; 1910: 0.44; 1920: 0.14). This was not, however, the case in rural areas where the correlations between age structure and mortality were either nonexistent or negative (1887: −0.29; 1900: 0.09; 1920: −0.17). The reason for this divergence can be found in the different structure of mortality in the town and countryside. If adult mortality were relatively more important in the towns, this would explain the apparent contradiction in the correlations. To

---

[22] Redondo, 'Descenso de la mortalidad infantil'; P. Hauser, *La geografía médica de la Península Ibérica, i. Climatologia y evolución médica ii. Demografía, morbilidad y mortalidad; iii. Morbilidad, mortalidad y suicidio* (Madrid, 1913).

[23] Knodel, *Decline of Fertility*, 174–87; L. Henry, *Manuel de démographie historique* (2nd edn., Paris, 1970), 104–5; E. van de Walle, 'Infant Mortality and the European Demographic Transition', in Coale and Cotts Watkins, *Decline of Fertility in Europe*.

[24] G. Ferrari and M. Livi Bacci, 'Sulle relazione tra temperature e mortalità nell'Italia unita, 1861–1914', in Società italiana di demografia storica, *La popolazione italiana nell'ottocento; continuità e mutamenti* (Bologna, 1985), 273–98.

test this hypothesis we calculated probabilities of dying for quinquennial age groups in rural and urban Spain for 1900 and 1910. The results are shown in Table 17.11 and confirm that differences between the mortality of adults in the towns and in the countryside were far greater than analogous differences in infant or child mortality. The urban–rural ratio increases with age and suggests that true differences in mortality are found in the adult age groups.

Table 17.11 Differential mortality in Spain, 1900 and 1910

Age group	1900			1910		
	Urban	Rural	U/R	Urban	Rural	U/R
0–1	200	181	111	169	150	112
1–4	240	210	114	179	164	109
20–25	56	46	122	45	35	129
30–35	54	40	135	61	44	139
40–45	83	57	146	77	50	154
50–55	155	99	157	128	86	149

The values shown are the probabilities of dying between the beginning and end of the age group shown, multiplied by 1,000. All are based on unweighted averages. See notes to Table 17.7 for further explanations.

Until the beginning of the twentieth century infectious diseases, particularly diseases of the digestive system, were a major cause of death in Spain and much of the rest of Europe, even though the importance of these diseases has since diminished rapidly.[25] These diseases particularly affect those age groups in which urban and rural mortality rates are most similar. Adult mortality, however, is determined primarily by the prevalence of diseases of the cardio-vascular system, the lungs, and non-infectious diseases of the digestive system, and, until the first half of the twentieth century, by malaria. A structural factor which must be kept in mind is the increasing tendency in Spain during this period to make use of the developing urban hospital system. It is possible that appreciable numbers of rural residents died in an urban hospital setting and that this exaggerated the importance of mortality differences. However, it is not clear how important that factor was.

In a closed population the age structure is a result of fertility and mortality, but in urban areas it is largely determined by the size of migration. The larger the migratory flow, the younger the population is likely to be, and, therefore, the lower mortality will be. In its turn, lower urban mortality would lead, other things being equal, to faster natural growth rates and would contribute to a relatively young age distribution.

In other words, overall mortality rates were certainly an indirect result of both in-migration and natural growth. As long as positive in-migration continued, this rather simplified model of growth was based on positive feedback: the heavier the migratory flows, the lower the death rate: a lower

---

[25] T. McKeown, *The Modern Rise of Population* (London, 1976); Moreda, 'Modernización demográfica'; J. Martínez Carrión, *La Población de Yesta en los inicios de la transición demográfica, 1850–1935* (Albacete, 1983), 298–337; Nadal, *Población española*, 154–61, 212–17.

death rate, in turn, would increase natural growth, and this in turn would contribute to accelerated growth, and the cycle would then begin again.

3. Conclusion

The differences in the behaviour of Spanish urban populations should by now be quite clear. In towns, nuptiality and fertility were appreciably lower than in rural areas, and mortality was higher. The differences are significant and ranged between 7 and 20 per cent. Even though the development of these variables was similar everywhere, there were certain variations in direction and intensity. The earlier decline of legitimate fertility and the more rapid reduction of infant mortality in towns are good examples.

Attempts to establish causal relationships between these and other variables have yielded results that are at best tentative. A number of factors have been singled out as being possibly significant in conditioning urban demographic behaviour, its evolution, and differences between town and country. None, however, has stood out as the only; or even the principal factor. The complexity of urban society makes it difficult to use simple or straightforward explanations. One of the major, albeit indirect conclusions of our discussion is that there is a multiplicity of often contradictory determinants of human behaviour in urban Spain. However, many of the key variables have been defined, and future researchers will need to integrate them in a more systematic manner to help our understanding of demographic behaviour.

In the final analysis, and in spite of its distinctive characteristics, the urban world continues to be intimately linked with the rural society that surrounds it. Reproductive behaviour in a town can only be analysed in relation to behaviour in its hinterland. During the period of this review there is no sign that this relationship was becoming weaker. The reality is clear; its explanation, though, perhaps less so. Our natural tendency to use economic and other quantifiable variables is stopped short in a situation where these do not explain all, indeed, they may explain very little, of the reality, in which cultural transfers seem to be so important. Migrants are the agents of these transfers who continually bolster up urban populations and in so doing create a bridge between the urban and the rural worlds. As long as a town's population originated largely from its surrounding area, the behaviour of the town's residents will never be truly emancipated from patterns prevailing in the countryside. Moreover, it was possible to move across the bridge in both directions and there is evidence that in their turn towns, and especially major cities, influenced behaviour in rural areas. The specific nature of these transfers, the variables which condition the strength of urban–rural ties and their development, and the mechanism of their diffusion remain to be determined and will become the subjects of future research and controversy.

Their importance cannot be questioned, especially if we consider that they provide the key to the diffusion of innovative behaviour in the Europe of the late nineteenth century and early twentieth centuries. To begin with we must strive for a more thorough and perceptive understanding of migrants and migration as pivotal elements in this world of urban–rural transfers.

18 Economic and Demographic Implications of Working-Class Housing in Early Victorian Leeds

MINORU YASUMOTO

Department of Economics, Komazawa University, Setagaya-ku, Tokyo, Japan

Is it possible to establish that the economic and environmental factors which shaped the life of the Victorian working classes had a discernible effect on their demography, for instance by affecting adult and infant mortality, as some social reformers were claiming at the time? In this chapter I attempt to test this assertion using a case-study. My data are taken from a computer tabulation of the enumerators' books for the city of Leeds at the census of 1851.[1]

My basic problem was to find an accurate definition of working-class families in terms of the data that are available. I have thus defined the working class in Leeds in terms of housing exclusively occupied by them, i.e. back-to-back or 'through' housing which can easily be identified on the large-scale Ordnance Survey map for the city which gives the situation in 1850.[2] The relevant streets which consist of back-to-back housing form the sample on which this study has been based. I prefer this method to more conventional ones, such as obtaining the occupations of individual inhabitants from the census returns, or studying the population of areas in which the inhabitants were mainly labourers; but, to provide a basis for comparison, I have also used information relating to people living in terraced houses to which smallish gardens were attached, and which can also be distinguished on the map for 1850. Their inhabitants may be taken as belonging to the middle or lower middle class. A typical example representing each type of housing is given in Figs. 18.1 and 18.2.

I am indebted to Professor N. Yamamoto of the Department of Economics, Wakayama University; Mr Takayuki Takai of the Data Processing Centre, Kyoto University, and to Dr Kevin Schurer of the ESRC Cambridge Group for the History of Population and Social Structure for the input format and program for my present research project of computer tabulations of the enumerators' books of the Census of 1851 for the city of Leeds. This study has been awarded a Grant-in-Aid for Scientific Research for the years 1984–6 by the Japanese Ministry of Education, Science, and Culture.

[1] Public Record Office, Enumerators' Books, 1851, HO107/2319–21, 2329.

[2] British Library, Ordnance Survey Plan OST(57), (1/1056), for the city of Leeds, sheets 1–20.

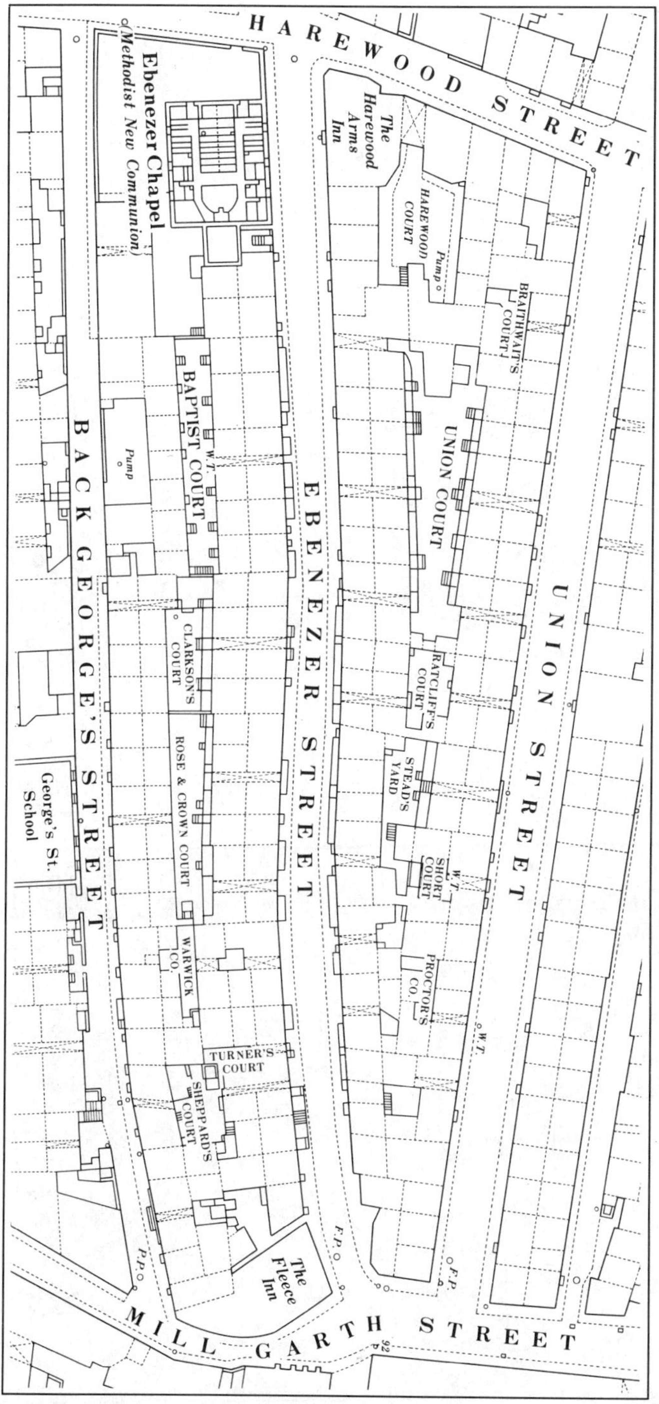

Economic and Demographic Implications 301

Figure 18.1. Working-class housing (back-to-back houses)

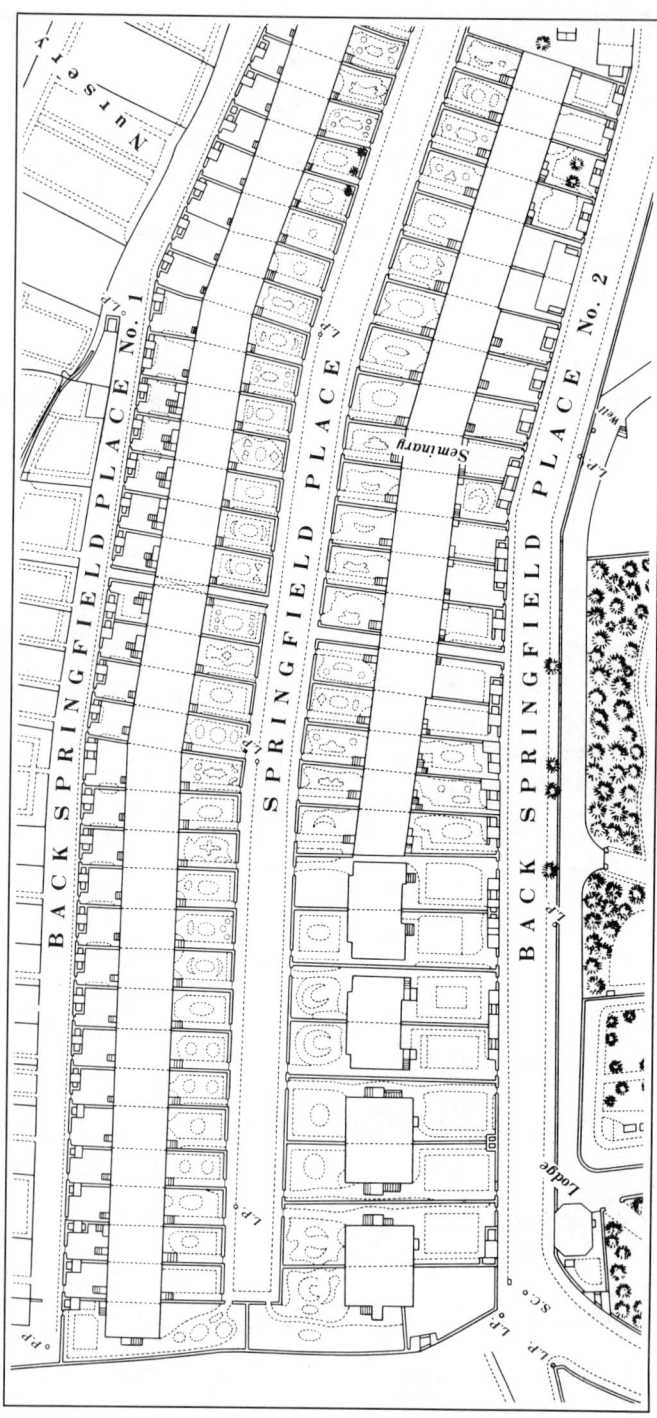

Figure 18.2. Middle-class housing (terrace houses)

Of the approximately 586 streets which were recorded in mid-nineteenth-century Leeds, more than 60 per cent (some 370) contained back-to-back houses.[3] I have studied eight streets consisting of back-to-back houses, all containing cellar dwellings, which were frequently castigated for their filthy condition by contemporary critics.[4] This seems a less arbitrary method of selection and definition. The size of the sample and other features of this type of housing are shown in Table 18.1. The inhabitants of these houses will be referred to hereafter as Group A.

Table 18.1 Sample of the working-class population

Name of street	Houses	Households	Population	Type of housing[b]
Ebenezer Street	68(1)[a]	68	315	38 back to back 11 through[c]
Goulden's Buildings	24(0)	27	189	24 back to back 4 (cellars)
Harper Street	37(0)	33	215	33 back to back 11 through
Hope Street	59(3)	58	254	2 (cellars) besides back to back
Nelson Street	50(2)	52	255	41 back to back 9 through 4 (cellars)
Off Street	46(1)	45	300	53 back to back 1 (cellar)
Sykes Yard	14(0)	21	85	14 back to back 1 upper room 5 cellars
York Street	148(1)	165	936	1 flat 7 single rooms 4 cellars, besides back to back
Total	446(8)	469	2,549	

[a] The figures in brackets represent uninhabited houses.
[b] The figures for type of housing are taken from Beresford, 'The Back-to-Back House in Leeds', p. 127. According to the lists drawn up by Professor Beresford, all these streets contained cellar dwellings. Yet only two of these streets (Sykes Yard and York Street) were shown as containing cellars in the enumerators' books. The figures in brackets are estimates based on the assumption that a back-to-back house which contained more than two households might be regarded as containing cellars.

Middle or lower middle-class housing shown on the 1850 map spread over 30 'terraces', and consisted of 468 houses, 51 of which were uninhabited. The population of 2,548 persons was almost exactly the same as in Group A and will be referred to as Group B. As another yardstick for comparison I also studied the rural population of Methley, a village dependent on commercial agriculture and coal-mining, situated on the outskirts of Leeds and consisting

---

[3] M. W. Beresford, 'The Back-to-Back House in Leeds (1787–1937)', in S. D. Chapman (ed.), *The History of Working-Class Housing—A Symposium* (Newton Abbot, 1971), 129–32; R. Baker, *Report on the Condition of the Residences of the Labouring Classes in the Town of Leeds, in the West Riding of York* (Leeds, 1841), 20.
[4] Beresford, 'The Back-to-Back House in Leeds', 127.

of 435 houses (15 of which were uninhabited) with a population of 1,902 (Group C).

1. General demographic features

In this section we briefly examine the demographic features of each of these populations, as distinct from the various features of the household or co-residing group which is the unit of analysis used in this study. A glance at Fig. 18.3 which depicts the age distribution of each population brings out certain features. For instance, the proportion of females aged 20–24 in the population in Group B is extraordinarily high, amounting to 17.7 per cent of the total female population of 1,603 women, whereas that aged 15–19 in Group C is fairly low (6.4 per cent). A relatively high proportion of men in Group A are in the age-group 20–24 (12.2 per cent). Another odd feature is the low percentage of men aged 30–34 in Group C, amounting to only 4.7 per cent.

In Fig. 18.4 we see the sex ratio for each type of population (males per 100 females). There is an anomaly in Group B, where the number of females is more than three times that of males, whereas in Group C there are relatively few females between the ages of 15 and 19, and few men aged 30 to 34. The sex ratio for the city of Leeds as a whole, regardless of age, is 93.6, most similar to that in Group A, compared with 58.2 in Group C (Table 18.3).[5]

The high proportion of females aged 15–19 and 20–24 in Group B, and 20–24 among males in Group A, and the unusual values of the sex ratio in the three younger age groups in Group B mentioned above are explained by an unusually high proportion of servants in Group B, and of lodgers in Group A. Their age structures are shown in Table 18.2. The distribution has a maximum

Table 18.2 Age distribution of lodgers and servants

Age	Lodgers in Group A				Servants in Group B	
	Male	%	Female	%	Female	%
0–9	54	11.2	43	15.9	0	0.0
10–14	25	5.2	14	5.2	23	3.9
15–19	38	7.9	25	9.2	143	24.2
20–24	101	21.0	62	22.9	198	33.4
25–29	67	13.9	27	9.9	105	17.7
30–34	57	11.8	40	14.8	52	8.8
35–39	41	8.5	15	5.5	29	4.9
40–44	38	7.9	20	7.4	19	3.2
45–49	15	3.1	9	3.3	11	1.9
50–54	19	3.9	5	1.8	8	1.4
55–59	16	3.3	0	0.0	2	0.3
60+	11	2.3	11	4.1	2	0.3
Total	482	100.0	271	100.0	592	100.0

[5] *Census of 1851*, Population Tables II: Ages, Civil Condition, Occupations and Birthplaces of the People, 1852–3 (1691–II) LXXX viii, Pt. ii, 669.

Economic and Demographic Implications 305

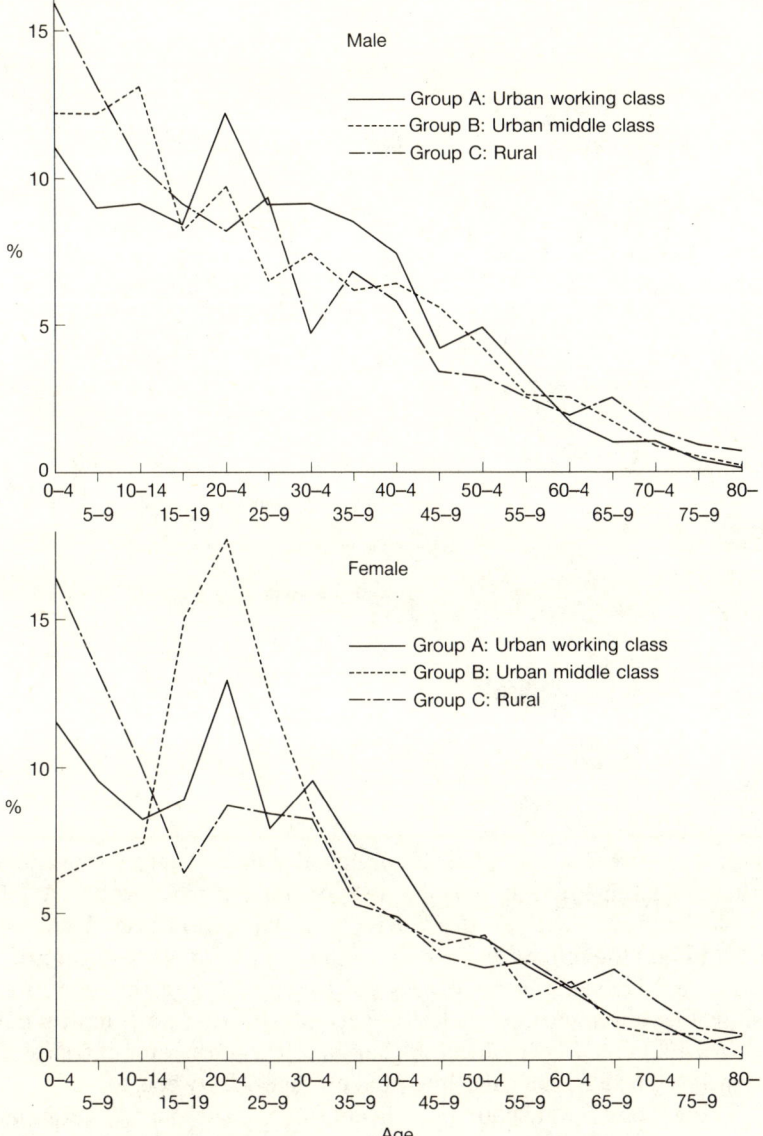

Figure 18.3. Age structure in Leeds

in the age group 20–24 in both populations. The proportion of lodgers of both sexes in the total population in Group A is almost 30 per cent, while 36.9 per cent of the female population in Group B were resident servants (Table 18.4).

The large majority (more than 74 per cent) of women working in the households of Group B are female servants who originated elsewhere. Similarly, more than three-quarters of the lodgers, both males and females,

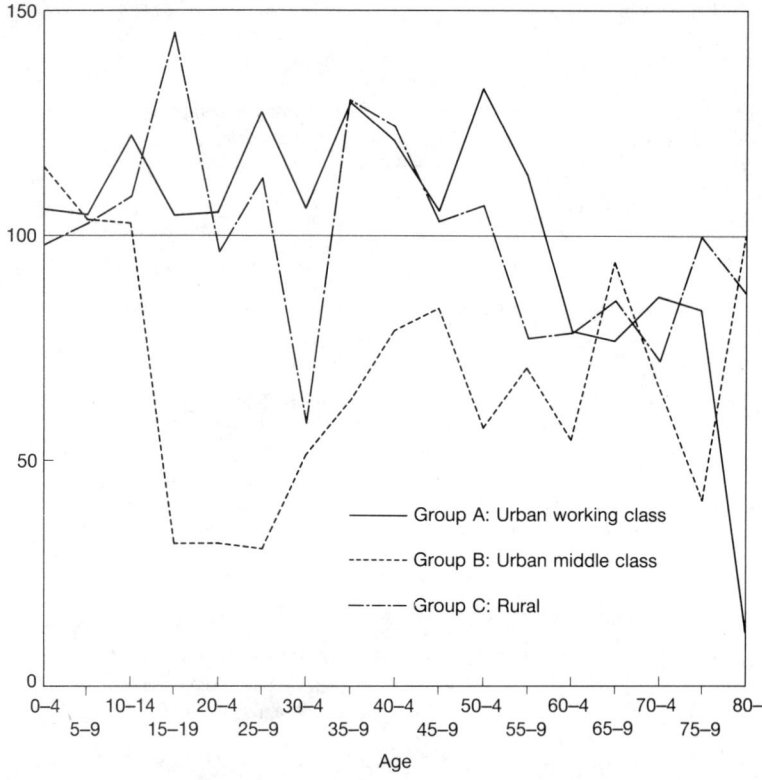

Figure 18.4. Sex ratio in Leeds

were born outside Leeds. Ireland, the principal source of migrants, supplied more than one-third of the population of lodgers in Group A. The distribution by birthplace of the different groups shown in Table 18.5 demonstrates that the migration patterns of the two groups were different.

In Table 18.6 we see figures relating to the nuptiality of this population. These show that among women below the age of 44 the proportion who never married was much greater in Group B than in either of the other groups. The distinction is particularly clear at the younger ages. Between the ages of 20 and 24, 54.2 per cent of the women in Group A were ever married, compared with only 7.8 per cent in Group B. The difference was also larger, though not quite so pronounced, in the age-group 25–9 (75.6 compared with 26.1 per cent). Among men, differences in nuptiality were pronounced in the three youngest age-groups (15–29), where the proportions ever married were also lowest in Group B.

The low proportion ever married in Group B may well be explained by the large number of female domestic servants in that group, most of whom, as is well known, were unmarried. In that group, of 592 female domestic servants

Table 18.3 Age distribution and sex ratio

Age	Group A					Group B					Group C				
	Male	%	Female	%	Sex ratio	Male	%	Female	%	Sex ratio	Male	%	Female	%	Sex ratio
0-4	147	11.0	139	11.5	105.8	114	12.2	99	6.2	115.2	151	15.8	153	16.2	98.7
5-9	120	9.0	115	9.5	104.3	114	12.2	110	6.9	103.6	126	13.1	123	13.1	102.4
10-14	121	9.1	99	8.2	122.2	122	13.1	119	7.4	102.5	101	10.5	93	9.9	108.6
15-19	112	8.4	107	8.9	104.7	76	8.2	241	15.0	31.5	87	9.1	60	6.4	145.0
20-24	163	12.2	155	12.9	105.2	90	9.6	283	17.7	31.8	79	8.2	82	8.7	96.3
25-29	121	9.1	95	7.9	127.4	61	6.5	199	12.4	30.7	89	9.3	79	8.4	112.7
30-34	121	9.1	114	9.5	106.1	69	7.4	135	8.4	51.1	45	4.7	77	8.2	58.4
35-39	113	8.5	87	7.2	129.9	58	6.2	92	5.7	63.0	65	6.8	50	5.3	130.0
40-44	98	7.4	81	6.7	121.0	60	6.4	76	4.8	78.9	56	5.8	45	4.8	124.4
45-49	56	4.2	53	4.4	105.7	52	5.6	62	3.9	83.9	34	3.6	33	3.5	103.0
50-54	65	4.9	49	4.1	132.7	39	4.2	68	4.3	57.4	31	3.2	29	3.1	106.9
55-59	42	3.2	37	3.1	113.5	24	2.6	34	2.1	70.6	24	2.5	31	3.3	77.4
60-64	22	1.6	28	2.3	78.6	23	2.5	42	2.6	54.8	18	1.9	23	2.4	78.3
65-69	13	1.0	17	1.4	76.5	16	1.7	17	1.1	94.1	24	2.5	28	3.0	85.7
70-74	13	1.0	15	1.2	86.7	8	0.9	12	0.7	66.7	13	1.4	18	1.9	72.2
75-79	5	0.3	6	0.5	83.3	5	0.5	12	0.7	41.7	9	0.9	9	1.0	100.0
80+	1	—	8	0.7	12.5	2	0.2	2	0.1	100.0	7	0.7	8	0.8	87.5
Total	1,333	100.0	1,205	100.0	110.6	933	100.0	1,603	100.0	58.2	959	100.0	941	100.0	101.9

Table 18.4 Proportions of lodgers and servants

	Group A				Group B				Group C			
	Male	%	Female	%	Male	%	Female	%	Male	%	Female	%
Lodgers	482	36.2	271	22.5	46	4.9	14	0.9	38	4.0	10	1.1
Servants	7	0.5	36	3.0	27	2.9	592	36.9	35	3.6	46	4.9
Others	844	63.3	898	74.5	860	92.2	997	62.2	886	92.4	885	94.0
Total	1,333	100	1,205	100	933	100	1,603	100	959	100	941	100

Table 18.5 Birthplaces of sample
(a)

	Group A				Group B			
	Male	%	Female	%	Male	%	Female	%
Leeds	476	36.0	511	42.5	494	53.1	653	40.7
Ireland	347	26.2	291	24.2	7	0.7	18	1.1
Elsewhere	501	37.8	400	33.3	430	46.2	932	58.2
Total	1,324	100.0	1,202	100.0	931	100.0	1,603	100.0

(b)

	Lodgers				Servants			
	Male	%	Female	%	Male	%	Female	%
Leeds	90	18.9	58	21.6	3	11.1	152	25.7
Ireland	161	33.8	100	37.2	0	0.0	13	2.2
Elsewhere	226	47.4	111	41.3	24	88.4	427	72.1
Total	477	100.0	269	100.0	27	100.0	592	100.0

Table 18.6 Proportion of the population ever married

Age	Group A		Group B		Group C	
	Male	Female	Male	Female	Male	Female
15–19	2.7	6.5	—	0.4	—	5.0
	(1.4)	(2.9)	—	(1.2)	—	(7.3)
20–24	28.8	54.2	7.8	7.8	29.1	48.8
	(42.3)	(56.3)	(11.5)	(26.1)	(36.4)	(60.6)
25–29	62.0	75.18	32.18	26.1	71.9	72.2
	(80.0)	(77.0)	(46.3)	(54.9)	(79.7)	(77.0)
30–34	70.2	83.3	66.7	43.7	86.7	77.9
	(90.5)	(88.4)	(77.6)	(70.7)	(90.5)	(83.1)
35–39	81.4	89.7	82.8	54.3	83.1	84.0
	(94.3)	(90.1)	(92.0)	(75.4)	(87.1)	(91.3)
40–44	73.5	92.6	86.7	64.5	92.9	95.6
	(93.2)	(98.3)	(92.7)	(83.3)	(96.2)	(97.7)
45–49	83.9	94.3	96.2	79.0	97.1	97.1
	(97.6)	(100.0)	(98.0)	(85.7)	(97.0)	(96.9)
50–54	90.8	95.9	94.9	72.1	96.8	96.6
	(97.7)	(97.6)	(97.3)	(83.0)	(96.7)	(96.4)
55–59	85.7	94.6	70.8	79.4	95.8	100.0
	(100.0)	(97.2)	(76.2)	(78.1)	(95.7)	(100.0)
60+	94.4	97.3	96.3	81.2	95.8	95.3
	(100.0)	(96.7)	(96.1)	(83.6)	(98.5)	(96.3)
Total	60.0	72.2	56.4	33.5	66.4	73.1
	(75.7)	(77.0)	(66.6)	(60.3)	(74.1)	(79.9)

Figures in bracket exclude servants, lodgers, boarders, and visitors.

only 9 were married and 23 were widowed, in contrast with the situation in the other two groups. If we consider the proportions ever married in each population excluding servants, lodgers, and boarders and visitors of both sexes, the general picture remains basically the same, although the contrasts are a little less sharp, as the figures in brackets in Table 18.5 show. The low propensity to marry among women in Group B seems to apply not only to resident servants but also to the autochthonous population, in which women tended to marry later than in the other two groups.

The basic differences in the structure of the different groups which we have described from an aggregate analysis of the enumerators' books can be explained mainly as a feature of the in-migrant population. Bearing this factor in mind we may now proceed to consider some features of the labour force in each of the three groups.

2. Labour force

Age-specific labour-force participation rates are shown graphically in Fig. 18.5 and indicate that among men these rates were similar in all age groups, except the two youngest (10–14 and 15–19) and the two oldest age groups (55–59 and 60+). For women, however, there is a difference between the different groups, both as regards the age distribution and the peak value. The highest rate for women (73.5 per cent) is found in Group B in the age group 20–24. This is easily explained by referring back to the figures in Table 18.2 in which the age structure of resident domestic servants is shown. The second-highest rate is found for women aged 15–19 in Group A. The contribution made by women to the labour force is lowest in Group C in all age groups. The picture is completely changed, however, if resident servants, lodgers, boarders, and visitors are excluded from the population: the relevant data are plotted in Fig. 18.6. The curves for Groups B and C shift downwards, and the distribution becomes distorted, particularly for the younger age groups. This tendency is reinforced by very high participation rate among younger women in Group A. The difference in patterns is much smaller for men; the labour-force participation rate among men in Group C lies midway between that of Groups A and B, as can be seen from the overall distribution.

The principal occupations recorded for women in the enumerators' books in Group A were mill workers (120), employed in the textile industry in Leeds (flax, woollen and worsted, cotton and silk) and comprising 30.5 per cent of all gainfully employed women in the urban working-class population, followed by domestic servants (48 or 12.2 per cent) and dressmakers (23 or 5.9 per cent). Among men in Group A the list is headed by 182 labourers (industry defined or undefined), 123 mill workers employed in the textile industries, and 88 boot and shoe makers including cordwainers, in a total working population of 966. In Group B there are 723 working members of the female population, their main occupation being that of domestic servant (592 or 81.9 per cent). Among the male working population living in middle-class or lower middle-class housing and consisting of 545 persons, merchants dealing in wool, cloth, wines, and spirits head the list (86 or 15.8 per cent), followed by 55 manufacturers (10.1 per cent) of different goods, and 52 clerks to merchants (9.5 per cent). In the rural population of Group C the main

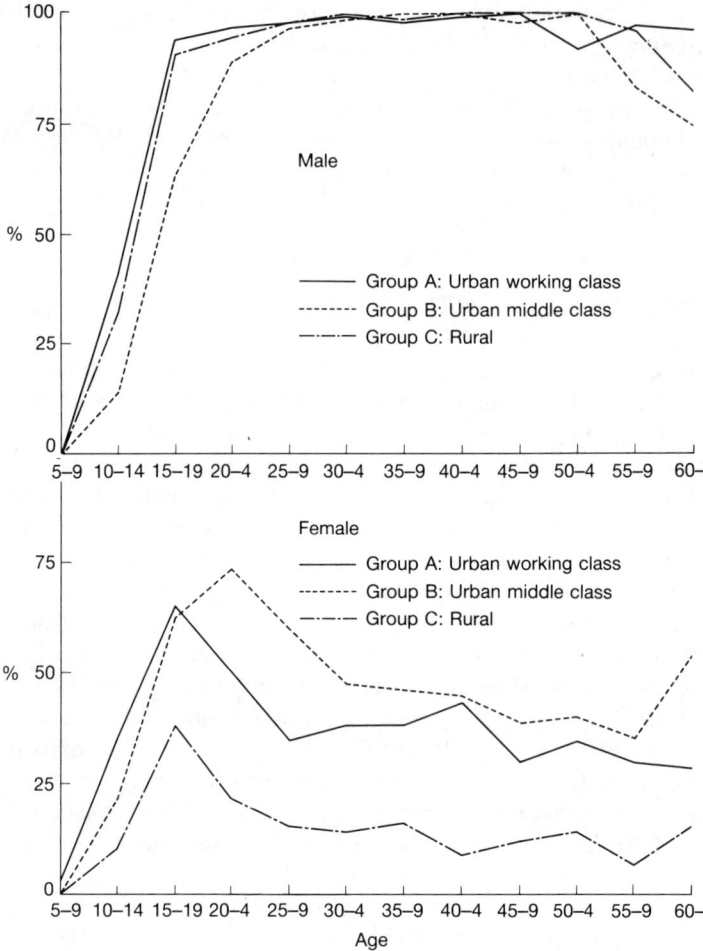

Figure 18.5. Overall labour-force participation rate

occupations of the female working population were domestic servants (43 or 44.3 per cent), dressmakers (17 or 17.5 per cent), and agricultural workers (11 or 11.3 per cent). Among men the principal occupations were coal-miners (197 or 33.9 per cent), agricultural labourers (118 or 20.3 per cent), and farmers (27 or 4.6 per cent). The total male working population amounted to 581.[6]

It is of interest to note that labour migration, as measured by the proportion of the working population born outside Leeds in relation to the total population born outside Leeds, was highest among women aged 15–19 in Group A and 20–24 in Group B. The proportion in Group A reached a

[6] Cf. M. Yasumoto, 'Industrialization and Demographic Change in a Yorkshire Parish', *Local Population Studies*, 27 (Autumn, 1981), 20–1.

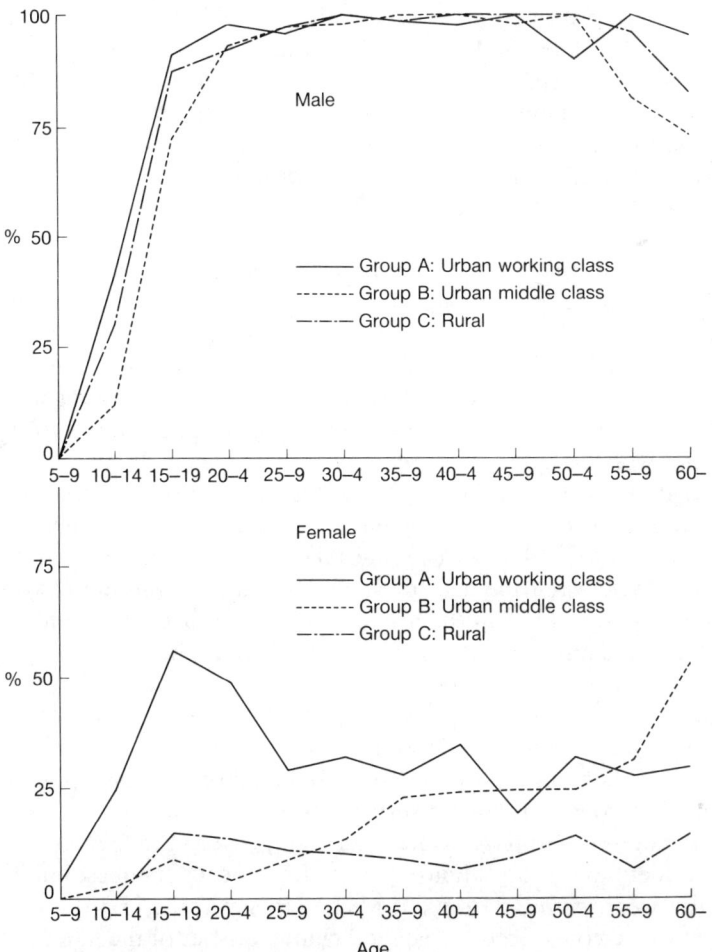

Figure 18.6. Labour-force participation rate excluding resident servants, lodgers, boarders, and visitors

maximum (62.0 per cent) in the age-group 15–19, which suggests that there was an influx of workers from the adjacent rural parishes who settled in the city as lodgers, the main 'in-migrant' labour force already noted in Group A. It should be remembered in this context that, as we already noted earlier, the percentage of the total female population aged 15–19 in the villages of Group C was as low as 6.4 per cent. These girls were prepared to move from the countryside in search of employment in the growing centres of industry in the town or the industrialized villages, such as the urban textile industry.

This conclusion is supported by figures relating to the age distribution of those employed in the Leeds textile industry, as well as by their relative wage rates, expressed as the average standing weekly wage (i.e. not including piecework) paid to women, compared with that paid to men in different age groups. Most of the 2,113 female workers reported to the Factory Commission for the year 1833/34 as being employed in Leeds wool textile factories were aged between 15 and 19 (612 or 29.0 per cent), the second-largest group being those between the ages of 10 and 14 (591 or 28.0 per cent). Among the 2,795 men employed, the proportion was largest in the age group 10–14 (687 or 24.6 per cent), compared with only 523 or 18.7 per cent in the age group 15–19.

Among women workers employed in the flax industry of whom there were 1,552, 656 or 42 per cent were aged between 15 and 19 and 527 or 34 per cent between 10 and 14. This is in contrast with the situation for male workers, of whom 159 were aged 15–19, and 407 aged between 10 and 14.[7] In the worsted and flax-spinning industries relative wage rates were somewhat higher for the younger women workers; for instance, the ratios of girls' wages to those of boys among worsted spinners were 1.2 for those below 10 years, 1.036 for those aged 10–12, 1.025 for those aged 12–14, 1.089 for those aged 14–16, and 0.97 for those aged 16–18; for flax spinners the ratios were 1.033 times those of boys for girls aged 12–14 and 1.043 times those of boys for the age group 14–16.[8] Thus girls between the ages of 15 and 19 enjoyed the most favourable employment opportunities in the urban textile industries and, up to the ages of 16–18, received higher wages than boys of the same ages.

The peak in age-specific labour migration rates, which is found among women aged 20–24 in the population in middle- or lower middle-class housing in Group B, on the other hand, is likely to be explained by the in-migration of domestic servants from the surrounding countryside. It is also possible that households in Group B recruited servants from the rural parishes, as well as from the families in Group A. More than one-quarter of the female domestic servants resident in Group B housing came from Leeds families, but 72.1 per cent of them were recruited from outside Leeds (see Table 18.5*b*).

So far we have considered the general characteristics of the labour force in each group. In order to clarify some of the features to which we have already referred we next look at labour-force participation of household members, excluding servants, lodgers, and visitors in each group. These figures make it possible to assess the differences in the structure of households depending on the numbers of workers and dependants (Table 18.7). The figures show the average number of persons, excluding servants, lodgers, boarders, and visitors in the household, and are based on 469 households in Group A, 417 in Group B, and 420 in Group C. Although the size of family predictably is smallest in Group A (3.63 compared with 4.09 for Group B and 4.16 for Group C), the number of working females (the fourth variable) is highest and

---

[7] Royal Commission on Employment of Children in Factories, *Second Report* (1834) (167), xix, 23, 26.

[8] Royal Commission on Employment of Children in Factories, *Supplementary Report*, Pt. II (1834) (167), xx, 71–352.

Table 18.7 Working and dependent members of households

Variable	Group	Mean	Standard deviation	t	d.f.	Probability (two-tailed)
Family size	A	3.63	1.90			
	B	4.09	2.21	−3.32	826.1	0.0009[a]
	C	4.16	2.08	−3.99	887.0	0.0001[a]
Number of male working members	A	1.15	0.81			
	B	1.09	0.74	1.16	884.0	0.2454
	C	1.21	0.75	−1.28	887.0	0.2002
Number of male dependent members	A	0.60	0.88			
	B	0.82	1.15	−3.25	772.3	0.0012[a]
	C	0.88	1.05	−4.32	820.9	0.0001[a]
Number of female working members	A	0.49	0.73			
	B	0.29	0.61	4.37	880.3	0.0001[a]
	C	0.14	0.39	9.07	733.6	0.0001[a]
Number of female dependent members	A	1.37	1.14			
	B	1.88	1.41	−5.87	798.2	0.0001[a]
	C	1.93	1.31	−6.75	834.5	0.0001[a]
Total working members	A	1.64	1.02			
	B	1.38	0.79	4.20	867.8	0.0001[a]
	C	1.35	0.80	4.62	872.4	0.0001[a]
Total dependent members	A	1.97	1.57			
	B	2.71	2.11	−5.83	763.9	0.0001[a]
	C	2.81	1.86	−7.21	823.9	0.0001[a]
Number of working sons	A	0.30	0.61			
	B	0.28	0.63	0.37	884.0	0.7086
	C	0.28	0.62	0.37	887.0	0.7135
Number of working daughters	A	0.19	0.51			
	B	0.05	0.25	5.32	694.2	0.0001[a]
	C	0.05	0.23	5.39	676.5	0.0001[a]
Total working children	A	0.49	0.87			
	B	0.33	0.69	2.96	871.8	0.0032[a]
	C	0.33	0.68	2.97	871.8	0.0030[a]

[a] Significant at the 1% level for a two-tailed test. The first value of t shown is for the difference between Group A and Group B, the second for the difference between Group B and Group C.

that of dependent females (the fifth variable) lowest in Group A, and the difference is statistically significant. Women contributed significantly to the economy of the household in this group.

This conclusion is reinforced by another index, the proportion of working wives in each group. In Group A nearly 20 per cent of wives (56 out of 285) were recorded as having had some occupation, in Groups B and C the numbers were only 4 and 7 (1.4 and 2.1 per cent respectively). The amount of child labour, particularly that of girls, was higher and the contribution made by resident sons and daughters to the household economy was more important (the ninth variable in Table 18.7). This is confirmed by the labour-force participation rates of daughters, which in Group A came to 24.6 per cent, 55.4 per cent, and 64.9 per cent for the age-groups 10–14, 15–19 and 20+ respectively; the corresponding figures for Groups B and C were, respectively, 0 per cent, 5.8 per cent, and 16.3 per cent, and 0 per cent, 13.9 per cent, and 26.8 per cent.

In this context it is instructive to notice a difference between the urban working class and the rural population as regards the economic value of children, which is seen in the figures in Table 18.8. These have been constructed from model production and consumption schedules, age distributions, and age-specific labour-force participation rates of children living in their parents' households for working-class populations in Group A, and rural populations in Group C.[9]

I have attempted to measure the contribution made to the parental household by co-resident children, as well as the costs they caused their parents. The figures given in Table 18.8 have been used for this purpose. Two different sets of wage rates prevailing in Leeds and the rural areas of Yorkshire have been used as a proxy for the contribution made by children. Wage rates for male and female workers employed in the flax and woollen factories in Leeds in 1833 have been used to represent urban wage rates, whilst unweighted average wage rates for male agricultural labourers and coal-miners and for female agricultural workers in the West Riding of Yorkshire in the same year have been regarded as representing wage rates in the rural areas (see Table 18.8a). These figures have been used on the assumption that most of the children of urban working-class families were employed in these industries and that those in rural areas worked either on the land or in the mines.

The relative wage rates of children in different age groups have been multiplied by the proportion of co-resident children of different ages in the two groups and by their labour-force participation rates, and the resulting

Table 18.8a Economic value of co-resident offspring: relative wage rates

Age	Urban: wage rates for Leeds flax and woollen factories, 1833				Rural: Wage rates of agricultural labourers and coal-miners in West Riding of Yorkshire, 1833			
	Male		Female		Male		Female	[a]
	Average per week in d.	Rate	Average per week in d.	Rate	Average per week in d.	Rate	Average per week in d.	Rate
5–9	27.4	0.112	32.9	0.134	35.3	0.144	32.4	0.132
10–14	49.0	0.200	46.1	0.188	58.1	0.237	48.6	0.198
15–19	97.6	0.397	70.7	0.288	133.8	0.545	60.0	0.244
20–54	245.6	1.000	82.2	0.335	211.0	0.859	81.0	0.330

[a] Wage rates of agricultural labourers only.

[9] E. Mueller, 'The Economic Value of Children in Peasant Agriculture', in R. G. Ridker (ed.), *Population and Development: The Search for Selective Interventions* (Baltimore, 1976), 107, 118; E. A. Wrigley and R. Schofield, *The Population History of England 1541–1871. A Reconstruction* (London, 1981), 445; Royal Commission on Employment of Children in Factories, *Second Report*, 23, 26; PP Agriculture, *The Present State of Agriculture and Persons employed in Agriculture in the United Kingdom* (1833) (612), v. 112, 117; PP Agriculture, *The State of Agriculture and Causes and Extent of the Distress* (1836) (79), viii. 53; PP Agriculture, *The Employment of Women and Children in Agriculture* (1843) (510), xii. 282–350; Leeds Archives Department, Middleton Colliery Collection, MC 153, fos. 25–34; J. H. Lenton, 'Wages in the Leeds Area, 1770–1850', M.Phil. thesis, University of Leeds, (1969), 107; Royal Commission on Employment of Children in Mines, *Report* (1842), 154–5, 218–19.

products have been summed as an index of the contribution made by children to the parental household. Similarly, the consumption of children of different ages has been represented as a proportion of the consumption of an adult (Table 18.8c) and multiplied by the proportion of co-resident children, and the products have been summed to obtain an index of the burden of dependency which co-resident children caused to their parents. The results suggest the following conclusions. The dependency burden caused by the age distribution of co-resident children as consumption units is higher in Group A than in Group C (67.20 compared with 63.72 for males, and 56.45 compared with 53.45 for females), but the difference is small and amounts to only some 5 or 6 per cent altogether when both sexes are taken into account (see Table 18.8c). Conversely, as is shown in Table 18.8b the predominance of the importance of children as contributors to urban working-class families is obvious. The figures come to about 20 per cent more in Group A than in Group C (1983.02 compared with 1650.83) and differ by a factor of more than 4 (671.67 compared with 146.8) for contributions made by daughters, and by 45 per cent for both sexes combined when rural and urban families are compared.

These points are brought out even more vividly in Fig. 18.7 where the figures in Table 18.8 are plotted by age of head of household. Total contributions by children in urban working-class families were higher in all age groups of heads of household than in rural familes whereas there is no discernible difference in the consumption of children between urban and rural working-class families. In Fig. 18.7b the relative contribution to production and consumption by children is shown as the ratio of those for working-class families in Group A to that of rural families in Group C broken down by age of head of household. In households with younger heads the economic value of children appears to be higher in urban working-class families.

At this juncture it would seem that the figures for relative wage rates which have been used as indices of the contribution made by children to the parental household are fairly robust for purposes of comparison. It would, however, be unwise to use them as a basis for claiming that urban working-class families were better off than rural families, unless it could be proved that other conditions, such as employment or the cost of living in the town were no worse than in rural areas. Calculations have been made relating to the cost of living and employment in Leeds and rural areas respectively.[10] There exists

---

[10] The following sources have been used for data for these calculations: Leeds Archives Department, Harewood Archives, Labourers' Account Books, HAR 185 (198): *Facts and Figures. A Periodical Record of Statistics, October 1841*, 5; E. J. Hobsbawm, 'The British Standard of Living', *Economic History Review*, 2nd series 10: 1 (1957), 56–7 for employment and wage rates in Leeds; PP Accounts and Papers, *Comparative Statement Showing the Conditions of 48 Men in the Parish of Westoning Whose Employment has been Irregular and 30 Men whose Employment has been Regular, 1834 and 1837* (1837–8) (359), xviii, pt. II, (328), 46–7, and *Result of an Inquiry into the Comparative Statement of Labourers in Westoning Parish* (1837–8) (439), xviii, pt. III, (452), 56–7 for employment, wage rates, and cost of living in rural areas; *Return Relative to Removal of Labourers from Agricultural to Manufacturing Districts* (1843) (254), xvi. 45–9 for the family incomes of the Leeds working-class families; G. Rimmer, 'Working Men's Cottages in Leeds 1770–1840', *Publications of the Thoresby Society*, 46 (1961), 199.

Table 18.8b Economic value of co-resident offspring: production units

Age	Male							Group A/Group C
	Group A: Urban working class			Group C: Rural				
	Production units (wage rate)	(1)	(2)	(3)	Production units (wage rate)	(1)	(2)	(3)	
0–4	0	26.6	0	0	0	30.2	0	0	—
5–9	0.112	22.2	1.2	2.98	0.144	25.4	0.9	3.29	91
10–14	0.200	22.5	41.9	188.55	0.237	19.7	27.9	130.26	145
15–19	0.397	15.9	93.4	589.57	0.545	12.1	86.8	572.40	103
20–54	1.000	12.8	93.9	1,201.92	0.859	12.6	87.3	944.88	127
Total				(1,983.02)				(1,650.83)	(120)

Age	Female							Group A/Group C
	Group A: Urban working class			Group C: Rural				
	Production units (wage rate)	(1)	(2)	(3)	Production units (wage rate)	(1)	(2)	(3)	
0–4	0	29.9	0	0	0	32.6	0	0	—
5–9	0.134	22.5	3.7	11.16	0.132	27.2	0	0	—
10–14	0.188	16.7	24.6	77.23	0.198	18.3	0	0	—
15–19	0.288	15.3	55.4	244.11	0.244	8.6	13.9	29.17	837
20–54	0.335	15.6	64.9	339.17	0.330	13.3	26.8	117.63	288
Total				(671.67)				(146.8)	(458)

Contribution by co-resident offspring of both sexes made to the household economy

Age	Group A: Urban working class			Group C: Rural			Group A/Group C
	Male	Female	Both Sexes	Male	Female	Both Sexes	
5–9	2.98	11.16	14.14	3.29	0	3.29	430
10–14	188.55	77.23	265.78	130.26	0	130.26	204
15–19	589.57	244.11	833.68	600.79	29.17	629.96	132
20–54	1,201.92	339.17	1,541.09	944.88	117.63	1,062.51	145
Total	(1,983.02)	(671.67)	(2,654.69)	(1,679.22)	(146.80)	(1,826.02)	(145)

Column (1) represents age distribution of co-resident offspring shown as percentages.
Column (2) represents age-specific labour participation rates of co-resident offspring shown as percentages.
Column (3) represents contribution to production made to the household economy by co-resident offspring converted from production units (wage rate) × (1) × (2).

Economic and Demographic Implications 317

Table 18.8c Economic value of co-resident offspring: consumption units

Age	Model consumption units	Male Group A (4)	Male Group C (4)	Group A/ Group C	Model consumption units	Female Group A (4)	Female Group C (4)	Group A/ Group C	Both sexes
0–4	0.320	8.51	9.66	88	0.320	9.57	10.43	92	90
5–9	0.520	11.54	13.21	87	0.480	10.80	13.06	83	85
10–14	0.820	18.45	16.15	114	0.680	11.36	12.44	91	104
15–19	1.000	15.90	12.10	131	0.800	12.24	6.88	178	143
20–54	1.000	12.80	12.60	102	0.800	12.48	10.64	117	109
		(67.20)	(63.72)	(105)		(56.45)	(53.45)	(106)	(106)

Column (4) figures represent economic burden brought about by co-resident offspring converted from model consumption units × age of co-resident offspring.

318 *Minoru Yasumoto*

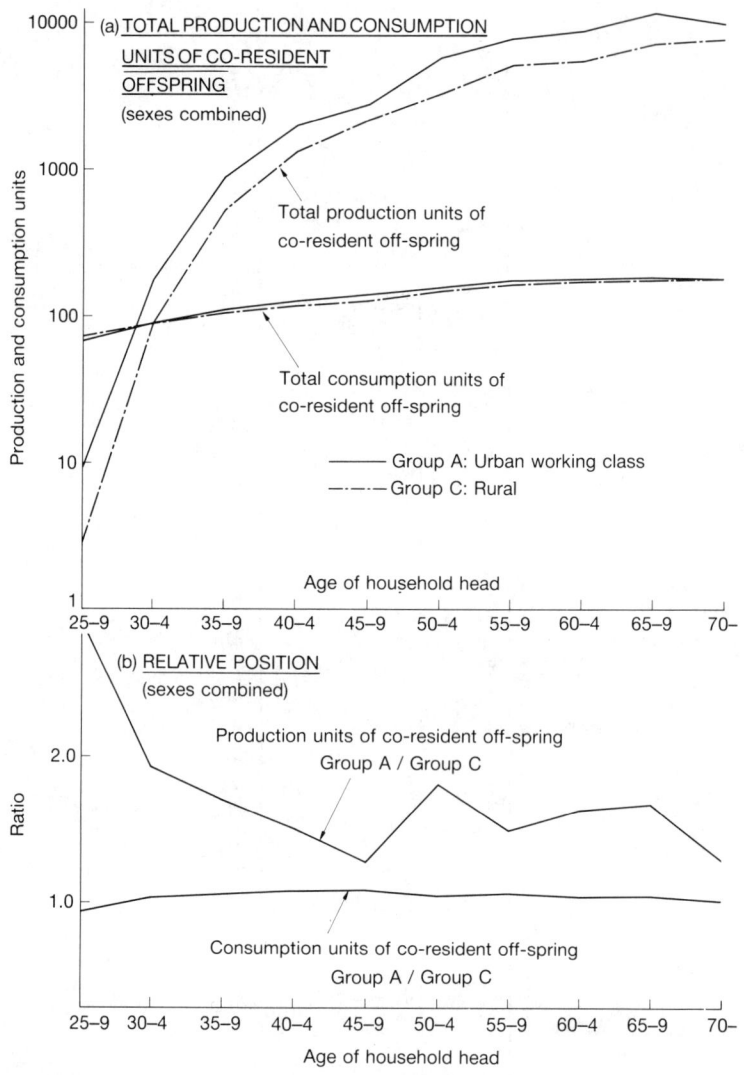

Figure 18.7. Contribution made by co-resident offspring to the household economy

information which has made it possible to estimate the average length of employment during the year for the 35 'trades' in Leeds in 1839, most of which concern men employed in craft-based workshops for an average of 10.5 months per year.[11]

Space does not permit a full explanation of these figures, but the following hypothesis seems reasonable. There seems to be no reason to believe that the

[11] For the persistence of craft-based workshops in Leeds, see D. Ward 'Victorian Cities. How Modern?', *Journal of Historical Geography*, 1:2 (1975), 141–3.

Leeds working class were less favourably situated in respect of regularity of employment than those working in rural areas of the West Riding at the end of the eighteenth century (on average an agricultural labourer worked for 222.34 days during the year) or those in a parish of Bedfordshire who worked for 34.1 weeks during the year. However, as the employment of unskilled workers who may have been more vulnerable to unemployment is not included in these figures, they may not be entirely representative of employment conditions for the totality of Leeds working-class families during the early nineteenth century. However, even unskilled workers in towns like Leeds, with a more diversified economy,[12] seem to have been provided with more regular employment than those in 'mono-culture' or port towns like Liverpool or Manchester, where employment for the mass of unskilled workers was completely irregular, or than in the rural areas where there was seasonal intermittent unemployment during the slack period after the harvest had been gathered.

Evidence relating to the cost of living in Leeds and in a rural parish of Bedfordshire is of interest for a comparison of this cost in early Victorian English towns compared with that in rural areas. The evidence available to us at the moment is not sufficient to measure the standard of living in urban centres. But it is possible to compare the proportion of income spent in urban and rural families on rent and fuel, as well as the weekly wages earned by heads of households. These comparisons show that the proportion of total income spent by agricultural labourers on housing was similar to that spent by urban workers (8.5 compared with 8.1 per cent) out of a total weekly average wage of 145*s*. 3*d*, although the amount going on rent was much lower for the rural families (12*s*. 4*d*. per week compared with 24*s*. for urban working-class families).[13] However, the expenditure on fuel by Leeds working-class families was much lower proportionately to income than in the countryside. It amounted to 3.0 per cent of total family earnings of 296*s*. 4*d*. per week, and 4.5 per cent of the average wage of the head of the household of 201*s*. 5*d*., when corrected for employment during the year, whereas rural labourers in Bedfordshire spent 10.6 per cent of total family income and 14.3 per cent of the weekly wage of the head of household (107*s*. 9*d*.). This suggests that urban working-class families would not have been significantly worse off as regards regularity of employment or cost of living than families who lived in rural areas.

The relatively favourable conditions enjoyed by urban working-class families could be one factor that explains migration from the countryside to the industrial centres where there were better opportunities for employment as well as relatively higher wages, so that the standard of living was certainly

---

[12] M. Yasumuto, 'Urbanization and Population in an English Town: Leeds during the Industrial Revolution', *Keio Economic Studies*, 10: 2 (1973), 87.

[13] For the situation in the city of York at the end of the 19th cent. cf. B. S. Rowntree, *Poverty: A Study of Town Life* (London, 1902), 165.

no worse than in the countryside. The contributions made to the urban working-class household by co-resident children could also have been responsible for aspects of the demography of the urban working class, as shown in its age structure, fertility, and general demographic behaviour.

Another inference that can be drawn is that household heads in Group A would live with their children, particularly those between the ages of 10–19, when the children's earning power was likely to be high, for longer than those in Group C because the economic value of children was likely to be greater in towns such as Leeds than in rural areas where there were few opportunities for children to be employed. A comparison of the age distribution of the eldest co-resident child in the three groups, shown in Table 18.9, supports this view. There is a tendency for children to stay in households of Group A for longer than in those in Group C, and this is reflected in the peak of the age distributions in these groups.

Table 18.9 Age distribution of eldest co-resident child (either sex)

Age	Group A		Group B		Group C	
	Number	%	Number	%	Number	%
10–14	60	30.0	35	18.6	58	31.0
15–19	65	32.5	41	21.8	50	26.7
20–24	33	16.5	54	28.7	33	17.6
25–29	18	9.0	24	12.8	19	10.2
30–34	10	5.0	17	9.0	8	4.3
35–39	10	5.0	8	4.3	14	7.5
40+	4	2.0	9	4.8	5	2.7
Total	200	100.0	188	100.0	187	100.0

3. Demographic implications of working-class housing

In this final section we consider the demographic implications of working-class housing in urban centres during the nineteenth century. The figures in Table 18.10 show the average difference in age between successive children living in the same household. The first three columns show the mean difference in age between the first and second, the second and third, and the third and fourth child respectively; an overall average is given in the fourth column. To control for the effects of children leaving home which would tend to lengthen the interval, and also in order to take account of possible differences in marital fertility, the information is given by age of wife (i.e. the mother of the children concerned).

The general trend is for the age differences between successive children to be longest in Group A and shortest in Group B, with Group C occupying an intermediate position about half-way between. In almost all the variations of Table 18.10 the difference between the age of the eldest and the second child is greatest in Group A (the only exception being the case where the mother was between 55 and 59 years old). If we look at the overall average age difference (i.e. the difference for different birth orders combined) the same

Table 18.10 Intervals between co-resident children

Age of wife	Group	Interval between 1st and 2nd		Interval between 2nd and 3rd		Interval between 3rd and 4th		Interval between 1st and 4th	
		Number of cases	(1) Mean	Number of cases	(2) Mean	Number of cases	(3) Mean	Number of cases	(4) Mean
20–24	A	12	2.17	2	3.00	1	2.00	15	2.27
	B	3	1.67	2	2.25	1	1.00	6	1.83
	C	6	2.50	1	3.00	—	—	7	2.57
25–29	A	22	3.00	11	3.00	3	5.30	36	3.19
	B	20	2.00	11	1.91	2	1.00	33	1.91
	C	36	2.22	17	2.88	8	2.25	61	2.41
30–34	A	29	3.24	19	3.00	8	3.38	56	3.18
	B	32	2.38	25	2.52	17	2.24	74	2.39
	C	43	2.49	33	3.09	21	2.10	97	2.61
35–39	A	39	2.95	33	4.21	16	3.69	88	3.56
	B	27	2.89	24	2.83	16	2.31	67	2.73
	C	28	3.18	26	2.46	22	2.91	76	2.86
40–44	A	31	5.10	20	3.95	14	3.50	65	4.40
	B	24	3.33	19	2.74	15	2.53	58	2.93
	C	27	3.96	22	3.41	17	3.41	66	3.64
45–49	A	19	4.37	12	4.42	8	5.13	39	4.54
	B	25	4.16	23	3.30	15	2.93	63	3.56
	C	21	5.81	17	3.47	10	3.90	51	4.58
50–54	A	13	5.15	5	3.20	3	3.67	21	4.48
	B	21	4.33	14	2.93	11	2.91	46	3.57
	C	15	5.27	11	3.55	8	3.75	34	4.35
55–59	A	9	3.67	4	3.00	3	5.67	16	3.88
	B	10	4.70	6	2.50	3	5.67	19	4.16
	C	11	3.73	7	3.43	5	4.60	23	3.83

holds true. The differences are particularly marked for the younger wives, where the figures are less affected by children who have left home.

If age of mother is left out of account, the same trend is found. The average age difference between the first two children is 4.02 years in Group A compared with 3.32 years in Group B. The figures for the age difference between the second and third child are 3.70 and 2.88 years, and those for the difference between the third and the fourth child are 3.89 and 2.62 years respectively. The differences between these values turn out to be statistically significant.

The evidence suggests that these differences may have been associated with differences in infant and child mortality. The larger differences found in Group A may be interpreted as implying that age gaps between co-resident children were larger in that group because some of the intervening children may have died, particularly in the case of the younger mothers. It is, of course, too simple to argue in terms of the age difference between successive children, given that there may have been fertility control, and possibly differential fertility depending on the mother's age at marriage, all of which makes the situation more complex. Yet it is not impossible that there may have been an important difference between the infant and child mortality rates of the two urban population groups. If this were the case, our case-study supports the widely quoted contention that congestion, poor sanitary conditions and defective sewerage, all of which were found in urban working-class housing, bore a high degree of responsibility for the higher rates of infant and child mortality, as these rates are a very sensitive indicator of conditions of life.[14] More direct supporting evidence is provided in Fig. 18.8.[15] The distribution of ages at death in populations of Group A has been derived from information on the place of residence of deceased persons contained in the parochial and nonconformist registers of Leeds for the period 1820–54. For both males and females infant mortality was highest among the urban working class, and mortality in that group remained substantially higher up to the ages of 5–9. Clearly, infant and child mortality were sensitive to environmental factors, such as housing and sanitary conditions.

Adult mortality, too, could have been affected by overcrowding and deteriorating standards of health in this type of working-class housing. This is confirmed by figures relating to the incidence of widowhood and widowerhood. Because of the incidence of remarriage these would not, by themselves, reflect adult mortality alone, but could be used as an index for comparative purposes. The proportion of widows in the total female population was highest in Group A (10.3 per cent), second in Group B (6.7 per cent), and least in Group C, though the difference between the latter two groups is not

---

[14] Rowntree, *Poverty*, 204–9.
[15] Calculated from *Fifth Annual Report of the Registrar General* (1843), 142–3, 164–5, Leeds Archives Department, Leeds Parish Church Registers (1820–54); Public Record Office, Nonconformist Registers, 239 I (RG4/3753, 4105); 231 IV (RG4/3731); Methley Parish Church Registers (1820–54), Leeds City Council.

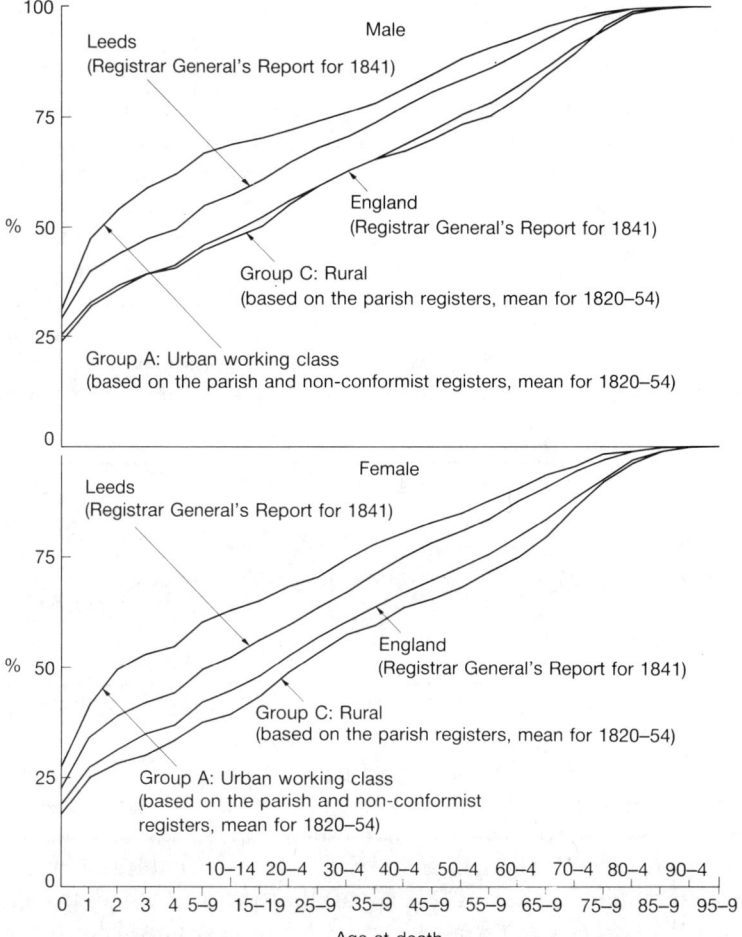

Figure 18.8. Distribution of age at death (cumulative)

significant. Widowers, too, were found most frequently in Group A (5.3 per cent), followed by Group B (3.2 per cent), and Group C (2.9 per cent).

The lowest maximum in the age distribution of widows is found in Group A for the age-group 40–44, which contains 17 (or 13.7 per cent) of the 124 widows in that group. Another peak occurs in the age-group 55–59. In Group B, on the other hand, the maximum occurs in the age-group 60–64, with 19 out of a total of 108 widows. It comes latest in Group C where 16.1 per cent of widows are in the age-group 65–69. The figures for the age distribution of widowers also indicate that the maximum occurs earliest in Group A in the age group 50–54 with 14 out of 71 widowers (19.7 per cent), compared with 16.7 per cent in the age group 70–74 in Group B, and 32.1 per cent in the age-group 75+ in Group C. It would appear that the environment in which working-class families were living reduced their expectation of life compared with that of the middle or lower middle classes, whose sanitary conditions were better.

Another aspect of working-class demography worth mentioning is that their family life-cycle differs from that found in the middle or lower middle classes or that of rural families. We have already seen that both men and women in Group A tended to marry earlier and began their families at a relatively lower age, especially in comparison with the situation among the middle or lower middle class in Group B. This evidence is supported by the implications of age-specific nuptiality rates and headship rates and also by the difference between the ages of husbands and wives. In Group A the average difference among 331 couples was 2.10 years, compared with 3.65 years among the 280 couples in Group B, and the figures in Table 18.11 which show

Table 18.11 Nuptiality and fertility

Group	Mean age at first marriage		% of co-resident children	
	Male	Female	Aged 0 (wife's age 40–54) %	Aged 0–4 (wife's age 44–49) %
A: Urban working class	26.96(24.43)[a]	23.90(24.04)	22.6	36.8
B: Urban middle or lower middle class	30.48(28.59)	31.75(26.45)	4.2	20.0
C: Rural	26.24(24.86)	25.19(23.41)	7.4	33.3

[a] Figures in parentheses are the ages at marriage for those excluding resident inmates (lodgers, servants, and boarders) and visitors.

estimates of fertility and nuptiality in each of the groups also support this statement. The singulate age at marriage [16] is calculated from the age-specific proportions ever married shown previously in Table 18.6. It is clear that age at marriage is lowest for women in the working class, or at least lower than for the urban middle classes. The age of the youngest child living in the household, which is here taken as a proxy for the age at which women in the working class stopped bearing children, indicates that working-class women continued child-bearing for longer than those in other groups. They married earlier and had more children than those in the middle class, and their children continued to live in the parental household for longer. However, higher infant and child mortality brought about a structure of working-class households which meant that households were smallest, the number of children living in the household lowest, and the labour-force participation rate highest in that group.

This explanation is supported by the figures in Table 18.12 in which we see the mean number of co-resident children broken down by the age of the wife. Among wives in their twenties the number of children living in the household in Group A exceeds that in Group B, whereas the reverse is true for women

[16] J. Hajnal, 'Age at Marriage and Proportions Marrying', *Population Studies*, 7 (1953), 129–31.

Table 18.12 Average number of co-resident children by age of wife

Age of wife	Group	Number of cases	Mean	Standard deviation	Coefficient of variation
20–24	A	33	1.18	0.97	82
	B	18	0.89	1.29	145
25–29	A	43	1.58	1.24	78
	B	43	1.53	1.26	83
30–34	A	53	1.89	1.50	79
	B	52	2.37	1.64	69
35–39	A	58	2.50	1.73	69
	B	39	3.08	2.31	75
40–44	A	45	2.58	2.04	79
	B	38	3.05	2.60	85
45–49	A	38	1.63	1.58	97
	B	33	3.52	2.38	67
50–54	A	28	1.64	1.76	107
	B	31	2.65	2.27	85
55–59	A	18	1.61	1.53	95
	B	16	2.00	1.54	65
60+	A	23	0.52	0.77	149
	B	19	1.73	1.21	70
Total	A	339	1.82	1.65	91
	B	289	2.44	2.10	86

aged over 30. This is likely to be a consequence both of the higher childhood and infant mortality in Group A and the difference between the family life-cycles of the two populations which is witnessed by the fact that the maximum in the number of co-resident children (2.58) occurs for wives aged 40–44 in Group A, compared with a maximum of 3.52 for wives aged 45–49 in Group B. A similar difference is found between urban working-class families and rural families. Referring back to Fig. 18.7b, which shows the relative position for heads of different households, it would appear that the position in working-class households is most favourable at an earlier age of the head than among rural families.

We may conclude that the analysis of the enumerators' books does, indeed, show that there was a difference between the demography of urban working-class households and other social groups, which is significant enough to merit further study based on larger samples and a more relevant classification of different types of housing. More extensive research is needed to confirm this provisional outline which might help in a fuller understanding of the economic and demographic idiosyncracies of urban working-class families in early Victorian England.

Appendix

*Humphrey Boyle's Estimate of Living Costs in 1832**

Least possible sum per week for which a man, his wife, and three children can obtain a sufficiency of food, clothing & other necessaries—Feby. 12th, 1832.

	s.	d.		£	s.	d.
Rent 2/-, fuel 9d., candle 3d.	3	0	Brout up . . .		14	6½
Soap 3d., soda 1d. blue & starch 1½d.		5½	Vegetables 1d. per day			7
			Salt, pepper, mustard, vinegar			2
Sand, black lead, bees wax & c.		2	7 pts. beer 1½d.			10½
Whitewashing a cottage twice a year		½	Water			1
			Schooling for 2 children			6
1½st flour for bread—2/6d.	3	9	Reading			2
¼st flour for puddings—2/8d. st.		8	Wear & tear in beds, bedding, brushes, pots, pans, & other household furniture			6
Eggs 2d., yeast 1½d.		3½				
1½ pints milk per day at 1¼d.	1	1				
¼ stone oatmeal 2/2d		6½	Clothing: husband 1/2d., wife 8d.		1	10
1 lb. treacle 3½d., 1½ lb. sugar at 7d. lb.	1	2	each child 4d.		1	0
1½ oz. tea at 5d., 2 oz. coffee 1½d.		10½				
5 lb. meat 6d.	2	6				
	14	6½		£1	0	3

Besides the sum required for the fund which it is agreed every workman [ought] to lay in store for sickness and old age, I have set nothing down for butter, not being certain whether it is essential to health, although it is to be found in almost every cottage where the weekly income is not more than half the amount I have stated as necessary for the proper support of a family: tobacco, although it is in very general use, I have omitted for the same reason; neither have I reckoned anything for religious instruction, which is thought by great numbers of the people as necessary to their happiness as is their daily bread: something, therefore, ought to be allowed for it.

The above is not made out from my own knowledge of housekeeping only; I have elicited from the most intelligent & economical of my acquaintances their opinion upon the most weighty items of expenditure, which, if correct, would have made the amount rather more than is here set down. If, upon the most strict enquiry, no material alteration can be made in the detailed estimate of the necessary weekly expenditure of five persons, I conceive that a case will be made out that the average earnings of workmen are not sufficient for the proper support of their families; and will prove at the same time that if greater economy was practised, if less was spent at the public house, there would be a much greater degree of comfort in the workman's cottage than is to be met with at present.

H. Boyle.

* In family records of Boyle & Son, Leeds.

Economic and Demographic Implications   327

Table A.1 Employment

Urban	Rural
	Harewood Parish (West Riding of Yorkshire, 1793–97)
	Number of agricultural labourers: 38
	Average length of employment per annum: 223.34 days
	Employment through the year: 71.6%
Leeds (1839)	Westoning Parish (Bedfordshire, 1834)
Number of trades: 35	Number of agricultural labourers: 66
Average length of employment per annum: 10.5 months	Average length of employment per annum: 34.1 weeks
Employment through the year: 87.5%	Employment through the year: 65.6%

Table A.2 Cost of living

Urban

Proportions of rent, fuel, and others in the income of working-class family in Leeds in 1832 per week

	Rent (24d.) %	Fuel (9d.) %	Food (151d.) %	Clothing (34d.) %	Others (25d.) %
1. Family income in Leeds (296s. 4d.)	8.1	3.0	50.9	11.5	8.4
2. Average weekly wage for a male workman in Leeds in 1839 (227s. 7d.)	10.5	4.0			
3. Weekly wage for a male workman, corrected for employment per year in Leeds in 1839 (201s. 5d.)	11.9	4.5			

Rural

Proportions of rent, fuel and others in the income of rural families in Westoning Parish in 1832 per week

	Rent (12s. 4d) %	Fuel (15s. 4d.) %	Others (115s. 4d.) %
1. Family income in 1837 (145s. 3d.)	8.5	10.6	79.4
2. Average weekly wage for a male labourer in 1837 (108s. 8d.)	11.4	14.2	
3. Average weekly wage for a male labourer, corrected for employment per year in 1837 (107s. 9d.)	11.5	14.3	

19 Demographic Aspects of Urbanization in the Lower Yangzi Region of China, c.1500–1900

TS'UI-JUNG LIU
The Institute of Economics, Academia Sinica, Nankang, Taipei, Taiwan, Republic of China

According to Skinner's definition, the lower Yangzi region was the most urbanized region of China by the end of the nineteenth century.[1] In this chapter I attempt to relate the phenomenon of urbanization to demographic characteristics of the region, on the basis of data collected from local gazetteers and genealogies. Since these two sources are completely different I should first point out that at the present stage we can only consider some case-studies which will illustrate the similarities and dissimilarities between rural and urban areas in the lower Yangzi region.

In the first section we shall trace urbanization in the region from the Tang-Song transition to the Ming and Qing periods. In the second, we shall study the demographic characteristics of some urban and rural populations obtained from genealogical data. In the third, we shall try to relate the statistical findings relating to demographic characteristics to other factors, such as popular attitudes and institutional arrangements, depending for this on literary sources from the Ming and Qing periods. This will lead us to the conclusion that, in late imperial China, there did exist dissimilarities between the urban and the rural populations in the lower Yangzi region.

1. The phenomenon of urbanization

Many historians have demonstrated that the prospect and distribution of urban centres in China differed before and after the Tang-Song transition (c.800–1000). The lower Yangzi valley during Song times stood out as the most economically developed region with the largest concentration of urban centres and this has been studied in some detail by Shiba.[2] He has pointed out that southward migration speeded the process of urbanization in the lower

---

[1] G. W. Skinner (ed.), *The City in Late Imperial China* (Stanford, 1977), 211–29.
[2] Y. Shiba, 'Urbanization and the Development of Markets in the Lower Yangtze Valley', in J. Winthrop (ed.), *Crisis and Prosperity in Sung China* (Tucson, 1975), 13–48.

Yangzi valley and in the south in general. The percentage of city dwellers during the twelfth and thirteenth centuries varied from 7 per cent in She county (in modern Anhui) and 13 per cent in Yin county (in modern Zhejiang) to 38 per cent in Dantu county (in modern Jiangsu). Moreover, from the data relating to stations for collecting commercial tax on goods in transit in 1077, he analysed the distribution and operation of the urban economic hierarchy in regional cities, local cities, and in central and intermediate market towns. In short, the essentially self-sufficient rural economy of the pre-Tang period was transformed and became more specialized, commercialized, and urbanized. This process was called by scholars 'mediaeval revolution in market structure and urbanization'.[3] In this respect the lower Yangzi valley outranked other Chinese regions.

With this historical background in mind, in this section we shall concentrate on the development of urbanization in the lower Yangzi valley during the Ming and Qing periods (1368–1911). In the discussion that follows, I shall rely mainly on studies that are based on material found in the local gazetteers.

First and foremost, during the Ming and Qing periods many large market towns emerged which specialized in the grain trade or in handicraft manufactures. This development was closely related to agricultural production in the region having become more commercialized and to its emergence as the most important area for the production of cotton and silk goods during the period.[4] A careful scrutiny of the local gazetteers showed that around the Lake Tai and Yangzi delta region there were altogether fifty-two towns which specialized in cotton goods, twenty-five which specialized in silk goods, and thirteen which specialized in the grain trade. Of these only one specialized in both grain and cotton goods, whilst there were eighty-eight other towns each of which specialized in one staple only.[5] This gives a picture of a highly specialized system and of division of labour in the area, especially in its core region.

We should note, however, that not all these towns maintained their prosperity throughout the Ming–Qing era. Nor did they grow or decline at similar rates. Most of the cotton towns were located around the Yangzi delta, and their growth or decline was much affected by shifts in transport routes. The silk towns tended to be in the Lake Tai area. They gained in importance during the late Ming period, and continued to grow during the Qing era; they even recovered quickly after the interruption caused by the Taiping rebellion. Their growth undoubtedly depended on the expansion of the silk trade and in turn helped to accelerate the commercialization of agricultural production in

---

[3] M. Elvin, *The Pattern of the Chinese Past* (Stanford, 1973), 164; Skinner, *City in Late Imperial China*, 23.

[4] Liu Ts'ui-jung, 'Specialization in Production in South China during the Ming–Qing Periods' (in Chinese), *Ta-lu tsa-chi*, 56: 3–4 (1978), 1–35; Liu Shih-chi, 'Specialized Market Towns in the Jiangnan Area during the Ming-Qing periods' (in Chinese), *Shih-huo Monthly*, 8: 6–7 (1978). 274–91, 326–37, 365–80.

[5] Liu Shih-chi, 'Specialized Market Towns'.

the surrounding rural areas. During the course of their development, the concentration of population and commercial functions of some of these towns even surpassed those of the county or prefectural city. The towns which specialized in the grain trade were mainly located around Suzhou which was the largest city in the lower Yangzi region during the mid-nineteenth century. This situation reflected a shift in agricultural production from the lower Yangzi core area to the middle Yangzi valley during the seventeenth century. Thus the rice area around Lake Tai became deficient in grain and had to rely on shipments from Hubei and Hunan during the early Qing period and thereafter on shipments from Sichuan.[6]

Some scholars have tried to consider the quantitative aspects of urbanization in addition to changes in the nature of the towns, by investigating changes in the total number of towns. For instance, a study of the Lake Tai area showed that by the end of the eighteenth century there were altogether thirty-six towns in Wujiang, Tongxiang, Guian, and Wucheng counties. Only sixteen of them were founded between 1368 and 1795, the others were either direct descendants of towns which already existed at the beginning of the Ming dynasty, or revivals of such towns. Moreover, the increase occurred mainly during the eighteenth century.[7] In a more comprehensive study which covered eight prefectures and one sub-prefecture situated in the core area of the lower Yangzi region it was shown that the number of market towns in this area increased consistently throughout the Ming and Qing periods. According to this study the estimated number of market towns at the beginning of the twentieth century was between 1,162 and 1,344. It was estimated that fifty-six of them contained at least 1,000 households, and of these ten contained more than 10,000 households by the end of the eighteenth century. In some counties remarkably high percentages of the population were recorded as urban. For example, in Wujiang county in 1744, the households of the twelve market towns in the county accounted for 35 per cent of all households in the county. In Changshou and Zhaowen counties together, in 1903 the eighty towns in those counties contained 19.6 per cent of their total population. Basing himself on this evidence, Liu Shih-chi has suggested that both Rozman's estimate that 7 per cent of the population in Jiangsu province during the nineteenth century were urban, and Skinner's estimate of an urban population in the lower Yangzi region of 7.4 per cent in 1843 and 10.6 per cent in 1893 were too low.[8]

---

[6] Liu Shih-chi, 'Specialized Market Towns'; Chuan Han-sheng, 'The Grain Trade in Suzhou during the mid-Qing period' (in Chinese), in *Zhongguo jingjishi luncong (Studies in Chinese Economic History)* (Hong Kong, 1972), 567–82.

[7] Shih Chin, 'Peasant Economy and Rural Society in the Lake Tai Area, 1368–1840', Ph.D. diss., University of California, Berkeley (1981), 92–3.

[8] Liu Shih-chi, 'A Quantitative Analysis of Market Towns in the Jiangnan area during the Ming–Qing periods' (in Chinese), *Ssu-yu-yen*, 16: 2 (1978), 128–49; id., 'Some Reflections on Urbanization and the Historical Development of Market Towns in the lower Yangtze Region, ca. 1500–1900', *The American Asian Review*, 2: 1 (1984), 1–27.

Demographic Aspects of Urbanization

Since the classification of urban centres by attributed rough population size could raise problems, and the data from local gazetteers could be inconsistent because of their varying quality, it is difficult to arrive at a precise measure of urbanization in pre-census China. Moreover, a recent attempt to estimate the degree of urbanization throughout Chinese history, in which it was suggested that urbanization reached its peak during the twelfth century when 22.4 per cent of the population were supposed to live in towns, and that there was a trough in the nineteenth century when the percentages urban were 6.9 per cent in 1820 and 7.0 per cent in 1893, has been shown not to be plausible, particularly on the basis of historical evidence relating to the lower Yangzi region.[9] I shall, therefore, in this chapter abandon attempts to estimate the percentage of urbanization from problematic classifications and population figures.

2. Demographic characteristics

During the past few years there have been some studies in historical demography based on data collected from Chinese genealogies. Although the results are as yet meagre, they do provide basic information on which to base a discussion of the demographic characteristics of past Chinese populations. This section is based on these case-studies, which have been selected to contain both rural and urban populations in the lower Yangzi region. The findings which relate to marriage, fertility, mortality, and migration are discussed below.

2.1 Marriage

We shall begin with two examples which illustrate differences in marriage behaviour between rural and urban families. In Table 19.1 we see information relating to the Yan family, residing at Qingqi, a market town in Tongxiang county, Zhejiang, and in Table 19.2 we see the case of the Zhou lineage, residing in a rural district south of the county town of Wujin, Jiangsu. In both tables the data have been arranged by generation showing numbers of recorded males and in-marrying females classified by their marital status. Some special individual events are given in notes below the tables.

Comparing these two cases we may note the following points:

1. The percentage of unmarried men aged 50 and older was, in general, negligible. In the Yan family there is no record of any man dying unmarried at an age exceeding 50 years; in the Zhou lineage there were altogether twenty-five such men in generations 53 to 61 and they amounted to only 1.4 per cent

---

[9] Chao Kang and Chen Chung-yi, 'Urban Population in Chinese History' (in Chinese), *Shih-huo Monthly*, 13: 3–4 (1983), 109–31; Liang Keng-yao, 'Remarks after Reading "Urban Population in Chinese History"', ibid. 132–7.

Table 19.1 Marriages of Yan family: an example of the urban population

Generation	Year of birth known	Recorded males						Recorded in-married females					
		Married	Engaged	Unmarried Died before 50th birthday	Age at death not known	Still alive[h]	Total	First wife	Second wife	Third wife	Fourth wife	Concubine	Total
1	?	1					1	1					1
2	1558	1					1	1				1	2
3	1597	3					3	3					3
4	1621–38	6					6	6					6
5	1653–77	6			3		9	6	2	1		1	10
6	1673–1713	10					10	10	4				14
7	1701–46	11			4		15	11	2			3	16
8	1726–88	16[a]			4		20	15				6	21
9	1756–1829	27	1[b]		3		31	27	4			7	38
10	1791–1854	39		5[e]	10		54	40[f]	5[g]	3		5	53
11	1815–81	31	1[c]	7	5	9	53	31	6	1	1	1	40
12	1842–92	8	2[d]	1	1	20	31	8	2				10
13	1871–1890	0				7	8	0					0
Total		159	4	13	30	36	242	159	25	5	1	24	214

[a] One man was uxorilocally married to a member of the Shen family.
[b] Died at age 35.
[c] Died at age 23.
[d] Aged 13 and 15 respectively in 1892.
[e] One man who died aged 40 was not married because he was an epileptic.
[f] One woman recorded as first wife after a predecessor to whom her husband was engaged died before marrying; another woman was engaged and died before marrying, but was not recorded as first wife.
[g] One woman was engaged but died before marrying.
[h] Still alive in 1892, when the family genealogy was compiled.

Source: Qingqi Yanshi jiapu (The genealogy of the Yan family at Qingqi).

Table 19.2 Marriages of Zhou lineage: an example of the rural population

Generation	Year of birth known	Recorded Males						Recorded in-married females					
		Married	Unmarried				Total	First wife	Second wife	Third wife	Fourth wife	Concubine	Total
			Died before 50th birthday	Died after 50th birthday	Age at death not known	Still alive[b]							
46	1365[a]	1					1	1					1
47	1399–1401	2					2	2					2
48	1422–28	3					3	3					3
49	1488–52	4					4	4					4
50	1466–76	8					8	8					8
51	1496–1523	29			1		30	29					29
52	1522–70	40	4		5		49	40	2				42
53	1542–1620	54		1	9		64	54	6				60
54	1575–1637	74[c]			8		82	73	5				78
55	1592–1697	80	2	1	14		97	80	8	1		3	92
56	1620–1720	78[c]	1		41		120	78	6	1			85
57	1644–1760	122[c]	1	4	14		141	121	8	1			130
58	1656–1807	143	5	7	28		183[d]	143	7	2			152
59	1704–1814	170[c]	10	4	37		221	170	16	2	1	1	190
60	1729–1845	185[c]	14	4	36		239	185	19			1	205
61	1739–1890	138	13	4	41	4	200[d]	138	10	1			149
62	1774–1902	88	16		37	8	149	88	4				92
63	1798–1904	46	2		18	29	95	46	5				51
64	1821–1903	13	2		7	29	51	13	1				14
65	1899–1902					5	5	0					0
Total		1,278	70	25	296	75	1,744	1,276	97	8	1	5	1,387

[a] This man moved to Shilipai in Wujin county to start this lineage.
[b] For those still alive in 1904 when the genealogy was compiled, the birth years for those in Generation 61 were 1882–90, in Generation 62 1882–1902, in Generation 63 1867–1902, and in Generation 64 1887–1903.
[c] In these generations, there were cases of uxorilocally married men; Generation 54 and 57 each had one such man but the surname of wife was not recorded; Generations 56, 59, and 60 each also had one such man but the surname of wife was recorded.
[d] Generation 58 one man and Generation 61 two men were adopted by other families (Shi, Hun, and Wang) and details of their marriages and deaths were not known.

Source: *Biling Shilipai Zhou shi zongpu* (The genealogy of the Zhou lineage in Shilipai village in Wujin county).

of all recorded males. It would seem that marriage was even more universal in the town than in the countryside. In both examples, there are cases of unmarried men who died at ages below 50, or whose age at death was unknown (most of them are only known as having died young). Such men probably died before being able to marry and cannot be regarded as single survivors. In both cases, a fair number of men who were still alive when the genealogies were compiled are listed; they were still young and likely to marry in due course.

2. The remarriage rate of men may be investigated by computing the rate of second and third marriages (calculated as the ratio of second to first wives, and of third to second wives respectively). In the Yan family, taking all generations together, these ratios came to 15.7 per cent, and 20 per cent respectively. In the Zhou lineage they were 7.6 and 8.2 per cent. The ratios in the Yan family were higher and those of the Zhou family lower than the average computed for twenty-three families and lineages in the lower and middle Yangzi regions,[10] which came to 11.3 per cent for second, and 10.8 per cent for third marriages. When differences between these twenty-three groups are compared, it seems that the rates were lower for lineages in rural areas than for those in towns. Neither the Yan nor the Zhou genealogies record any cases of remarriages of women who had married into the family. It has been found in previous studies that there were more women in the rural areas who remarried after the death of their husband.[11]

3. Men generally remarried after the death of their wives, but they could also take a concubine or concubines during their wives' lifetime. Concubinage was permitted by Chinese law, though the regulations differed in different periods. For instance, Ming law permitted the common people to take concubines only after a man had reached the age of 40, provided that he had no son. However, this restriction was relaxed by Qing law.[12] Rules and instructions adopted by a family or lineage could also influence the marriage behaviour of its members. Whether a man could afford to take a concubine also depended on his wealth. These institutional and economic conditions may help to explain the difference found in the rates of concubinage (number of concubines divided by the total number of in-marrying women) in different generations of the same family, or in families of different social and economic groups. For example, in the Yan family, the ratio of concubines to wives was 11.2 per cent, whereas in the Zhou lineage it only came to 0.4 per cent. The fact that the Yans were town dwellers, whereas the Zhous had engaged in farming for many generations makes this difference easily comprehensible.

---

[10] Liu Ts'ui-jung, 'The Growth and Migration of Population during the Ming-Qing Periods' (in Chinese), in Hsu Cho-yun et al. (eds.), *Papers from the Seminar on Chinese Social and Economic History* (Taibei, 1983), 288.

[11] Ibid. 289.

[12] Chen Guyuan, *Zhongguo hunyinshi (A History of Marriage in China)* (Taibei, repr. 1975), 68–9.

Furthermore, among the 24 concubines in the Yan family, only one was taken by a man (born in 1558) during the Ming period.

4. We should also note in passing that uxorilocal marriage was found both in the Yan family and the Zhou lineage. There was only one such Yan marriage in the eighth generation, whilst there were five in the Zhou lineage in generations 54, 56, 57, 59, and 60. Though the reason for these occurrences was not mentioned in the genealogies, the men concerned could all have been very poor.

2.2 Fertility

The fertility of Chinese populations in the past can be reconstructed from the genealogies. Conjugal families can be reconstituted from the vital dates relating to parents and sons (those for daughters were not generally recorded), and these can be used to construct fertility rates. Here we shall study estimates relating to two lineages in the core and one at the periphery of the lower Yangzi region for cohorts of first wives and husbands. The Yan family will also be studied as an urban example. Age-specific fertility rates (ASFRs) and their sums (total fertility or TF) relating to male births to first wives are listed in Table 19.3 and in Table 19.4 they are listed for the husband. The following points from these tables may be noted.

1. The estimates of total fertility derived from the weighted average of the three lineages showed that in general the fertility of husbands exceeded that of first wives. The unweighted estimates for the Yan family gave the same result. This was obviously due to the fact that a husband's fertility was affected by remarriage, as the births of all sons born to the first wife, other wives, and concubines were taken into account. The difference between the fertility of the husband and that of the wife was particularly marked in the Yan family, as the remarriage rate in that family had also been higher.

2. When looking at changes over time it would appear that cohort fertility of both husbands and first wives who were born during the eighteenth century tended to be higher than that of others. In the case of the Wang lineage in Tongcheng, Anhui for which data are available for the period 1400 to 1800, it would appear that total fertility also peaked in the cohorts born between 1448 and 1497. In the Zhu lineage in Jiangdu, Jiangsu, total fertility was also high for those born between 1548 and 1597. Whether these findings have any implications for population growth in China during the sixteenth century remains uncertain. At any rate, the findings that total fertility was higher for cohorts born during the eighteenth century seems at least plausible in the light of our knowledge that the population of China as a whole increased during that century.

3. The difference between the fertility of the urban and the rural populations in the past remains a puzzle for the student of Chinese historical demography. The estimates in Tables 19.3 and 19.4 indicate that, on average,

Table 19.3 Fertility: male births per first wife

Lineage	Cohorts	No.	Age-specific fertility rates							Total fertility
			15–19	20–24	25–29	30–34	35–39	40–44	45–49	
Zhou	1698–1747	31	0.045	0.124	0.100	0.087	0.087	0.000	0.000	2.22
	1748–97	91	0.029	0.110	0.111	0.096	0.073	0.028	0.000	2.24
	1798–1817	35	0.034	0.091	0.102	0.126	0.056	0.023	0.000	2.16
Weighted average		157	0.033	0.109	0.107	0.101	0.072	0.021	0.000	2.22
Cumulative			0.033	0.142	0.249	0.350	0.422	0.443	0.443	
Zhu	1548–97	30	0.073	0.108	0.119	0.080	0.072	0.017	0.010	2.40
	1598–1647	38	0.042	0.086	0.106	0.098	0.071	0.027	0.007	2.19
	1648–97	62	0.019	0.091	0.113	0.093	0.048	0.027	0.004	1.98
	1698–1747	96	0.027	0.121	0.118	0.087	0.069	0.020	0.016	2.29
	1748–97	179	0.028	0.115	0.112	0.096	0.092	0.033	0.005	2.41
	1798–1817	84	0.033	0.098	0.082	0.116	0.055	0.032	0.000	2.08
Weighted average		489	0.031	0.108	0.108	0.096	0.077	0.028	0.007	2.28
Cumulative			0.031	0.139	0.247	0.343	0.420	0.448	0.455	
Wang	1398–1447	14	0.071	0.086	0.100	0.100	0.043	0.000	0.014	2.07
	1448–97	23	0.026	0.130	0.139	0.061	0.122	0.046	0.010	2.67
	1498–1547	48	0.079	0.125	0.072	0.052	0.045	0.023	0.021	2.09
	1548–97	44	0.091	0.068	0.064	0.042	0.048	0.043	0.022	1.89
	1598–1647	60	0.057	0.100	0.080	0.069	0.069	0.036	0.022	2.17
	1648–97	153	0.056	0.116	0.110	0.107	0.075	0.048	0.008	2.60
	1698–1747	234	0.057	0.117	0.155	0.120	0.097	0.053	0.007	3.03
	1748–97	245	0.050	0.124	0.123	0.127	0.083	0.042	0.004	2.77
	1798–1817	62	0.029	0.136	0.110	0.063	0.102	0.023	0.000	2.32
Weighted average		883	0.055	0.117	0.120	0.103	0.082	0.043	0.009	2.65
Cumulative			0.055	0.172	0.292	0.395	0.477	0.520	0.529	
Yan	1597–1842	43	0.047	0.125	0.101	0.072	0.057	0.046	0.000	2.24
Cumulative			0.047	0.172	0.273	0.345	0.402	0.448	0.448	

Sources: Biling Shilipai Zhou shi zongpu (see Table 19.2); Weiyang Jiangdu Zhu shi shixiou zupu (The tenth edition of the genealogy of the Zhu lineage in Jiangdu); Tongcheng Wang shi zougpu (The genealogy of the Wang lineage in Tongcheng); Qiuqqi Yen shi jiapu (see Table 19.1).

Demographic Aspects of Urbanization 337

Table 19.4 Fertility: male births per husband

Lineage	Cohorts	No.	Age-specific fertility rates								Total fertility
			15–19	20–24	25–29	30–34	35–39	40–44	45–49	50–54	55–59	
Zhou	1698–1747	47	0.013	0.060	0.080	0.124	0.057	0.069	0.050	0.021	0.000	2.37
	1748–97	109	0.013	0.068	0.089	0.099	0.074	0.061	0.035	0.014	0.000	2.27
	1798–1817	45	0.004	0.071	0.080	0.118	0.093	0.035	0.020	0.009	0.000	2.15
Weighted average		201	0.011	0.067	0.085	0.109	0.074	0.057	0.035	0.015	0.000	2.27
Cumulative			0.011	0.078	0.163	0.272	0.346	0.403	0.438	0.453	0.453	
Zhu	1548–97	42	0.024	0.106	0.110	0.132	0.077	0.052	0.020	0.025	0.017	2.82
	1598–1647	49	0.012	0.041	0.110	0.049	0.104	0.053	0.037	0.051	0.007	2.32
	1648–97	105	0.010	0.038	0.071	0.085	0.073	0.085	0.056	0.021	0.022	2.31
	1698–1747	120	0.012	0.082	0.112	0.087	0.076	0.046	0.033	0.013	0.006	2.34
	1748–97	269	0.018	0.079	0.097	0.090	0.088	0.062	0.026	0.007	0.006	2.37
	1798–1817	145	0.015	0.077	0.105	0.103	0.068	0.042	0.019	0.004	0.003	2.16
Weighted average		730	0.015	0.072	0.099	0.091	0.080	0.058	0.030	0.013	0.008	2.33
Cumulative			0.015	0.087	0.186	0.277	0.357	0.415	0.445	0.458	0.466	
Wang	1398–1447	14	0.000	0.100	0.143	0.071	0.043	0.000	0.029	0.000	0.030	2.08
	1448–97	31	0.026	0.123	0.095	0.095	0.081	0.064	0.040	0.018	0.019	2.81
	1498–1547	71	0.048	0.110	0.100	0.079	0.061	0.037	0.031	0.018	0.017	2.51
	1548–97	67	0.075	0.066	0.072	0.027	0.040	0.041	0.016	0.019	0.018	1.87
	1598–1647	84	0.057	0.057	0.075	0.083	0.065	0.052	0.070	0.036	0.024	2.60
	1648–97	173	0.028	0.091	0.116	0.098	0.091	0.069	0.037	0.013	0.004	2.74
	1698–1747	289	0.019	0.078	0.116	0.109	0.103	0.076	0.042	0.014	0.004	2.81
	1748–97	327	0.021	0.074	0.103	0.125	0.107	0.070	0.040	0.022	0.011	2.87
	1798–1807[a]	57	0.021	0.071	0.083	0.082	0.094	0.053	0.077	0.023	0.000	2.52
Weighted average		1,113	0.029	0.080	0.103	0.101	0.091	0.064	0.042	0.019	0.010	2.70
Cumulative			0.029	0.109	0.212	0.313	0.404	0.468	0.510	0.529	0.539	
Yan	1597–1832[a]	50	0.050	0.089	0.094	0.053	0.083	0.031	0.047	0.042	0.017	2.53
Cumulative			0.050	0.139	0.233	0.286	0.396	0.400	0.447	0.489	0.506	

[a] Since the Wang genealogy was compiled in 1866 and the Yan genealogy in 1892, to avoid including those who had not completed their reproductive lives the cohorts were cut off 10 years earlier than those of the first wives.

Sources: See Table 19.2.

total fertility for the two lineages in Jiangsu (Zhou and Zhu) was lower (2.22 and 2.28 respectively for the first wife) than that for the one lineage in Anhui (Wang: 2.65 for the first wife). However, the difference between them may reflect that one was resident at the periphery and the other two in the core region, rather than that they were respectively urban and rural. It can be argued that the core of the region must have been more urbanized than the periphery. Total fertility for Yan first wives (2.24) was similar to that among the Zhou and the Zhu. Since only a very small number of Yan first wives were observed (43 born between 1597 and 1842) it would seem wise at the present stage of the research to treat the representativeness of these figures for the urban population with caution.

4. As regards the ASFRs there are some irregularities caused by small numbers. It was clear, however, that ASFRs for first wives reached a maximum in the age-groups 20–24 and 25–29, and those for husbands in the age-groups 25–29 and 30–34.

Here it may be appropriate to present some figures relating to widowhood among first wives, which might explain some of the variation in total fertility between the core and the periphery. In Table 19.5 we see the number of widows as a percentage of first wives among the Zhu (core) and the Wang (periphery). The widows were classified by their birth cohort and age at widowhood into two broad age-groups. When we compare the figures in Table 19.5 with those in Table 19.3 it is clear that total fertility in both the

Table 19.5 Percentages of widows among first wives

Cohort	Number of first wives		Widowed at age 20–44				Widowed at age 45 or over			
			Zhu		Wang		Zhu		Wang	
	Zhu	Wang	No.	%	No.	%	No.	%	No.	%
1548–97	30	44	4	13.3	8	18.2	8	26.7	20	45.5
1598–1647	38	60	7	14.3	17	28.3	11	28.9	24	40.0
1648–97	62	153	16	25.8	27	17.6	23	37.1	53	34.6
1698–1747	96	234	13	13.5	30	12.8	23	24.0	82	35.0
1748–97	179	245	31	17.3	42	17.1	57	31.8	68	27.8
1798–1817	84	62	19	22.6	17	27.4	27	32.1	12	19.4
Total	489	798	90	18.4	141	17.7	149	30.5	259	32.5

Sources: Weiyan Jiangdu Zhu shi shixiou zupu (The tenth edition of the genealogy of the Zhu lineage in Jiangdu) (1881 edn.); Tongcheng Wangshi zongpu (The genealogy of the Wang lineage in Tongcheng) (1866 edn.).

Wang and the Zhu lineages was lower in those cohorts in which the proportion of young widows was higher. Changes over time were quite consistent. The fertility rates estimated in Tables 19.3 and 19.4 were based on data relating to conjugal families in which information about vital dates was complete. Families for which this information was incomplete were excluded from the calculation. To investigate what difference it would make if both types of family were taken into consideration, the data were arranged by number of sons in each family, classified by the father's cohort, and this is

Demographic Aspects of Urbanization

shown in Tables 19.6 and 19.7 for the Zhou and Wang lineages respectively. These tables listed families with different numbers of sons (ranging from 0 to 9) according to their father's birth cohorts and divided them into two groups: those in which the father had died before reaching the age of 50 and those in which he died at age 50 or over.

When the two lineages are compared it is striking that the mean number of sons in the Zhou lineage (1.6) was lower than that of the Wang (1.8). Both

Table 19.6 Number of sons in families classified by father's cohort and ages at death: Wujiu Zhou Lineage

Classification	1400 cohorts b. 1398–1447			1450 cohorts b. 1448–97			1500 cohorts b. 1498–1547		
	d50+	d−50	All	d50+	d−50	All	d50+	d−50	All
No. of sons									
0	0	0	0	1	0	1	4	8	12
1	3	0	3	3	0	3	10	7	17
2	2	0	2	4	0	4	10	4	14
3				2	0	2	7	1	8
4				1	1	2	3	0	3
5				0	0	0	3	0	3
6				1	0	1			
7				1	0	1			
Total no. of sons	7	0	7	34	4	38	78	18	96
No. who died young	0	0	0	0	0	0	0	2	2
No. of families	5	0	5	13	1	14	37	20	57
No. of remarriages	0	0	0	0	0	0	4	0	4
Average no. of sons per family	1.4	0	1.4	2.6	4.0	2.7	2.1	0.9	1.7
% who died young	0	0	0	0	0	0	0	11.1	2.1
% re-married	0	0	0	0	0	0	10.8	0	7.0
% of families without sons	0	0	0	7.7	0	7.1	10.8	40.0	21.1

Classification	1550 cohorts b. 1548–97			1600 cohorts b. 1598–1647			1650 cohorts b. 1648–97		
	d50+	d−50	All	d50+	d−50	All	d50+	d−50	All
No. of sons									
0	12	11	23	6	10	16	11	12	23
1	14	10	24	25	11	36	24	32	56
2	20	6	26	17	7	24	24	17	41
3	5	3	8	13	2	15	12	5	17
4	3	3	6	2	1	3	9	3	12
5	2	1	3	1	2	3	6	0	6
6				0	1	1			
7				1	0	1			
Total no. of sons	91	48	139	118	51	169	174	93	267
No. who died young	2	3	5	14	6	20	15	7	22
No. of families	56	34	65	34		99	86	69	155
No. of remarriages	5	1	6	8	2	10	9	4	13
Average no. of sons per family	1.6	1.4	1.5	1.8	1.5	1.7	2.0	1.4	1.7
% who died young	2.2	6.3	3.6	11.9	11.8	8.6	7.5	8.2	
% re-married	8.9	2.9	6.7	12.3	5.9	10.1	10.5	5.8	8.4
% of families without sons	21.4	32.4	25.6	9.2	29.4	16.2	12.8	17.4	14.8

Classification	1700 cohorts b. 1698–1747			1750 cohorts b. 1748–97			1800 cohorts b. 1798–1848		
	d50+	d−50	All	d50+	d−50	All	d50+	d−50	All
No. of sons									
0	11	22	33	13	37	50	9	66	75
1	44	39	83	35	56	91	17	54	71
2	40	19	59	37	31	68	17	33	50
3	17	13	30	25	14	39	15	15	30
4	9	4	13	6	4	10	4	5	9
5	1	0	1	1	3	4	3	1	4
6				1	0	1	0	1	1
7									
Total no. of sons	216	132	348	219	191	410	127	196	323
No. who died young	14	12	26	14	12	26	21	72	93
No. of families	122	97	219	118	145	263	65	175	240
No. of remarriages	7	2	9	16	10	26	6	16	22
Average no. of sons per family	1.8	1.4	1.6	1.9	1.3	1.6	2.0	1.1	1.4
% who died young	6.5	9.1	7.5	6.4	6.3	6.3	16.5	36.7	28.8
% re-married	5.7	2.1	4.1	13.6	6.9	9.9	9.2	9.1	9.2
% of families without sons	9.0	22.7	15.1	5.9	25.5	19.0	13.9	37.7	31.3

Classification	Total		
	d50+	d−50	All
No. of sons			
0	67	166	233
1	175	209	384
2	171	117	288
3	96	53	149
4	37	21	58
5	17	7	24
6	2	2	2
7	2	0	2
Total no. of sons	1,064	733	1,797
No. who died young	80	114	194
No. of families	567	575	1,142
No. of remarriages	55	35	90
Average no. of sons per family	1.9	1.3	1.6
% who died young	7.5	15.6	10.8
% re-married	9.7	6.1	7.9
% of families without sons	11.8	28.9	20.4

For d50+ read: died on or after 50th birthday; for d−50 read died before 50th birthday. Those whose age at death was unknown were included in the group dying before their 50th birthday.

Sources: See Table 19.2.

values are less than the average total fertility of husbands listed in Table 19.4, because families for which information was incomplete, and also families without any sons, have been taken into consideration.

If we consider changes over time, movements in the average number of sons per family in both lineages were similar though slightly different in magnitude. The percentage of sons who died whilst still young (generally before their fifteenth birthday) amounted on average to 10.8 per cent among the Zhou and to 13.1 per cent among the Wang. The trend over time in this

Table 19.7 Number of sons in families classified by father's cohort and age at death: Tongcheng Wang lineage

Classification	1350 cohorts b. 1348–97			1400 cohorts b. 1398–1447			1450 cohorts b. 1448–97		
	d50+	d−50	All*	d50+	d−50	All	d50+	d−50	All
No. of sons									
0	0	0	0	0	1	1	0	1	1
1	4	0	4	6	7	13	11	5	16
2	2	0	2	4	2	6	4	6	10
3	0	0	0	5	4	9	6	3	9
4	0	0	0	3	3	6	6	6	12
5	1	0	1				2	1	3
6							0	0	0
7							0	1	1
8									
9									
Total no. of sons	13	0	13	41	35	76	71	62	133
No. who died young	0	0	0	2	2	4	0	0	0
No. of families	7	0	7	18	17	35	29	23	52
No. of remarriages	0	0	0	0	0	0	4	1	5
Average no. of sons per family	1.9	0	1.9	2.3	2.1	2.2	2.5	2.7	2.6
% who died young	0	0	0	4.9	5.7	5.3	0	0	0
% re-married	0	0	0	0	0	0	13.8	7.4	9.6
% of families without sons	0	0	0	0	5.9	2.9	0	4.4	1.9

Classification	1500 cohorts b. 1498–1547			1550 cohorts b. 1548–97			1600 cohorts b. 1598–1647		
	d50+	d−50	All	d50+	d−50	All	d50+	d−50	All
No. of sons									
0	12	12	24	9	31	40	5	16	21
1	20	23	43	29	25	52	20	34	54
2	19	18	37	17	17	34	20	12	32
3	17	10	27	14	6	20	16	11	27
4	7	2	9	7	3	10	8	6	14
5	2	3	5	1	0	1	5	1	6
6				0	0	0	2	0	2
7				0	0	0	1	0	1
8				0	2	2			
9									
Total no. of sons	147	112	259	136	105	241	184	120	304
No. who died young	2	1	3	18	21	39	11	13	24
No. of families	77	68	145	75	84	159	77	80	157
No. of remarriages	7	10	17	6	3	9	12	2	14
Average no. of sons per family	1.9	1.7	1.8	1.3	1.5	2.4	1.5	1.3	
% who died young	1.4	0.9	1.2	13.2	20.0	16.2	6.0	10.8	7.9
% re-married	9.1	14.7	11.7	8.0	3.6	5.7	15.6	2.5	8.9
% of families without sons	15.6	17.7	16.6	12.0	36.9	25.2	6.5	20.0	13.4

variable was not as regular as that in the average number of sons. However, it is of interest that fathers belonging to the cohorts born in the 1800s lost a fairly high percentage of their sons (28.8 per cent among the Zhou and 26.3 per cent among the Wang). This would imply that child mortality increased during the nineteenth century. We shall consider movements in mortality

Classification	1650 cohorts b. 1648–97			1700 cohorts b. 1698–1747			1750 cohorts b. 1748–97		
	d50+	d−50	All	d50+	d−50	All	d50+	d−50	All
No. of sons									
0	7	24	31	27	63	90	38	126	164
1	48	28	76	72	88	160	66	181	247
2	42	33	75	59	84	143	56	91	147
3	34	18	52	61	38	99	57	66	123
4	31	7	38	45	22	67	45	29	74
5	8	4	12	21	10	31	22	13	35
6	6	2	8	7	2	9	11	6	17
7	3	0	3				8	0	8
8							0	4	4
9							0	2	2
Total no. of sons	455	208	663	700	520	1,220	761	828	1,589
No. who died young	28	18	46	34	48	82	115	132	247
No. of families	179	116	295	292	307	599	303	518	821
No. of remarriages	15	11	26	41	17	58	45	43	88
Average no. of sons per family	2.5	1.8	2.3	2.4	1.7	2.0	2.5	1.6	1.9
% who died young	6.2	8.7	6.9	4.9	9.2	6.7	15.1	15.9	15.5
% re-married	8.4	9.5	8.8	14.0	5.5	9.7	14.9	8.3	10.7
% of families without sons	3.9	20.7	10.5	9.3	20.5	15.0	12.5	24.3	20.0

Classification	1800 cohorts b. 1798–1817(46)[a]			Total		
	d50+	d−50	All	d50+	d−50	All
No. of sons						
0	4	241	245	102	515	617
1	10	265	285	294	656	950
2	15	120	135	238	383	621
3	13	55	68	223	211	434
4	12	31	43	164	109	273
5	3	18	21	65	50	115
6	1	5	6	27	15	42
7	0	1	1	12	2	14
8				0	6	6
9				0	2	2
Total no. of sons	158	921	1,079	2,666	2,991	5,577
No. who died young	35	248	284	245	484	729
No. of families	68	736	804	1,125	1,949	3,074
No. of remarriages	19	87	106	149	174	323
Average no. of sons per family	2.3	1.3	1.3	2.4	1.5	1.8
% who died young	22.2	27.0	26.3	9.2	26.6	13.1
% re-married	27.9	11.8	13.2	13.2	8.9	10.5
% of families without sons	5.9	32.7	30.5	9.1	26.4	20.1

[a] For those who died at ages 50 and over, the observation ended in 1817.

Source: Tongcheng Wang shi zongpu (see Table 19.3).

later; here it will be sufficient to note that Chinese genealogical records relating to mortality are incomplete, and that it is particularly difficult to estimate child mortality, as vital dates were not generally available for those who died young.

The frequencies of remarriage listed in Tables 19.6 and 19.7 are limited to second marriages, i.e. a man who married for the third time was only counted once. There was no discernible trend in the percentage of remarriages.

It is striking that in the two genealogies considered, the percentages of families without any sons were fairly high and quite similar (Zhou: 20.4 per cent; Wang: 20.1 per cent). A peak was reached for the cohorts of 1550, and again for the cohorts of 1800. In the latter cohort, almost one-third of fathers had no sons. This suggests that there was a decrease in the fertility of men during the nineteenth century. The high percentage of families without sons was closely related to the practice of adoption in Chinese families. But we shall not consider this subject here, as it is more important for family history than for historical demography.

2.3 Mortality

I have mentioned that Chinese genealogies provide only meagre data for the estimation of childhood mortality. Another deficiency in the genealogical records relating to mortality is that, even for adults, the number of those whose dates of birth and death were known was smaller than that of those for whom only the date of birth was given.[13] The first defect makes it almost impossible to estimate childhood mortality from genealogical data directly. An indirect solution would be extrapolation based on model life tables. Alternatively, all the data relating to one family or lineage could be combined, especially where the numbers are small.

In this chapter our discussion of mortality will be based on two life tables (see Table 19.8) which have been constructed for one group of urban and one of rural males. The urban group included members of the Yan family from Qingqi, the Zhou family from Nanxun (both towns around Lake Tai), and the Qin lineage from the city of Guiji (the county town of Shaoxing) along the Hangzhou bay. For the table of rural males, those belonging to the Wang lineage of Tongcheng were selected.

As may be seen from Table 19.8, the observed number of deaths of urban males was small, even though data from three genealogies were combined. In both parts of the table the numbers of observed deaths of males below the age of 15 was very small. Therefore, the values of $q(x)$ were computed from data beginning with the age-group 15–19 and ending with that of 80+. The values were then graduated and extrapolated to the beginning of life.[14] The results show that the mortality of members of these two populations was much the same, with a slight excess for the urban group. However, as the urban section was based on relatively small numbers this finding can only be regarded as provisional.

We shall use the table for the Wang lineage to investigate changes in

[13] Liu Ts'ui-jung, 'The Demographic Dynamics of Some Clans in the Lower Yangtze Area, ca.1400–1900', *Academia Economic Papers*, 9: 1 (1981), 115–60.

[14] Yuan I-chin, 'Life Tables for a Southern Chinese Family from 1365 to 1849', *Human Biology*, 3: 2 (1931), 157–79. The model life table used was Coale and Demeny's Model West table, levels 7 and 8 respectively.

mortality over time. Male adults in that family were divided into six cohorts: the 1500 cohort, born between 1498 and 1547, all of whom had died by 1627; the 1550 cohort, born between 1548 and 1597, all of whom had died by 1677, and so on to the 1700 cohort, born between 1698 and 1747, all of whom had died by 1827, and a final 1750 cohort, born between 1748 and 1782, all of whom were dead by 1862. Life tables constructed for these cohorts based on adult deaths yielded an expectation of life at age 15 amounting in successive cohorts to 41.88 years, 34.14 years, 37.87 years, 42.61 years, 40.53 years, and 38.01 years respectively. The highest mortality was experienced by the 1550 cohort, all of whose members had died by 1677. This seems reasonable as the transition crisis of the Ming–Qing period occurred during the lifetime of

Table 19.8 Life tables for urban and rural males

Age	Urban Qingqi: Yan b. 1558–1872 Nanxun: Zhou b. 1719–1887 Guiji: Qin b. 1615–1861				Rural Tongcheng: Wang b. 1400–1782			
	No.[a]	$q(x)$	$l(x)$	$e(x)$	No.[a]	$q(x)$	$l(x)$	$e(x)$
0–1	—	0.1821	10,000	34.39		0.2056	10,000	35.53
1–4	2	0.1065	8,179	40.97	16	0.1203	7,944	43.63
5–9	2	0.0316	7,308	41.69		0.0322	6,988	45.43
10–14	1	0.0227	7,077	37.97		0.0232	6,763	41.86
15–19	3	0.0316	6,916	33.79	21	0.0322	6.606	37.79
20–24	12	0.0441	6,697	29.82	48	0.0454	6,393	33.97
25–29	16	0.0606	6,402	26.08	84	0.0504	6,103	30.46
30–34	11	0.0824	6,014	22.60	103	0.0651	5,703	26.95
35–39	19	0.1104	5,518	19.40	110	0.0744	5,418	23.65
40–44	15	0.1463	4,909	16.50	130	0.0950	5,015	20.35
45–49	19	0.1914	4,191	13.90	174	0.1404	4,539	17.32
50–54	30	0.2473	3,389	11.60	193	0.1812	3,902	14.63
55–59	13	0.3153	2,551	9.59	217	0.2489	3,195	12.31
60–64	14	0.3969	1,747	7.85	173	0.2641	2.400	10.56
65–69	10	0.4936	1,054	6.36	176	0.3651	1,766	8.46
70–74	15	0.6065	534	5.12	133	0.4346	1,121	6.88
75–79	3	0.7356	210	4.16	97	0.5607	634	5.25
80+	1	1.0000	56	3.73	76	1.0000	270	3.74

[a] No. is the observed number of deaths.

Sources: *Qingqi Yanshi jiapu* (*The genealogy of the Yan family at Qingqi*) (1892 edn.); *Nanxun Zhou shi jiapu* (*The genealogy of the Zhou family at Nanxun*) (1911 edn.); *Guiji Qin shi zongpu* (The genealogy of Qin lineage in Guiji) (1911 edn.); *Tongcheng Wangshi zongpu* (The genealogy of the Wang lineage in Tongcheng) (1866 edn.).

members of this cohort. Life expectancy in succeeding cohorts improved, up to the cohort whose members had died by the end of the eighteenth century, which shows that mortality could have been increasing during the nineteenth century.

This trend in the mortality of the Wang lineage seems to fit in with the general political and economic changes that occurred in China throughout the period of observation. But the Wangs were primarily rural residents; what

2.4 Migration

In the preceding discussion we have considered some aspects of nuptiality, mortality, and fertility in urban and rural populations of the lower Yangzi region. A major force which would affect the pace of urbanization in any period or place is the amount of rural–urban migration. This topic, too, will be illustrated in this chapter by means of some case-studies.

For example, it has been found in a study of lineages at Linghuzhen, a market town which specialized in trade in silk goods in Guian county, Zhejiang, that the founders of thirty-five of the fifty-nine lineages resident in the town by the end of the eighteenth century had moved into the town from elsewhere. The distribution of these migrants by their date of arrival in the town is shown in Table 19.9. During a long span extending over 435 years, the

Table 19.9 Date of arrival of migrants to Linghuzhen

Period	Number of years	Number of migrants	Migrants per decade
1360–98	38	6	1.6
1399–1521	122	10	0.8
1522–1620	98	5	0.5
1621–1722	101	6	0.6
1723–95	72	8	1.1

Source: Shich Chin, *Peasant Economy and Rural Society*, 109–10.

Table 19.10a Frequency of migration in each generation in the Wang lineage in Tongcheng

Generation	Number of males recorded	Number of migrants (year of birth in parentheses)	% of migrants %
10	158	3 (?)	1.9
11	131	5 (2?, 1609–74)	3.8
12	197	3 (1672–1710)	1.5
13	355	4 (2?, 1660–1712)	1.1
14	506	9 (1?, 1715–58)	1.8
15	722	19 (4?, 1714–1808)	2.6
16	742	25 (6?, 1775–1836)	3.4
17	635	24 (1?, 1738–1825)	3.8
18	392	12 (2?, 1804–51)	3.1
19	189	5 (1804–1826)	2.6
Total		109	

first and the fifth periods stand out as being more favourable to geographical mobility than the others, if migration is measured by the number of migrants per decade (in the first period the number was 1.6 and in the fifth, 1.1). Information on place of origin of the migrants shows that, between 1360 and

1798, twenty-six came from the western part of Zhejiang. Among them fourteen came from villages and seven from other towns. Seven came from the eastern part of Zhejiang, five from Anhui, three from Jiangsu, and one from as far away as Henan. Even this single example, which relates to one town only, reveals a great deal of information about rural–urban migration, and can be seen to reflect changes in political, social, and economic conditions.[15]

Another case relating to migrants among members of the Wang lineage is considered below. In Table 19.10 migrants in this lineage are classified by the

Table 19.10b Destinations of out-migrants in the Wang lineage in Tongcheng

Province	Number	First known year of birth	Last known year of birth
Anhui	29	1609	1824
Shaanxi	18	1714	1794
Jiangsu	4	1797	1852
Guangxi	4	1674	1712
Jiangxi	2	1660	1799
Zheijiang	1	1808	
Henan	1	1763	
Guangdong	1	1758	
Fujian	1	1819	
Zhili	1	?	
Not known	47	1672	1851
Total	109		

Source: Tongcheng Wang shi zongpu (The genealogy of the Wang lineage in Tongcheng) (1866 edn.).

frequency of migrants in each generation and by the destinations of the out-migrants. Table 19.10a shows that the percentage of migrants was never very high, but that a large number of the out-migrants who belonged to the Wang lineage were born during the eighteenth and early nineteenth centuries. Table 19.10b shows that, apart from those whose destinations were unknown, the Wangs tended to move quite a distance away from their place of birth. Since in most of these cases the genealogy only gives their destination as a county or a province, it may not be right to think of them all as moving to the county town or the provincial capital. However, it is known that those who moved to Jiangsu, Jiangxi, Zhejiang, Fujian, Guangdong, and Zhili were bound for the town. Moreover, many of those who moved to Shaanxi and also those who moved to unknown destinations were engaged in trade. All this suggests that the migration movements of members of the Wang lineage were similar to the major migration streams in China during the eighteenth century, and that they tended to move to towns rather than rural areas, as did those from the Wei and Li lineages in Hunan province.[16]

[15] Shih Chin, 'Peasant Economy and Rural Society', D. H. Perkins, *Agricultural Development in China, 1368–1968* (Chicago, 1969).
[16] Liu Ts'ui-jung, 'Growth and Migration of Populations', 303–14.

Demographic Aspects of Urbanization 347

There is still no comprehensive study of rural–urban migration in the lower Yangzi region as a whole. The major difficulty lies in the lack of systematically collected statistics. All that one can say is that rural–urban migration is likely to have been increasing from the late nineteenth century onwards, as Shanghai grew to become the largest city in modern China.[17]

To sum up this section, we should consider five points. First, the rural and urban populations in the lower Yangzi region differed in their nuptiality, and particularly in their rates of remarriage. Secondly, as regards fertility, this was slightly lower in the core of the region than at the periphery, and the fertility of men who lived in towns was higher, because of their higher rates of remarriage. Thirdly, as far as we know at the moment, mortality levels were similar in the urban and the rural populations. Fourthly, small-scale studies on individual towns and lineages appear to show evidence of migration from the countryside to the towns, particularly during the eighteenth and nineteenth centuries. However, large-scale systematic studies of this subject will be needed in the future. Finally, we may note that the findings relating to demographic characteristics and their changes over time went in parallel with general changes in political and economic conditions during the period studied.

3. Other factors related to demographic characteristics

In this section we shall focus on attitudes, mentality, and institutional arrangements which may be related to demographic characteristics of the population in the lower Yangzi region, with an emphasis on urban populations. Since information on this subject remains scanty, our discussion must be regarded as tentative, although it does provide useful insights into the demographic characteristics that we have found so far.

Although the remarriage of widowers was a normal phenomenon, marriage to much younger women was ridiculed.[18] Moreover, although concubinage was regularly practised in the towns, stories were told during the Qing period about righteous men who rescued unfortunate girls from becoming concubines and helped them to contract proper marriages, and these men were ultimately rewarded for their efforts.[19] A concubine was usually obtained by

---

[17] Liu Shih-chi, 'The Development of Market Towns in Jiangnan after the Taiping Rebellion' (in Chinese), *Shih-huo Monthly*, 7: 11 (1978), 547–76; M. Elvin, 'Market Towns and Waterways: The County of Shanghai from 1480 to 1910', in G. W. Skinner (ed.), *The City in Late Imperial China* (Standford, 1977) 441–74; C. W. Pannell, 'Recent Growth and Change in China's Urban System', in L. Ma and E. W. Hanten (eds.), *Urban Development in Modern China* (Boulder, Colo., 1981), 91–113.

[18] Chu Jiaxien, 'Jian-gu shou-ji' (1695 edn.), 1/11a-b, in *Bi-ji xiao-shuo da-quan xyu-bien (Additional Collection of Notes and Stories)* (Taibei, repr. 1962), vol. 13.; Chu-Jiaxien, 'Jian-gu shi-ji', 4/12b-13a, ibid., vol. 15.

[19] Liang Gungchen, 'Bei-dong-yuan bi-lu san-bien' (1845 edn.), 2/6b, in *Bi-ji xiao-shuo da-guan (A Collection of Notes and Stories)* (Taibei, repr. 1962), vol. 23; Chen Kangqi, 'Lang-qien ji-wen'(1880 edn.), 2/8b, ibid., vol. 22.

purchase, and some wealthy men were able to afford to be generous and provided matchmakers with opportunities to profit.[20]

As regards remarriage of widows it would appear that only during the Qing period were remarried women looked down upon. Cases in families of scholar–officials were cited to show that 'remarried women were not considered to be anomalous' during the Song dynasty.[21] However, Qing customs in the lower Yangzi area meant that remarried women were treated differently in the marriage ceremony and they were often bitterly criticized.[22] In these circumstances it is not surprising that there are countless cases in the literature of women who were praised for their virtue![23] Most local gazetteers contain chapters which tell stories of virtuous women, or at least list their names. In additon, philanthropic organizations were founded in many cities for the support of poor widows. For example, in Wujin county a *jingjietang* (literally a Hall for Respectable Charity) was founded in 1796 to support 300 virtuous widows every year.[24] In Jiangdu county a *lizhentang* (literally a Hall for Determinative Chastity) was founded in 1840 to support young widows less than 30 years old, and a *xulijyu* (Office for the Assistance of Poor Widows) to distribute subsidies to widows of the poor gentry class, and a *baozhenju* (Office for the Protection of Virtuous Widows) were set up in 1881 to provide pensions for widows who had decided not to remarry.[25] This evidence of the attitudes towards the remarriage of men and women in Imperial China in the lower Yangzi region supports our contention that the fertility of husbands exceeded that of first wives.

The reason for the rather moderate level of marital fertility in the lower Yangzi region in Ming–Qing China may well lie in the fact that estimates based on genealogical records underestimate true fertility, as only recorded sons were counted. Could there be other reasons besides deficient data? It is well known that infanticide was practised as a means of population control in traditional China.[26] However, during the Qing period homes for foundlings (*yuyingtang*, literally homes for nursing babies) were set up in cities in the lower Yangzi region by members of local élite groups.[27] At least forty-five

---

[20] Cai-heng-zi, *Chung-ming man-lu* (1877 edn.), 1/25b-26a, in *Bi-ji xiao-shuo da-quan*, vol. 14.

[21] Lu Jingan, 'Leng-lu za-shi' (1856 edn.), 1/10b, in *Bi-ji xiao-shu da-quan xyu-bien*, vol. 13; Chu Jianxien, 'Jian-gu san-ji', 1/11a, ibid., vol. 14; Qien Yung, 'Lyu-yuan cung-hua' (1870 edn.), 23/6a–b in *Bi-ji xiao-shuo da-quan*, vol. 17.

[22] Cai-heng-zi, *Chung-ming man-lu*, 2/12b; Chu Jiaxien, 'Jian-gu shou-ji', 4/8 13b.

[23] Lu Jingan 'Leng-lu za-shi', 6/8a–b; Zhu Meishu, 'Mai-you-ji' (1874 edn.), 4/8b in *Bi-ji xiao-shu da-quan*, vol. 10.; Huang Jyunzai, 'Jin-hu qi-mo' (1895 edn.), 5/1b–2a, ibid., vol. 11; Zhu Mouxiang, 'Ming-zhai xiao-shi' (1811 end.), 4/1b–12a, 5/12a–b, ibid., vol. 13.

[24] *Wujin Yanghu hozhi* (*A Combined Local Gazetteer of Wujin and Yanghu Counties*) (1866 edn.), 5/25b, p. 15 nn.

[25] *Jiangdu xyu xienzhi* (*Additional Gazetteer of Jiangdu County*) (1885 edn.) (Taibei, repr. 1970), 12b/18–21.

[26] Chu Jiaxien, 'Jian-gu liu-ji', 3/2b–3a, in *Bi-ji xiao-shuo da-quan xyu-bien*, vol. 14; Chen Kangqi, 'Lang-qien ji-wen', 10/3b; G. Rozman, *Population and Marketing Settlements in Ch'ing China* (Cambridge, 1982), 35–8.

[27] S. Fuma, 'The Beginning of "shan-hui" and "shan t'ang" ' (in Japanese), in K. Ono (ed.), *Min–Shin jidai no seiji to shakai* (*Politics and Society in the Ming-Qing Periods*) (Kyoto, 1983), 210–19.

such homes were founded between 1655 and 1736 in county towns or prefectural capitals.[28] The motive behind the founding of such institutions was partly the revulsion felt by members of the élite classes against the practice of infanticide, but it was also true that economic development had made available more funds which could be used to set up and support these organizations. In short, the effectiveness of infanticide as a measure of population control in the lower Yangzi region during the Qing period would have been checked, provided these foundling homes were functioning properly.

Since age at marriage was generally quite low in traditional China,[29] late marriage could not have acted as a preventive check. It is, however, noteworthy that the literature of the Ming–Qing period contains references both to contraception and to abortion. For example, in an essay written in memory of his mother, Gui Youguang (1507–71), a famous scholar from Kunshan, mentions that she had suffered when giving birth to her seven children (four girls and three boys, of whom two of the girls died when they were very young), and did not want to conceive again. She took some kind of drink, concocted by an old woman, which contained two spirals. As a result, she lost the power of speech, though she did not conceive again, and died a year later at the age of 25.[30]

Though this story does not suggest that the potion was particularly effective, it is revealing that the idea of contraception did exist, and that birth control was practised in the area as early as the beginning of the sixteenth century. Moreover, there were women mentioned in the contemporary literature who specialized in the provision of abortifacient drugs who were known as *yaopo* (women pharmacists), and who were skilled in providing abortions.[31] However scanty this evidence is, it does suggest that the practice of abortion could have affected the fertility of traditional women in the lower Yangzi region.

There were other customs relating to birth: women who specialized in midwifery (*wenpo*) are mentioned in the Qing literature, but were also known during earlier periods. Stories about the skills of these women who practised in the lower Yangzi region are told, and some of them became very wealthy.[32] Moreover, there were many medical and psychological procedures designed

---

[28] Liang Ch'i-tzu, 'Foundling Homes in the Lower Yangzi Area during the Seventeenth and Eighteenth Centuries' (in Chinese), in The Institute of the Three Principles of the People (ed.), *Papers on the Maritime History of China* (Taibei, 1984), 97–130.

[29] G. W. Barclay et al., 'A Reassessment of the Demography of Traditional Rural China', *Population Index*, 42: 4 (1976), 609; Liu Ts'ui-jung, 'The Demography of Two Chinese Clans in Hsiaoshan, Chekiang, 1650–1850', in S. Hanley and A. Wolf (eds.), *Family and Population in East Asian History* (Stanford, Calif., 1985).

[30] Gui Yougang, 'Zhenchuan xienshing ji' (Collected Works), in *Si-bu cung-kan ci bien* (Shanghai, 1919–22) 25: 328.

[31] Chu Jiaxien, 'Jian-gu liu-ji', 4/10a; Zhu Meishu 'Mai-you-ji', 4/8b–9a.

[32] Chu Jiaxien, 'Jian-gu liu-ji'; Yu Yueh, 'Cha-xiang-shi xyu-chao', 5/9b, in *Bi-ji xiao-shuo da-quan xyu-bien*, vol. 16; Zhu Mouxiang, 'Mai-you-ji', 7/6b–7a; Lu Changchun, 'Xiang-yin-lou bin-tan', 1/16a, in *Bi-ji xiao-shuo da-quan*, vol. 10.

to assist women who had experienced difficulties in childbirth.[33] These matters may be relevant for any future studies of infant mortality in China, a topic that has not so far been studied in Chinese historical demography.

Finally, we must mention institutions for the relief of the poor, help during famines, and the provision of coffins and burial grounds for poor persons and vagabonds. Some studies of famine relief in traditional China already exist.[34] Their functioning would undoubtedly have reduced the numbers of deaths during periods of food crisis. As regards poor relief, organizations such as *yangjiyuan* (asylums for the relief of the poor), which were established by the state, and *pujitang* (asylums for general relief), which were set up by local people, operated in most cities during the Qing period. Their object was to provide shelter for the aged and to distribute alms to widows and orphans.[35] Provided these organizations functioned effectively, the support they provided will undoubtedly have saved the lives of many of the poor.

The provision of coffins and graveyards was considered to be an important philanthropic duty, at least during the Qing period. Such establishments were mentioned in many local gazetteers. Thus, between 1824 and 1841, in Wujin county, offices were set up in seventy-two rural districts to provide coffins for those who died on the roads or rivers, and these establishments kept close contact with the *cunrentang* (literally, Hall of Benevolence) which was set up in the county town.[36] Quite apart from the fact that these provisions constituted charitable acts which would provide a return for the benefactors, the proper disposal of the bodies of those who died on the roads and rivers was an important hygienic measure for the protection of the environment.

4. Conclusion

Urbanization in the lower Yangzi region during the Ming and Qing periods developed not only through an increase in the number of market towns, but also through the specialization of towns in trading in particular commodities.

Studies based on a number of genealogies show that the proportion of remarried men tended to be higher in the towns than in the country and that this raised urban fertility. Mortality in the towns probably did not differ much

---

[33] Chu Jiaxien, 'Jian-gu yu-ji', 4/5b,·'The Beginning of "Shan-hui" ' vol. 17; Qing-cheng-zi, 'Zhi-i xyu-bien', 4/4b–5a, 7a, in *Bi-ji xiao-shuo da-quan*, vol. 22; Yu Yueh, 'Cha-xiang-shi xyu-chao', 21/2b–3a.

[34] P. E. Will, *Bureaucratie et famine en Chine au 18ᵉ siècle* (Paris, 1980); L. M. Li, 'Introduction: Food, Famine and the Chinese State', *Journal of Asian Studies*, 41: 4 (1982), 687–710; R. Bin Wong and P. C. Perdue, 'Famine's Foes in Ch'ing China', *Harvard Journal of Asiatic Studies*, 43:·1 (1983), 291–331; Liu Ts'ui-jung and Fei Ching-han, 'Preliminary Study on the Operation of the Ch'ing Granary Systems' (in Chinese), *Academia Economic Papers*, 9: 1 (1978), 1–29; Liu Ts'ui-jung, 'A Reappraisal of Functions of Granary Systems in Ch'ing China' (in Chinese), *Academia Economic Papers*, 8: 1 (1980), 1–31.

[35] Fuma, 'The Beginning of "Shan-hui" ', 205–7; *Wujin Yanghu hozhi*, 3/32a–33a.

[36] Ibid. 5/31a–34a.

from that of the rural population. Migration from the country to the town during the eighteenth and late nineteenth centuries around Shanghai also resulted in increased urbanization. Finally, qualitative information on institutions relating to marriages, births, and deaths can be used to give a better understanding of the quantitative data presented in this chapter.

20 The City
Agent or Product of Urbanization

PAUL M. HOHENBERG

Department of Economics, Rensselaer Polytechnic Institute, Troy, New York 12181, USA

In this chapter I shall attempt to distil a consensus from all the chapters contained in this volume. I shall also draw on the discussions that took place at the seminar, where the papers on which these chapters are based were first delivered. That this task has been entrusted to one who is not himself a demographer by profession suggests that my task is to look at some of the broader issues that have been raised. It should, however, be remembered that the core of this volume consists of the research efforts: it remains true, to recall Goethe, that 'God is in the details'.

In what follows, I shall offer a personal commentary on some of the issues that have been raised, rather than attempt a balanced or comprehensive summary. The unifying thread, however, will be the question of the city's autonomy, the extent to which in the past urban communities have controlled or conditioned population or other processes which, in turn, shaped their development. By focusing on urban autonomy, the historical continuity of urbanization will be emphasized, since earlier urban settlements compensated for their inferiority in numbers by their distinctive cultures and powers. In this connection, I can venture a single comment regarding the important issues of data and measurement, issues which are not otherwise dealt with here. I share de Vries's view that, on balance, the increase in urbanization has been overstated. In early modern Europe, for instance, the proportion of the population which lived in sub-threshold but genuine towns was quite substantial. Later incorporations of suburbs and satellite towns into larger agglomerations also bias the statistics in the direction of increased concentration.

1. Urbanization and the changing urban population

The inevitable preliminary question is: what do we mean here by urbanization? This question is put not because we want to be bogged down in definitions, issues relating to data, or sterile methodological controversies, but to bring out more clearly the context within which we focus on population dynamics. It seems useful to pose the issue by a series of questions, which indicate the position or positions that were taken up during the seminar discussions.

1. Is urbanization a single and unique transformation of society, a shift from predominantly rural to predominantly urban living, or is it more generally a change in the life and population of towns? Replies to this question were largely implicit in the papers that were presented, but some clear-cut differences of opinion developed during the discussion and will be reflected in this chapter.

2. When discussing urbanization are we concerned with a process which is specifically linked to cities and their inhabitants, or is urbanization merely a synonym (to be sure one with particular connotations and emphases) for a more general social transformation, which can also be described as the rise of capitalism, industrialization, development, modernization, etc., etc.? In this seminar, the concentration on population dynamics helped to keep the focus on settlement patterns.

3. When dealing with the growth of urban life are we mainly concerned with a shift in the proportion of the urban population? Or is it the development of specialized functions—activities other than the production of food and simple commodities for local consumption—that best captures the phenomenon of urbanization? In our discussions, the focus on people was countered by arguments that stressed the relative importance of functional criteria for urban development.

4. Since specialization is a consequence, as well as a precondition, of exchange, is the degree of integration of urban systems perhaps its truest measure? Such systems are political and administrative as well as commercial, either because order is necessary for a trade-based division of labour, or because the exercise of organized power depends on the capture of a growing surplus. It was generally agreed that system concepts and approaches were good servants for the historian, but that they made bad masters.

5. Finally, is urban life no more than a mere count of heads, or an account of the material and political base of activity? There is an urban culture distinct—not least in its demographic aspects—from that which prevails beyond the city walls. Whilst no one would disagree with this point in principle, during the seminar aspects that bound town and country together, rather than their separateness, were stressed.

I cannot give a definite answer to these rhetorical questions; my purpose is to stress that measures of the extent or progress of urbanization will yield different results depending on the answers given to them. I simply pose a challenge, that of retaining the specific nature of urbanization while linking it, none the less, with other large-scale societal processes. I do so because I know from recent work with Lynn Hollen Lees of the University of Pennsylvania how difficult this challenge is to meet.[1] In the context of the seminar, the task

---

[1] P. M. Hohenberg and L. H. Lees, *The Making of Modern Europe, 1000–1950* (Cambridge, Mass., 1985).

was to retain the emphasis on population and the vital revolution, whilst remembering that those who live in towns work, live, and reproduce in specific spatial, social, economic, political, and cultural settings.

I shall illustrate why it seems to me important to keep urbanization and urban change distinct from other social processes. In doing so I shall develop the theme of urban autonomy. It has been commonly assumed, and it is sometimes explicitly argued, that cities grow, at least for some of the time, because they are forced to absorb a surplus of people from an over-populated countryside. I shall return to the subject of urban growth in relation to overall population dynamics, because I believe that it requires a more complex explanation than rural overspill. Here, I shall content myself with pointing out how improbable such a view is, at least for the earlier stages of urban society.

The urban enterprise is an extraordinarily fragile and tenuous one in a relatively poor society. I believe that we have not been sufficiently impressed by its persistence in the face either of so many conflicts and catastrophes, or of the potential for profound clashes of values between urban life and the prevailing rural order. In most circumstances, the regular provisioning and policing of an urban population is a very taxing task for urban society: to add an uncontrolled number of destitute rural migrants would be to invite disaster. Yet, a society which is sufficiently well organized to operate a complex system, such as a town, would certainly not be content to remain passive. It would accept and retain only those who can fit in, and would have views about the place that they should occupy. In the larger view, moreover, urbanization is associated with rural success rather than rural failure; eloquent evidence of this was provided during the seminar. In addition, a high degree of mobility, including a gross movement from country to town, is far from uncommon without overall urbanization or population growth. Odense, Cuenca, Edo, and even nineteenth-century England, seen from the vantage point of Liverpool, clearly show that mobility and net urban growth through migration are distinct concepts.

Thus the view that urbanization results from rural 'push' factors underestimates the autonomy of cities, particularly in weakly centralized or incompletely developed societies. Yet, as I shall argue at the end, large social transformations, not least general urbanization itself, can reduce urban autonomy. The consequences are daily brought home to the inhabitants of large cities.

2. Urbanization and economic history

We have learned much about past developments and hazards of urban life, and have come to doubt certain aspects which used to be regarded as well established. The insights provided by social scientists have enriched our understanding and produced new subjects for investigation, as well as new tools for historical research. However, the study of urbanization and population dynamics has also shed new light on a number of major topics concerned with the functioning and development of societies. I shall only touch on three: the demographic transition, or, more generally, social mechanisms for the control of fertility and demographic responses to the social and natural environment; the establishment of modern economic growth or—to use a less pedantic term—the Industrial Revolution; and the economic history of pre-industrial, traditional, or transitional societies.

2.1. Demographic transition

One powerful idea that has emerged from the papers and the discussion is that different communities pursue population equilibrium in different ways, and that much light is shed on distinct demographic processes when these are looked at in this larger 'ecological' perspective. Urbanization itself, where this term is now used simply to denote a single transition to a much larger proportion of the population living in towns, can be regarded as a roundabout way for controlling population size, a long-term preventive check. 'Roundabout' is a key work here, for there is ample evidence that in the short or medium term urbanization generally yields increasing or sustained population growth. Young migrants to the town make room for new families in their area of origin, whilst at the same time bringing about an age structure in the towns which is conducive to high fertility. Although the fertility potential is frequently not realized, because the social system restricts nuptiality, and rapid urban growth and high densities tend to keep mortality high, it does offer the prospect of further growth through positive natural increase. Eventually, however, urban couples begin to control the sizes of their families and new norms or attitudes diffuse to the surrounding countryside and bring about a new long-term homeostasis.

Focusing on urbanization also highlights a rather fascinating problem, namely why there was not an explosive increase in mortality during the nineteenth century. This, rather than the question why the fall in mortality was so slow, seems to me to be the real problem. Consider the inequalities brought about by the rapid accumulation of population, or the backwash effects on societies that were left behind in development. Consider also the conditions of housing, water supply, sewage disposal, and medical services (or the lack of them) in the new or fast-growing agglomerations. Finally, consider the echo effect on infant mortality of higher fertility, coupled with a lower age at marriage and the shift to wage labour. Bideau's conjecture that some force must have been operating from the late eighteenth century onwards to reduce infant and child mortality is, indeed, intriguing.[2]

---

[2] A. Bideau, 'La Variabilité régionale de la mortalité des enfants en France au début du XIXe siècle', paper contributed to session 1 of the seminar.

But the most powerful and far-reaching contribution that the study of urbanization makes to the larger field of historical population studies may well be that it has restored the study of mobility to its rightful central place. The clear lesson to be drawn from the papers presented at the seminar is that mobility much exceeded gross migration which, in its turn, was greater than net migration to urban areas. The movement from the countryside to the town, on which so much attention has been focused is little more than a residual category in the larger phenomenon of population movement. When we come to think of the actual people involved, the 'permanent' urban migrant can almost be viewed as merely a *sojourner* who died before moving on again. Of course, to put it in this way is a distortion, but it serves as a useful correction to exaggerated views of migration and urbanization as social and spatial dislocations.

Mobility is more pervasive than it has conventionally been given credit for, and can be found even when other movements are weak or absent. Moreover, it is mobility which most clearly conditions urban demographic processes. There are abundant examples of this. Life-cycle or career-stage migration will modify the age structure of the city population and probably also overall fertility; the pace of gross in-migration to a city with limited employment opportunities will affect the migrants' rate of leaving as well as their mortality; and the movement between different towns will both follow and help to shape the urban system. If occupational and social mobility are added to geographical mobility, the way becomes open to pursue not only the social consequences of urbanization, but to do justice to changes in the countryside which were—understandably—not given the recognition they merit during our deliberations.

2.2. The onset of modern economic growth

The concept of the Industrial Revolution is enjoying one of its periodic booms. This time the emphasis is placed on structural change, and studies of urbanization afford a welcome opportunity for a general-equilibrium approach. I should like to consider some of the questions raised by Wrigley in his chapter and draw attention to some parallels between Britain and Japan in connection with urban systems. The discussions certainly brought out the strong relationships that existed between food supply (including improvements in transport), demographic processes, and urbanization.

It appears that improvements in the productivity of labour played the principal part both during the early modern period and in the nineteenth century. In the latter case they actually over-explain the very considerable upsurge in urbanization, as Bairoch has shown in his chapter in this volume. The reason, of course, was not that labour was so scarce a resource—to some extent urban settlements can grow their own populations—but that non-producers of food needed to be fed, and it is hard to imagine the mobilization of very large surpluses with static productivity. The experience of eastern and Mediterranean Europe makes it clear that attempts to achieve urbanization by ever greater rural exploitation are self-limiting, if not self-defeating.

The view that agricultural intensification, or higher land yields, played a minor role relative to labour productivity makes me uneasy for at least two reasons. The first is the evolution of agricultural technology, which was on balance land-saving and labour-using (in Hick's sense) at least until 1850. Another, even more basic objection is brought about by simple arithmetic. Since rural population increased and land area did not, output per head cannot have grown faster than output per acre. What seems to have happened is that technological progress made more of the land usable for cropping or intensive grazing, whilst non-agricultural employment absorbed large amounts of rural labour at a low opportunity cost in terms of output of food, etc. It must be remembered that this was the time when the well-tended landscapes of Europe and the networks of market centres were in the process of full development and when there was a rich diversity of manufacturing and service functions in villages and towns. Data which emphasize labour productivity and play down the improved use of natural resources fail to capture this important (and transient) phase in the larger story. Finally, recall that agricultural land is subject to depletion. Technical change and tangible investments were required to maintain—let alone to increase—crop yields.

Although much of my attention has been devoted to continuities in the process of urbanization, there is one respect in which the notion of urbanization as a massive one-time shift in population contributes to our understanding of development. I have long felt that a true understanding of growth and development can only be obtained by going beyond its beginnings and by focusing on the pitfalls to sustained progress. Urbanization in the wider sense of viable city systems goes back a long way in all sorts of societies, but it was limited by inelasticities, particularly in food, but perhaps also in the supply of urban services, which constrained the size of individual towns, and in markets for services and manufactures supplied in cities. I agree that labour-surplus models are quite useful, particularly those that focus on the elasticity of the supply of labour. But I have been struck by the paucity of cases in which urbanization can be shown to have faltered or been constrained by the lack of human raw material. Barriers to urban development can more often be traced to high nominal wages and so back to the food supply. Thus, it is quite appropriate to emphasize the stimulating effects of towns on rural production; what Hla Myint has called the 'vent for surplus'.[3] I only wish that there was more direct evidence of such stimulation than simply the growth in demand for rural produce.

Of course, modern economic growth is not the British Industrial Revolution writ large and extended successively to more and more societies.

[3] H. Myint, *Economic Theory and the Underdeveloped Countries* (Oxford, 1971).

There is a rich literature that deals with the implications of being a follower rather than a leader, of market-driven compared with state-led development, of resource–population balance, culture, and other factors. We are far from having clarified the implications of these modes of development for urbanization, let alone answering the more subtle question whether the pre-existing urban system played a part in the success of development, or shaped it in certain ways. Here, too, I believe that concepts of urban systems applied with imagination as well as caution can help, and I shall return briefly to the question in that context.

2.3 The early modern economic context

We take it for granted that the development of population and urbanization during the industrial era must be studied in the light of the economic metamorphosis. Despite doctrinal differences and revisions, we do not lack explanatory models. No comparable framework is available to help us in integrating the large and growing store of historical information relating to early modern cities, their people, and their economies. Even without censuses and aggregate statistics our knowledge continually widens and deepens. But non-specialists, and particularly those concerned with future transformations, are conscious of the absence of integrative models to set against those of the medieval or industrial–capitalist systems and which could be used with the wealth of data and useful generalizations that are available.

For me it was the study of urbanization that demonstrated how fragmentary is our vision of the early modern era, in spite of such deservedly well-known efforts as those of Wrigley to think in general equilibrium terms. My own efforts 'to save the phenomena' draw heavily on the work of the late F. Braudel.[4] Clearly, traditional or transitional societies in Europe, and certainly in Asia, were neither immobile nor unchanging in time or in space. 'Modern' elements, such as towns, non-agricultural production for the market, population movements, and effective social and individual controls on fertility were present and made a difference. Cities, in particular, were remarkably viable and resilient, were organized in genuine systems, and were integral to the functioning of the society despite its continuing rural and even agrarian character.

Our effort to model the early modern economy as a background to the study of urbanization was focused on economic conditions. Long-run variations in population resulted in more or less intensive Ricardian competition for land, and a corresponding fluctuation in the distribution of income between wages on the one hand and surplus or rent on the other. The larger the number of people, the greater the share of rent, and rents accrued to urban élite groups, or were at least spent in the towns. The coincidence that has been noted between the maxima in urban and overall populations thus involves more than a spill-over.

[4] F. Braudel, *Civilization and Capitalism, 15th to 18th Centuries*, 3 vols. (London, 1981–2).

One implication of this is that urban societies tended to flourish during periods when rural populations were encountering increasing distress. If confirmed, this finding can help to account for the difficulty historians have experienced in sorting out 'pull' and 'push' factors in migration, and in characterizing the differences between migrants and those who did not move. Mobility resulted from distress as well as from opportunity, and these forces, paradoxically, may have waxed and waned together. Whilst migrants tended to leave the least favoured rural situations for the most promising prospects in towns, other things being equal, it is also true that urban migrants were often relegated to subordinate positions, tolerated rather than welcomed, and their chances of survival and succession were smaller than those of the natives. It may be true on balance that rural conditions stimulated or retarded mobility, but that opportunities in the towns governed both the rate of true migration, and the selection of permanent urban dwellers. Whilst those least adapted to rural conditions were perhaps also most likely to leave the village, they would only remain in the towns provided they were qualified to do so by temperament and skills. Migrants could be the flotsam of village society, or those most fitted for life in the towns, and possibly both at the same time.

Migration to the towns helped populations at both ends adjust to changing conditions and thus stabilized the system whilst conditioning its eventual transformation. At the same time, economic conditions stimulated movements which were large in relation to their net effect on the proportion of the population which was urban. Of those who moved, most were fated to move again soon, or to die during their wanderings. Thus stability of residence, notably for town dwellers, must be seen as a privilege rather than as a sign of backwardness.

Manufactures played an important part in the early modern economy as viewed by our model. Many, though not all, historians accept the value of the concept of proto-industrialization as a label; I believe that its scope may be extended to cover the direct as well as the indirect roles of the town in secondary production. Moreover, it is impossible to grasp the nature of the mobility revolution, whether in town or in the country, without giving full weight to non-agricultural producers and their proletarianization during the pre-factory period.

One of the principal features of the proto-industrialization model is that the spread of domestic industries removed social barriers to family formation, and thus increased overall fertility. It is interesting to compare the situation of Verviers with that of the communes of the Barentin in Normandy.[5] In the one case, we have a large 'urban village' which tended to export population during its proto-industrial heyday; in the other there is no evidence that fertility was high or even stable: a French, rather than a proto-industrial pattern. In

---

[5] See the contribution by M. P. Gutmann to the seminar, 'How do Urban and Rural Industrial Populations Grow? Migration and Natural Increase in Verviers and its Hinterland'. See also ch. 16 by J. P. Bardet in this vol.

neither case, however, do we find the 'classic' pattern associated with proto-industrialization.

We may summarize these remarks on economic relations during the 'transitional' phase with a simple model. In Fig. 20.1 I have divided the economy into three sectors rather than two, and the principal flows between sectors are shown. Those that, in my view, have received less attention in the analysis of urbanization than they deserve have been underlined. They include the flow of simple manufactures between the rural sectors, with urban enterprise and finance sharing in the profits, the drain of rents from the countryside, and the migration of a rural proletariat to the towns. The first of these is, of course, essential for the proto-industrialization hypothesis. The flow of rents to the towns for sumptuary consumption or investment in monumental buildings, on the other hand, is characteristic of a system with limits to both growth and urbanization. Finally, the movement of landless and often non-agricultural persons to the new industrial settlements is integral to the mobility revolution, the mechanization of industry, and the radically increased pace of urbanization.

3. Urban systems

Few topics in the study of urbanization are so compelling and at the same time so challenging as the external relations of towns. Exchange constitutes the *raison d'être* of urban settlement, while imports of food, fuel, and (usually) people are essential to the continuation of town life, to say nothing of urban growth. Moreover, any given centre engages in more than bilateral exchange; it often serves as a relay or junction in a chain of connections which involve many places and elements. Nor is exchange restricted to tangibles: goods,

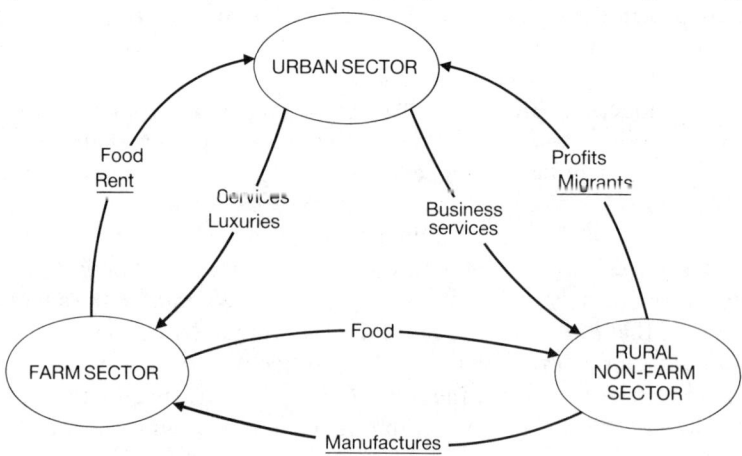

Figure 20.1. Intersectoral flows in a transitional economy

persons, or money. Power, ideas, tastes, and attitudes flow to and from cities, refined, simplified, or perhaps adapted at each station on the way.

From an analytical point of view, system concepts promise great insights. Whilst much can be learned by going beyond simple urban–rural dichotomies to distinctions of size or function among urban settlements, urban systems are constructs that not only recognize complexity but attempt to organize it. At the same time, the more formal models, such as those that focus on hierarchies of population size, have yielded as much frustration as help to students of the history of urbanization. Certainly, the discussions in the seminar testify to this ambivalence, particularly when the Latin American perspectives offered by Carol Smith were juxtaposed to those for Europe and Asia.[6] In this intellectual thicket, I can only diffidently offer the dual-system view that Lynn Hollen Lees and I applied in our recent synthesis of long-run European urbanization. Yet I hope to show that this approach can go some distance towards clearing up some puzzles with which the participants in the seminar had to wrestle.

I begin with the central theme of one of the sessions: the relation of agricultural productivity to the growth of urbanization. Wrigley argued the case for a strong linkage between these two variables in the case of England, and stressed that the country's lead in urbanization was both greater and more lasting than in industrial production. Others, however, pointed out that high farm output per head could limit urbanization by raising labour costs, and offered the cases of Holland and northern Italy as examples of precocious but arrested development. In the dual-system perspective, the issue takes on a somewhat different aspect.

To dramatize my point, imagine a wall erected across England from the Severn to the Wash, or from Bristol to King's Lynn. Between 1700 and 1850 the two regions thus defined developed in ways which are not incompatible with such a separation. On one side there was a relatively autarkic Merrie England, on the other the emerging workshop of the world. Leaving aside the distortions of this historical fantasy, what clearly distinguishes the two regions is their urban system. The array of central places in the south and east, more than ever totally dominated by London, supported strong economic progress with remarkably little additional urbanization. Most of the tremendous urban growth outside London occurred to the north and west of our imaginary wall. The mushrooming towns and emerging conurbations of that region in fact formed the highly industrialized core of a world economy. A far-flung overseas periphery provided food and raw materials and an equally elastic appetite for manufactures. Nearby regions furnished some food, but chiefly contributed the human input, as proto-industry and meagre farming were concentrated and modernized or displaced. This type of urbanization corresponds to what we have called the network system, with functional rather than numerically defined urban hierarchies, adaptive and flexible

---

[6] See ch. 2.

spatial relations, and linkages which were strongest between complementary, functionally specialized places. By contrast, central places form geometrically regular hierarchies of similar towns, with new functions simply added as one moves up the order. This pattern was maintained in southern England.

Although the pace was slower and the geography less neat, the French experience was similar. During the nineteenth century, farming made regular progress, but market centres and provincial capitals grew very little despite the administrative status conferred upon them by the Revolution.[7] Rapid urban growth was confined to the industrial regions and major transport centres, with the exception of Paris which paralleled London as the dominant or primate capital. The Dutch and Italian experience also becomes clearer in the dual-system perspective. Having lost their place at the centre of the early European world economy, their regional urban systems were larger than was required by the most intensive agricultural economy. The result was urban stagnation or—in percentage terms—even retrogression. The principal change was the emergence of a more marked hierarchy in city-size distribution, typical of central-place systems. By contrast, network cores tend towards an oligarchy of leading cities.

Even if the idea that modern agriculture needs only a relatively modest regional urban framework is accepted, the central-place system of rural England still stands out in this respect. The case of Japan may offer a further clue. As Rozman has pointed out, in that island nation there was a relatively smaller development of intermediate regional towns than in China.[8] The presumption is that both Britain and Japan were able to substitute water transport, notably along their coasts, for overland carriage. The many intermediate centres typical of continental systems could be bypassed and trade channelled through a few gateway ports and junctions.

4. Conclusion

Urbanization is more than the transformation of a society from a situation in which it consists mainly of producers of food living on the land to one in which a few farmers feed an array of moulders of metal and pushers of paper who crowd together on a small fraction of the surface area. If these are the macro-outlines of the process and its numerical end points, they provide no hint of the historical experience between the beginning and the end, nor of the role of cities or their people. Very far back in the past, the development of a more settled, productive and complex rural society was closely tied to the rise of cities, which demanded greater efforts from the toilers on the land and yet provided the stimulus which we—significantly—call civilization. These cities were windows on the future for a society still huddled together against the

[7] See ch. 5.   [8] See ch. 4.

unknown. They introduced and fomented change, but they also permitted the established order to resist threats to its stability, whether by absorbing misfits or making it possible for individuals or communities to specialize.

Cities in a predominantly rural society developed effective mechanisms for coping with threats from all quarters. Recall that they housed the agents of the dominant powers who could feel threatened by urban values and ambitions: the feudal magnate, the absolutist ruler, the churchman with his hegemony over morals. Perpetually condemned to an exchange with the outside world, cities organized the space around them, and sometimes distant places as well to ensure both food and profit for themselves. Always attractive to ambitious or desperate outsiders and periodically in need of them to make up a natural deficit, cities continued to fight to preserve their control and to retain the value of citizenship, the consciousness of belonging to a place rather than to a person. It was also the city that introduced the idea of an environment largely man-made and which men could therefore control and be responsible for. And it was the city that shifted the social pecking order away from full dependence on property and status to a much greater emphasis on income and achievement. The effect of urbanization on population growth was first positive and then negative, as nuptiality increased and legitimate fertility declined.

It may be thought that mass urbanization would glorify and promote urban values and give cities even greater control. Rural life has certainly been permeated by urban ideas and artefacts. But in adapting their culture for export, city dwellers have in large measure lost their sense of place and civic identity. The great transformations which produced modern industrialized nation-states actually reduced urban autonomy. As societies became urbanized, cities not only dissolved spatially into conurbations and metropolitan areas, but their civic institutions and distinctive cultures faded into tourist shows. Interestingly, rural-based regional identities have, at least in Europe, been far more resilient and so helped some cities of the second rank to reaffirm their heritage.

From earliest times, cities under direct rule were far less able to control their human, social, and physical environment. As a consequence, the populations of capitals could grow without reference to economic circumstances. The central power was forced to cope with the multitudes, to provide them with bread and circuses. Yet the deep coffers and strong police powers of modern states could not ensure as much order and amenity as attentive city fathers had provided in more modest places and with more modest means. In spite of all the cultural excitement and cosmopolitan energy of imperial Rome, absolutist Paris, and Petersburg, Vienna, or Naples, living conditions in these towns for the mass of people were as bad as in the worst industrial slums that capitalism could create.

The irony is that the states of the twentieth century, whether socialist or *laissez-faire*, industrial or developing, democratic or authoritarian, find themselves in much the same situation as their predecessors. High taxes, comprehensive welfare programmes, sophisticated planning and bureaucracy; none of these rearguard actions have achieved more than an alleviation of urban ills. Regions boom or stagnate, despite more and more plans; primacy flourishes or festers from Moscow to Tokyo, from Calcutta to São Paulo. So far, the People's Republic of China has managed to control urbanization, if not urban congestion. But there, too, the large modern city in all its grandeur is more and more the product of an urbanized society and less and less, as it so often was in history, an actor.

Index

Aachen 86, 89
Abrams, P. 49 n.
Adams, D. W. 172 n.
agricultural labour, productivity of 134, 135, 136, 139–40, 146–8, 151, 195
agriculture 27–8, 31, 33, 102–3, 104–7, 109–10, 112, 116–20, 123, 131–2, 134, 154, 199–204, 212, 220, 287, 310, 314, 319, 329–30, 357, 361, 362
   see also agricultural labour, productivity of; crop yields
Ahlberg, G. 222 n., 227, 228, 229, 231 n.
Ahlström, G. 120 n.
Akerman, S. 165 n., 170 n., 172 n., 183 n.
Aldcroft, D. H. 141 n., 142 n.
Altona 89
Amsterdam 16, 56
Angyal, 48
annexation 46
Appleby, G. 34 n.
Argentina 32, 38, 39, 137 n.
   city-size distribution in 23–4, 28
Arriaga, E. E. 47 n.
Auerbach, F. 21 n., 75 n.
Augsburg 86, 89, 93, 94, 97, 98
Augustyn, B. 10 n.
Australia 32, 137 n.
Austria 8, 90
Avenel, G. d' 140

Bacon, F. 265 n.
Bagwell, P. S. 141 n.
Bailly, A. 142 n.
Bairoch, P. 113, 134 n., 135 n., 137 n., 138 n., 139 n., 140 n., 141 n., 142 n., 144 n., 145 n., 149 n., 150 n., 356
Baker, R. 303 n.
Bamberg 86
Barcelona 291
Barclay, G. W. 349 n.
Bardet, J.-P. 244 n., 253 n., 265 n., 273 n.
Barentin-Pavilly (France) 265, 267, 281
Baskin, C. W. 22 n.
Beckman, M. J. 30
Béguin, H. 144 n.
Belgium 10
Bengtsson, T. 130, 195 n.
Benzing, J. 90 n.
Beresford, M. W. 303 n.
Berlin 88, 89, 98, 99, 231
Berry, B. J. L. 21–2, 25 n., 29 n., 30, 31, 32 n., 34 n., 50

Bideau, A. 174 n., 355
Bin Wong, R. 350 n.
Birdsall, N. 290 n.
Birmingham 108
birth control, and family formation 243–4, 246, 252, 253–4, 257, 258–63, 264–81, 291, 293, 322, 349
   French model 264–81
Blaschke, H. 89 n.
Blayo, Y. 165 n., 168, 169
Bongaarts, J. 183 n.
Bonnet, L. C. 265 n.
book fairs 90, 93–4, 99
Boonstra, O. W. A. 19 n.
Braudel, F. 4, 13 n., 358
Brazil, 32, 37
Bremen 86
Breslau 86, 88, 89, 90
Bromley, R. D. F. 35 n.
Bruford, W. H. 98 n.
Brünn 98
Brunswick 88
Brutzkus, E. 32 n.
Buenos Aires 23–4

Cai-heng-zi 348 n.
Caldwell, J. C. 172 n., 177 n.
Cambridge 107
Canada 32, 137 n.
Caniage, J. 174 n.
Cantillon, R. 74 n.
Cardoso, F. H. 36 n.
Carlsson, B. 113 n.
Carlsson, S. 228, 239
Carter, H. 75 n.
Chao Kang 331 n.
Chen Chung-yi 331 n.
Chen Guyuan 334 n.
Chen Kangqi 347 n., 348 n.
Chester 107
Chile 39, 137 n.
China 22, 49, 61, 62–73, 328–51, 364
   birth control in 349
   city-size distribution 25, 27, 31
   comparisons with urban Europe 66, 71–2
   fertility patterns, urban and rural 335–43, 348
   infanticide in 348–9
   marriage patterns, urban and rural 331–5, 347–8
   midwifery in 349–50
   mortality patterns, urban and rural 343–5, 350

China (*cont.*):
  19th-century urbanization 63–70
  philanthropy and poor relief 350
  pre-1800 city populations 63, 328–9
  rural–urban migration patterns 345–7
  urbanization in lower Yangzi region, c.1500–1900: 328–51
Christaller, W. 22 n., 48, 100
Chu Jiaxien 347 n., 348 n., 349 n., 350 n.
Chuan Han-sheng 330 n.
city-size distribution
  allometric growth model 29, 75
  forms of 20–4, 75–6
  immature urban systems 24–8, 41
  mature urban systems 29–33
  primate urban systems 33–9, 41
  summary of 39–42
  see also rank-size distribution
city size and fertility, correlation between 291
city size and mortality, correlation between 294–6
Clapham, J. H. 110 n.
Clark, C. 32 n., 141
Clark, J. 166 n.
Cliff, A. 48 n.
climate 150, 296
Coale, A. J. 19 n., 283 n.
Cole, W. A. 12 n.
Coleman, D. C. 106 n.
Cologne 86, 89, 93, 94, 97, 98
Colombia 37
colonialism 34–7, 38
contraception, *see* birth control
Cooley, C. H. 148
Copenhagen 158, 159, 160, 231
Corsini, C. 165 n.
Coventry 107
Crafts, N. F. R. 107 n.
Crofts, J. 141 n.
crop yields 134–5, 137–9, 142–6, 150–1, 357
Cuenca 15, 16, 168–85, 354
Czechoslovakia 32

Da Molin, G. 165 n.
Danzig 86, 93
Davis, K. 167 n., 244
Deane, P. H. 12 n.
Deloche, J. 141 n.
Denmark 13 n., 14, 130 n., 152–64
Deprez, P. 284 n.
Dessau 98
de Vries, J. 26, 27, 29, 41, 44 n., 47, 51 n., 59 n., 62, 63, 67, 69, 71, 72, 76 n., 78, 80 n., 86, 88, 103, 106 n., 110, 206 n., 352
de Zeeuw, J. W. 11 n.
Diedericks, H. A. 16 n.
disease 297
domestic servants 172–6, 206–12, 219, 223, 227, 228, 231, 239–40, 288, 304–5, 306, 308–9, 309–10, 312

Dresden 89, 98
Dupaquier, J. 265, 279, 281
Düsseldorf 89, 98

Eberhardt, H. 98 n.
economic variables 29–31, 32, 35–8, 104–5, 109, 298, 354–60
  see also wages and incomes
Edo (later Tokyo) 63, 67, 69, 206–8, 210, 211, 212, 214, 216, 219, 354
Eisenstadt, S. N. 36 n., 38 n.
El Salvador 22
El Shakhs, S. 25 n., 27 n., 31 n., 34 n.
Elvin, M. 329 n., 347 n.
Emden 86, 93
Engelen, T. L. M 19 n.
England 5–6, 12, 49, 56, 61, 102–3, 104, 106–12, 300–27, 354, 361–2
  Corn Laws, repeal of 116, 118
  emigration from 111
  pre-industrial urbanization in 102–12
  urban population distribution c.1700 48
Erfurt 88, 93, 98
Eulenburg, F. 93 n.
Europe 6–9, 26–8, 32, 45, 61–2, 66, 71–3, 108, 110–11, 137–40, 142–3, 243, 282
  city-size distribution in 26–8
  comparisons with urban East Asia 71–2
  crop yields in 137, 143
  productivity of agricultural labour in 139–40
  urban percentage, interpretation of 45–6
European Fertility Project 57
Evans, A. M. 30 n.
Exeter 107
exports 113, 115, 116, 118, 119, 121, 123, 150, 154, 245

Faletto, E. 36 n.
family formation, marriage 215, 216–18, 304–9, 323–5, 355
  Chinese model 331–5, 347–8, 349
  Spanish model 286–91, 298
  Swedish model 222–6, 228, 229–42
  see also fertility; fertility decline
Farr, W. 103
Fasserman, H. 76 n.
Fei Ching-han 350 n.
Ferrari, G. 296 n.
fertility, birth rates 53, 55–8, 103, 125–8, 153, 154–7, 161, 182–3, 222, 243–63, 264–81, 283, 285, 296, 320–2, 324–5, 355
  Chinese model 335–43, 348
  Spanish model 286–93
fertility decline 245–63, 289–90
  Geneva model 245–57, 258, 262–3
  Rouen model 245–54, 255
Findley, S. 166 n., 180 n.
Flensburg 158, 159
Fogel, R. W. 142 n., 144

Index 367

France 17–18, 61, 77–83, 102, 106–7, 108, 244–63, 264–81, 359, 362
  French Revolution 74, 77–83, 279, 281, 362
François, É. 74 n., 89 n.
Frankfurt 89, 90, 93, 94, 99
Freeman, W. J. 141 n., 142 n.
Freiburg 93
Frey, A. 48 n.
Fridlizius, G. 113 n., 117 n., 121 n., 122 n., 125 n., 128 n., 188 n., 198 n., 199 n., 201 n.
Friedlander, D. 57 n.
Frijhoff, W. 93 n.
Fuma, S. 348 n., 350 n.

Gadd, C.J 120 n.
Garden, M. 18, 263
Gardlund, 228
Garrison, W. L. 22 n., 30
Geneva 17, 244–63
Germany 84–100, 106–7, 282
  administrative capitals, importance of 88–9, 98
  cultural and intellectual indices 90–100
  16th–18th-century urban network 84–100
  urban population analysis 84–90
Gibrat's Law of Proportionate Effect, *see* city-size distribution: allometric growth model
Giessen 98
Ginsberg, N. 21 n., 22
Gloucester 107
Goertz, G. 135, 150 n.
Goethe, J. W. von 352
Goldfriedrich, J. 90 n., 94 n.
Goldscheider, C. 166 n.
Goldstein, A. 183 n.
Goldstein, S. 183 n.
Göteborg 116, 187
Gotha 98
Göttingen 97, 98
Graz 98
Great Britain 32, 137, 140, 282, 362
  see also England
Guatemala 40
  urban distribution in 28, 33, 35
Guatemala City 35, 40
Gui Youguang 349
Gustafson, U. 227, 228, 229 n.
Gutmann, M. P. 359 n.

Haggett, P. 48 n., 144 n.
Hajnal, J. 324 n.
Hall, J. W. 69 n.
Hall, P. 32, 41 n.
Hamburg 86, 89, 90, 93, 97, 123, 124
Hammel, E. A. 181 n.
Hanover 88, 89, 98
Harris, C. D. 25, 80 n.
Harris, J. R. 166 n.
Harris, W. D. 36 n.
Hart, S. 56 n.

Haswell, M. 141
Hauser, P. 296 n.
Hay, D. 32, 41 n.
Hayami, A. 61, 67, 214
Heidelberg 93
Helsingborg 188, 199
Henry, L. 248, 258, 273 n., 279, 286 n., 296 n.
Hirschmeier, J. 213 n.
Hobsbawm, E. J. 317 n.
Hochstadt, S. 165 n.
Hogan, D. P. 165 n., 172 n.
Hohenberg, P. 48, 49
Hoselitz, B. F. 105 n.
Houdaille, J. 286 n.
housing 288, 300–27
Houston, R. 106 n.
Huang Jyunzai 348 n.
Hungary 32

illegitimacy 222, 223–5, 288, 289
illiteracy 287
imports 136, 150
Industrial Revolution 74, 112, 140–1, 148, 149, 282, 356–8
industry and industrialization 150, 162, 194–8, 226–7, 245, 290–1, 309–12, 314, 356–8, 359–60, 361
infanticide 348–9
Ingolstadt 93
inheritance patterns 181, 288
Israel 32
Italy 12–13, 49, 106–7, 146, 361, 362
Itō, S. 62 n., 219 n.

Japan 9–10, 13, 15–16, 32, 37, 49, 61, 62–73, 206–19, 362
  apprenticeships in 212–14, 216, 219
  castle towns 208, 210
  comparisons with urban Europe 66, 71–2
  18th- and 19th-century migration patterns 214–18
  18th- and 19th-century urban employment patterns 206–19
  marriage and family formation in 215, 216–18
  19th-century urbanization 63–70
  pre-1800 city populations 63
  sex ratio of migrants 214–16
Jefferson, M. 21 n., 81
Jena 93
Jeorger, M. 279
Johansen, H. C. 13 n., 153 n.
Johnson, E. A. J. 34 n.
Johnson, G. A. 24 n., 27, 29 n., 75 n., 76 n., 80 n.
Jonsson, U. 188 n., 221 n., 222, 224 n.
Jörberg, L. 113 n., 131, 195 n.

Kasarda, J. D. 32 n.
Kassel 89, 93

Index

Kelley, A. C. 53 n.
Kertzer, D. I. 165 n., 172 n.
Keyfitz, N. 43 n., 55, 57 n.
Kiesel, H. 99 n.
King, G. 107 n.
Kito, H. 214 n.
Knodel, J. 286 n., 289 n., 291 n., 296 n.
Kobe 67
Kohl, J. G. 148
Königsberg 86, 89, 93
Kowaleski, S. A. 76 n., 80 n.
Krantz, O. 114, 121 n.
Kyoto 66, 68, 206, 208, 211, 214, 216

labour market, analysis of 205–6
Lachiver, M. 165 n., 266
land tenure and inheritance 181
Landskrona 188, 199, 201
Laslett, P. 111 n., 165 n., 168, 169 n., 170 n., 205, 206 n.
Latin America 23–5, 27, 31, 33–5, 36–9, 40, 136, 172, 361
Laux, H. D. 285 n.
Lawton, R. 165 n., 177, 284 n.
Lee, E. S. 166 n., 177 n.
Leeds
  household members, labour-force participation of 312–18, 324–5
  labour force analysis 309–20
  living costs, 1832 example 325–6
  nuptiality pattern 304–9
  standards of living and employment compared with rural areas 315–20, 324–5
  wage rates 314–18
  workers' age distribution 304–5, 311–13, 320
  working-class housing, demographic implicatons of 320–5
Lees, L. H. 48, 49, 83, 353, 361
Leighton, A. C. 141 n.
Leipzig 89, 90, 93, 94, 98, 99
Le Mée, R. 78 n.
Lenton, J. H. 314 n.
Lepetit, B. 78 n., 141 n.
le Roy Ladurie, E. 102
Lesthaeghe, R. 291 n.
Lewis, O. 225
Li, L. M. 350 n.
Liang Ch'i-tzu 349 n.
Liang Gungchen 347 n.
Liang Keng-yao 331 n.
Linz 98
literacy 279–80
Liu Shih-chi 329 n., 330, 347 n.
Liu T'sui-jung 18, 329 n., 334 n., 343 n., 346 n., 349 n., 350 n.
Liverpool 108, 354
Livi Bacci, M. 289 n., 291 n., 296 n.
London 12, 48, 103, 104, 108, 123, 149, 361

Losch, A. 22 n.
Lotka, A. J. 75 n.
Lu Changchun 349 n.
Lu Jingan 348 n.
Lund 188, 199, 201
Lutz, C. H. 35 n.
Lyons 81

McGreevey, W. P. 141 n.
McKeown, T. 297 n.
McNeill, W. 167 n.
McPherson, J. 30
Madden, C. H. 27 n.
Madrid 291
Magdeburg 86, 89, 93, 97
Mainz 89
Malmö 116, 117, 118, 121, 125–30, 133, 186–8, 192, 198, 199, 201
Malthus, T. R. 106 n.
Manchester 108
Mannheim 89, 98
marriage, see family formation
Martínez Carrión, J. 297 n.
Massey, D. S. 183 n.
Matović, M. R. 223 n., 225 n., 226 n., 230 n., 231 n.
Mehta, S. K. 31 n.
Mendels, F. F. 290 n.
Menken, J. A. 183 n.
Mera, K. 39 n.
Merlin, P. 144 n.
Methley, see Leeds
Meulan (France) 18, 266, 267–8, 270, 274
Meusel, J. G. 94 n.
Mexico 37, 38
Meyer, B. H. 141 n.
midwifery 349–50
migration and in-migration 40, 41, 53–60, 111, 128–31, 150, 205–6, 255–7, 284, 285, 287, 288–9, 291, 297–9, 305–6, 310–12, 319, 328–9, 355, 356, 359
  Chinese model 345–7
  Danish model 152–64
  French model 276–81
  Japanese model 214–18
  Spanish model 165–85
  Swedish models 186–204, 220–2, 226–9, 240–2
Montgomery, A. 221 n.
Moreda, P. 285 n., 297 n.
Morrison, P. A. 166 n.
Morse, R. 34
mortality, death rates 53, 55–8, 103, 110, 125–8, 154–5, 156–7, 161, 174, 215, 220, 222, 263, 273, 274, 283–4, 285, 286, 289, 322–4, 325, 341–2, 355
  Chinese model 343–50
  Spanish model 293–8
Moscow 25

Index   369

Mottu-Weber, L. 141 n.
Mueller, E. 313 n.
Mullan, B. P. 183 n.
Münch, P. 99 n.
Munich 93
Myint, H. 357

Nadal, J. 285 n., 297 n.
Nakabe, Y. 66 n.
Netherlands, The 9, 10–12, 47, 48, 49, 103, 106–7, 361, 362
  historical urbanization of 47, 48
Neuberger, E. 167 n.
New Zealand 32, 137 n.
Nicolas, J. D. 286 n.
Norberg, A. 165 n., 170 n., 172 n., 183 n.
Norrköping 220
North, D. C. 121 n.
Norwich 107
Nuremburg 86, 93, 94, 97, 98

O'Brien, P. K. 142 n.
Odense 14, 15, 152–64, 354
Ohlsson, R. 192 n., 195, 199 n.
Osaka 66, 68, 206, 208, 210–11, 213, 214, 216, 219
Osaka, M. M. 9 n.

Pannell, C. W. 32 n., 347 n.
Paris 81, 264 n.
Peking 25
Perdue, P. C. 350 n.
Perkins, D. H. 346 n.
Perrenoud, A. 248 n., 252 n., 257 n., 263 n.
Persson, C. 221 n., 224 n.
Peru 38
Petit Quevilly 265
Philipov, D. 55
Philippines, The 3
Phythian-Adams, C. 208 n.
Poland 32
Pollard, S. 45 n.
Ponsard, C. 75 n.
population, urban percentage of 44–6, 53, 143, 145
population mobility, see migration
Portes, A. 24 n., 32 n., 34 n., 35 n.
Portugal 22
Potsdam 89, 98
Potter, R. G. 183 n.
Poussou, J. P. 172 n.
poverty 221–3, 224–6, 278, 335, 350
Prague 86, 93
Pred, A. 43 n.
Princeton Fertility Project 19
Prussia 90
publishers and publishing 90–9
Pumain, D. 75 n.

Qing-cheng-zi 350 n.
Quezaltenango (Guatemala) 28

railways, see transport systems
rank-size distributions, rank-size rule 21–5, 27, 29, 30–2, 35, 37–8, 41, 49–53, 67–8, 69, 75, 76, 82–3
Ratzel, F. 148
Redondo, R. G. 294 n., 296 n.
Regensburg 86, 93
Reher, D. S. 181 n., 284 n., 286 n., 288 n.
Rémond, A. 141 n.
Renard, C. 265 n., 279
Renes, J. 10 n.
Renouard, D. 141 n.
Ricardo, D. 5, 101, 102–3
Richardson, H. W. 29, 30 n., 75 n., 83 n.
Rimmer, G. 315 n.
Ringrose, D. R. 172 n., 173 n.
Ringwalt, J. L. 141 n.
roads, see transport systems
Roberts, B. 34 n., 40 n.
Robson, B. T. 27 n., 48 n., 75 n.
Roel, A. E. 244 n.
Rogers, A. 43 n., 53–4, 55
Rouen 17–18, 244–63, 265, 267–8, 269–70, 273–8, 279–81
Roumois (France) 265, 267, 281
Rowntree, B. S. 319 n., 322 n.
Rozman, G. 49, 61 n., 63 n., 66 n., 67 n., 69 n., 75 n., 214 n., 348 n., 362
rural surplus 104–5, 134–5
Russell, J. C. 26, 28, 50
Russia 27, 49, 61, 137
  city-size distribution in 25

Saibante, M. 75 n.
Saito, O. 212 n., 213 n.
Salisbury 107
Salzburg 98
Sanchez, B. 286 n.
Sandberg, L. G. 113
Schofield, R. S. 12 n., 111 n., 165 n., 244, 293 n., 314 n.
Schön, L. 114, 116 n., 119 n., 131, 132 n.
Seville 291
sex ratios 55–6, 214–16, 227, 228, 231, 239, 287, 288, 304, 306–8
Shachar, A. 38 n.
Sharlin, A. 56 n., 57, 110 n., 205–6, 243 n., 293 n.
Sheffield 108
Shiba, Y. 328
Shih Chin 330 n., 346 n.
shipping, see transport systems
Shrewsbury 107
Simon, H. 29 n.
Singer, H. W. 75 n.

370 Index

Skinner, G. W. 4, 25, 28, 31 n., 38 n., 61, 64–6, 67, 75 n., 76 n., 80 n., 328, 329 n., 330
Smith, A. 102, 103, 104–6, 112
  Wealth of Nations 104–5, 112
Smith, C. A. 22 n., 24 n., 27 n., 28 n., 31 n., 33 n., 35 n., 40 n., 50–1, 75 n., 76 n., 361
Smith, H. D. 67 n.
Smith, T. C. 66 n., 210 n., 218–19
Snell, K. D. M. 106 n.
Socolow, S. 35 n.
Söderberg, J. 188 n., 220 n., 221 n., 224 n.
Soetbeer, A. 124
Soly, H. 10 n.
Sotteville 265
Souden, D. C. 111 n.
Spain 15, 16, 18–19, 106, 146, 168–85, 282–99
  censuses in 282–4
  mortality patterns 293–8
  nuptiality and fertility patterns 286–93, 298
  urbanization pattern summarized 284–5
Stephenson, C. 182 n.
Stockholm 15, 16, 114, 116, 125, 128, 186, 187, 188, 220–42
  family formation patterns 222–6, 229–42
  migration, effect of on family formation 240–2
  migration (1860–90) 226–9
  migration pattern, pre-industrial 220–2
Strasburg 86
Stuttgart 89
Sundbärg, G. 144 n.
Sunderland 108
Sussman, G. D. 273 n.
Sweden 6, 15, 16, 113–33, 186–204, 220–42
  agricultural productivity, growth of 116–20, 123, 131–2, 193
  agricultural workers, migration of 193–4, 198–204
  commercialization of economy (1810–70) 113–33, 186
  dual labour market in 125–31
  foreign trade and economic growth 113, 115, 116, 118, 119, 121, 122–5
  Freedom of Trade Ordinance (1846) 221
  industrialization in 193, 194–8
  inequalities in income 131–2, 194–8, 199–204
  merchant houses, role of 122–5
  migration and in-migration 128–31, 187–98, 199–204
  transport sector productivity, growth of 120–2
  urbanization in the south (1820–60) 198–204
  wage differences and migration in 19th century 194–8, 199, 204
  see also Stockholm

Taiwan 32
Third World concerns 33–4, 36, 37, 40, 221

Thoen, E. 10 n.
Tilly, C. 44, 290 n.
Tisdale, H. E. 47
Todaro, M. P. 166 n., 167 n., 172 n., 177 n.
Tokyo 211
Totman, C. 9 n.
Toutain, J. 145 n., 148
transport costs 134, 137, 140–2, 145–6, 148–9, 150
transport systems 104, 120–2, 132, 135, 136, 144, 150, 154
Treadway, R. 283 n.
Trieste 86
Tübingen 98
Tugault, Y. 264 n.

Ulm 97
Unger de Zarate, A. 183 n.
United States of America 7
  city-size distribution in 21, 22, 27, 32
  crop yields in 137, 142–3
urban hierarchies 27–8, 30, 37–8, 40, 41–2, 48, 59–60, 78–81, 108
urban primacy 21–5, 27, 32, 33–9, 41, 42, 50–1
urban systems
  central-place theory 30, 38, 48–9, 75, 76, 100, 362
  external relations of towns 360–2
  problems in historical application of 48–53
urban transition, problems in historical application of 53–9
urbanization
  and changing urban population 352–4
  demographic transition 355–6
  early modern economic context 358–60
  econometric analysis of 135–6
  and economic history 354–60
  modern economic growth, onset of 356–8
  in pre-industrial societies 101–12, 165–85, 328–51
  problems in historical application of 43–8
  Tilly's definition of 44
  Tisdale's definition of 47
Utterström, G. 193 n.

Valencia 291
Vance, J. 49
Vandenbroeke, C. 10 n., 284 n.
van de Walle, E. 296 n.
van der Woude, A. M. 11 n., 19 n., 56, 110 n., 205–6, 219
Vapnarski, C. 20 n., 23–4, 27, 28, 43 n.
Verhulst, A. 10 n.
Vexin (France) 18, 265–6, 267, 269, 279, 281
Vienna 88, 89, 93, 98, 222
von Thünen, J. H. 7, 8, 104, 144 n.

wages and incomes 131–2, 194–8, 311–12, 314–18, 319–20
Wakabayashi, K. 216 n.

Walker, M. 89 n.
Wallerstein, D. 37 n., 45 n.
Walton, J. 24 n., 32 n., 34 n., 35 n.
Ward, B. 30 n.
Ward, D. 317 n.
Warsaw 86
Watkins, S. C. 19 n.
Weimar 98
wet-nursing 174, 252, 263, 273–6, 281
White, C. 141 n.
Wilcox, P. 165 n.
Will, P. E. 350 n.
Williamson, J. G. 53 n., 55 n., 56, 57 n., 194–5
Wittenberg 93, 94
Wittman, R. 99
Worcester 107
Wrigley, E. A. 12 n., 59 n., 103 n., 105 n., 107 n., 108 n., 109 n., 110 n., 111 n., 166 n., 244, 293 n., 314 n., 356, 358, 361

Xenos, P. 3

Yasumoto, M. 311 n, 319 n.
Yokohama 67
York 107
Ystad 201
Yu Yueh 350 n.
Yuan I-chin 343 n.
Yugoslavia 32
Yui, R. 213 n.

Zarate, A. 182 n.
Zelinsky, W. 43 n., 54–5
Zhu Meishu 348 n.
Zhu Mouxiang 348 n., 349 n.
Zipf, G. K. 21, 30 n., 75 n., 76, 166 n.
Zuiches, J. J. 166 n.
Zumkeller, D. 248 n., 252 n.